D0207806

Duff Pattullo of British Columbia

Duff Pattullo of British Columbia

ROBIN FISHER

UNIVERSITY OF TORONTO PRESS

Toronto Buffalo London

© University of Toronto Press 1991
Toronto Buffalo London
Printed in Canada

ISBN 0-8020-2780-6

Printed on acid-free paper

Canadian Cataloguing in Publication Data

Fisher, Robin, 1946–
Duff Pattullo of British Columbia

Includes bibliographical references.
ISBN 0-8020-2780-6

1. Pattullo, Thomas Dufferin, 1873–1956. 2. British Columbia – Politics and government – 1933–1952.* 3. Prime ministers – British Columbia – Biography. I. Title.

FC3826.1.P37F5 1991 971.1'03'092 C90-095666-6
F1088.P37F5 1991

The excerpt from *The Confidential Clerk*, copyright 1954 by T.S. Eliot and renewed 1982 by Esme Valerie Eliot, is reprinted by permission of Faber and Faber, Ltd, and Harcourt Brace Jovanovich.

This book has been published with the help of a grant from the Social Science Federation of Canada, using funds provided by the Social Sciences and Humanities Research Council of Canada. Publication has also been assisted by the Canada Council under its block grant program.

For the boys,

Manu and Keri

Contents

Preface

There's always something one's ignorant of
About anyone, however well one knows them;
And that may be something of the greatest importance.
T.S. Eliot, *The Confidential Clerk*

If, as some continue to believe, the subject of a biography speaks for himself, the preface is the place where an author may speak of his subject. Thomas Dufferin Pattullo reached the height of his career during the depths of the Depression when, in 1933, he became premier of British Columbia. He had more than thirty years experience in business and politics behind him, and eight years as leader of his province before him. Today, fifty years after his defeat as premier in 1941, he is not well remembered, even in British Columbia. Yet Duff Pattullo was a man of consequence. Four premiers have dominated British Columbia politics in the twentieth century: two were Liberals, two were conservative in the 'small c' sense of the word, though one them joined Social Credit. Of the four – Richard McBride, John Oliver, Duff Pattullo, and W.A.C. Bennett – I believe that Pattullo was the most significant. He was striking and exceptional as an individual, and he was important to, and even representative of, the history of this province in the first half of the twentieth century. Though he came from Ontario, he identified so closely with his adopted region that I have called this book *Duff Pattullo of British Columbia*.

I also wrote this biography because a number of colleagues to whom I must listen, if not heed, insisted it was ill-advised. Indeed, as some Canadian historians abhor biography and others disparage regional history, this book may seem twice misguided. When I began this work, biography had fallen into disrepute among Canadian historians as more and more of them became convinced that the life of an individual, particularly if white, male, and a politician, was far less interesting and significant than the lives of many people. The rise of the so-called new social history led to a preoccupation with class, gender, and race, on which biography supposedly throws little light. I hope that this biography will help disprove such claims. At the same time, I should be quite clear that, for this historian , the individual matters as much as the group. And some people *are* more important than others.

Though political biography was once one of the grand traditions of Canadian historical writing, few biographies have been written of regional leaders. This gap in the literature exists largely because the timing was bad. As regional history came into vogue, political biography fell into disrepute. These two developments were related. Since political biographies were mostly of national figures and perpetuated central views, regional historians concluded that biographies of political leaders were not the best way to explain regional distinctiveness. Consequently, with some notable exceptions, there are few good biographies of regional politicians, particularly in western Canada.[1]

I began to look at the life of Duff Pattullo because a provincial premier who was so unanimously condemned by the historians of central Canadian politics was bound to be extremely interesting. Historians of Ottawa politics sometimes forget even the name of British Columbia's premier in the 1930s.[2] When they do get his name right, Pattullo usually features only as a saboteur of the recommendations of the Rowell-Sirois Commission on Dominion-Provincial Relations. Without much consideration of his background or his ideas, Pattullo is denounced as an unthinking and dogmatic opponent of Ottawa's attempt to centralize further Canadian government. Historians who believe that 'the Liberal way' was the William Lyon Mackenzie King way refer to the 'reckless "Duff" Pattullo.' He is seen as one 'of these questionable Liberals' because he decided to use public money to build a bridge as a depression-time works project.

Sometimes such historians find the very thought of Duff Pattullo so distressing that they become confused about basic points. One author has suggested that Pattullo, like King, came from a 'genteel, middle-class Presbyterian and Liberal' family, but, despite this, he came to power 'without social prestige' and his election 'symbolized the rejection of middle-class leadership.'[3]

Eastern authors have got away with such nonsense largely because British Columbia historians have done little to counteract it. Much of the province's history is still unwritten, and the biggest gap grows bigger every day: the twentieth century. Margaret Ormsby remarked, almost thirty years ago, that we in British Columbia 'are ignorant of the mainsprings of our political development,' and the point is almost as valid today as it was then.[4] Since Ormsby pointed out some of the 'neglected aspects of British Columbia's history,' Martin Robin's singular survey of west-coast politics, *The Company Province*,[5] has appeared to mixed reviews. There has been some writing on the chequered history of the Co-operative Commonwealth Federation (later the New Democratic Party), particularly in the form of graduate theses, though it has been in power less than any other major provincial party. Social Credit has also received a little scholarly attention. But the Liberals and the Conservatives, it would seem, are almost forgotten at the provincial level. More work needs to be done on those leaders and parties that have dominated the government benches in British Columbia. And Pattullo is no exception. Apart from an oft-quoted article by Ormsby, also written nearly three decades ago, no one has considered his life and career in any detail.[6]

Yet his biography is more than a life of Duff Pattullo: it is also the history of a region. Though regionalism has been much discussed by Canadian historians, they have never been precise about its definition. If, as Pattullo argued, Canada is made up of five regions, the one province that most clearly qualifies as a region, even if there is some fuzziness at the northern border, is British Columbia. Duff Pattullo did not merely come to live in this westernmost region, he also became of it. The rhythm of his life – as he moved from local frontier development in the beginning, to building a provincial economy in the teens and twenties, to struggling with the national context in the thirties – is very much the pattern of British Columbia's history in this century. Pattullo's politics were thus born of his region. Seeing things from the periphery rather than the centre, it is hardly surprising that he came to view the Canadian confederation in a way that was very different from the Ottawa men. And, just as Pattullo presented another perspective on Canada before the Rowell-Sirois Commission, this biography offers an approach to Canadian history and politics that is different from the centralist interpretation perpetuated by the Rowell-Sirois historians.[7]

Within his particular province, Duff Pattullo was first and foremost a politician. He was one of those men 'defined by the world,' whose sense of self was comparatively weak until he developed a public persona and for whom politics was a way of life.[8] His private life usually took second place to his public career, and many of his personal relationships suffered as a result. In stretches of this biography, readers will learn less of the private Pattullo than they might wish. They will also learn that Pattullo was a man's man who operated in what was, to a large extent, a man's world. The towns of the western frontier, like the political life of British Columbia in the 1920s and 1930s, were dominated by males. Pattullo enjoyed the power and privilege of his gender and he also paid the price of these prerogatives. His personal relations with women, especially those who were close to him, were often less than satisfactory. To the extent that this biography looks at masculine British Columbia it could be described, to take in vain the title of a colleague's book, as 'redinking Canada.' The connoisseurs of British Columbia history will appreciate this savour of tradition, particularly as represented by certain references to Richard McBride.

There is one final point to make. Even though no life can be recaptured wholly, as it was, it does not necessarily follow that all biography is ultimately fiction.[9] And yet every subject does not speak for itself. Rather, biographies are created by historians who may miss points of vital importance and tend to see what they are looking for, but who try to present a clear and accurate likeness. Sometimes, as I wrote, I wondered if I could hear Duff Pattullo saying over my shoulder that I had got it all wrong:

that it was all 'misinformation and misinterpretation,' as he would have put it. I can only hope that these were the moments of overactive imagination.

Like all books, this one was not written alone. The first debts that I incurred were to some archival friends. When they were both fairly new to what was then the Provincial Archives of British Columbia, Kent Haworth and Terry Eastwood devoted time and energy to organizing the Pattullo Papers. The collection had languished for many years and was even held 'in reserve' for a time, until these two put it in order and drew up a detailed inventory. When I later began reading the material, it was an object lesson in how historians are served by dedicated archivists. Nearly as useful were the times we three spent talking about Duff over coffee at the 'ptomaine palace.' Later Kent, as archivist for the University of Toronto, was again very hospitable and helpful. Though he is now in Nova Scotia, I hope he is still enough of a west-coaster to enjoy the heading to the first chapter. Terry has also moved on to another position, but the staff of what is now the British Columbia Archives and Records Service has continued to be friendly and helpful. I am also grateful for the assistance I received from Special Collections at the University of British Columbia Library and University of Victoria Library, Yukon Territorial Archives in Whitehorse, Rick Stuart and the staff of Parks Canada in Dawson City, Prince Rupert City Hall and the Prince Rupert Public Library, University of Calgary Library, Provincial Archives of Manitoba, Archives of Ontario, University of Toronto Archives, Queen's University Archives, University of Western Ontario Library, Woodstock Public Library, Woodstock Museum, and, last but never least, the National Archives of Canada. None of the research in any of these places would have been possible without the financial assistance of the Social Sciences and Humanities Research Council.

My second set of obligations is to the relatives of Duff Pattullo, particularly his daughter Doris Collison, who was helpful in every possible way while never attempting to influence what I wrote. For the conversations we had, the letters and photographs she let me use, and the insights she provided, I am more grateful than I can say. I will always regret that I did not get this book written in time for her to read the final version. I must also thank her daughters and especially Beth Pattullo for her recollections and assistance, even to the extent of letting me stay in her house during one of those Victoria summers. I hope this book does justice to the name she holds so dear. Ethelwyn and Adam Zimmerman, along with other family members in Toronto, were also forthcoming about their relative. All of these people provided perceptions that could not be found on paper.

Many colleagues also helped me write this book, some without even knowing it and they shall remain nameless. I should, however, like to thank Edward Ingram for his timely and forthright admonitions. Chris Anstead, Robert Bothwell, Douglas Cole, George Emery, Michael Fellman, Stephen Gray, Hugh Johnston, and Howard Kushner all made helpful comments and observations as I was doing the research and writing. Patricia Roy and John English not only were true colleagues along the way, but also took the time to read and criticize the manuscript. I appreciate the enthusiastic interest that Gerry Hallowell and Laura Macleod of the University of Toronto Press took in this project and the editorial skill of Rosemary Shipton, who fine-tuned the manuscript.

Mary-Ellen Kelm, who survived living with two men, made many helpful suggestions, one of which she now disowns. Without her, the book would still be unfinished. And, finally, I have dedicated this book to my sons, knowing they will take it as very slight recompense for the time I have stolen from them to write it.

During the research on this book I once spent a few days up the coast at Prince Rupert working on the records in City Hall. Since my time was short, a staff member kindly let me have an office so I could keep working after five o'clock. During the evening, Peter Lester, who has followed in Duff Pattullo's footsteps as mayor of Prince Rupert, arrived for a council meeting. In contrast to Pattullo who served as mayor for only one year, Lester was then, I believe, the longest serving mayor of any Canadian city. Somewhat taken aback to see a total stranger in one of his offices, he demanded, 'What are you doing here.' Searching for a quick reply, I replied lamely, 'Well, it's a long story.' Now, at last, here it is.

Duff Pattullo of British Columbia

CHAPTER 1

Woodstock, Ontario

'The field is so limited for one of my great capabilities'

Like most British Columbians of his generation, Duff Pattullo came from somewhere else. And, as with any immigrant, the place from whence he came was a part of the baggage he brought with him. Thomas Dufferin Pattullo was born on 19 January 1873 in Woodstock, Ontario, the third child and second son of George Robson and Mary (Rounds) Pattullo.

The young Pattullo's immediate forebears were Scottish, not Italian as many were later to suppose. Pattullo, or Pattillo, is a fairly common lowland name, probably originating in Fife where it is perpetuated in a tiny hamlet called Pittillock. By the fifteenth century some of the Pattullos had moved across the Firth of Tay to settle in Forfarshire, part of the present county of Angus, and there, in the town of Kerriemuir, Duff Pattullo's great-grandfather, Alexander Pattullo, was born in 1775. Alexander pursued a military career, serving in a number of local regiments before becoming a non-commissioned officer in the forty-second Highlanders: the famous Black Watch. Demobbed after the end of the Napoleonic wars, Alexander was in his forties, married for a second time, the father of seven children, and looking for a new career. But prospects were few in the depressed and unsettled conditions that prevailed in Scotland in the years immediately after 1815. With the final defeat of Napoleon, thousands of old soldiers like Alexander Pattullo were looking for work at a time when rural Scotland was suffering a crisis that had been building up for decades. Traditional methods of farming had depleted the land to the point where it could no longer support a growing population. Agricultural improvements and the resulting clearances produced an exodus from the countryside. Scotland was simply overcrowded. So Alexander Pattullo, like many others, looked for new land and sought new opportunities in the new world.

When the Pattullo family came to Canada in 1820, Alexander, at the age of forty-five, was probably thinking more of his children's future than his own. 'Having the means to cultivate a New Farm,' he applied for and was granted 100 acres of land in the township of Caledon.[1] In the backwoods of Peel County, the fifth concession west of the village of Caledon was not prime farm land. Its tough ground would yield only with long, hard work. Yet, as the Pattullos settled among McGregors and Camerons, the rolling, wooded hills of Caledon must have reminded the newcomers in many ways of home. Having established his family on this new land, Alexander survived for only eight years, but his sons continued to farm in Caledon until the middle of the century. The census of Canada West for 1851 shows that Halket Pattullo, aged forty-two, was living with his wife and nine children in a log house in Caledon.[2] The fact that the family was still living in a log house indicates that they had not made their fortune. Halket, the third son of Alexander, had married Jane Robson. Their seventh child, a son, was born in 1845 and named George Robson Pattullo.

Duff's father spent his early years in Caledon until 1855, when the family moved to Blenheim Township in Oxford County where Halket had purchased 100 acres comprising the north half of Lot 13 on the Fifth Concession.[3] The gently sloping land of Blenheim was far superior to that of Caledon. The Pattullo farm was in a rich, fertile area, one concession south of the little village of Drumbo. When Halket Pattullo died, ownership of the land was to be assumed by the eldest son, Alexander.[4] Even on this better land, the farm would only support one family, so Halket's younger children were obliged to earn their living in other ways. Two sons, Thomas and William, left Oxford County to seek their fortunes in the goldfields of British Columbia.[5] But it was largely through the careers of George Robson and his younger brother, Andrew, that the Pattullo name was to become prominent within the boundaries of Oxford.

As befitted the son of a farmer, George Pattullo always extolled the virtues of rural life, but it was in the towns of Oxford and the immediate vicinity that he was to make his way. He attended primary school in Blenheim Township and high school in Dundas, and briefly it seemed that he might make a career of school teaching. The classroom of a little school in Drumbo was not, however, entirely to his liking and certainly it did not absorb all of a young man's energy and ambition. While in Drumbo he courted and married Mary Ann Rounds, the seventeen-year-old daughter of the popular local doctor, James Burley Rounds. The Rounds family came from Burford, the township immediately to the south of Blenheim, but James practised for most of his life in Drumbo. He married Eliza Berry in 1848 and Mary, their first child, was born two years later. Dr James Rounds was a well-known and much loved member of local society and was active in municipal politics, serving as both councillor and reeve in Blenheim.[6] In such a small community the Pattullos and the Rounds must have been well acquainted. Although the Rounds were Baptists and the Pattullos Presbyterians, the two families shared an interest and involvement in Reform politics. Members of both families had also gone west in search of gold. James Rounds's uncle, Ransford Rounds, had led a party overland for the California goldfields in 1852. Ransford himself died on the way, but other members of the party arrived and settled in California. James's brother, Charles Rounds, farmed near Drumbo and in 1878 purchased land from the Pattullos.[7] So George Pattullo and Mary Rounds would have known each other for several years before they were married in 1867.

Though their connections with the village were strong, the young couple did not stay long in Drumbo. While he was still teaching, George Pattullo became the local correspondent in Drumbo for the Paris *Transcript*. Newspaper work was more to his liking than school teaching and the proprietor of the *Transcript*, Robert Patterson, was impressed enough with

George's ability to suggest that he become the managing editor of the paper. Pattullo took up the offer and held the position for nine months, long enough to confirm his growing interest in journalism. Then, late in the summer of 1870, George Pattullo made a decision that was to determine the course of his life. The Woodstock *Sentinel* had been established in 1854 by John McWhinnie and Alexander Hay and had remained in the McWhinnie family ever since. But now the paper was up for sale and, although he had very little experience in the editorial end of running a newspaper and absolutely none on the business side, George decided to buy the operation. With his wife and their first child, Ethelwyn, who was born two years earlier, George Pattullo moved to Woodstock and began a new career as owner and editor of a local newspaper. The Woodstock *Sentinel* appeared for the first time under the Pattullo name on 1 October 1870.

Centrally located in the rich agricultural lands of Oxford, Woodstock had, by 1870, established its position as the commercial and administrative nucleus of the county. Yet even its most avid boosters could not have described Woodstock's growth as spectacular. The grandiose plans of John Graves Simcoe to develop the area in the 1790s had come to very little other than the arrival of the first few settlers from the United States. Simcoe had proposed that a road be built from Burlington Bay on Lake Ontario inland to the Thames River and on to the site of his planned provincial capital named London. His plans also called for a town to be built at the point where his road, Dundas Street as he named it, met the Thames. When Simcoe left the colony in 1796, the 'Governor's Road' was mostly just a blazed line and the town of Oxford had failed to emerge from the forest.[8] It was not until the early 1830s, and the arrival of a group of British half-pay officers, that any significant development took place on the site of what was to become Woodstock. Credit for founding the town should probably go to Andrew Drew, who arrived in Upper Canada in 1832 representing his partner Rear-Admiral Henry Vansittart and anxious to make money from developing land. He chose a townsite on the southwestern tip of Blandford Township bounded by the Thames River to the west and Dundas

Street to the south. Drew had the land surveyed, named the first streets, and began to build.[9] By 1835 a post office had been opened and two years later Woodstock, as it was now called, was made a district town.

But still development was slow. Woodstock remained isolated from the major trade routes and was unable to compete with the larger centres of Brantford, Hamilton, and London. There was a major influx of population into Oxford County in the late 1840s and Woodstock's prospects improved with the development of new transportation links. Roads were upgraded and a group of local men formed a company to build a railway connecting Woodstock with Lake Erie at Port Dover. While progress on that scheme was delayed, the first locomotive passed through the county on the Great Western Railway.[10] With the avenues of commerce opened, Woodstock could develop and prosper as an agricultural supply town. By the time the Pattullos were establishing themselves there in the 1870s, Woodstock was the county town and judicial seat for Oxford, its population approached 5000, and three railways crossed its boundaries. The continued importance of farming to the town's economy was acknowledged by the annual agricultural shows held on the fair grounds on the west side of the town, but the townspeople were also proud of their retail stores and some secondary manufacturing had been established by local entrepreneurs. Outside observers may have felt that Woodstock's growth was stimulated by the business generated 'by the demands of the wealthy section in which it was located, rather than the inherent energy or enterprise of the businessmen within.'[11] Yet, by exploiting the advantages of its location and building on its role as an administrative centre, Woodstock had become a solid community that could look forward with some certainty to steady, if not spectacular growth. It was the kind of place where a young man who was prepared to learn through experience might venture into the newspaper business with a fair chance of success.

Not that the new owner of the *Sentinel* was welcomed with open arms by everyone in Woodstock. George Pattullo later recalled that the editor of the conservative paper, the *Times*, commented that it boded ill for both business and journalism in

Woodstock that the *Sentinel* had fallen into such inexperienced hands. Pattullo, who seldom conceded that any Tory spoke the truth, later confessed that in this case perhaps the editor of the *Times* had a point. Even the proprietors of a Liberal paper thought they saw an opening in Woodstock following the sale of the *Sentinel*. The owners of the *Review* that had hitherto been published in nearby Princeton suddenly moved their paper to Woodstock in time to appear on the same day as the new *Sentinel*.[12] The expectations of his competitors notwithstanding, George Pattullo overcame his lack of experience and quickly turned the *Sentinel* into a successful local newspaper that was to continue publishing under the Pattullo name for thirty-three years. Operating out of his office on Dundas Street in the centre of town, he began by publishing once a week on Friday morning. The four-page newspaper included two pages of Canadian and overseas news, one page of local information and advertisements, and a final page devoted to selections of edifying verse, advice for farm and garden, and a section headed 'Humorous.' The politics of the new newspaper, as the masthead proudly announced, were 'Reform.' Like any local newspaper, the *Sentinel* also carried personal announcements. The issue for Friday, 24 January 1873, gave notice of the birth of a son to G.R. Pattullo and his wife on the previous Sunday, the nineteenth.[13]

Thomas Dufferin Pattullo was baptized the following June in Knox Presbyterian Church at the same time as his brother, James Burleigh Rounds Pattullo, who was two years older. The future premier of British Columbia was named Thomas after his uncle, who was in the Cariboo, and Dufferin after the Earl of Dufferin, who, as governor general of Canada, had visited Woodstock a few months before Duff was born.[14] As he grew up he preferred Dufferin, presumably because it had a little more panache than plain Tom. When Duff was born the family lived in a house on Finkle Street that was rented from D.W. Karn, who owned an organ factory in town.[15] During their first nine years in Woodstock, the Pattullos moved several times from one rented house to another, even living for a while among the town's elite on Vansittart Avenue. By the end of the decade George Pattullo was sufficiently certain of his own position to purchase a home. At the east end of Woodstock, Dundas Street rose up a gentle incline before it stretched away towards Hamilton. On the crest of the rise, on the corner of Hincks Street, named for the great reformer, Duff's father bought six lots in 1879 and three more on adjacent Centre Street the following year.[16] He soon owned the best part of a city block – space enough for a large house, extensive lawns, trees, gardens, an orchard, and a number of farm animals to supply the household necessities. The house was a substantial, two storied, brick structure with a wrap-around veranda. Inside it was expansive and roomy, with a big country kitchen and breakfast room, and, in the front of the house, a good-sized drawing room that was put to constant use since there were always relatives and other guests to stay.

It was here, at 'Burnside,' that Duff grew up. The large house and spacious grounds required constant upkeep, and his earliest childhood memories were of working around the home: tending the fire places in the house, pushing a hand mower over what seemed like miles of lawn, minding the animals, or sorting bushels of apples in the spring. Yet life was not all work in the younger years. He was also later to recall how he and his brothers and sisters always had a lot of fun,[17] and, as boys, he and James were particular playmates. They amused themselves as most boys would in such surroundings: after they had eaten all they could they fought with apples in the orchard, tossed dice behind the currant bushes, let loose a prize game cock in the neighbour's hen house and rejoiced at its clarion call of victory, and then sat on the huge gate posts at the end of the drive and challenged every passing boy, who was not too big, to mortal combat. It was in this same context that Duff showed at an early age the independence that was such an important part of his personality. One of his responsibilities was to milk three cows morning and afternoon. Young Duff soon found, however, that this chore was taking too much of his spare time after school when other boys were playing baseball. So, while his father was out of town, he sold the cows. He quite expected to be reprimanded when his father returned, but to his surprise he was commended for his enterprise, especially when his father found that he had put the proceeds, more than $150, in the bank.[18] Duff never came to care much for animals, later observing that 'I am very fond of cats and dogs. I am also fond of lions and tigers, and am thrilled with the industry of ants and bees but I do not like to consort at close quarters with any of them.'[19] And yet throughout his life, no matter how far away he travelled, he always remembered the house and gardens of Burnside with great affection.

His parents, particularly his father, were an important influence on his early life and they too were recalled with warmth in his later years. Duff probably inherited his determination and will in large part from his mother. Mary Pattullo was a striking rather than beautiful woman, her strong features indicating a strength of character that Duff was to display more as he grew older than he did as a young man. As the eldest daughter of a busy local doctor and politician, Mary undoubtedly learned to assume family responsibilities at an early age. Like her father, her husband was also a man who pursued both his career and his interests with enthusiasm. Publishing the morning *Sentinel* took George Pattullo out of the house in the evenings, and his increasing involvement in public affairs meant he was often away from home. Mary Pattullo ran the house and cared for the children, bearing another child almost every two years until there were seven. Ethelwyn was the first, followed by James and Duff, then two daughters, Pearl and Kate. Duff's younger brother George was born in 1879 and Mary came three years later. Mary the mother loved her children and missed them sorely on those occasions when she was away from home with her husband. In 1883 they were both absent for several months while he was working for the Ontario government. Mary Pattullo wrote often to 'my two big boys, Ma's champions,' as she called Duff and his older brother James, 'and my dear little helpmate Wynnie,' the eldest daughter.[20]

Sadly, however, the family circle was abruptly broken the following year when Mary died giving birth to her eighth child, Andrew. Duff was eleven when he lost his mother and the event left a sharp memory that was made all the more poignant by the fact that his mother died on 8 April, his father's birthday.

Little details of that day remained with him forever. After many years he could still recall meeting his father in the morning and giving him a china matchbox for his birthday and later in the day his father picking him up at the foot of the stairs. By evening the sacrifice had been made: the baby survived but the mother did not.[21] George Pattullo later remarried. His second wife, Frances Camilla Biggar, was from an eminent family but never replaced their mother in the hearts of the Pattullo children, and Wynnie played a large part in raising the younger ones.

There was a pattern of untimely death on the male side of the Pattullo family through the generations. When Duff was six his grandfather, Halket Pattullo, took his own life, and later his uncle Andrew with whom his father was very close did so too. Andrew Pattullo committed suicide in 1903 while on a speaking tour of England. In 1936 Duff's youngest brother Andrew, who like his namesake uncle spent much of his life struggling with poor health and alcoholism, also killed himself. While the possibility of suicide may run in families and perhaps prompted Duff to take chances, it was the death of his mother that affected him most of all. Like many children who lose a parent, he may not have absorbed his grief. On the fateful day, by his own recollection, he was more involved in his father's birthday than the awareness that his mother was dying in an upstairs bedroom. The unexpected loss as a child perhaps explains Duff's willingness to take risks as a young man, in an effort to explore his own self-destructive impulses. He would also, in his early twenties, put the love of his father very much to the test.

In the meantime, in the absence of his mother, Duff's father was the single most important individual in his life. Through later childhood and adolescence his father was his guiding light. Like Duff, all the Pattullo children grew up with a great deal of fondness for 'the governor,' or 'bops' as they affectionately called him. George Robson Pattullo had handsome, open features – good looks that his sons would inherit. A ready sparkle in his eye indicated a nimble sense of humour. As a writer he liked to play with long words and his son remembered his amusement 'as he dilated upon the coruscations and scintillations of genius.'[22] George Pattullo was genial and ingenuous, liked to socialize, took a genuine interest in people, and was usually willing to see the better side of them. These were all characteristics that Duff later shared to a greater or lesser extent. Along with these major traits, Duff also acquired some little habits from his father, including the practice of early rising. The day started at Burnside at 4 AM. The governor loved to get up early in the morning and Duff 'did not mind' once he was up.[23] It was a habit that the son retained, and through his working life he would often feel he had the jump on other men by starting his day earlier. Duff was also to follow the example of his father to a considerable extent when he came to make choices of career.

When Duff was a child, much of his father's time was taken up with improving the fortunes of 'the daily Pattullo,' as the *Sentinel* came to be known, particularly to angry Conservatives. During the 1870s George Pattullo built up the *Sentinel* from merely one among many to the leading newspaper in the county. By 1881 it billed itself as having a larger circulation than all the other local papers in Oxford combined, and therefore the best advertising medium in the district. Pattullo and Company also claimed to have the largest printing house in the province outside the main centres, and they solicited all types of book and job printing.[24] The Pattullo family's involvement in the Liberal party meant that the *Sentinel* also picked up a certain amount of patronage in the form of political advertising and printing, although, inevitably, they sometimes complained they were not getting enough.[25] By the end of the 1870s the *Sentinel* was well established and, as George Pattullo spent more and more time on politics and public affairs, he spent less time on his newspaper. He brought his younger brother Andrew in as a junior partner and, in 1878, the *Sentinel* was amalgamated with the other Reform newspaper in Woodstock, the *Review*. The Woodstock *Sentinel-Review* was edited jointly by the two Pattullo brothers for a couple of years, but in 1880 Andrew bought out George's interest and continued as sole editor while sharing ownership with a series of partners including a nephew named Andrew Laidlaw. Pattullo and Company published their first daily edition in 1886 and Andrew remained proprietor and editor of the *Sentinel-Review* until a few months before his death.

In nineteenth-century Ontario there was a close association between party politics, particularly Reform party politics, and the partisan 'party' press. Involvement in the Reform or Liberal party was also a family tradition among the Pattullos. The patron saint of the Reform newspapermen politicians was, of course, the editor of *The Globe* in Toronto, George Brown, who had been the member for South Oxford in the 1860s. As a boy, George Pattullo was impressed with Brown's power as a platform orator and had written to him for advice on how to become a newspaper editor. Although he was unknown to the man he sought to emulate, he received a kindly and practical reply.[26] So it was quite natural that, during his early years in Woodstock, Pattullo should take as much interest in politics as in the *Sentinel*. Indeed, the two were closely intertwined. Only a few months after his arrival in Woodstock, Pattullo was a prominent member of a committee of Reformers preparing for a forthcoming visit by Alexander Mackenzie and Edward Blake. After the two Liberal leaders had been to town, the *Sentinel* was littered with headlines trumpeting the 'Magnificent Reception' that 'Glorious Old Oxford' had given 'to the People's Champions.' Pattullo's *Sentinel* also revelled in Liberal electoral victories, and none more so than the defeat of John A. Macdonald and the Tories in the federal election of January 1874. That campaign had been a battle 'of honesty against dishonesty – morality against immorality – electoral purity against electoral corruption – an honest system of Government against a corrupt system of Government – in a word, a battle of Right and Wrong,' and the editor of the *Sentinel* was overjoyed to announce that 'right has triumphed ... gloriously.'[27]

While all Liberal victories were to be savoured, George Pattullo became more involved in the provincial than the federal party. In 1872 the premier of Ontario, Edward Blake, and his treasurer, Alexander Mackenzie, left provincial politics for Ottawa, and Blake handed the premiership over to Oliver Mowat. Shortly thereafter it afforded George Pattullo 'no ordinary degree of pleasure' to report that, of all the constituencies offered, the new premier had selected North Oxford. There were, wrote Pattullo, great advantages for Oxford in being represented by the first minister of the crown.[28] There were also to be great advantages for George Pattullo in an increasingly close association with Mowat and his Liberal machine.

Duff Pattullo later recalled that Oxford County 'was a heavy producer of dairy products and young Liberals.'[29] He might well have added that his father played a very important role in the latter. George Pattullo was part of an effort in the late 1870s to organize the Ontario Liberal party on a province-wide basis. In 1876, at a convention in Toronto, he and James Young, a member of the House of Commons, were put in charge of a committee set up to begin the process of establishing a centralized party structure.[30] Two years later he became secretary of the Ontario Reform Association and, as chief Liberal organizer, he was often away from home, particularly during the run up to the 1878 federal election. The euphoria of four years earlier was, alas, not to be repeated and Liberals were dismayed when the voters rejected their politics of purity and returned the old rascal himself: John A. Macdonald. Deeply disillusioned, George Pattullo was tempted to quit his post in the party but was convinced to stay on until the next provincial election. Meanwhile, he conducted a post-mortem on the Liberal demise by sending out a questionnaire asking local correspondents in the ridings to comment on the reasons for the electoral defeat and the state of Liberal organization in their area. The Liberals had lost the election for a number of reasons, but important among them was their over-confidence. They were so convinced of their own rectitude that they felt all they had to do was inform the people of their policies and virtue would triumph.[31] It was a form of political optimism, or perhaps naîvety, that was to be a part of Duff Pattullo's later political career.

While his father often half-heartedly warned the young Pattullo to stay out of the political arena, Duff grew up amid politics and discussions of politics. He frequently accompanied his father as he went about the county to political meetings. Liberal leaders of the day were often guests at the Pattullo home. Mowat frequently stayed at Burnside during campaign trips to his North Oxford constituency, as did Richard Cartwright, who was the member for South Oxford for a time. On one overwhelming occasion there was a visit from a group of men whose names sound like a roll-call of late nineteenth-century liberalism in Canada: in addition to the premier of Ontario, Honoré Mercier, W.S. Fielding, Edward Blake, Richard Cartwright, and David Mills were all in Woodstock at the same time.[32] George Pattullo corresponded with Wilfrid Laurier, whose portrait hung in the Pattullo living room. The Pattullos were also acquainted with another Liberal couple living in nearby Berlin who had a son nearly two years younger than Duff named William Lyon Mackenzie King. While they did not have the same family connections back to the Rebellion of 1837, the Pattullo home was steeped in Reformism and its patriarch continued to be deeply involved in the Liberal party of Oliver Mowat.

Duff learnt his politics from his father and he would remember many of these early lessons in Mowat Liberalism in later life. Oliver Mowat remained premier of Ontario for twenty-four years partly through his efficient use of patronage, and George Pattullo was one cog in this big machine. Like a host of other supporters, Duff's father was rewarded for services rendered with a post that enabled him to continue working for the party. In 1886 James Ingersoll, who had been registrar of Oxford County for more than fifty years, died and George Pattullo was appointed to replace him. It was not the first position that Mowat had given to Pattullo, but this one was permanent. George held the position until his death thirty-six years later. He drew his income as a proportion of the fees collected for land transactions and, by the mid-1890s, it amounted to about $2500 a year. The duties of the county registrar were not onerous; the position was a sinecure that gave the office-holder plenty of time for party work. Mowat wrote to Pattullo to say he was pleased to have 'had this opportunity to secure the comfort of you and your family.'[33]

As well as providing for his supporters, Mowat has been said to deserve the title 'father of the provincial rights movement in Canada,'[34] and in this context, too, George Pattullo played a minor role. No issue epitomized more the effort to protect and expand Ontario's jurisdiction than the dispute with the federal government over the location of the boundary with Manitoba. During the summer of 1883 both Ontario and Manitoba were trying to establish administrative control over Rat Portage, as Kenora was then known. In the midst of the controversy, Pattullo was appointed a commissioner for Ontario and sent to Rat Portage to gather information and to oversee the province's interests in the area. In August, when a public meeting was called to consider the question of obtaining municipal incorporation from Ontario, George Pattullo was the spokesman for the Ontario side in a debate with John Norquay, the premier of Manitoba. Pattullo must have been persuasive because his views carried the day.[35]

Many Ontario Liberals were, of course, much more enthusiastic about advocating provincial rights for Ontario than they were about conceding the same rights to other provinces. Reformers supported western expansion because they believed it was in the interests of 'Empire Ontario.' Those in the west who resisted this imperialism were merely obstacles to be removed. Thus Louis Riel was described as 'this foul murderer' in the Woodstock *Sentinel*, and one of Duff Pattullo's earliest and most vivid memories of Toronto was cheering with his father at the return of the troops who had suppressed the North-West Rebellion in 1885.[36] A few years later, however, once Manitoba was safely in Liberal hands, George Pattullo could write to the newly elected premier, Thomas Greenway, and advise him 'to stand unflinching by the Province, to insist upon its fullest rights being recognized at Ottawa and elsewhere.' Pattullo also thought, needless to say, that Greenway should 'expose fully' the misdeeds of Norquay and the Conservatives over the past ten years.[37]

There was more to Mowat Liberalism than patronage and provincial rights. Mowat himself was pragmatic and cautious, but under the calm surface the reform current still flowed. Governing through a long period of depression, Mowat moved away from the old *laissez faire* individualism of an earlier generation of Liberals. He recognized the possibility of a more active state that when necessary, or when pushed, would intervene to regulate social and economic development. Mowat was eclectic rather than doctrinaire in his approach to policy making: he took good ideas from wherever they came and was particularly prone to turning the recommendations of royal commissions into legislation. To ensure the continued development of agriculture he introduced various forms of government assistance to farmers, including loans to allow them to drain land. Mowat not only confirmed the agricultural roots of the Reform tradition in Ontario, he also used the power of the state in the new sectors of the late nineteenth-century economy. He asserted Ontario's right to control its own bountiful resources. Government regulation of mineral deposits was tightened. In the late 1890s the provincial government, in an effort to eliminate the export of sawlogs, took steps to convince lumber companies to do their processing in Ontario.[38] Mowat fostered the opening up of new land and tried to attract the immigrants to settle it. He was willing to spend money on public works: on roads and railways, on buildings, and on fire protection in the forests. He felt that the state should intervene in a modest way between capital and labour, and passed legislation to regulate working conditions and to establish a minimal form of arbitration. Mowat also increased the role of the state in social areas. Health was seen as more of a public responsibility, there was legislation to protect children, as well as government action on education.[39] Two and three decades later many of these policies would have echoes in British Columbia after George Pattullo's son became minister of lands and then premier.

When Oliver Mowat withdrew from provincial politics in 1896 it was the end of an era for Ontario, and George Pattullo became less active in party affairs. Not that the Pattullos were absent from the scene. Mowat was replaced as the member for North Oxford by Duff's uncle, Andrew Pattullo. When the Ontario legislature met in 1897, the new member for North Oxford recalled the efforts of the absent champion of provincial rights in Ontario and thereafter he continued to be a supporter of the Mowat line.[40] As president of the Ontario Good Roads Association, Andrew Pattullo was an active promoter of the Mowat policy of improved roads. A fountain erected in his memory that still stands in front of the Woodstock Museum in the centre of town bears witness to his contribution in this area. He also advocated improved methods of dairying and served as president of the Western Dairyman's Association. Andrew was an accomplished orator and, at the time of his death in 1903, he had been in England for three months speaking publicly in support of Joseph Chamberlain's campaign for imperial preference.

Andrew's Pattullo's death was a great shock to the family as it was to Ontario. Duff's younger brother, George, was working for a London newspaper and staying with his uncle at the time. Andrew was in poor health, he found the speech-making exhausting, and he was, perhaps, disappointed by some of the adverse reaction in the British press to his ideas. He killed himself on 29 December, during that sometimes depressing hiatus between Christmas and New Year when, for active people, life seems to stand still. The younger George found his uncle's body with his throat cut by a razor. Andrew had left a note with the three words, 'Forgive me George.'[41] It was undoubtedly meant for his nephew, but it might equally well have been addressed to his brother in Woodstock. There had been tension between the two brothers as, a generation later, there would be between Duff and George, yet the personal loss was hard to bear. Political life went on. In 1911 another recently appointed leader of the Ontario Liberal party was looking for a safe seat and found it in the riding of Oliver Mowat and Andrew Pattullo.[42] The new member for North Oxford was a man who would later play an important part in Duff Pattullo's political career. His name was Newton Rowell.

When his brother Andrew became the politician in the family, George Pattullo gave more time to other forms of public service, though these too were a part of the Mowat legacy. A decade earlier, in 1885, Mowat had appointed George Pattullo as secretary of the Niagara Falls Park Commission. Ever since he became premier, Mowat had been under pressure to clean out the undesirable elements operating around Niagara Falls, but he had deflected all suggestions to establish a publicly owned park. By 1885 he was caught between the demands of the politically influential private interests who wanted to develop the area and the force of public opinion that was building up in favour of a public park. In an effort to disentangle the situation, Mowat established the Niagara Falls Park Commission to investigate the matter and select a suitable private company to run the park. To the premier's surprise his commission, impressed by the New York State Reservation at Niagara, recommended provincial rather than private ownership of the Canadian side. As Mowat pondered, George Pattullo threw his weight behind the idea of a free public park. He wrote to Mowat to point out the political implications of the popular support for a government-run park and the success of New York State's operation. He did not expect much objection to the cost, arguing that it was now 'a recognized duty of Governments' to preserve natural wonders and he cited the American precedents of Yosemite and Yellowstone. Pattullo's views were influential. Mowat adopted virtually all of them when, in 1887, he finally introduced legislation to create Ontario's first publicly owned park.[43]

The Niagara area was of great historical significance as well as scenic beauty and George Pattullo's participation in the politics of conserving one of Ontario's natural wonders was a prelude to his efforts to preserve other aspects of the province's heritage. He was a prime mover in the formation of the Oxford Historical Society in January 1897. At a meeting held in his office he was elected the first president.[44] Some of the impetus to form the society came from Pattullo's friend, James Coyne, of St Thomas. Coyne was in many ways Pattullo's counterpart in Elgin County: active in the West Elgin Reform Association, he was an unsuccessful Liberal candidate in 1886 before being appointed registrar for Elgin County. The Oxford Historical Society initially affiliated with the Pioneer and Historical Society of Ontario and in June 1897 Coyne was made president of the provincial organization. With the encouragement of George Ross, the minister of education, Coyne reorganized the society and expanded its activities, a process which led to the formation of the Ontario Historical Society a year later. When the act to incorporate the new society was passed in 1899, Andrew Pattullo guided it through the Ontario legislature. George Pattullo joined the executive of the society in the same year, just as it entered what has been called perhaps the most active period of its history.[45] In 1904 he was elected president of the Ontario Historical Society and in 1905, when he gave his presidential address, the annual meeting was held at Niagara-on-the-Lake, a town with potent associations with the Loyalists and the War of 1812. That same year he led a delegation that was largely responsible for convincing the federal government to preserve Fort George where, wrote Pattullo, 'the soil has been reddened and made sacred with the life blood of these brave men who so nobly fought to repel the invader and preserve the unity of the Empire, all for Britain's glory.'[46]

The leaders of the Ontario Historical Society at this time saw history as mythology. They sought to validate and explain the present by perpetuating and popularizing an acceptable view of the past. They were advocates of the Loyalist tradition, the imperial connection, and national patriotism. They organized local celebrations of these aspects of Canada's past and were preoccupied with erecting monuments and raising flags. In later years Pattullo wrote to Coyne on the letterhead of the Oxford Patriotic Association, of which he was vice-president.[47] George Pattullo was the only person in the history of the Ontario Historical Society to serve as president on two separate occasions and in 1919 when, reluctantly, he held the office again, the annual meeting was held on his home ground in Woodstock. On this occasion his presidential address was a paean of praise for Oxford County and its early pioneers.[48] There was always a strong element of local boosterism in the activities of the affiliated societies. The society also made more substantial and lasting contributions to the understanding of Ontario's past. Pattullo was a strong supporter of the society's new publication *Papers and Records,* which appeared for the first time in 1899 and was later to carry his presidential address. Pattullo brought his political influence to bear in the society's effort to convince the Ontario government to establish a provincial archives. Once again his views carried some weight among Liberal politicians and, in 1903, the province appointed the first Ontario archivist.

Although George Pattullo worked hard for the province's historical society, just as he had done earlier for the provincial Liberal party, he remained a Woodstock man. He loved the place and was never tempted to leave. 'After fifty years in a quiet little town' he did not regret that he had resisted the blandishments of the big cities. He had had his chances to move to one of the larger centres but he thought 'more can be got out of life here than in the glare, the din and the hub-bub of the city.'[49] His commitment to the community was also revealed by his involvement in public service and good works at the local level. He took a particular interest in the younger generation in Woodstock, serving at different times as president of the Woodstock Children's Aid Society and chairman of the Public School Board. There is no evidence that he neglected his own children, but as Duff and his brothers and sisters came of age their father gave much of his time to the local community as well as to various provincial organizations.

The Pattullo children grew up in comfortable circumstances. The family was not immensely wealthy, but they lacked for nothing and were secure enough, particularly after their father was made registrar of Oxford. The household was a substantial one and the fact that it included domestic servants was a measure of the family's wealth and status. George Pattullo was a well-known and highly regarded figure in the local community and undoubtedly, in the eyes of his children, he played an important role on the larger stage. Within the small world of Woodstock the children had every advantage: comfort, security, and social position. Some of them, especially Duff's cautious and circumspect elder brother James, were able to conform to expectations. But for Duff, the safe and secure sphere of his early life began to be limited and restricting. In later years he often said that as a boy he had lamented the fact he was growing up 'in a too prosaic age.'[50] As he became a young man there was within him a strong desire to kick over the traces – to cut loose and find his own way in the wider world. Unlike his father who was satisfied with Woodstock, Duff had inherited something of his uncles who had gone west to seek their fortunes. While he tried to settle into a career in his hometown, that other part of his personality was not to be denied. For a while it looked as though Duff might become the black sheep of the much respected Pattullo family.

He did not, for example, follow his father in matters of faith. George Pattullo was a Scottish Presbyterian and religion was an important element in his life. As for many in mid-nineteenth-century Ontario, the church was a source of stability and order in a changing world. And there were very close links between religion and politics. Particularly in Oxford County, many Presbyterians were, like George Pattullo, also Reformers. His son, however, grew up in an age of growing secularization and with a generation that often questioned the religious certainties of their parents. As a boy, Duff went to Woodstock's Knox Presbyterian Church with his father, but when he could make the choice he did not attend. George Pattullo was out of town for an extended period in 1886 and was surprised to learn by letter that his thirteen-year-old son was not going to church as was their custom.[51] As an adult Duff followed his own inclination and rejected the narrow Calvinism of his father's beliefs. In later life he would explain that he was never a communicant of the Presbyterian church.[52] Though he described himself as an adherent, he did not attend church regularly and religion was not important to him.

His father had more influence on his schooling. Like all the older Pattullo children, Duff went to school at the Woodstock Collegiate Institute. It was originally a grammar school and by 1881, a few years before Duff started school, it had become so overcrowded that a new building had to be erected. The substantial new school was on Riddle Street near the centre of town. Now known as the Woodstock Collegiate and Vocational Institute, it became a high school in 1886. The Pattullos claimed in their *Woodstock Directory* published two years later that the local collegiate institute was one of the best in the province.[53] As in all things when he was young, Duff was encouraged in his school work by his father. George Pattullo and his sons corresponded when he was out of town and he urged them to try hard to improve their writing.[54] Duff's early schooling may have been made difficult by the fact that he was left-handed. Yet other students remembered him as a handsome, curly-haired boy who was bright and self-assured. He did well in examinations and was envied by all.[55] He gave his first public speech at high school and recalled he had every confidence in his views but approached the platform with trepidation about his ability to express them.[56] Duff had a natural, quick, but somewhat undisciplined intelligence. In 1890, his final year, he took university matriculation courses in English grammar, English composition, English literature, history, arithmetic, algebra, Euclid, Latin, French, and German. He passed them all except French, but he did not go on to university.[57]

When he left school at seventeen his formal education was over but his learning continued, as the cliché goes, in the school of life. He found a career, at least for a while, as a junior clerk in Molson's Bank. It was not easy to get a position in a bank and his father's influence may well have been a factor in securing the job. On the corner of Dundas and Perry streets, Molson's Bank was located in the centre of the town's business district. Duff worked a block along the street from the *Sentinel* building and his father's registry office was just one block north on the corner of Hunter and Graham streets. It was a tight little world and, although it was looked upon as a 'gentleman's job,' the work at the bank was not very exciting.[58] In the days before typewriters, part of his task was to hand copy all correspondence into the copybook, and he was also responsible for posting the daily mail. It was all pretty routine and tedious stuff, and as time went on there were increasing signs that Duff was restless. He tended to assume too much responsibility for one in such a junior position and he later confessed that he probably would eventually have been fired had he not resigned. Since he always arrived first in the morning and opened the bank, he had all the keys and combinations, including the one to the treasury. Once a customer, who frequently borrowed a few thousand dollars before catching a train on business out of town, came in on a Saturday when there was not enough cash in the till. It was near the end of the day, the manager had left and the customer was in a hurry, so Duff opened the treasury and lent the man the money he needed. He was a little uneasy until Monday when all turned out well, but clearly Duff had too much initiative, ambition, and, above all, self-confidence to be satisfied for long with the dull routine of a junior bank clerk.[59]

Furthermore, at $4.00 a week, the position did not pay well and Duff was soon living beyond his means. In an effort, perhaps, to escape from the boredom of his working days, he made sure that he enjoyed his evenings and days off. He began to develop a reputation among the young men of Woodstock for painting the town red, but to unwind fully he went elsewhere. On one occasion, close to the end of his time at the bank, he took the Friday train to the London Hunt Club ball. He got tied up with a lawyer who was pursuing a young lady in London with her mother. To Duff the mother was young enough to look better than the daughter, and it was quite an evening as the lawyer bought champagne all through the night. Duff recalled that a friend 'stood me on my head at train time but I was all in and returned to Woodstock on the afternoon train.' He did not arrive at work on Saturday morning to open up for all the farmers, and his father was not amused. Although Duff sat next to him at meals, 'the governor' did not speak to him for three months, not because of the bender in London but because he had failed in his responsibility at the bank. The combination of a low-paying job and high living after hours was disastrous. By the time that he was twenty-one Duff had run up a personal debt of nearly $700.[60]

Finally he could stand it no longer. He came of age in 1894 and began to make his own decisions. He told the bank manager he was going to quit his job and leave town. He went to his father's office to talk to him but could not bring himself to reveal his intentions. So he expressed his feelings by letter instead. 'I have long wondered,' he told his father, 'whether I must continue in this life of worse than mediocrity, whether I may not rise above which hitherto I have been, whether I may not turn aside from the rut in which I have been travelling, and whether I may not be capable of something beyond that which now seems to be my prospect ... Banking has become so distasteful to me I simply abhor it.'[61] He said he would have left long ago had it not been for his debts. Even now he knew that others would impugn his motives, but in his own mind he was not leaving to escape his creditors. He hoped his father would protect him from them. He would, in any event, make something of himself and he wished his father would not have cause to regret the birth of his second son. His sole reason for leaving was, he said, 'that I may fulfill my ambitions ... I say I *shall* be something further or fail in a hard struggle.'[62] With this intention Duff left the small town where he had spent his first twenty-one years and headed out for the big city where, he thought, the action was.

There was more than a touch of instability in the Pattullo family and for the next several months in New York Duff lived close to the edge. This period of his life was painful at the time and afterwards he remained sensitive about it. Many years later, after time had softened the sharp edges of the experience, he wrote in more detail, looking back on his doubtful past with some equanimity and a good dash of romanticism. Yet, even then, he covered himself by adopting a fictional device. Under the *nom de plume* of 'John Burnaby' he wrote a series of letters describing a young man's adventures in New York. The letters were not mailed, but they could only have been written by Pattullo and clearly they describe his own experience. 'John Burnaby' wrote to two lady friends named 'Lilian' and 'Sibil.' 'I ... long to spread my wings and cleave the regions of the unknown,' he told Sibil, and to Lilian he confided 'I do not exactly like the idea of leaving Canada but you see the field is so limited for one of my great capabilities.'[63]

Compared to the security of little Woodstock, the bustling, raucous city of New York rendered a hard reality. And Duff was now on his own. For the first few days he stayed at the Grand Union Hotel and enjoyed the theatres and bars. But he soon had to find more modest quarters in a rooming house on 12th Street near Washington Square, and from there he began the search for employment. 'Skirmishing around New York' that summer it seemed that no one required 'a gentleman' of his 'peculiar talents.' He attempted to bring in some money by selling insurance but without much success since, he concluded, 'New York is perennial. It does not require insurance.' Trying to sell encyclopedias was no more lucrative and he ended up working as an usher in a restaurant. There the handsome, young Pattullo may have made a hit with the female patrons, but he certainly did not make much money. Broke and lonely, he began to think of home. He could smell the perfume of lilacs and roses on the air as, in his imagination, he ascended the hill to Burnside. But he did not return. He was still searching, although he was not very clear for what. As he put it, 'the wild furious search goes on for that which will never be found.' He had not yet 'been sufficiently buffeted upon the waves of adversity' and felt that he had more to learn in this hard school.[64]

By fall Duff was sinking lower and lower as the possibility of failure and poverty weighed heavily. He later claimed he had toyed with the idea of joining a filibustering expedition to Cuba but decided he was too young to die, either by the sword or from some tropical disease.[65] Escaping from financial problems by going off to the wars was never to have much appeal to him. Since he had been in New York he had often walked along the west-side docks to his lodgings on 12th Street and so, instead of going to Cuba, he signed on to a cattle boat bound for London. It was to be the worst experience of his life. The conditions on board were appalling, and the crew was made up of the worst of London and New York's 'wharf rats.'[66] After crossing the Atlantic on this unsavoury vessel he spent ten unpleasant days in London, sleeping in a dockside doss house. He considered going to South Africa before shipping back to New York on the same steamer. Returning to America 'seemed like coming out of a dark heavy drama into a light sparkling comedy. London the drama, New York the comedy.'[67] Like New York, Duff was still bouyant. He had tested the waters and had not gone under. Thoughts of home began to flow in on him again: recollections of those golden days of childhood when life was easy and uncomplicated. Yet he did not return immediately and instead found a temporary position as a tax collector in suburban New York. But within a few weeks he was back in Woodstock.

As in the parable, the father welcomed the prodigal home. Duff later recalled that 'My good father sent me a draft and advice, both of which I accepted.'[68] For his part, the son was not quite the same callow young man who had left home a few months earlier. Having so vividly encountered failure in his youth, he would live for the rest of his life with its possibility in the forefront of his mind. In the longer term it might drive him towards success, to seek new opportunities in distant places, but now he decided to hold still for a bit and take stock of his life and that of others. For during his sojourn away he had learned some general lessons along with the personal ones.

He had rubbed shoulders with the poor and the unfortunate in two of the world's largest cities and believed he could sympathize with their plight in a real and not just a sentimental way. As he reflected on the experience, he thought he understood the source of socialism, though he rejected it as a form of ignorance. He had 'seen men grind their teeth at the "antics" as they call it of the rich. They have been taught to feel that the rich are the oppressors and they the oppressed. Born to squalor ... they have been inoculated with a belief in the tyranny of wealth. They have a hazy knowledge that all men are born equal and that inequality is usurpation by somebody. It is the same as the war of capital and labour. There is no reciprocation of feeling or ideas. Labour writhes under the heel of capital and capital but presses the harder.'[69] Much of Pattullo's learning was intuitive, based on experience rather than the bookish kind. While he was in New York he had, as he put it, 'picked up a lot of information but no money.'[70] Now, back in Woodstock, even if Duff had changed, his old financial problem remained. Having seen a little of what lay beyond, he felt he could stay in Woodstock for a while, but he may well have been thinking already about the west.

In the meantime, immediate practicalities had to be considered. Duff was still in debt and he needed a job. This time he followed his father's footsteps into newspaper work. For short time he edited *The Reformer* in Galt. The newspaper was, naturally, a Liberal one. As the Dumfries *Reformer* it had been owned formerly by James Young, a political acquaintance of George Pattullo, who had sat at different times in the House of Commons and the Ontario legislature. Now Andrew Laidlaw, who had been associated with Duff's uncle on the *Sentinel* and was related to the Pattullos by marriage, owned the *Reformer*. In

1896 a daily edition was brought out in addition to the regular weekly edition, and that is perhaps why Duff was brought in as editor. He still lived in Woodstock and the same year his father appointed him as deputy registrar of Oxford County. Both of these positions provided useful experience that would serve him well in the future. As a newspaper editor he learned how to write clear direct prose, and as deputy registrar, as at Molson's Bank, he became familiar with office organization and routine. Under his father he was also introduced to the procedures for handling land titles. But while the experience was useful, neither position paid very much and Duff's financial problem persisted.

About the time that Duff began as editor of the Galt *Reformer* in an effort to make a little money, another man, away in the farthest corner of Canada, struck it rich beyond his wildest dreams. In mid-August 1896, under the shadow of King Solomon Dome, George Washington Carmack, or perhaps one of his Indian partners, dipped a pan into the waters of Rabbit Creek and took out a quarter of an ounce of gold. Four dollars' worth in one pan was a phenomenal find. Carmack asserted the discoverer's right to a double claim and staked out 1000 feet of the creek before heading to the nearest settlement at Forty Mile to register his claim and spread the news. Rabbit Creek was soon to be renamed Bonanza Creek and the great Klondike gold rush was on. The following summer, as the word rippled out around the world, men everywhere dropped what they were doing and, hooked by the lure of Yukon gold, were reeled north.

Living in Woodstock and editing a paper in Galt, Duff Pattullo was initially unmoved by these events. In the summer of 1897 Woodstock, along with the rest of the British empire, enthusiastically celebrated sixty years of Queen Victoria's rule. As he watched the parade on Dundas Street, listened to the speeches given by his father and his uncle Andrew, and then in the evening saw the grand fireworks display in the newly named Victoria Park, Duff hardly thought that within a few weeks he would be on his way to one of the most distant reaches of Victoria's empire. That same summer the recently elected Liberal government in Ottawa was becoming more and more concerned about the rapid influx of a largely alien and potentially unruly population of miners into the Yukon. The public, caught up in the fervour for empire, began to demand that Canada's rights in the area be defended, and the government responded by moving to establish a degree of administrative control over the far-off frontier. In September the minister of the interior, Clifford Sifton, announced the appointment of Major James Morrow Walsh to lead a party of officials that would leave shortly to set up a territorial government in the Yukon. Another member of the Liberal cabinet of 1896 was Sir Richard Cartwright, who owed George Pattullo a favour. When Cartwright lost an election in Kingston, Duff's father had found him a safe seat in South Oxford. Now Pattullo called in the debt by asking the minister to use his influence to obtain a position for Duff on the Walsh party. Duff Pattullo was duly sent a letter from the Department of the Interior informing him that he had been appointed to Walsh's staff at a salary of $75.00 a month plus expenses.[71]

In mid-September 1897 there was a big family gathering at Burnside. Duff's older sister Ethelwyn, or Wynnie as she was known, married a young barrister named Adam Ballantyne, the son of a former speaker of the Ontario legislature who lived in nearby Stratford.[72] The day was bright and clear, and the lawns and gardens of Burnside never looked better. The bride was attended by her three younger sisters, Pearl, Kate, and Mary, and the Pattullo boys, James, Dufferin, George, and Andrew, as always, enjoyed the conviviality. They were not to know that it was to be the last time the family would be all together at Burnside. Duff, on his way to Ottawa to join Major Walsh, left on the evening train with the honeymooners. Throughout the rest of his life family ties remained very important to him and he would return many times to Woodstock to visit, but never to stay. He was leaving forever the familiar, established surroundings of his hometown for a town in the northwest that had just begun. Dawson City was a long way, both physically and psychologically, from Woodstock, Ontario, and it was a place that might make or break a young man yet to prove himself.

CHAPTER 2

Dawson City, Yukon

'You will never reach the heights by refusing to climb'

Duff Pattullo left for Dawson City because he thought it would be a grand adventure. And so it was. But it was also to be much more than that. As he took the train to Ottawa on the first leg of his journey in the fall of 1897, Duff, at twenty-four, was an individual who had yet to find a place for himself. He seemed to be one of 'the men that don't fit in.'[1] He had tried many things, but none had been entirely to his liking. Outwardly, to be sure, he was cocky and self-assured, but this outer ebullience hid an inner uncertainty about himself and his future. Still, he was off to play a part in the last great gold rush: to participate in the madness that engulfed the Yukon as the nineteenth century came to an end and the twentieth began. And while others dug for gold, Duff would test his mettle.

Leaving Woodstock, Duff no doubt recalled his Uncle Thomas who had gone to California and then up to British Columbia at the height of the Fraser River gold rush. He may have dimly remembered, as a three year old, seeing his uncle come to Burnside with Cariboo gold in his pockets. Later he had probably read the articles on conditions in gold-rush British Columbia that his uncle wrote under the name of 'Tillicum' for the *Sentinel*. Thomas Pattullo was an easy-going, generous man who struck it rich and then lost it all before he died in the Barkerville hospital.[2] Duff was certainly reminded of the uncle after whom he was named when, on the trail to Dawson City, he met

Captain Jack Crawford, the 'poet scout' of the west. Crawford had known Thomas Pattullo and he reckoned that Duff looked just like a smaller version of his uncle. As was his wont, Captain Jack celebrated this meeting with the nephew by knocking off some verse on the death of Thomas that Duff passed on to his father.[3] But George Pattullo gave little thought to poetry, and he had more mundane things than adventure on his mind when he sent his son to Dawson. Perhaps recalling that his brother had made money on the goldfields before he lost it, George Pattullo had assumed Duff's debts, which now amounted to $1800, in the expectation that, with a steady government job, his son would pay them off.[4] George Pattullo also naîvely thought that far-away Dawson would be a place where a restive young man would be removed from the temptation to spend money on riotous living.

The truth was that Duff was departing from the ordered world of Woodstock where debt was a stigma and heading for a rough and tumble frontier where fortunes were made and lost on a daily, if not an hourly basis. Like any immigrant, he turned his back on his past and set his face to the future. His early years in southern Ontario could not be entirely erased, but, like other Pattullos before him, he now sought new opportunities in a different place. Duff Pattullo was still a young man and he was heading for the promised land and, while reality might well be different from expectation, it was all new and exciting. Though he brought his background with him, he responded with enthusiasm to the new land. He would soon become a westerner.

Unlike his foray to New York, which had been an individual enterprise, Pattullo went to Dawson as part of a well-organized group. Arriving in Ottawa, he quickly found he had at least one thing in common with the others in the party that was being assembled for the Yukon: that political influence, and not necessarily natural ability, was primarily responsible for his appointment. Duff claimed that thousands had applied for positions and he acknowledged the strength of his father's political pull.[5] The leader, Major James Morrow Walsh, was a personal friend of Sifton, but the veteran of the North-West Mounted Police and the hero of earlier dealings with Sitting Bull and the Sioux was also a popular choice with the public. Initially Duff, too, was impressed with the major's courage, confidence, and organizational ability. Later, however, both Pattullo and the public would revise their views. Other members of the party included T.H. McGuire, appointed judge of the Yukon Provisional District Court; F.C. Wade, who was to be crown prosecutor and registrar of lands; two inspectors of mines, J.D. McGregor and Captain H.H. Norwood; Captain H.A. Bliss went as an accountant; and the major's brother, Philip Walsh, went along in charge of transport. Duff was billed as the stenographer and typist of the party but was, in fact, secretary to Walsh. The title of secretary went to A.J. Magurn, a Toronto *Globe* correspondent whose real task was to write newspaper reports that would reflect well on the government. In all, the party numbered fifty or more and it was elaborately fitted out for Arctic conditions. Pattullo reported that each member was given an 'eider down quilt, a pair of blankets, a wolf skin robe, a rubber sheet and a belt and a brace of revolvers with one hundred rounds of ammunition.' He had to provide other supplies himself and these included: 'water tight boots, moccasins, rat skin socks, chamois vest and drawers, heavy underclothing, musk ox mittens, corduroy suits, rubber skins for fording, oil skin suit, coon skin coat and cap, deer skin leggings.'[6] If nothing else, providing for the expedition must have seriously depleted a number of species of wildlife. Thus equipped, the Walsh party, accompanied by the minister of the interior, Clifford Sifton, left Ottawa and headed west.

Like the earlier gold rushes in British Columbia, the Klondike was to be a government-controlled frontier. Prior to the discovery at Bonanza Creek, the Canadian government had established a minimal form of administration in the Yukon. In 1895 Inspector Charles Constantine and a small force of North-West Mounted Police were sent in to establish dominion authority and the Canadian, rather than American pattern of mining regulation. By the fall of 1897 the earlier trickle of miners into the Yukon had become a flood, and the fast-moving developments demanded a more vigorous assertion of federal authority.

So Major Walsh and his party were sent to set up an administration in the territory.

Unlike the earlier gold rushes to the west coast, however, the Klondike was controlled by a government that was far removed from the situation and had little first-hand knowledge of conditions on the frontier. Stumbling through the smoke of events, government ministers in Ottawa tried to quell the fires of political opposition with measures that were often inappropriate to the situation on the goldfields. Local officials were appointed because of Ottawa connections, and regulations devised by the federal government often had to be revised and then revised again, as they created more problems than they solved. Duff Pattullo was a part of this federal operation when he left Ottawa but he would soon recognize its deficiencies. Leaving Ontario for the farthest west, he was to learn to appreciate the federal club from the other end.

Pattullo and the rest of the Walsh party departed from Ottawa by train on 25 September 1897. They stopped in Winnipeg for a day's rest and Pattullo sensed for the first time the expansiveness and optimism of the west as it was beginning to open up. Naturally he still saw things in accustomed terms, as he commented on the 'Imperial Canadian spirit' that was growing in the west and, as in the east, had received great impetus from the Jubilee celebrations. But he already recognized that something new and vigorous was coming to life. 'No western Canadian,' he reported, 'has any doubt about the future.' They were all certain that with increased population would come development on a grand scale. He claimed that the people of the west saw the Yukon expedition as 'an advertisement for Canada and for Canada's varied natural resources such as they have never before had.'[7] Pattullo was invigorated by the whole enterprise, and he wrote to his father that he was feeling 'as strong as an ox for the great undertaking.' An old problem still dogged him, however, as he continued to run up debts. There had been various expenses on the trip out and in Ottawa 'there were about a dozen fellows all putting up the champagne and that cost me $15 at a crack.' While in Winnipeg he had to draw another $100 against his father. 'You have no idea,' he explained in a letter, 'of the little expenses which run up like blazes.'[8]

Leaving Winnipeg, the party socialized its way towards Vancouver. Pattullo found the prairie landscape of no special interest, but the mountains were a new world. As the train wound its way through the Rockies he was deeply moved by the wild grandeur of the scenery that was so unlike the gentle, man-made geography of rural Ontario. His thoughts and feelings outstripped his ability to express them and his words were rather maudlin. But he felt the clear mountain air and saw the great rocky peaks that, even when miles away, seemed to stand right beside him. It was fall, and the mountain sides and valleys were covered with 'stately trees and luxuriant shrubs with their varied hues and beautiful autumn tints.'[9] By the time he reached Vancouver, Pattullo had seen enough of British Columbia's spectacular natural beauty to know that he had come to another place: one that was unique, special, and different from the one he had left.

Arriving in Vancouver on 1 October, the party spent a day preparing for the passage up the coast on the vessel *Quadra*. They were joined by William Ogilvie, who Pattullo met for the first time. Ogilvie knew the territory into which they were heading, since he had spent several years exploring and surveying in the Yukon and had advised the federal government as it developed policy for the area. He now accompanied Walsh's men on the next part of the journey towards Dawson. Amid the clicking of cameras and the cheering of the crowd on the dock, the *Quadra*, under Captain John Walbran, pulled out of Vancouver. Duff Pattullo began the first of what would be many trips up the British Columbia coast. The weather was better than it often is in the first week of October, but in rough seas off the Queen Charlotte Islands Duff worried that his inadequate shorthand would fail him completely when he took dictation from Sifton. He was relieved when the minister returned his notes with only a few changes, saying that the work was fine given the conditions. Somehow Pattullo was in his element on the coast; while others went down with seasickness, he was feeling 'like a fighting cock.'[10] There were lighter moments and, when the seas were calmer, they played Ogilvie's gramophone for entertainment. Duff was particularly fond of opera. After calling in at Port Simpson, the *Quadra* continued north and, steaming up Lynn Canal on 9 October, it approached the ramshackle town of Skagway: the port of entry to the Yukon.

In 1897 Skagway was an instant outpost of American freedom, enterprise, and somewhat *laissez faire* attitude towards law and order. In contrast to their grand entry into Canadian towns, the representatives of dominion authority received no welcome in Skagway. Since there was no civic government, no city officials greeted them. For the young Pattullo it was not a great loss, since 'the inevitable addresses from these high officials were also wanting – a cause of general thankfulness.'[11] Yet, for his own part, Pattullo was determined to keep up appearances. While others changed clothes in anticipation of roughing it, Duff prepared to go ashore in a Wilfrid Laurier stand-up collar and a grey fedora. Captain Bliss had already warned him that his collars could not be packed over the mountain pass, not knowing that Pattullo also had a couple of white flannel suits stashed away in his gear.[12] There was no wharf at Skagway, so however elaborate the preparations the actual process of getting ashore was somewhat undignified. The men of the party had to scramble 'over barges, scows, houses, boats, planks, logs, rails, and posts' until they reached dry land. The main street ran from the foreshore towards the mountains behind, and walking along it for the first time was Pattullo's initiation to a wide-open, freewheeling, western boom town. Hundreds of frame houses and huts were being thrown up in short order. The business section was dominated by hotels, saloons, real estate and mining agencies, and, as Pattullo understated it, everybody was 'advertising himself and his wares in the most striking and conspicuous fashion.' People of all classes and all walks of life were randomly thrown together – a 'heterogeneous host,' all rubbing shoulders as they struggled through a sea of mud. 'There is a large sprinkling of gamblers and women of the street,' wrote Pattullo, 'but there are respectable people too.' Presumably having investigated the matter with some interest, he also reported that the cost of liquor meant there was little drunkenness in Skagway.

Duff estimated that 'it would cost a fellow about $25 before he could get even a moderate jag on.'[13]

Like most gold rushes, the Klondike was a largely male frontier. Though a tiny minority, there were women in Skagway. Yet for Pattullo they too seemed to be separated by gender stereotypes. In a revealing piece of social commentary he noted: 'Two ladies especially attract the visitor's attention, one a female packer, known as Texas Bill, who carried goods over the pass the same as men. Her dress was of the bifurcated pattern and she also had a wild western swagger. The other was a different type, Mrs Scoville, wife of the correspondent of the New York World. She accompanied her husband to this territory and is now on her return. She had suffered great hardships and was nearly exhausted when she reached Skagway from Lake Bennett. She was a pretty little woman, cultured, quite young, and despite the hardships undergone appeared to have enjoyed the rough experience.'[14]

Skagway was the entrance to the White Pass route into the Yukon. Pattullo climbed up the hill as far as the station manned by the North-West Mounted Police at the summit and he was appalled by what he saw. The human misery and strain as men trudged up the pass was bad enough, but even worse was the sight of the oxen and horses falling off the side of the trail and dropping to their deaths below in what became known as Dead Horse Gulch. Other animals collapsed from exhaustion and died where they lay in the middle of the trail. It has been said that Pattullo insisted he saw an ox trying to fling itself over the cliff rather than tread the terrible trail.[15] Down in Skagway he was impressed by the optimism of the people. Even those who had known hardship and had bitter or pathetic tales to tell still hoped that good fortune would overtake them. But up on the trail there was only hard reality and Duff heard stories of big, strong men starting over only to return in a couple of weeks looking twenty years older and unrecognizable to their friends. Already his advice to those thinking about coming to the Klondike was that they would be better off to stay at home.[16]

At the same time, now that he was there, Duff was giving some thought to his own future in this new land. In contrast to the other individuals who passed through Skagway, Pattullo was a member of a government expedition. Yet, like the gold-seekers, he had his eye out for the main chance. He had seen the down-side of the Klondike experience on the White Pass trail, but he had also noted there were many opportunities for making money in Skagway. He intended to work hard as a member of the civil service, but he also conceded that 'a little of the yellow has a temptation for me.'[17] The two would not necessarily be contradictory. He told his father that Major Walsh was pleased with his work and did not see why he should not be a valuable man to the Department of the Interior. At the same time, the major had indicated that he might take Pattullo into a scheme to make money.[18]

Meanwhile, Pattullo had his own plans for raising a little cash. He had arranged to write accounts of the journey and forward them to his father, who was to syndicate them in the *Globe* and as many other eastern newspapers as possible. His letters were, of course, published in the *Sentinel* too, and Andrew Pattullo was able to score some good political hits in editorials by using information provided by Duff. The popular view of, and enthusiasm for, the Klondike in the south was very much the creation of newspaper reporters who sold copy by adding plenty of colour and hyperbole. Purple prose was their stock in trade. Pattullo hoped to sell his stories and the proceeds were to be credited to his account, but he did not peddle fiction and his writing was crisp and direct. In his letters to his father, Duff described how the expedition prepared to tackle the infamous Chilkoot Pass.

While Pattullo and the rest of the party remained in Skagway, Walsh, Sifton, and Ogilvie went ahead to reconnoitre. They went in over the Chilkoot Pass as far as Tagish Lake and back down the White Pass. On his return, Sifton said he would not send his worst enemy over the White Pass and so the party moved over to the other branch of the Lynn Canal and the rival town of Dyea. The supplies and equipment were manhandled across the shallows and mud flats and put ashore above the high-tide mark. As Walsh's men prepared to move up to the Chilkoot Pass they knew that, having crossed the shoreline, the going would soon be a lot tougher. By now it was the last week in October and winter would soon be upon them. Walsh tried to conceal his apprehension with a bit of bravado, saying to Duff, 'I hope it is raining and snowing on that pass like the devil just to see what it is like.'[19] He was soon to have his wish.

At first the trail inland was easy and inviting, but the land soon revealed its true nature when they reached the canyon of the Dyea River. The trail was in a 'deplorable condition.' It was littered with logs and boulders and the defile was so narrow that they had to lift their legs up to the horses' necks to prevent them from being crushed on either side. 'Capt. Bliss' monumental figure was too much for his charger,' so he was frequently obliged to get off his horse, but Pattullo and Philip Walsh rode right through without dismounting. They were told afterwards that what they had done was extremely dangerous. Had the horses missed their footing the riders would have been hurled hundreds of feet below. But, wrote Pattullo, 'Fortune favoured us' and they arrived safely at Sheep Camp at the far end of the canyon.[20]

Located in a basin at the foot of the mountains, Sheep Camp was so named because it had been a meeting place for sheep hunters. Now the area was a constantly moving chaos of men and equipment. The stampeders paused only briefly at this point to assemble their supplies and gather their physical and mental resources as they contemplated the final assault on the Chilkoot. The summit was now only about four miles away and in good weather the top of the pass was visible from Sheep Camp. But most of the 3500 foot ascent from Dyea to the top still had to be climbed. To make matters worse, the weather turned nasty as the Walsh party arrived at Sheep Camp. A strong south wind blew in sleet and snow and the packers who began ferrying supplies up to the final slope returned with the news that the summit was impassable.

The next day Walsh directed Pattullo to lead the first group on the next stage: the climb to the Scales. The wind was stronger and had swung around to the north, so it was tearing down the pass into their faces. By the time they reached the great boulder known as the Stone House, snow was building on the trail. It was up to their armpits in a couple of hours. The last part of the day's climb was on hands and knees, but they finally crawled, exhausted, up to the Scales.

They were now at the base of the final hill, on a flat area of ground known as the Scales because everything was reweighed prior to the final climb. Pack animals could not carry loads any further and so, before the first tramline was built in December 1897, manpower was the only way to get supplies over the summit. But gale-force winds and driving snow could make the slopes impassable for days. Not knowing how long they would have to wait for the weather to clear, Pattullo and the others dug out the snow and put up their tents on the bare rock. The huge projecting stones meant that when they threw down their blankets at night, it was 'like sleeping on church steeples.' There were no trees above Sheep Camp, so they had to send back down for firewood. The wind picked up even more overnight and they had to build a six-foot wall of snow around the tent to prevent it's being ripped away in the gale. 'Truly,' wrote Pattullo, 'we had struck the proverbially roughest spot on the whole trail.' They soon decided that only something frightful would prevent them from crossing the summit at daylight.[21]

With the wind raging around them they had little sleep, but the gale subsided about four in the morning. By nine o'clock it was clear and the sun glistened on the newly fallen snow. Already the packers were coming and going, some of them with huge loads, taking the baggage to the top. They also made the way easier for those who followed by breaking in the trail. Pattullo's climb up the 700 feet from the Scales to the top of the Chilkoot was even a little anticlimactic after what had gone before. They struck camp at 10:30 in the morning and joined that single strand of humanity that was slowly drawn up the final, seemingly perpendicular slope to the top of the pass. Duff reached the top at 11:10. In his matter-of-fact prose he noted: 'Distance from Sheep Camp about five miles. Distance from Dyea from 18 to 20 miles. It seemed a hundred.'[22]

That climb up the 'Golden Stairs' was made by most of the stampeders of 1897 as they slaved to get enough supplies over the top to permit them to cross the international border. These men and their endeavours provided an image that, more than any other, epitomized the Klondike quest. The scene affected Pattullo deeply. As a member of a government expedition that included a large cohort of Indian packers, he only had to cross the Chilkoot once. Individual stampeders had to climb the pass over and over again. The Canadian government required that a miner have one ton of supplies before he could cross the international border at the top of the pass and fifty pounds was about as much as the average man could carry in one load. For many, the process of lugging their goods and chattels up the final slope took weeks. Now he had crossed 'the awful divide,' Pattullo reflected for a moment on the plight of those with whom he shared the trail. It seemed to him 'that for the man in search of riches the glamour of gold must lose some of its brilliancy and in its place come the gloom of stern reality darkening his expectations ... To see the despair written on men's faces as they carry their packs up and up the awful hill is almost enough to make one's heart ache.' He had already realized that 'sentiment won't do away up in the Klondike. Every man who comes here must be willing to take life risks and be willing to stand every imaginable hardship.'[23]

Such was the reputation of the Chilkoot Pass that many thought, once they had reached the top, their troubles were over. But, as Pattullo soon found, they had just begun. The Walsh party pushed on around Crater Lake and beyond to Lake Lindemann, where they prepared to travel by boat down the Yukon River. It was already early November as they started across Lake Bennett and winter was rapidly closing in. A group under Judge McGuire went on to Dawson while the rest moved more slowly, carrying supplies and establishing depots every thirty-odd miles. After Lake Bennett, they crossed Tagish and Marsh lakes and then went downriver, through White Horse Rapids and Miles Canyon, towards Lake Labarge. The temperature continued to drop and a slick of ice was beginning to form on the water. Pattullo had allowed his beard to grow and had assumed a rather biblical appearance when, at one point, they were forced into a cove on Lake Labarge by rough weather. Some other men that Pattullo knew were sheltering there and one friend rushed up, gave him a hearty slap on the back, and said, 'Jesus Christ, how are you? I did not expect to see you here.' To which Pattullo replied, 'Old friend, you can expect to meet Jesus anywhere.'[24] When he left Lake Labarge and started down the Lewis River, as that section of the Yukon was then known, he did not realize that he would soon come very close to meeting his maker.

As they proceeded downriver, further and further north, the conditions became more and more treacherous. On 17 November they camped for the night about six miles beyond the Big Salmon River. They had only gone a few miles the next morning when Pattullo's boat came surging round a bend in the river and up ahead was a fearful ice jam. Approaching the jam, the ice was ground up for several yards along each shore with a channel of slush and ice running down the centre of the river. The leading boats were struggling to shore and the men in Pattullo's boat attempted to cross to the same side. They collided with a block of ice and were carried downstream for some distance, but eventually got close to the shore. J.J. Freeman, travelling in another boat, leapt out of the wrong side, went through the mush ice, and drowned. The Indians guiding Pattullo's boat quickly appreciated the situation and laid tent poles on the ice and started across on snowshoes. When Pattullo began to follow, the poles had gone through the ice and the strings on his snowshoes were frozen and impossible to tie. So with the snowshoes in his hands he began to inch ashore on all fours, encouraged and urged on by Bliss. Twice his leg went through the ice, but he held on. For a fifteen-minute eternity he crawled across the ice and eventually stood on firm ground. Once safe, he was convulsed by fear. Later that evening, when he had recovered somewhat, he wrote to his father that he 'would not go through the 15 minutes crossing that slush again for all the gold in the Yukon.'[25]

Pattullo had survived the disaster, but the expedition had lost many of its supplies and the river was clearly unsafe for further travel. They spent a few days at the spot they named Freeman's Point after their lost comrade. After taking stock of the situation, the party retreated to Big Salmon River to spend the rest of the winter. They would not reach Dawson before spring breakup.

After weeks of constant activity and a close brush with death, Pattullo had some time for reflection as he cooled his heels for a couple of months at Big Salmon in temperatures that often went down to sixty below. He was defensive about having not reached the objective. In his letters home he emphasized what the expedition had achieved – making it so far and establishing supply posts along the way – rather than what it had not. Even at a distance he realized that all was not well in Dawson City during the winter of 1897–8. He wrote about the steady stream of men who passed through the camp, not going in, but heading out to the coast. Food shortages were chronic in Dawson through that winter and many disillusioned men simply left in disgust. Some of the retreating miners felt they had been misled and told Pattullo they reckoned this to be the 'greatest country in the world for liars.'[26] He noticed how selfish men became when the chips were down. In that relentless climate, to share one's food might only mean that two would starve, so people learned not to ask of others. Walsh's men did not face such immediate problems, yet, according to Pattullo, they learned to 'surmount our hardships up here with a bouyancy that I didn't think possible and many little things that down east we would consider rough we now think luxurious.'[27]

While Pattullo appreciated the need for individual self-reliance, he also advocated government initiative to solve the social and economic problems of the Yukon. He felt that the present rush was not justified by the conditions and that those like William Ogilvie who were speaking publicly and enthusiastically about the unlimited riches of the area were 'simply outrageous.' It was not that Pattullo thought the Yukon lacked potential, it was just that appropriate government action was required to develop it. Otherwise there would be the 'biggest burst of an inflated boom' and the Liberals in Ottawa would 'not feel it lightly.'[28] He particularly urged the need for a Canadian transport route into the territory. The Yukon River was too uncertain and the season too short for safe and reliable transportation. A railway link would make access easier for the miners and bring in an adequate food supply at cheaper rates. He was careful to note in his letters written for publication that government policy would be made by government, but he nevertheless pointed out that 'development cannot proceed without the means thereof.' Without a transportation route the area would remain idle, but with it 'development will go forward in this country which would astonish the world.'[29] As he was to do at other times and in other circumstances, he advocated 'broad liberal policies' for the Yukon. 'Our policies,' he wrote, 'should be as broad as our country itself.' It was as though he saw a parallel between the underdeveloped west and his own lack of financial success, for there 'is always a time in the growth of a nation as of a youth, when it may be stunted or made strong, healthy and prosperous. Now is Canada's time.' And Pattullo called upon the Canadian government and the Canadian people to take hold of the situation or run the risk of relinquishing the untapped wealth of the Yukon to others.[30]

The federal government was unsuccessful in its efforts to have a Canadian railway put through to the Yukon and Pattullo was not able to do much about his own finances. By the time the Walsh party was ready to move in the early spring of 1898, Pattullo had decided that the idea that a man could make money easily in the Yukon was an eastern misconception, yet he still had some hope of 'turning over something before the year ends.'[31] He applied to the minister of the interior for a salary increase, but without the support he expected from Major Walsh. In fact, things were wearing a little thin between Duff and the major. Miffed that Walsh would not recommend him for a raise in pay, Pattullo wrote to his father that he should not be surprised if he quit his job as secretary to the commissioner. He said that Walsh had a fearful temper and blamed him for everything that went wrong. 'In fact it has been nothing short of the very devil, but,' he added smugly, 'I have stood it all ... The Major can do as he damn pleases.'[32]

Major Walsh, while unaware of Pattullo's admonition, was nevertheless following the advice. When the weather improved in the early spring he moved, not on to Dawson City, but back to Lake Bennett. There was talk of an American relief expedition being sent to the Yukon and Walsh wanted to be sure that nothing untoward happened at the border. There was no international incident, but on 3 April there was a tragic natural disaster near the boundary. An avalanche ripped down the Chilkoot Pass close to the Scales and took the lives of more than sixty people. Walsh and Pattullo went down to do what they could to help. For the rest of the month, while he waited for Walsh to give the word to move out, Pattullo found it 'ducedly monotonous' in Bennett.[33] It was 3 May before they finally struck north for Dawson City.

They first retraced their steps of last fall: past Big Salmon and on to Freeman's Point. On 13 May they ran the feared Five Finger Rapids with ease in the low river and the following day they reached the old Hudson's Bay Company post of Fort Selkirk. Located half a mile downstream from where the Lewis and Pelley rivers joined to form the Yukon proper, Fort Selkirk was, according to Pattullo, the finest location they had seen since the coast. There were twenty or so squared log houses, a trading post, and a mission all set down in superb surroundings. Away to the north east was 'a magnificent range of mountains which look as if a great velvet drapery had been thrown over them in folds graceful beyond the artist's hand.'[34] While the expedition paused for a couple of days, Pattullo explored the area. Following the Dalton Trail for a short distance one morning he contemplated the scene about him, later recording that 'the inspiration seized me of what a freedom there was about the life around me, away from the conventionalism and affectation of the age, and of how much I preferred the wild trail to a London thoroughfare, even though there were no "fine places round the corner" at which to quench one's thirst.' Not that he was completely taken in by the grandeur around him, for he added that 'I think differently now that I am back at camp and would not at all mind one of those "fine places around the corner." '[35] His acquaintance with the watering holes of Dawson would be one reason why he got to know Fort Selkirk more intimately the next winter.

Refreshed by a few days' rest at Selkirk, Walsh and his men floated their Peterborough canoes out into the Yukon River for the last stretch down to Dawson. The river was flowing free of ice but the spring run-off was causing the water to rise, so travel was fast but hazardous. By the latter part of May there was virtually no darkness and they were able to put in long hours. Four days after leaving Selkirk, on Saturday, 21 May, they broke camp at 6:30 on a bright, crisp morning. A little over an hour later Pattullo's canoe swept round a big bend in the river and there, just beyond the mouth of the Klondike River, was their objective: Dawson – 'the City of Gold.'[36]

After the long winter, Pattullo had at last made it to Dawson City – and that in itself was an achievement. Yet at first glance Dawson did not seem like much of a city, and its aspect was hardly golden. Not that there was any lack of people. Indeed, for a few weeks that year Dawson was the largest Canadian city west of Winnipeg. But the throngs of men only increased the problems of a town that was ill-prepared to receive and accommodate them. To the approaching newcomer in the spring of 1898 it scarcely seemed like the San Francisco of the north. The sand bar along the shoreline of the Yukon was strewn with boats and supplies as thousands of stampeders poured into the city. Up along the river bank ran Front Street, which was already lined with one- and two-storey log buildings. Some were warehouses for the commercial companies, but most housed saloons and dance halls. Front Street, or First Avenue, was the façade and the centre of activity. Behind it, although the streets were laid out in a grid pattern, there were few other signs of order. Log cabins, shanties, and tents were scattered, apparently at random, over the townsite and up the side of Moosehide Mountain behind. On the surface it seemed like total chaos. Soon after Pattullo arrived, further confusion was created when the rising waters of the Yukon River that had brought the Walsh party so rapidly down from Selkirk began to inundate the town. For a while much of Dawson was under five feet of water and Pattullo recalled that he 'had a libation from a canoe in one of the numerous bars on Main Street.'[37] Dawson City was being built on a swamp and, at the best of times, drainage and sanitation posed major problems. In July 1898 a typhoid outbreak sent many men to the overcrowded hospitals. With thousands of miners milling through the muck and filth, Dawson at its height was like no place on earth.

Pattullo took it all in and, like many others, was soon able to overlook the seamier side of Dawson. To him it was 'a jolly place.'[38] Front Street thronged with life, the saloons were packed, and the dance halls were romping. There was a magic, carnival atmosphere, but this was not the wild west and the town was not out of control. Looking beyond the surface confusion, Pattullo saw an orderly, sober, and law-abiding crowd living under the influence of British institutions. There were many of the features of more established societies: banks, newspapers, and a telephone service. There were five churches, and if the sabbath was not exactly, as Pattullo claimed, observed as in any other town in Canada, it was nevertheless observed. Pattullo was not alone in comparing Dawson favourably with Skagway, pointing out that the type of men who were the terror of the population in the American town were not present in Dawson. Those who had arrived hoping to make a quick fortune without effort found 'no vacant lots on easy streets' and were already thinking about leaving. And Pattullo thought that the territory would be better off without them. What it needed was sturdy prospectors and hard workers who would bring lasting development.[39] Brand new and bursting at the seams, Dawson in 1898 was perhaps an exaggeration, or perhaps it just epitomized the Canadian west at the turn of the century. Certainly Pattullo found it exciting, different from the outside, and in many ways congenial. One evening during a quieter moment he wrote to his father in far-off Woodstock about this new place and the men who had come there. 'We have had heavy rain tonight, and the sky has just cleared; the air is cool, there is the same solemn stillness broken only by the choir singing in the Jesuit church at the foot of the hill; the Yukon flows quietly on with its secrets of gold; the dreamers wonder if a fortune is coming to them and the plain practical man is hoping to reap his reward by hard and arduous labour.'[40] Both Pattullo and the city he had come to were a mixture of dreams and practicality. Having arrived, Pattullo was observing others and learning about himself, for, like many of the stampeders of 98, he had been on a journey much greater than the one to Dawson City.

Pattullo and the rest of the Walsh party had, of course, come to Dawson to establish an administration and consolidate the rule of law. It was not until 13 June 1898 that the Yukon Territory Act, establishing a separate political entity, came into effect. Under the act, the territory was to be governed by a commissioner and an appointed council.[41] Pattullo had his first taste of governing when he served briefly as secretary to the Yukon Council in the summer of 1898. By the time Walsh arrived in Dawson, however, he had already resigned as commissioner and Sifton had appointed William Ogilvie as his replacement. During the couple of months he stayed in Dawson, Walsh gathered information for his report to the Canadian government and tried to deal with some of the more immediate problems. Many matters required his attention. Not least of them was the controversy that swirled around the operations of the Gold Commissioner's Office. Both the gold commissioner, Thomas Fawcett, and his office were bitterly attacked throughout 1898 by the *Klondike Nugget*, which publicly voiced the views of disgruntled miners. While it was true that Fawcett was not a very able administrator and certainly not all members of his staff were above reproach, it was also clear that the gold commissioner laboured under great difficulties. Apart from the sheer volume of paperwork involved in processing thousands of mining claims, local officials had to implement a system that was constantly being revised by Ottawa. The Gold Commissioner's Office was badly housed and understaffed. Office efficiency was not enhanced when, during the flood of June 1898, the lower floor was under a foot of water and all work had to be removed to the second level.[42] Walsh, who took a personal interest in the process of establishing mining claims, looked into the problems of accommodation and staffing and tried to reassure the miners that their grievances would get a fair hearing in Ottawa. But Walsh was not in Dawson long enough to do anything thoroughgoing even if he had been inclined to, and certainly his involvement in the Dominion Creek fiasco, when one of his employees used prior knowledge to stake claims, did little to inspire confidence.[43]

By 2 August Walsh was on his way out again and Pattullo went with him. Walsh was leaving for good but Duff intended to return to Dawson. On the trip out Pattullo met another man from Woodstock whose family home, 'The Firs,' was just up Dundas Street a little way from Burnside. Joe Boyle, the putative 'King of the Klondike,' had already seen the possibility of large-scale hydraulic and dredge mining. He had made a number of trips between Dawson and Ottawa in an effort to get a lease to a stretch of the creeks long enough to allow such mining.[44] Boyle's comings and goings, like Pattullo's, were reported in the Woodstock *Sentinel*. By now travel on the Yukon River had become much easier. This time Walsh and Pattullo travelled most of the way to Bennett by steamer, then on foot over the Chilkoot again to catch a boat to Seattle and from there a train across Canada. Pattullo spent a few days with his family in Woodstock before going to Ottawa to assist Walsh with his report to the government. He came back to Burnside from his adventures in the north feeling fit and well and it was noted that he had put on thirty pounds since he left home a year ago.[45]

Pattullo was ready to return to Dawson by the end of September. He was not making the trip back alone for he had convinced his brother James, or 'Burt' as Duff called him, to give up his law practice in Toronto and establish himself in Dawson. There was plenty of litigation over mining claims and not many lawyers in the Yukon in 1898. It was said that some lawyers were able to make as much as $5000 a month in Dawson, and Duff no doubt painted the opportunities in the north in glowing colours for his brother.[46] They had played together as children and now, from the time they went to Dawson, Duff and Burt became very close, in spite of, or perhaps even because of being very different personalities. Duff, although becoming a little more controlled, still had a reckless streak. He was willing to gamble and take risks. His brother remained cautious and calculating, and throughout his life often had a steadying influence on Duff, advising him to think again before rushing headlong into some new scheme. Duff valued his brother's advice even if he did not always follow it. Nor was James Pattullo a complete bore. He and Duff often went out on the town together and on one evening when they were 'having a jollification,' Duff recalled they 'out caroused Caruso.'[47] As a younger man, at least, James also had enough fire in him to respond to Duff's enthusiasm for the northwest and to leave Toronto for Dawson City. Once there he enrolled as a barrister and solicitor and set up a very lucrative practice, first with his partner from Toronto, H.E. Ridley, and later on with H.S. Tobin.[48]

Duff Pattullo's own position was less clear as he returned north. Earlier he had assumed that he would, as a matter of course, become the secretary to the new commissioner of the Yukon, but William Ogilvie vetoed that idea. At Pattullo's request, Sifton had therefore appointed him to be the clerk responsible for the abstracts in the Gold Commissioner's Office. Along with this appointment, Duff also carried other government dispatches back to the Yukon. He arrived in Dawson in late October in running ice just in time to commute the death sentence of Frank Nantuck and to confirm the fate of four others convicted of murder. Faith Fenton, a *Globe* reporter in Dawson, was so anxious for a scoop that she had already sent out a report of the hanging of all five and she now had to arrange with Colonel Sam Steele to send a police dog team to retrieve her premature account.[49] In the case of the murderers, Ottawa's directions were eventually followed, but in the matter of Pattullo's own appointment they were ignored, and it was to be several months before he began work in the Gold Commissioner's Office.

Back in Dawson there was still general dissatisfaction with the office of the gold commissioner. Accusations of incompetence were flying thick and fast as the *Klondike Nugget* led the charge against the Canadian officials. Miners particularly objected to the fact that mining records were not open to the public. The Gold Commissioner's Office had neither the staff nor the space to allow public access, but many quickly concluded that nefarious deeds were taking place behind closed doors. The *Harper's Weekly* correspondent, Tappen Adney, expressed the prevailing opinion on the creeks when he claimed that the clerks in the office sold information and allowed some individuals to jump the queues and register claims ahead of others who had been waiting for days. 'It became recognised by everyone who was obliged to deal with the office that the only way of getting even what belonged to him was to bribe an official.'[50] It was partly to meet such criticism that Sifton had decided to put Pattullo's registry office experience to good use and to send him back to Dawson as abstracts clerk to organize the abstracts of deeds and make them available for public inspection. Sifton had also instructed Ogilvie to clean up the Gold Commissioner's Office. But that was going to take some time and, meanwhile, the accusations did not go away. In October 1898 Ogilvie was appointed as a one-man commission of inquiry to investigate the miners' charges. He waited until the following February before conducting hearings, by which time the critics had lost much of their steam and Thomas Fawcett had already been replaced as gold commissioner. Ogilvie's report exonerated Fawcett of any malfeasence, but some clerks were removed from the office because of serious doubts about their honesty. In this context Ogilvie felt he had to be very careful about who he allowed to work in the Gold Commissioner's Office, so when Pattullo returned to Dawson the commissioner overrode the appointment made by Sifton and, instead of becoming abstracts clerk, Duff was banished to Fort Selkirk for the winter, where he performed the duties of timber agent.

While Pattullo may have been captivated by the natural environment at Selkirk when he passed through in the spring, he had not planned on spending a winter isolated in that tiny community. Nor did he intend to be denied a position that he considered to be rightfully his. Even before he left Dawson for Selkirk he had written directly to the minister of the interior to complain. He began by pointing out to Sifton the chaos in the Gold Commissioner's Office. Abstracts were being written out by clerks who knew nothing of the work and signed by a gold commissioner who did not have the time to examine them. Pattullo said he had been 'informed by clerks in the Gold Commissioner's Office that the state of the records is disgraceful and that none but the men already there could make head or tail of them.' Along with his own interests, Pattullo felt that those of the public would be much better served if he were to organize the records of the Gold Commissioner's Office in Dawson rather than being shunted off to Selkirk where the crown timber agent already had too many assistants. He therefore asked Sifton to reverse Ogilvie's decision.[51] Pattullo was no doubt assisted in his petition by his father's political connections. In fact, on the very day that Pattullo wrote to the minister, Sifton was visiting Woodstock at George Pattullo's invitation.[52] Of course it took nearly two months for Pattullo's letter to reach Ottawa and by then Duff was already in Selkirk. Implementing Sifton's original instruction to put Pattullo in the Gold Commissioner's Office was further delayed by an increasingly pointed exchange of letters in which Ogilvie defended his decision to send Duff south.

The commissioner of the Yukon was somewhat put out that the minister should question his overturning of the instruction regarding Pattullo because he assumed he had been given a free hand with appointments. While Ogilvie may have been an excellent surveyor who knew the Yukon Territory intimately and, as commissioner, there is no doubt he faced a host of pressing matters that demanded long hours of work, the fact remained that he had very little administrative experience. He created problems for the Department of the Interior by lacing his correspondence with personal comment and innuendo, with the result that many of his letters could not be put in the official files. In Pattullo's case he did not hold back.

Ogilvie clearly held a low opinion of Dufferin Pattullo and he did not hesitate to explain why to Sifton. The new commissioner was very critical of his predecessor and Pattullo was discredited in Ogilvie's eyes by his association with Walsh. In an initial letter, Ogilvie wrote that Pattullo was 'very often termed Major Walsh's pimp by some of the best people here.'[53] In a following letter Ogilvie rose briefly above the level of street gossip and added the more substantial point that he had heard Pattullo continued to represent the interests of Walsh and others who had mining claims in the area. Ogilvie felt that, given the storm of protest over the Gold Commissioner's Office, new appointees should not represent the interests of particular individuals. He also regarded Pattullo's personal behaviour as inappropriate for a government official in a sensitive and perhaps vulnerable position. On his return to Dawson, Pattullo had asked the commissioner for a week off to store his outfit away and to prepare to take up his duties. According to Ogilvie, Pattullo also took time out for some recreation. He and a friend lost money in a gambling den and were threatened with a beating when they were unwilling to pay. Pattullo, as ever, had his wits about him and told his attackers that his friend was the commissioner's son and if he were hurt there would be trouble. Ogilvie's son was not well known in Dawson and Pattullo and his friend created enough uncertainty to allow them to escape and enjoy the joke. Ogilvie, however, was not amused, either by the escapade or by Pattullo's drinking and 'rebellious spirit.' Ogilvie even claimed that James Pattullo was glad that Duff was being sent to Selkirk because 'Dawson was not a good place for the boy.' It was the kind of thing that Burt might have said, but again Ogilvie had nothing solid and did 'not wish the brother's name to be brought into the matter.' Thinking that a little discipline would be good for Pattullo, Ogilvie sent him off to Selkirk and hoped that Sifton would support the move since 'it is better for things to be dealt with here than at Ottawa.'[54]

It was on this last point that Ogilvie made his major error: a miscalculation that would eventually lead to his resignation. For things, of course, were not decided in Dawson, and Sifton wrote to his subordinate to point out that fact. The minister said he had appointed Pattullo knowing his behaviour had sometimes left something to be desired but he was prepared to make 'some allowance ... for a young fellow placed in Dawson City.' Whether or not Pattullo was looking after anybody else's claims was, to Sifton, 'a matter of comparatively small importance.' In any event, he knew that Pattullo was capable and, unlike most of the other clerks, had experience in a registry office. Pattullo had been appointed to organize the records in the Gold Commissioner's Office and to make the abstract books available for public inspection. It was not onerous work, according to Sifton, and the gold commissioner ought to be able to see in a week if Pattullo were able to do it properly. There was, therefore, no good reason for changing Pattullo's appointment. Furthermore, wrote Sifton, it was quite impossible for him to send a man to Dawson with a specific commission and allow his appointment to be cancelled when he got there. He was prepared to give Ogilvie a certain amount of latitude, but he had to remind the commissioner that the administration of the Yukon was a departmental matter, that he was the minister responsible, and that 'as long as I have the responsibility I propose to exercise the power.'[55] Sifton made it as plain as he could that he controlled patronage appointments in his department. Accordingly Ogilvie was obliged, in April 1899, to bring Pattullo back to Dawson, where he began work in the Gold Commissioner's Office.

Having finally got the position to which he had been appointed, Pattullo, perhaps for the first time in his life, knuckled down and gave all his energy to doing the job well. He had a position of some responsibility, and it was certainly a challenge to establish a system of records keeping out of the shambles of the Gold Commissioner's Office. Some effort had already been made under the new gold commissioner, E.C. Senkler, to reorganize the office, but Senkler was really too busy with his other work, particularly the court cases, to pay much attention to the day-to-day running of the office. Supervising the work of twenty or so clerks, establishing proper procedures, and ensuring a regular flow of paper were to be Pattullo's tasks. One of the problems facing the Gold Commissioner's Office was that in the early months of the gold rush it had been deluged with thousands of claims and related documents. By the spring of 1899 the pressure had eased a little, but the office had never caught up with the backlog. Within a week of his return to Dawson, Pattullo had assessed the situation and written to his superiors to request an allocation to employ clerks to work in the evening and complete the unfinished paperwork. Pattullo also pointed to the need to employ better qualified people for the regular day's work.[56] Another major hindrance to office efficiency was the total unsuitability of the building in which it was housed. The office was located in the government reserve on Front Street at the south end of Dawson City. The gold commissioner no longer had to share the two-storey log building with other departments, but the office was still cramped, dark, and badly organized. The public area was on the lower floor but most of the records were kept on the upper level, so a great deal of time was wasted running up and down the stairs. Pattullo noted that on one average day seventy-nine bills of sale were recorded that entailed 158 trips upstairs.[57] The clerks were presumably in good physical shape, but their work was slow and those kept waiting for attention often became angry. The acquisition of a more competent staff and adequate office space would have to wait, but Pattullo nevertheless took charge of the office and set to with a will to bring order out of the chaos of its records.

When Pattullo took over he found that the records could not have been in a worse state if they had been deliberately arranged that way.[58] Documents were not properly written up; they were often submitted on scraps of paper, written in pencil, and many did not show clear title. Hundreds of bills of sale, mortgages, and other agreements had never been put through the records; there was no receiving book for registering documents; and no indexing and numbering system by which they could be readily found. Relocations were not systematically kept. No check was made on current work, let alone on past transactions, so errors were common and often entries were left off the records altogether. Because it was virtually impossible to follow the history of a particular claim, no reliance could be placed on the abstracts issued from the office.

Through the summer of 1899 Pattullo worked long hours to deal with these various problems. First he insisted that all documents must be submitted on substantial paper, written in ink, and, most important, all must show title in the proper form. To start with, he said, 'there were a few kickers' who thought that the Gold Commissioner's Office should not adjudicate on title, but Pattullo argued that every document issued should be prima facie evidence of title, and gradually the lawyers and miners fell into line.[59] Once accepted in the office, all documents were assigned a number, registered in the receiving book, and filed in numerical order. Because they were filed according to the date received, the documents relating to a particular claim were scattered through the files, making a system of recording all transactions on each claim essential. Using volumes he had brought in with him the previous fall, Pattullo instituted a system of record books for mining claims that served much the same function as the lot and concession abstract index in the Oxford County registry office. In Dawson they were arranged geographically by the various creeks. Each volume was started in the middle page, which was reserved for the discovery claim on each creek. All subsequent claims were numbered consecutively from the first, both up and down the creek, and were placed either before or after the discovery claim in the record book according to their location. All transactions on each claim, from the initial crown grant on, were recorded, and the abstracts indicated the date, the nature of the transaction, the parties involved, and the number of the relevant document. These record books were open to the public and were an essential reference for the office clerks. With this system in place, any document could be found in as little time as it took to run up and down the stairs. Pattullo instituted a system of checking current work at the end of every day and also at the end of the month. The huge backlog of unprocessed transactions was written up and put through the books.[60] By the end of the summer, the public had access to abstracts on all placer mining claims that were, as far as past errors permitted, accurate and reliable.

All was not perfect, but by most accounts Pattullo's reorganization of the Gold Commissioner's Office was very successful. Never modest, Duff himself claimed there had been a vast improvement and that the public was beginning to have some confidence in the work of the office. Greater efficiency could be achieved with new offices, competent clerks, and proper supplies, but he was satisfied with what he had done.[61] Others were too. Word had got back to Sifton that Duff was doing well and he passed the comment on to George Pattullo.[62] Even the sceptical Ogilvie had changed his mind. He was impressed enough with Pattullo's work to send him to Stewart River in August to inspect the mining recorder's office there, and he had to admit, in his official report written in September 1899, that 'Mr Pattullo has proven himself an intelligent, pains-taking and industrious official.'[63] Ogilvie said much the same thing in private. James Pattullo wrote to his father that Duff was first-rate: 'He has got the G[old] C[ommissioner]'s office in decent shape & has earned great praise: the Commissioner told me only yesterday, he was a God-send to him.' James added, however, that he was sure Duff was sometimes discouraged. While he was working like a Trojan it was so far 'without apparent result.'[64] What he meant was that Duff was not being rewarded by the government for all his hard work. At the beginning of the year Ogilvie had suggested to Sifton that an assistant gold commissioner be appointed to handle the routine of the office.[65] Now that he was doing the job, Pattullo felt he should officially be given the position.

He wrote several times to Sifton to argue his case. After a few months back in Dawson, Pattullo had discovered some of the real reasons why Ogilvie had sent him to Selkirk the previous fall and he felt it necessary to go over some old ground in defence of his claim to the new position. He noted that all government officials in the Yukon were subject to rumour and innuendo and were therefore obliged 'to defend their characters against a lying and absolutely unscrupulous foreign element. The amount of false swearing which has been done here is simply unparalleled in the history of the world.'[66] Pattullo asserted, however, that any investigation would show he was above reproach. He had resisted countless offers to share claims so that by now men had stopped even asking him. Contrary to Ogilvie's earlier suggestion, he did not represent any outside concerns. He had purchased four or five 'interests' on his own account, but all, he regretted to say, were of little value. Nor did he have a drinking problem. Pattullo did allow that in the past he had made 'what might be called one or two "breaks," ' but now claimed he had not touched liquor for months.[67] Thus there was no good reason why he should not be appointed assistant gold commissioner and several reasons why he should. He had been doing the work effectively for several months and had saved the government a great deal of money by reorganizing the office. Some of the clerks had disputed Pattullo's instructions and his right to give them, so he felt he would have more authority within the office as well as in dealings with the public if he were made assistant gold commissioner. Needless to say, he also considered he was entitled to a salary in keeping with the new position.

For a while it looked as though his application might be successful. The gold commissioner appointed him as his assistant for a six-month probationary period, pending a final decision from the Department of the Interior. Pattullo must have thought he had the position in the bag, since he began to sign letters as assistant gold commissioner. He was, however, to be disappointed. Once again Ottawa overruled a local decision and this time it was to Pattullo's detriment. At a distance, Sifton apparently was not convinced that Pattullo had changed his personal habits enough to make him immune from undesirable influences. The Liberals were still taking a lot of political heat over their handling of Yukon affairs and Sifton did not need any more officials, particularly from the Gold Commissioner's Office, creating further embarrassment. Ironically, given what was to happen, Sifton probably would have been better off if he had employed Pattullo's proven ability rather than appointing someone who was new to the situation. But the minister could not read the future and, besides, Pattullo had already had a turn at the patronage trough and there were many others to satisfy. So in spite of Duff's entreaties and the efforts of his father, who wrote to Sifton once again on his son's behalf,[68] Pattullo was passed over and J.L. Bell was appointed assistant gold commissioner. Duff assumed that political considerations were involved, yet he complained of unfair treatment. Sifton replied crisply that he felt no obligation to appoint Pattullo to the permanent position. In recognition of his service he was prepared to increase his annual salary from $1200 to $1500, but that was all, and Pattullo could take it or leave it.[69] Since he had no choice, Pattullo took it. His day-to-day work did not change much with Bell's appointment. As chief clerk he remained responsible for office routine and he continued to complain to the department that his salary was not commensurate with his contribution.

While his professional role did not change much in the fall of 1899, his personal life did. During the summer, while he was whipping the Gold Commissioner's Office into shape, Duff met the recently widowed Lillian Miles. That same summer, about the time Duff and Lillian were getting to know each other, Ogilvie was forced to defend the employment of women as clerks in the Gold Commissioner's Office. Since there was a lack of qualified men, Ogilvie saw no harm in hiring respectable women to do the work. One of those whom he had employed needed the salary because she was a widow, and, Ogilvie wrote to Sifton, 'I may add a bona fide widow. You know what I mean.'[70] Lillian was also 'bona fide' and had just returned to Dawson to settle her late husband's estate. She was born Lillian Riedemiester in 1871 in Toledo, Ohio, and was one of three daughters of Otto Riedemiester who had been a lawyer. Lillian's father died before she met Duff. She had come to Dawson in 1898 with her first husband, Jerry Miles, a pharmacist who also had an interest in some claims out on the creeks. He may have had some of these claims in his wife's name, for the mining records for 1898 show that a Mrs J.J. Miles took out a free miner's certificate.[71] Like many a cheechako, Jerry Miles went out to the diggings when he should not have, was caught by cold weather, and froze to death. After her husband's tragic end, Lillian left Dawson and spent the winter with a sister in California, then returned the following summer. Before she met Duff she settled out of court with her husband's partner for $1500. Pattullo later claimed that she ought to have got $20,000 had the partner not robbed the estate. Still she acquired an amount that was equal to Duff's annual salary and, a year later, her mother died leaving a small estate. Lillian also owned what Duff called a house but was probably a cabin on the corner of Fifth Street and Sixth Avenue.[72]

Duff and Lillian had not known each other for long when they were married on the evening of Thursday, 30 November 1899. Both were, however, well known in Dawson and so the small ceremony attended by a few special friends was reported in the *Klondike Nugget*.[73] The private ceremony was conducted by a minister but took place in the bride's house. Marriage altered Duff's life somewhat. He moved from his room in the mess for government employees into Lillian's house and, although in later life they would spend a lot of time apart, in the early months of their marriage they were a close couple. Duff spent less time out on the town with the boys, and James wrote to his father that he had seen little of his brother since his wedding because he stayed pretty much to his house.[74] It was, of course, the middle of winter and when the weather warmed Duff would once again cut a figure on the streets of Dawson. Legend has it that on hot days he was partial to stepping out in a white duck suit. At twenty-six Duff still looked young and boyish and his new wife was an attractive woman with strong, classical features. Together they were a handsome couple as they took part in the social events of Dawson. Duff was always full of fun and he both enjoyed and contributed to the gaiety of social occasions.[75] But underneath the surface, like Dawson itself, Duff was changing. Marriage had added another element of stability to his life. When Bell was appointed assistant gold commissioner, Pattullo had asked if he could be sent as inspector of mines to Sulphur Creek, but he probably dropped the idea because he could not have taken his wife. He was soon commenting in his letters to his father on how aimless his existence would be without Lillian.[76]

Pattullo also observed that his financial position began to improve from the time of his marriage. He still owed money, both to his father and to his brother. Soon after they were married Duff assumed power of attorney over Lillian's finances and he began to pay off some of his debts. He was to wait many months before he actually received the salary increase promised by Sifton and he was unable to convince Ogilvie that he should get a living allowance in lieu of his room on the government reserve.[77] Although the peak of the gold rush had passed, the cost of living was still high in Dawson. The newlyweds lived in reasonable comfort and Duff's estimate of his monthly expenses included the $150 it cost Lillian and him to eat at restaurants.[78] But clearly he was not going to make a fortune in the government service. He continued to complain bitterly about the 'outrageous' treatment he was receiving over his salary. He told

Sifton that, given the responsibilities he had, he ought to get more than a mere $40 above the salary of a messenger boy of seventeen. He was now a married man, obliged to live the life of a gentleman and not as a 'squaw man,' and he said he should at least be given the increase he had been promised a year ago. Sifton finally admitted that Pattullo had a point and increased his salary to $2000 a year.[79] At the same time, the work in the Gold Commissioner's Office had become routine and no longer a challenge, so Pattullo began to think of another career. He was appointed vice-consul in Dawson for Norway and Sweden and he and his friends got a good deal of amusement out of the overenthusiastic *Nugget* reporter who wrote that Pattullo was well qualified for the position by virtue of his fluency in Swedish.[80] He also made plans to study law, but before they came to fruition there were, once again, personnel problems in the Gold Commissioner's Office.

Criticism of the office had become less noisy but could still be heard. In the spring of 1900 the *Klondike Nugget* objected to Assistant Gold Commissioner Bell's decision to end the public disclosure of mining records and old suspicions were aroused once again when that move was followed by the arrest of some staff members. There were renewed calls to clean out the office, but few changes were made and the sniping continued. Then, in the fall of 1901, Bell was suddenly suspended from his position, pending an investigation by the Department of the Interior of alleged 'maladministration of affairs in his office.'[81] In the meantime, Pattullo was once more called upon to fill in. When Bell's suspension was made permanent in November, so was Duff's appointment as acting assistant gold commissioner. But he was only acting assistant. As he had done before, Pattullo was expected to do the work of the assistant gold commissioner without the official title or the salary that went with the position.

Other changes were also taking place in the Gold Commissioner's Office. On the first weekend of December 1901 the office was moved from its old, cramped, and dingy quarters into the substantial administration building that had just been completed on Fifth Avenue in the government reserve. The new building was a large, two-storied, wood frame structure with a 160-foot frontage. One Dawson newspaper suggested that it was the largest building ever constructed in the north and even the *Nugget* congratulated the government on financing 'a magnificent building, magnificently finished.'[82] The interior was done in oiled, varnished British Columbia fir, and the rooms and offices were well lit by large windows and numerous electric lights. The building was heralded as indicative of the material progress and maturing civic status of the city. As large as it was, the administration building was always a problem to heat properly, but in every other way life was made much easier for Pattullo and the others in the Gold Commissioner's Office. The thirty-two people working in the office moved in over the weekend, opened for business on Monday, 2 December 1901, and from then on, Pattullo announced, the hours would be ten to six Monday to Friday and ten to one on Saturday.[83] The Gold Commissioner's Office took up one half of the ground floor at the north end of the building and the Gold Commissioner's Court was directly above. The largest room on the ground floor was the 1600-square-foot mining recording office. It was divided by a 90-foot U-shaped counter over which the public transacted most of its business. Behind it was a large work place with direct access to the brick vault where the records were kept. Pattullo had a commodious, well-lighted office at the back of the building directly off the recording office.[84] From there he was able to keep a close watch on the work as it was carried out. Altogether it was a much more satisfactory work place.

A few months after Duff occupied his new office, he and Lillian moved into a new house. They had bought three lots on Grant Street at the corner of Ninth Avenue in February 1902.[85] It was an area on the rise above the government reserve where a number of officials lived. Duff and Lillian built a log house and would live there as long as they stayed in Dawson. For Duff it was only a short walk across Minto Park to the back entrance of the administration building – a distance he no doubt appreciated on the cold, dark mornings of mid-winter. In the long, hot, summer evenings he could sit on his front porch and look down to where the Klondike River, muddied from the workings on its feeder creeks, met the clearer waters of the Yukon.

By 1902 the nature of gold mining on those creeks around Dawson was beginning to change. It was clear to some, including Pattullo, that the days of the individual placer miner working a 250-foot claim were numbered. The rich deposits of Bonanza, Hunker, and Eldorado creeks were being worked out and more efficient methods of mining were required. Pattullo had foreseen this development three years earlier. When he started work in the Gold Commissioner's Office he had argued that the mining records ought to be organized with a view to permanence and not just to meet the demands of a transient gold excitement. Long after the creeks were worked out under the present methods there would be a rich field for hydraulic operations.[86] By 1902 the first dredge on Bonanza Creek had demonstrated the great potential of that mining technique. Large-scale mining demanded larger working areas and at the forefront of the demand for more extensive concessions was the energetic entrepreneur A.N.C. Treadgold. He, and others like Joe Boyle, had persuaded the federal government to reserve long sections of creekbed for the big operators using the new technology. When notice of the Treadgold concessions was posted in the Gold Commissioner's Office in July 1901 there was an instant storm of protest. The free miners, not unreasonably, saw the concessions as a threat to their operations. So once again the lines were drawn and the battle raged over government mining policy.[87]

Pattullo took a position between the two extremes. He recognized that the nature of mining would have to change: that the 'day of the pick and shovel is gone by; modern methods must be introduced.'[88] He believed that placer mining could still be encouraged by increasing the size of claims to 1000 feet square. In a territory so vast there was plenty of room for all, and enlarging the size of claims would foster the development of outlying districts. At the same time he argued that around Dawson, where the coarse gold was worked out, it was necessary to encourage capital intensive operations. So, although he objected to some of the specific detail of the concessions, he favoured making grants of, say, one mile of unclaimed creekbed to the likes of Treadgold. He found much of the newspaper criticism of the concessions to be ill-informed objection to monopoly in principle rather than a detailed demonstration that this particular monopoly was iniquitous. At the very time that some were beginning to doubt that Dawson would survive, it was necessary to foster new development; it would not do to wait until the place began to decline. If Treadgold were successful, others would follow his example. If he were not, then no harm was done. Pattullo invoked the spirit of the builders of the Canadian Pacific Railway and said it was time to allow those with capital to venture it. He stated these views primarily in a letter to the commissioner marked 'For the information of the Minister,' and he also expressed them in public when a mass meeting was called to mobilize opposition to the concessions.[89] As it had done with earlier mining regulations, the federal government revised some of the provisions of the Treadgold concessions, but an inexorable trend had been set in motion. The individual miner was being replaced by large-scale operations. In the years that followed, gold production in the Yukon was kept up by the hydraulic miners and the massive dredges that ground noisily along the creeks transforming the landscape as they went.

As well as expressing views on general policy on the goldfields, Pattullo continued to supervise the routine of the Gold Commissioner's Office while he waited for the department's decision on the permanent position. This time he was more than optimistic and he really expected to be made assistant gold commissioner. Of course Duff always looked on the bright side, but even James thought he would be given the appointment.[90] All of the Pattullo family's considerable political influence was marshalled in support of Duff's claim. Both George and Andrew Pattullo wrote to Sifton urging that Duff be given the job on a permanent basis that he was doing so well. In January 1902 the cashier in the Gold Commissioner's Office, Thomas Middleton, disappeared and was later found to have killed himself. An investigation revealed he had defaulted on payments of about $1000. Not wanting his position jeopardized, Pattullo asked his father to go to Ottawa to make it clear he was in no way involved in the affair and to press the minister once more to give him the assistantship. Both his father and his uncle Andrew had already been told that it was unlikely Duff would get the job.[91] Pattullo did not know what was going on in the minister's mind, but as month after month went by without word even his eternal optimism must have begun to fade. It was nearly a year before a decision was made and once again Pattullo's hopes were dashed. F.X. Gosselin, the crown timber and land agent in the Yukon, was selected to take over the job Pattullo had been doing.

Duff Pattullo was again being penalized for his past behaviour. While there were political considerations in the Gosselin appointment and he too was a capable official, Pattullo was denied the position largely because Sifton was still unconvinced he was sufficiently stable to resist temptation. There were other reasons. James Smart, Sifton's deputy minister and right-hand man, visited the Yukon in the late summer of 1902 and, with time to spare in Whitehorse on the way out, he wrote at length to the minister on a number of matters. Smart had not enjoyed his stay in Dawson. He had spent most of his time closeted in the administration building and considered it to have been the worst experience of his official career. He was not impressed with the Gold Commissioner's Office and thought it would be a mistake to make Pattullo the permanent assistant. The humourless deputy minister presumably intended no pun when he conceded that 'Pattullo is certainly a very smart young fellow.' But Smart claimed that Pattullo did not have the confidence of the people. This alleged distrust was partly due to Duff's youthful appearance and lack of experience. More substantially, perhaps, people were apparently concerned that, as a lawyer involved in litigation over claims, James Pattullo might have undue influence on Duff. As acting assistant gold commissioner Duff certainly wrote numerous official letters to Pattullo and Ridley on matters relating to specific claims, but there is no evidence whatever of unwarranted collusion between the brothers. Even Smart admitted there was probably no ground at all for the suspicion. Yet the very existence of the possibility in the public mind, whether well founded or not, was enough to disqualify Pattullo, and Smart therefore recommended Gosselin for the position. Sifton's man was also in the Yukon to assess the political climate and, apart from Gosselin's competence, Smart noted that his appointment would not do the Liberals any harm among the French community in Dawson. French Canadians were a substantial element in the Yukon population and they had the ear of the Laurier government, particularly when it came to civil service appointments. A vigorous election campaign was being waged for a federal seat and the campaign committee of the Liberal candidate, J.H. Ross, argued that the only way to secure the French vote was to appoint a French Canadian as assistant gold commissioner.[92] So there were, as always, political considerations, but in the end it was probable that the brash, aggressive Pattullo had simply rubbed another stolid federal official up the wrong way.

Pattullo could understand the political factors involved in Gosselin's appointment even if he found them difficult to accept, and he might have stayed on in the Gold Commissioner's Office had insult not been added to injury. Gosselin was appointed at twice the salary Pattullo had been getting, so he claimed he was at least entitled to the extra pay for the time he was acting assistant gold commissioner. His view was endorsed by the gold commissioner and Senkler wrote to Smart recommending that, since two acting mining inspectors got mining inspectors' salaries, Pattullo should get the salary of the assistant gold commissioner. Smart's eventual reply was a telegram saying that 'Pattullo's wishes cannot be met regarding additional remuneration' and a confirmatory letter noting that Treasury Board regulations did not permit officers holding positions temporarily to have the full salary. For Pattullo that was the last straw. He wired Sifton his resignation, effective on 1 December 1902.[93]

The fall of 1902 was a trying time for Pattullo. As she was often to be, Lillian was unwell. She was not as strong as she appeared and frequently suffered from one malady or another. At work, Pattullo felt he had served well and been shabbily treated. He had been considering the possibility of another career and pursuing the idea of going into law. A special territorial ordinance enabled him to article in the Gold Commissioner's Office. On 6 October 1902 a judge signed a certificate recommending that he be admitted to the bar when he passed the appropriate examinations.[94] Although he was exploring other long-term possibilities, he still intended to stay on in the Gold Commissioner's Office as chief clerk just as he had done when Bell was appointed. But Smart's refusal to consider what Pattullo thought was a reasonable salary request was the ultimate outrage. On the surface his resignation seemed precipitous, but there were underlying causes. He had felt for some time that he had gone about as far as he could go in the government service. He recognized he was working in a system where ability was not necessarily the prime qualification for advancement and, if nothing else, Pattullo had a high regard for his own ability. After three-and-a-half years he was on top of the routine of the job and there was not the same challenge and sense of accomplishment as in the first few months. Or perhaps it was just that the job was no fun anymore. On the way into Dawson he had commented about a minor chore that it 'always seems to me if a fellow is going to have more trouble over a thing than the fun he is going to get out of it, he might far better leave it alone altogether.'[95]

And so Pattullo quit the government service. He was a generous, outgoing individual and genuinely popular in the Gold Commissioner's Office. One day just before he left he was called upstairs to the Gold Commissioner's Court to witness a testimonial from his fellow workers. They spoke of his fine work and the esteem in which he was held in the office. Gold Commissioner Senkler also commended his efforts and presented him with a gold watch. Pattullo was touched by these unexpected and kind words from the office staff and he recalled the many happy days he had spent in their company. He also received high praise from the often critical *Klondike Nugget*. He was acclaimed for his efficiency, his knowledge of every detail of his work, and his courteous manner with the public.[96]

Pattullo had tendered his resignation, but he did not intend to let the matter of his back pay die. He called again on his father and his uncle to do battle with the Department of the

Interior on his behalf. He had 'put a rotten office on a solid basis' and had been treated with gross unfairness by the department. And when he said the department he meant 'Mr Smart.' He told his father that he wanted the matter investigated by the minister and 'not by someone who makes a hurried trip into the country and who may jump to the conclusion that I am a young man with too much assurance.'[97] The Pattullos pressed Sifton, who earlier had refused to explain in writing why Duff had been denied the permanent position. He now wrote in some detail. The minister reiterated the reasons for Duff's being passed over a second time, regretted he had resigned in the way he did, and dismissed the application for the pay of assistant gold commissioner by saying it was 'absolutely impossible to entertain it at all.'[98] This time, however, Andrew Pattullo would not take no for an answer. He wrote again to argue that Duff should not be penalized for past lapses. In the early days in Dawson he would have been a 'rare bird' indeed had he not cut loose once in a while, but when warned by both the minister and his family he had stopped his drinking binges. Furthermore, with temptation and corruption all around him, he had kept his nose clean in the Gold Commissioner's Office. His work had not been criticized in any way, and in that he was unique in the entire department – 'from the Minister down,' added Andrew without delicacy. Perhaps Duff was hasty in resigning but, 'like all spirited fellows,' he was smarting under a perceived injustice. Things might have gone more smoothly had he been dealing directly with the minister rather than with Smart. In any event, Andrew Pattullo wanted Sifton to reconsider, arguing that surely precedents could be found for Duff to receive the salary of assistant gold commissioner. If this were not enough, he told Sifton that he intended 'running down to Ottawa to see you personally.' Finally Sifton relented, having also had word from Dawson that Duff had been a most effective officer and should have got the recognition he deserved.[99] There was a ministerial reconsideration and presumably precedents were found, for Duff received his back pay.

The extra money enabled Pattullo to pay off his debts. He wrote to thank his father for his good offices and to tell him that for the first time in thirteen years he did not owe any money. In the three years since his marriage he had paid off some $6000.[100] He now hoped that he had left the word 'debt' behind him forever. But that was not to be.

When he left the Gold Commissioner's Office Pattullo turned his back on the possibility of qualifying for the bar and, instead of emulating his brother's lucrative choice of career, Duff went into real estate. He joined with Emil Stauf to form the partnership of Stauf and Pattullo, real estate, mining, and financial agents. Stauf had been in Dawson since March 1899 when he had formed a partnership in real estate with C.K. Zilly.[101] The new firm of Stauf and Pattullo had their offices in the Northern Commercial Company's office building on King Street. James Pattullo had his law offices in the same building. It was, in every sense, the other side of town from the government reserve and the administration building. If the federal government was the largest operation in Dawson City, then the Northern Commercial Company was the second largest. Until 1901 it had been the Alaska Commercial Company, and it was both the oldest and the biggest commercial operation in Dawson. Its complex of buildings were at the heart of the city's business district and dominated the corner of Front and King streets. Its buildings faced the Yukon River, the highway of commerce, and King Street, or First Street as it had been known, was a major thoroughfare that led to the trail out to the gold fields.[102]

It was into this atmosphere of bustle and commerce that Pattullo moved in early 1903. Since they had offices in the same building, Duff and James spent more time together, particularly while Duff was alone over the summer of 1903. Lillian followed the example of many Dawson wives and took an extended trip to the outside for the summer. While she was gone Duff worked to build up his new business, dealing in residential and mining property and selling insurance. He was enthusiastic and optimistic about this new life. He had moved from the public to the private sector in the hope that his fortunes would improve: that energy and talent would be rewarded rather than being stifled by the hierarchical organization of a government department. But enterprise was not entirely free outside of government. The commercial world had its own, if different, restrictions and limitations. And 1903 was not a good year to go into real estate in Dawson City.

By then Dawson was in decline. The boom was over and miners were attracted to new fields, particularly in Alaska where the Tanana discovery of 1903 led to an exodus to Fairbanks. The miners were the first to leave, but they were followed by businessmen who saw greater opportunities across the border. From 1901, when there were 27,219 people in Dawson, the population dropped steadily until by the next census of 1911 there were only 8512.[103] As miners left the creeks, houses were deserted and places of business stood empty. Even James Pattullo began to have a hard time of it. In 1903 he was appointed crown prosecutor; or, at least, he was made half a crown prosecutor. Still wanting to spread patronage around, the federal government had given James the position jointly with J.C. Noel. It brought in a little extra income, but not enough to offset the decline in other work. One year later business had dropped to the point where James only expected to meet expenses.[104] Duff's line of work was even more immediately affected by Dawson's decline. Being well known and popular in Dawson, he had plenty of contacts, but the city hardly provided an expanding market on which to build a successful real estate business and, although many in town were no doubt increasingly concerned about their future, he was not able to sell much insurance either. Pattullo believed that 'Dame fortune always knocks once and when the opportunity arises to make a big hand legitimately, I will endeavour to seize it.'[105] Unfortunately few opportunities knocked on Duff's office door after he went into business in Dawson.

Partly for that reason, he devoted more time to activities outside of his work. Duff had always taken an interest in sports, though more as an observer than a participant. As editor of the Galt *Reformer* in 1897 he had arranged a special wire into the newspaper office to print a round-by-round description of a fight between Bob Fitzsimmons and Jim Corbett in Carson City. He was considered to be a reliable authority on prize fights.[106] While he was working in the Gold Commissioner's Office he helped to organize a strong civil service hockey team. Duff's generosity was often greater than his means and, when his team won a local championship in 1901, he presented each member with a set of custom-made gold cuff links.[107] At the same time he suggested that Dawson should send a team to compete for the Stanley Cup, claiming it could field a hockey team as good as any Canadian city.[108] It took a few years for the plan to come to fruition. When it did, Pattullo was actively involved in the organization of the Dawson team that was sent to Ottawa in December 1904. Joe Boyle, who like Pattullo was also a boxing fan, was to manage the team in the east. Dawson was wild with enthusiasm about its team sent forth to do battle for the Stanley Cup, but, as with many of Pattullo's schemes, the expectations were not realized. The Dawson team was soundly beaten by Ottawa in the first game and humiliated 23 to 2 in the second.[109] It was neither the first nor the last time that Pattullo's plans would come to grief in Ottawa. But win or lose, sport was an important social activity in Dawson. In winter Duff's enthusiasm was hockey and in summer it was tennis. Along with many leaders of Dawson society, Duff was a member of the tennis club and in 1903 he was elected its president.[110]

Pattullo had new responsibilities of a different kind when he became a father. His only daughter, Lillian Doris Pattullo, was born on 2 April 1905. She was named for her mother, but like her father grew up preferring her second Christian name. Duff was intensely fond of his daughter. He bestowed on his one child all of the love that his father had given to his many children. He gave of himself and his worldly goods, and imparted his particular enthusiasm and joy of life upon Doris. Not surprisingly, father and daughter were alike in many ways. Yet they did not share all things. Throughout his life Pattullo always kept his family life and his political career largely separated. He certainly did not bring his political trials home to the family in the evening, and Lillian and Doris were often unaware of his tribulations of the day.

After he left the Gold Commissioner's Office, Duff Pattullo became increasingly involved in politics, and particularly in the intense and internecine infighting that developed within the Yukon Liberal party. He had always been active within the party but kept a low political profile as long as he was in the government service. Almost as soon as he resigned there were rumours in Dawson that he would stand for election as alderman.[111] Although he did not do so immediately, his thoughts of a political career were probably a factor in his decision to leave the civil service. In February 1903 he was elected to the executive committee of the Dawson Liberal Club and, at the end of the year, he did declare himself a candidate for a place on the Dawson City Council.[112] Pattullo's first gambit in electoral politics was fairly low key as the brief campaign was not very vigorous. At the one meeting where the candidates stated their positions, Pattullo advocated a reduction in taxes and more autonomy for the city on financial matters. By election day on 9 January 1904 he was one of twenty-four candidates for six places. Pattullo was successful in his first try for electoral office. He polled the third highest of the candidates, with 259 out of the 638 votes cast.[113] While the election campaign may have been a mild one, the political fun and games started almost immediately after Pattullo was elected a Dawson City alderman.

The storms of Yukon politics in 1904 raged around the unfortunate personality of Frederick T. Congdon, the federally appointed commissioner of the Yukon Territory. Congdon had been a prominent leader of the forces opposed to the Treadgold concessions, so many in Dawson were pleased when he was made commissioner in March 1903. Pattullo had taken a different position in the debate on the concessions but raised no objection to Congdon in the early months of his rule. The commissioner, who had his eye on the Yukon seat in the House of Commons, organized a ruthless political machine. He took the use of patronage to new heights, even for the Yukon, in his effort to ensure the loyalty of followers and to buy off opponents. One of his henchmen, William Temple, extorted contributions from the owners of saloons and dance halls in return for immunity from prosecution.[114] Such methods soon alienated many Liberals and, as opposition grew, Congdon demonstrated his complete lack of political finesse. He referred to his opponents within the Liberal party as crooks and traitors and asserted that the best way to handle them was 'to take them by the throat.'[115]

Pattullo, along with many other Liberals in Dawson, was particularly offended by Congdon's machinations to establish a newspaper that would faithfully reflect his views. Given his family background, Pattullo knew as well as Congdon the political advantages of a subservient press and initially he was prepared to help the commissioner out. But he got badly burned in the process. In November 1903 Congdon had Temple attempt to bring about an amalgamation of the *Sun* and the *Record* and Pattullo was made manager of the joint paper. The deal fell through, however, and Temple had to return the $2500 that had been put into the venture. When Temple could not raise the money, Pattullo agreed to get the amount, plus another $500 for outstanding *Sun* bills, in return for a contract to do an equivalent amount of government printing. He arranged for the printing to be done by another Liberal newspaper, the *News*, while Congdon and Temple established a new paper called *The World*. Pattullo had been promised, but had not been given in writing, a contract to print the Yukon Year Book. He began to get apprehensive when some of Congdon's men put about the suggestion that the contract would go instead to *The World* in an effort to teach the young Pattullo a lesson. The matter was raised at a meeting of the Liberal Club and Pattullo, who was 'not generally given to equivocation,' explained his side of the story in clear terms.[116] He and a group of Liberals then met with Congdon to sort the matter out. At this point, according to Pattullo, a few polite and politic words from the commissioner would have settled the issue. But Congdon only became annoyed when his methods were challenged. He refused to honour the contract and when Pattullo threatened to go public with the story he was told 'to go to hell.'[117]

Pattullo had fallen into a political trap. Congdon was using the printing contract as leverage to force him into line. Such duplicity was too much for Pattullo. He, too, was a determined individual, and he was unwilling to submit to such bullying. He became a leading opponent of the Congdon forces even though, just months after paying off his father, he was once again in debt, this time to the tune of $3000. His decision to run for the City Council may have been partly motivated by the fact that Dawson aldermen received a salary of $1500.[118] But more important was his annoyance at the position he had been put in by Congdon. He warned Sifton that the commissioner was running amuck and would do great damage to the government if he were not restrained. During the Treadgold excitement Pattullo had taken Congdon to task for the damage he might do to the administration by opposing department policy, and Congdon replied 'he did not give a big d for the Minister of the Interior.' Now the commissioner told Pattullo he did not give a damn either for the Liberals of the Yukon or for his own position. 'A gentleman so entirely indifferent,' Pattullo suggested to Sifton, 'would seem to be in need of a guardian.'[119]

Pattullo was past playing that role, however, and began to attack Congdon, both from the Dawson City Council and within the ranks of the Liberal party. As chairman of the committee for fire, light, and water, Alderman Pattullo was responsible for the Dawson fire department. Every year there were major fires in the city and the competence of the fire brigade was always a hot political issue. Sometimes Duff tested its efficiency by setting up false alarms and then timing the fire brigade's reaction with a stopwatch. Fire fighting also consumed about three-quarters of the council's budget and, by 1904, with declining revenue and a large deficit, there was a desire to cut costs. Pattullo's committee decided to reduce the size of the fire department. Four men, including the captain, were dismissed and all were Congdon supporters.[120]

At the same time the conflict within the Yukon Liberal party over Congdon's methods had burst wide open. The battle lines were now clearly drawn between the 'Tabs,' as the Congdonites were known, and his opponents who were called 'Steam Beers.' Because it was alleged that Congdon refused to pay his bribery debts, his followers were disparaged as 'Tabs,' while his opponents were named 'Steam Beers' in honour of one of their leaders who was a beer manufacturer. In April 1904 the Yukon Liberal Association condemned interference by government employees in the affairs of the party and elected Pattullo to replace F.M.

Shepard as secretary. Shepard refused to hand over the books and monies of the association to Pattullo and the commissioner's supporters formed the rival Yukon 'Territorial' Liberal Association.[121] By now there was no moderation of sentiment or language on either side. While Pattullo wrote to both Sifton and Wilfrid Laurier to revile Congdon as 'unreliable, impolitic, autocratic, weak and wholly lacking in ordinary judgement,' a leading Congdon supporter informed the prime minister that Pattullo's group was nothing but a 'gang of bums.'[122]

Through the summer of 1904 the two groups of Liberals continued to blast away at each other and Pattullo was Congdon's most vociferous opponent.[123] The 'Steam Beers' held meetings to denounce Congdon publicly. Pattullo complained about his refusal to honour the Year Book contract, while others ventilated their outrage at his blatant use of patronage. Pattullo tried to persuade Liberal leaders in Ottawa to intervene in the situation and was disgusted when they would not. After appeals to Sifton proved useless, Pattullo threatened 'to publish from one end of Canada to the other a history of Yukon legislation from the time when you assumed office until today.' Wilfrid Laurier regretted the 'threatening tone' of Pattullo's letters, but showed how completely out of touch with the Yukon he was when he appealed 'for concessions and mutual forbearance' from the two sides.[124] While Laurier naïvely wished that Liberals would bury the hatchet, it was clear that the wounds already inflicted could not be healed and the party would be hopelessly divided for the next federal election. In June the Yukon Liberal Association met to nominate their candidate and put together a platform. Pattullo considered running but withdrew in favour of Thomas Kearney. The 'Steam Beer' program called, among other things, for an end to the meddling by civil servants in partisan politics. They were ready, or so they thought, to do electoral battle with the Congdon troops. Pattullo had already told Sifton that nothing less than the removal of the commissioner would settle the matter. For Pattullo there was a distinction between patronage and corruption, and Congdon and his gang were 'the coarsest grafting proposition ever inflicted on a community.' But even Pattullo, who observed that 'Denmark was never half as rotten as Yukon,' was hardly prepared for Congdon's next move.[125]

Since the Dawson City Council provided a base for Pattullo's opposition to Congdon, the commissioner removed that challenge to his power by the simple expedient of eliminating the council. When Dawson was incorporated three years earlier some citizens, particularly some businessmen and property owners, had opposed the move because they did not want to be burdened with city taxes. Now, with the city in decline, they feared that taxes would be increased, and a small group petitioned the Yukon Council to revoke the city charter and remove the elected aldermen. The petition gave Congdon the pretext he needed. He had the petitioners request a plebiscite on the question, refused to hear Pattullo and the other aldermen who objected, and then promised the citizens a rebate of one-third of their taxes if they voted to end the city charter. As if that were not enough, he then proceeded to rig the voting. He appointed the city clerk to run the election without any outside scrutiny. The aldermen responded by dismissing the clerk and electing Pattullo as acting chairman of the finance committee to oversee the election. The city clerk then locked himself and the assessment rolls in the city hall. Denied access to the building through the door, Pattullo climbed through a window and claimed he had found evidence of tampering with the voters' list.[126] But it was all to no avail. Those citizens permitted to do so voted overwhelmingly to revoke Dawson City's charter, and Pattullo's first stint as an elected representative came to an end when Congdon declared the result official on 19 September 1904.[127]

With that carpet pulled from under him, Pattullo became even more determined to see Congdon's removal. And he was soon to have the chance. In October Congdon did what Pattullo had suspected for several months he might do.[128] He resigned as commissioner and accepted the nomination of the Yukon 'Territorial' Liberal Association as a candidate in the coming federal election. With Congdon on the hustings, the Yukon Liberal Association withdrew their candidate and joined with the Conservatives to support Alfred Thompson, who agreed to follow most of the 'Steam Beer's' policies. The campaign was hard and vicious, and Pattullo was in the thick of it. James Pattullo, who declared he was enough of a Liberal loyalist to support the administration candidate, thought Duff should keep out of it. He advised his brother that if he wanted a political career he should lie low, wait until Congdon was out of the way, and then he would have a good chance at the Liberal nomination. When Duff and Congdon met and traded insults at a campaign meeting, James even tried to effect a reconciliation, but he 'could do nothing with Duff and Congdon is just as bull-headed.'[129] The political Pattullo was not one to back off from a fight, even when the better part of valour might have been in his own interest. In contrast to James, Duff Pattullo was already enough of a maverick to buck the establishment even within his own party, and certainly Ottawa's brand was no longer on him. As far as he was concerned, coercion and intimidation were running rampant in the Yukon and, whatever Ottawa thought, it had to be stopped. He self-righteously told Wilfrid Laurier, 'I suppose that I will not ... be less a good Liberal in fighting for that which is right, than dumbly submitting to that which I am certain is wrong.'[130] Pattullo was convinced that Congdon's men would once again try to prevent opponents from voting, and he was not mistaken. But this time they went too far in their efforts to edit the voters' lists. Three days before the election William Temple and some other Congdon supporters were charged with conspiracy to defeat the Election Act. On election day the 'Steam Beers' were finally victorious as Thompson defeated Congdon by a sound margin. It had been, said Pattullo, 'to say the least, an exciting election.'[131]

Pattullo's joy that Congdon was down was mingled with concern when it became apparent that he was not entirely out and his supporters were trying to have him reinstated as commissioner. Pattullo had 'always realized that this territory has been used for political purposes regardless of the needs of the territory.'[132] Now, having observed the excesses of the Congdon machine and the unwillingness of federal politicians to respond to demands for change, Pattullo was more critical of control from the centre. In that, as in other things, Pattullo had become a westerner. This time he hoped that Sifton would send them a good man, 'a western man who understood western ideas of doing business.' He further advised the minister that the new commissioner should not be a French Canadian. A number of French Canadians in the civil service had been prominent Congdon supporters and, although Pattullo said he had 'no antipathy whatever to Frenchmen as Frenchmen,' he had already warned Sifton that if one of their number were appointed commissioner it 'would precipitate a political fight which the boundaries of the Yukon could not confine.'[133] After some delay, the British Columbian W.W.B. McInnis was made commissioner and, with his appointment, Yukon politics began to settle down. The Congdonites tried to discredit the new commissioner and Pattullo rose to his defence,[134] but the strident voices of 1904 were now muted even though the rivalries had not entirely disappeared. Pattullo still complained to Ottawa when Congdon was returned to his old position as legal adviser to the Yukon Council and when 'Tabs' of doubtful credibility were given government jobs. Laurier grew more exasperated with the bickering and, when Pattullo forwarded a resolution of the Yukon Liberal Association criticizing the reinstatement of three Congdon supporters, the prime minister told him that 'were it not for the fact of my old political connection with and friendship for your family, I would not have noticed this resolution which is as insulting as it is untrue.'[135] The heat had gone out of the situation and, as the political temperature dropped, so did Pattullo's will to fight. Besides, along with most people in Dawson, he was increasingly preoccupied with economic rather than political problems.

Like the wild flowers of the north that bloomed so brightly because the season was short, Dawson also faded fast. Gold mining had not laid the basis for other forms of economic development. A visitor in the spring of 1908 thought that Dawson City gave the 'impression of respectability compelled by impoverishment, of the temperance that succeeds dissipation, of the bust after the boom.' Those who remained strove to cope with the straitened circumstances so that, while the boom had gone, business continued. Only slight vestiges of the old days when

Dawson 'was a hummer' remained. For the most part the town looked 'like a nicely washed young man of subdued demeanor' who gives a hint that he once led a wild life.[136] As he too settled into less exciting times, Pattullo perhaps gave a similar impression. Still the young man about town in his early thirties, he struggled to find financial success. But he was fighting a trend as people left, businesses closed, and the town looked more and more bedraggled. In 1907 he formed a new partnership with William G. Radford. Both men worked in the same line of business and hoped to improve their prospects by pooling their resources. Pattullo was the senior partner in the new firm and held three-fifths of the shares. Pattullo and Radford made some money but clearly Dawson City no longer provided sufficient scope for Duff's drive, energy, and ambition. Dawson was in decline and Pattullo did not want to go down with it. He needed new Chilkoots to climb. He hung on for another year, then in 1908 he left for greener pastures on the outside.

The Klondike had been a formative experience for Pattullo. In common with many who came and left, he was to look back on his days there as the best of his life. Not that he wallowed in Yukon nostalgia. He never cared much for the poems of Robert Service, save perhaps for the line about the hollow 'That's plumb-full of hush to the brim.'[137] He did, in later life, dash off some verse imitating the style of the bard of the Yukon which he entitled "Over The Chilkoot":

We was waitin' for the Major,
We was waitin' for the word
To surmount the orful Chilkoot,
What as everyone had heard
Was a roarin', ringtail snorter,
An' as much as life was worth,
But we only stood and trampled,
Waitin' for the Major's word.

Such a orful wind was blowin',
An' the snow was pilin' high,
An' we trampled, trampled, trampled,

Till we thought that we should die,
An' the wind kept blowin' harder,
An' the snow kept pilin' more,
An' a thousand feet above us,
We could hear the summit roar.

Pattullo's ditty goes on to describe going over the pass and then to express the belief that it was perseverance and devotion to duty that overcame obstacles like the Chilkoot.[138] Although he crossed the pass several times again, the exhilaration of facing the elements and getting to the top for the first time never left him. He was later fond of saying that 'you will never reach the heights by refusing to climb.'[139]

His favourite book about the Yukon was one he read in the 1930s called *Sourdough Gold*. Writing to congratulate its author, Mary Lee Davis, he described her work as 'a poem in factual expression and a symphony in philosophic thought.' In her book Davis explained how the true adventure of the north was not the physical struggle with the elements but the psychological search for one's self. Like Duff, she had gone to the Yukon in a turmoil of spirit and, during the time spent there, had put together the broken pieces of her life.[140] The Chilkoot and the river that it led to was the highway that carried the adventurer away from the accustomed world, away from the traditional supports, to a place where one had to learn to stand alone. The Chilkoot was the pass by which one crossed the height of land that divided the one world from the other, and the climb to the summit required more strength of will than physical stamina. Duff agreed with Davis's view that 'indomitable cheerfulness' was 'the most indispensable baggage a man could pack over the pass.' As Duff had written soon after his brush with death on the Yukon River: 'There is one thing this country teaches a man with special emphasis – to trust in providence!' And, he might well have added, not to worry. For both Davis and Pattullo, the Yukon was a 'graduate course' where one learned lessons for life.[141]

Duff's Yukon days stood out because of the 'complete change in environment in formative years.'[142] Dawson was an isolated society where the rest of the world was called 'the outside.' Pattullo had faced the rigours of the land in getting there and, having arrived, he found a place where he could fit in. He had proven to himself in the Gold Commissioner's Office that he could do a job and do it well. He could face a challenge with cheerfulness and optimism and he now assumed that sheer determination would overcome any obstacle. He had learned some political lessons too in that unruly classroom. He saw the need for government intervention to stimulate the development of a frontier area but also realized that, if carried to excess, it could become a burden on the territory. The Klondike was a frontier where people expected the government to deliver services but protested vociferously when it appeared to interfere with their economic objectives.

While Pattullo had become more disciplined and controlled, the gambler, willing to take a chance, was always in him. So when the hand was played out at Dawson, he had to move on. Duff was still looking for the big deals where the stakes were huge, and watching for the one card that was so high and wild he would never need to deal another. Sweeping up the jokers, he left Dawson for another frontier town where a new deck was about to be shuffled.[143] But unlike Dawson City, where at least there was a boom before the bust, in Prince Rupert the boom never really came.

CHAPTER 3

Prince Rupert, British Columbia

'This isn't a place for the faint hearted'

To Duff Pattullo, Prince Rupert seemed to offer a new beginning. Not that he was the same intemperate young man who had left Woodstock for Dawson City ten years before. At thirty-five he was now older, and in some ways wiser, as a result of his work and experience in the Yukon. Traits of the young Pattullo certainly remained and he was still willing to chance it all on a single throw. By now he had also imbibed the boomer mentality of the northern frontier. So when he heard that a new town was to be opened up he was eager to place huge bets both on its future and on his own. But he did not, as he had done with previous ventures, simply charge in as if there was no tomorrow. This time he intended to improve the odds by laying some groundwork.

Prince Rupert in 1908, like Dawson City a decade earlier, was a town that had only just begun. The west shore of Kaien Island, on Tuck Inlet, had been selected by the Grand Trunk Pacific Railway Company as the location of its western terminus. In a murky deal with the British Columbia government, the railway company had acquired 10,000 acres at a dollar an acre. In 1906, when the first survey party arrived, the proposed townsite was still covered with virgin rainforest. With the cutting of trees and the blasting of rock, some land had been cleared and a town was beginning to emerge among the stumps of fallen cedar. Center Street had been surveyed and cut, and ran as a planked road up from the foreshore. The alignment of some of the avenues that would run at right angles to the streets had been established. A few wooden buildings had gone up to replace the tents that had served the first pioneers. Down at the shore a section of railway line was being laid to connect up with the main line when it arrived. The company had also built a wharf to facilitate the entry of supplies, and retail stores were opening up to serve the growing population. It was rough and ready. As yet, it did not look like much, but a patch of wilderness had been cleared and the elements were being reordered to form a frontier town.

Like the Grand Trunk Pacific workers at Prince Rupert, Duff Pattullo was also laying out plans and checking the angles. He left Dawson at the end of the summer of 1908 and took a trip east to Woodstock and Ottawa. Moving from Dawson City to the Grand Trunk Pacific town of Prince Rupert was like moving from one Liberal enterprise to another and so the old political connections were worth keeping up. Pattullo tried to call on Wilfrid Laurier in Ottawa, and when he found that the prime minister was unavailable he left a note wishing him well in the forthcoming federal election.[1] More to the immediate point was the fact that the brother of his father's second wife, William H. Biggar, was general solicitor for the Grand Trunk Pacific Railway and a director of the Grand Trunk Pacific Development Company that handled the land dealings along the railway line. There is no evidence that Pattullo got any special favours from either company, but at the same time the family connection did not do him any harm and he was able to make contact with the senior officers in the two companies. He returned to the coast full of enthusiasm for the prospects in Prince Rupert.

The Grand Trunk Pacific had not yet opened the townsite for the sale of lots, so Pattullo planned his operations from Vancouver where he had set himself up in an apartment in the west end for the winter. His primary interest was in real estate and he was still the senior partner of the Dawson firm of Pattullo and Radford. Their idea was to open a branch office in Prince Rupert. For a while, Pattullo thought about taking a plunge into the hectic Vancouver real estate market. In the winter of

1908–9 the Terminal City entered one of its periodic growth cycles. As population flowed in and the city expanded, real estate and construction became the major areas of economic activity. Dozens of new firms sprang up overnight, all frantically speculating in Vancouver property. Pattullo was sorely tempted, but with his sights set on Prince Rupert he resisted the blandishments of Vancouver. Perhaps he missed an opportunity to make a lot of money, but Pattullo felt that some people would get badly burned when they were caught holding on to the outside property that was being snapped up so enthusiastically. While Pattullo did not invest in the city, Vancouver was certainly a good place to learn more about the real estate business. He made a number of useful contacts. Some offered advice and others said they would have Pattullo invest on their behalf in Prince Rupert. He also purchased calendars and novelties with Pattullo and Radford advertising on them so that he could make a big splash once the town was opened up for sale and he could move in. By the spring he was ready to go with the real estate side of the operation. He intended to buy heavily in Prince Rupert and hang on to the property until the railway arrived. Then he would make a killing. That, at least, was the plan.

But speculating in town lots was not going to be Pattullo's only business enterprise in Prince Rupert. As in Dawson, Pattullo and Radford would also handle rental accommodation and various forms of insurance. They hoped that this business would carry them through the dull times in the real estate market. Pattullo further diversified his interests by founding the Prince Rupert Construction Company in partnership with two Seattle men, George Driver and Romeyn Jansen. Once again Pattullo was the senior partner. He assumed there would be a great deal of building in the new town and this company was established to carry out all forms of construction, to operate a brick and tile works, and to engage in shipping and supplying.[2] Pattullo was also interested in the development of utilities in Prince Rupert. The memorandum of association setting up the Prince Rupert Construction Company provided for the possibility that the partners might establish a power company, and Pattullo himself was exploring the idea of forming another company to put in a telephone system. He even toyed with the idea of starting a newspaper and, although in the end he dropped it, he thought about bringing in his brother George to run the paper.[3] George Pattullo, who was six years younger than Duff, had worked on a number of newspapers in the east and was now making a name for himself in the United States as a writer of western stories. The two brothers were to keep in touch through most of their lives but they probably could not have worked with each other; it was perhaps best that George did not come to the coast in 1908.[4]

Pattullo certainly had plenty to occupy his active mind during that winter in Vancouver. His excitement about business prospects in Prince Rupert was only intensified by the frustration of waiting in Vancouver and watching others make money. 'Vancouver is going to be a wonder,' he wrote to his partner in Dawson, and he confessed he found it 'devilish tiresome' that he could not 'get in the game.'[5] He still received sage advice from his brother James, who was now a king's counsel in Dawson. In his letters James urged Duff not to put money into operations he did not have the time to run himself. If there was money to be made in Prince Rupert he would make it on his own with his own effort.[6] James no doubt offered similar admonitions in person when he was on a trip to the outside and the two met in a Vancouver hotel. Not having seem each other for six months, they got together at noon and did not leave the hotel until one the next morning. Duff later claimed they had spent $600 between them.[7] Duff said that a one-night stand was his limit, but there was no containing his enthusiasm for his business ventures. He had already told Radford that they 'ought to gamble a little,' and by February 1909 he had decided he would buy heavily in Prince Rupert. 'The men who have made the money out here are the men who have taken chances ... The big money is the chance money.' With business going from bad to worse in Dawson, Radford's heart may have sunk a little at this news, but Duff had absorbed the spirit of Vancouver on an upswing and there was no stopping him. 'This whole coast has just nicely started,' he wrote.[8] He was sure that his destiny lay with it, and, in particular, with the new town on the northern coast that was supposed to rival Vancouver itself.

By the end of February he was ready to go up to Prince Rupert to look over the townsite. He had an unsuccessful tussle with the Grand Trunk Pacific when he tried to get the company to give him a licence to build an office building. Apparently family influence did not have an immediate effect and Pattullo also expected that the retirement of Frank W. Morse as general manager of the Grand Trunk Pacific would nullify any advantage he had built up with the company.[9] The railway company tightly controlled the number of people who set up on the townsite before lots were available for sale. Pattullo was never easily deterred and he continued to press his case with the new management. He told them he was going to take a lot of Yukon capital into Prince Rupert and that Yukoners calling in on their way north in the spring 'will think that I am a very poor rustler if I am unable to rustle an office.' He found it difficult to understand why the company seemed to want to discourage the very development upon which the future of Prince Rupert depended. Indeed, it was exactly the kind of criticism that others had made of the Grand Trunk Pacific and which he had done his best to deny. But it was all to no avail. By the time the company relented somewhat, Pattullo had rented an office in an existing building.[10] The incident was an early indication to the extent to which the railway company would control the development of the town.

Nor did his first glimpse of the townsite do much to raise his spirits. Compared with Vancouver, or even Dawson City in the early days, Prince Rupert was hardly impressive. Those already on the site had built as cheaply as possible because the Grand Trunk Pacific only permitted people to erect a building on condition it was removed after the land was sold. In the spring of 1909 it took a considerable feat of imagination to see this ramshackle collection of tents and frame buildings as the new terminal city and gateway to the Orient. Even the weather was depressing. It seemed as though the rain never ended. It hung all about in thick, grey curtains and the oldtimers on the townsite explained to the newcomers that there were only two seasons on that part of the coast: the rainy season and August.

Still, there is more to the climate of a place than the weather, and Duff Pattullo's bubbling optimism could not be contained for long. Inspecting the townsite from the wooden sidewalks that had been built for the purpose, he declared there was good land for development. He set about building up his business and establishing his reputation as a man about town. He distributed his advertising and people began coming into his office. He had no land to sell, but he made valuable contacts and sold a few insurance policies. Along with George Driver, he was also working to get the construction company's operations rolling. To further enhance his image as a man on the move he brought the first automobile into town: a flashy red Auburn that cost $2500 to bring up to Prince Rupert. His 'swell auto' was evidently the 'talk of the town,' but with only a couple of miles of plank road on the whole townsite it was hardly necessary for transportation. On one occasion he took Chief Justice Gordon Hunter and some friends for a spin out to Seal Cove but ran out of gas, and they all had to walk back to town.[11] The automobile was a form of self-promotion rather than a means of getting around – an effort to show that Pattullo was going places more in the figurative than in the literal sense.

Pattullo quickly became a Prince Rupert booster, particularly in his letters to William Radford in Dawson City. Initially his partner found Duff's enthusiasm infectious. It was, no doubt, a good antidote to the ills of Dawson. 'Business here is rotten. Rents as tight as blazes,' was all that could be said about the Yukon end of the operation. They were certainly not selling any property there. So Pattullo and Radford relied on Prince Rupert to make their fortunes, and Radford was happy enough when Pattullo reminded him that he, as the senior partner, would take three-fifths of the profits in Prince Rupert as well as Dawson. Radford wrote that people returning to Dawson from the coast reported that Duff Pattullo was 'the best posted man on the Continent as to the townsite of Prince Rupert.'[12] Inevitably James was more cautious. He said no one returning from the outside looked on Prince Rupert as a place to invest because the town would not amount to anything until the railway was built. His view was that the only money to be made in real estate was through speculation and not by making a permanent commitment to the place. Duff would not be forewarned, however. He intended to go for broke no matter how long it took, and he was 'ready for a siege of ten years.' As he put it to James, 'This isn't a place for the faint hearted.' Radford also needed reassurance: 'I am playing for big things Billy. ... we shall sooner or later make a killing. I know that you are game and the right stuff.' Pattullo had no time for those who had doubts about Prince Rupert. He convinced himself, and anyone else he could, that 'she will be a hammer.'[13]

Both Duff Pattullo and the Grand Trunk Pacific Railway had great expectations for Prince Rupert. For the railway company it was to be the culmination of the new transcontinental railway. A port city to supersede Vancouver, it was supposed to be the entrepôt between Canada and the Orient: the entrance to the Northwest Passage. The topography of Kaien Island precluded the prosaic checkerboard layout of the company's prairie towns. Something more reminiscent of upper Westmount in Montreal was thought to be appropriate for Prince Rupert.[14] This grandiose vision of the new city was reflected in the town plan produced by the Boston architects, Brett and Hall, with its wide, sweeping streets and in the huge hotel, designed by Francis Rattenbury, that the company planned to build behind its station on the Prince Rupert waterfront. In that context Duff Pattullo's plans were a little more mundane, though they were supremely important to him. He merely wanted to acquire what had eluded him all his life: a small fortune. And so he staked his financial future in a town where the plans were elaborate and splendid, and almost too good to come true.

The Grand Trunk Pacific Railway was ready to throw open the townsite for the sale of lots by the end of May 1909. It advertised a series of auction sales and at the first, held in Vancouver, about 2000 lots were offered. The lots usually had a 25-foot frontage and most were sold in pairs. The company put a reserve value on all land, and a quarter of the price had to be paid immediately with the balance in annual instalments over the next three years. Other sales were held in Victoria, Seattle, and Tacoma, and some lots were sold in Prince Rupert itself.[15]

Pattullo attended the sales in Vancouver and Victoria and, caught up in the enthusiasm of the moment, he 'went in a little strong' on purchases.[16] He bought twenty-three lots at a cost of $33,565. Sixteen were in residential areas and seven were where Pattullo assumed the central business district would be located. He had two corner lots downtown on 3rd Avenue; one on 1st Street and one on McBride. These had cost him $8000 and $12,000, respectively, and he intended to hold them for speculation. He planned to build his own offices on an inside pair of lots one block down on 2nd Avenue, which was supposed to be the main commercial street. He purchased all these lots in partnership with Radford, his brother James, and Jack Horne, an old friend from the Yukon who also owned land in California. Each had a quarter share in the enterprise.[17] Neither Pattullo nor Radford had all the money to finance their shares. Radford brought other Dawson people in on his quarter and Pattullo borrowed from Horne to pay for his portion. Duff tried to get another family member, his brother-in-law Adam Ballantyne, to invest in Prince Rupert. But the Toronto lawyer had heard discouraging things about the Grand Trunk Pacific town: that the railway company had everything under its control and, with exorbitant prices being paid for land, outsiders had no chance of making money. He acknowledged though that Duff was living in a different world. 'I know quite well that you westerners, in your usual optimistic way, never believe prices are at the top and laugh at our slowness.' Pattullo's Prince Rupert enterprise was founded on optimism and borrowed money, but he was sure that, given time, the town would be a hummer. Meanwhile, he announced, 'it behooves us not to be discouraged by the knockers.'[18]

Such reassurance was necessary because Prince Rupert certainly had its share of detractors, and some were closer at hand than Toronto. Duff was concerned that James's former law partner, who was now practising in Vancouver, would persuade his brother that Prince Rupert was a bad investment. Ridley was 'a knocker from start to finish,' and Duff had never made a proposition to him 'that he was not a[s] dubious as hell about.' Once when Pattullo had suggested to him that he come in on a property deal, 'the expression on his face would cast a shadow over the sun.' Duff was rapidly coming to the conclusion that Vancouver people were 'a selfish greedy outfit' who could see nothing but Vancouver.[19] But not all of the 'knockers' were in Vancouver. In Prince Rupert itself the oppositionist newspaper, *The Empire*, warned that speculators who bought lots at inflated prices might not be able to afford to build on them. The development of the town would thus be retarded and, at least until the railway arrived, people would have to make the best of a bad bargain.[20] Even some of Pattullo's associates soon began to have doubts. But he would have none of it. 'You chaps will have to get together a little more nerve,' he advised Horne. Whether it was nerve or naîvety, Pattullo had no misgivings, at least not on the surface. This town, he told James, 'is going to be a wonder.'[21]

So Pattullo dug in for what he expected to be a long siege. He had a two-storied office building erected on his 2nd Avenue property at a cost of $4000.[22] He planned to use half of the ground floor for his own business and rent the other half. The upstairs floor was fitted out as living quarters. He had missed his family during the first months in Prince Rupert and once the building was ready they came up the coast to join him. Between business and politics he also had time for family things in Prince Rupert. Doris was nearly five when they moved there and father and daughter shared the outdoors together when he took time off from work. They went hunting, fishing, and berry picking, and Duff taught Doris to swim in a little lake across the harbour. He was immensely proud of his daughter, who was as active and irrepressible as he was. He could only describe her by saying that she was already what Prince Rupert was going to be: 'a wonder.'[23] Lillian figures much less in his letters from this period. She was often unwell while they were in Prince Rupert and she did not share fully in her husband's business and political interests. Doris was the bright spot, and it was from his outings with her on his days off that he drew some of his high spirits.

Pattullo continued to emanate energy and confidence, but remaining optimistic became increasingly difficult in the face of repeated business setbacks.

Pattullo did not expect to make his fortune quickly or easily in Prince Rupert. He recognized that he would have to 'do some tall rustling during the next few years' if he were to make big money.[24] He certainly did not plan to sit still and wait for things to happen. He began wheeling and dealing in real estate. He bought and sold city lots as well as some large tracts of potential farmland in the interior, but he bought more than he sold and so got further and further into debt as he waited for the railway to arrive. His speculations may have been injudicious, but in the frontier towns along the proposed railway lines of British Columbia they were certainly not unique. The problem was that no amount of energy and activity could compensate for those factors that were out of his control.

Within the townsite there was conflict over where the central business core should be. 'Outsiders' who, like Pattullo, had purchased lots at sales in the south wanted to centre the town around McBride and 2nd Avenue. Others felt hostility towards these men because they had bid lots in the area up beyond their value. The 'insiders,' men who had been on the site for some time and had mostly purchased their lots through local agents, wanted the business district to be located about five blocks west around 6th Street.[25] Gradually this tension was resolved in favour of the 'insiders,' and Pattullo found his most valuable property was on the periphery rather than in the middle of the business district.

An even more important obstacle to the realization of Pattullo's plans was the fact that Prince Rupert never lived up to its expectations. In its early years, development was held back because the railway did not arrive on schedule. As a Liberal enterprise, the Grand Trunk Pacific suffered with the defeat of Laurier and his party in the 1911 federal election. Late in the same year an economic downturn began to take effect, and its fortunes sank even lower when the president of the company, Charles Melville Hays, went down in the *Titanic* the following year. Every setback delayed the completion of the railway, and the first train did not arrive in Prince Rupert until April 1914. Much of the elaborate town plan remained uncompleted and the company's grand hotel never became more than a hole in the ground. The delayed arrival of the railroad was also disastrous for those speculating in Prince Rupert property. Some, who turned over their lots quickly, made a little money, but those, like Pattullo, who held on hoping for bigger things, never made much headway. There was a brief flurry of activity in the fall of 1909. Pattullo happened to be out of town and did not capitalize on it to the extent he might have.[26] His employees sold a few lots and the firm made a little money, but it was more tantalizing than profitable.

As always Pattullo maintained a bold front, but after less than a year in Prince Rupert it was clear he was not going to make a fortune in real estate. He hoped that the summer of 1910 might bring a revival, but it brought only disappointment. In June he admitted the real estate business was 'rotten.'[27] By the end of the year when he sent a financial statement to Radford it showed that, although the balance was on the right side of the ledger, expenses were high and profits were low: they had made $7434.34 in Prince Rupert. Pattullo's share of this amount was not much help because he was relying on profits to cover his payments on the land as well as on the money he had borrowed to purchase it. He was trying to sell the automobile and knew that, if he got rid of it at all, it would only be at a loss. He would no longer speculate about the future of Prince Rupert. He told Radford he would simply wait and see.[28] Nor was the news from Dawson City any better. Radford still reported that 'money is as tight as blazes here. Collecting rents is hard work.' Radford had told Duff months ago that any big money made by the partnership would have to be acquired at the Rupert end.[29]

Pattullo might have been able to look on the stagnant real estate market with more equanimity if any of his other business ventures had been doing well. But they too, it seemed, merely absorbed money. Although Pattullo and Radford represented a dozen insurance companies in Prince Rupert and employed two men in the office to handle the work, they barely sold enough policies to cover their salaries. The Prince Rupert Construction Company was Pattullo's other great hope and it had got off to a promising start. The Grand Trunk Pacific Development Company had judged the construction company 'to be entirely worthy' when it was granted a lease for waterfront property in May 1909.[30] The construction company also acquired forty acres of land up the Klyex River, a tributary of the Skeena, where there were substantial clay deposits and they had built a brick plant. The idea was straightforward enough. Having sold town lots through the real estate firm, the construction company would be able to do the building. Part of the problem, however, was that, with so many business interests, Pattullo was overextended, both financially and in terms of having the time to develop any one enterprise fully. The construction company was managed by one of the other partners, George Driver, and he quickly got into difficulties. Expenditure outstripped income and the books were badly kept. By early 1910 Pattullo had to bring in an outside auditor who found that a proper record of amounts expended was not being kept.[31] 'It is a pretty mess,' a disillusioned Pattullo told his brother. He felt that Driver had let him down as a friend. He was finding that business was much more cut-throat than it had been in Dawson and loyalty to friends was less of a consideration. From now on, he said, 'business is business' and he was ready to sell off the construction company.[32] For lack of a buyer he had to maintain his interest in the operation, but it really had become a burden. There was, as Pattullo would have said, no fun in it any more.

Other sidelines were more successful though not highly profitable. Along with a group of local businessmen, Pattullo had set up the telephone system in Prince Rupert. He continued the family tradition of involvement in newspapers with a $1000 interest in the *Prince Rupert Optimist*, later called the *Daily News*. The outlay was comparatively small but, unlike most of his other ventures, at least it brought a small financial return if not much consolation.

Business was restrained and so was Pattullo's optimism. And yet, no matter how bad his financial situation, he never became depressed. He had private doubts, but publicly he remained bright and outgoing. There were other things in life beside business. While he was not so young anymore, he was still the man about town. Like most frontier communities, Prince Rupert was a largely male culture. Men outnumbered women by nearly three to one in 1911 and Duff was one of the majority.[33] Well-known and popular, he was referred to as 'the genial gentleman' in the *Daily News*.[34] He enjoyed the social life of Prince Rupert, particularly going out with the boys. When the real estate exchange held its first banquet, Pattullo was there and the realities of the market were ignored as 'the live wires of the city made merry. For the first time they were all investors and the amount of property liquidated without glutting the market was surprising.' Pattullo joined in proposing one of the many toasts to 'the Real Estate Exchange; Prince Rupert's Salvation.' A week later he was one of a committee that prepared a welcome for Wilfrid Laurier. Again formality was quickly abandoned as the whole town celebrated the arrival of the Liberal leader. The *Prince Rupert Optimist* lived up to its name by asserting that Laurier had come 'to watch the progress of the Grand Trunk Pacific, his greatest political achievement,' and to see the town that was 'the most dazzling of the gems of commerce ... made by this new railway.'[35] Pattullo knew only too well that real estate could not be Prince Rupert's only salvation or even his own for that matter, and he was reminded of his political roots as he met the grand old man of Canadian Liberalism for the first time. In the midst of all his worries about business, Pattullo was already very active in local politics.

When it began, Prince Rupert was a company town. Every aspect of its initial development was controlled, either by the Grand Trunk Pacific Railway Company or by its associate in British Columbia, the Conservative government of Richard McBride.[36] Before long, however, the citizens wanted a say in the development and organization of their town. In March 1910 a bill to incorporate the city of Prince Rupert was introduced into the provincial legislature, though not before McBride had reassured the company that its interests would be protected and that it would have 'every opportunity ... to present its views.'[37] Among the townspeople, resentment continued to build over the stranglehold that these powerful outside forces had on Prince Rupert. Pattullo led a group of citizens who wrote to McBride and his attorney-general, William Bowser, asking for changes to the legislation, particularly with regard to water rights, in the interests of the city.[38] Pattullo had earlier travelled to Victoria to lobby the government to remember the needs of the city as well as those of the company. Once the City of Prince Rupert Incorporation Act was passed, the first local body elections were to be held and Pattullo toyed with the idea of running for mayor.[39]

His renewed interest in politics was against the advice of many of his friends. James was adamantly opposed to the idea of Duff running for office. He could see no good reason for it. Political involvement would only consume a lot of time and energy that would be better devoted to business. James allowed that, as mayor, Duff might be able to foster his business interests but added that it would never amount to much financially. 'If any money is made by the occupants of these positions,' he told Duff, 'history always has it that it is made dishonestly.' The first mayor of Prince Rupert would be extremely busy and the $2000 salary would hardly compensate for the setback that Pattullo's business would suffer. Rather than holding public office oneself, James thought it would be preferable to have one's friends there.[40] He claimed that most of Duff's other friends in Dawson also opposed the idea. Radford wavered on the issue, but was inclined to James's view. Lillian, too, was distinctly unenthusiastic about Duff's running for public office.

But Pattullo only took advice when it suited him. Like most politicians he could see the connections between public and private interest, and he felt that if he could improve the fortunes of the town then he would also add to his own. So, while he withdrew his name from nomination as mayor, he remained on the ballot for alderman. Pattullo revelled in the conviviality and banter of election meetings and he seemed to draw energy and confidence from the election campaign. He was somewhat concerned that the fact he employed a Chinese houseboy might count against him. Many in Prince Rupert were adamantly opposed to the employment of Asian labour, and a group called the Society of White Pioneers had promised to vote against anyone who did.[41] On election day his local popularity was demonstrated when he came third in a poll that elected eight council members from fifteen candidates.[42] Dissatisfaction with the way the government in Victoria had managed the town was also revealed in the defeat of the Conservative member of the legislature and government agent in Prince Rupert, William Manson, in the mayoralty contest. Although the election was not run on party lines, the majority of the first council, including the mayor Alfred Stork, were Liberals. Pattullo also took pleasure in the election of two other Yukoners besides himself to the council, while another member was a Prince Rupert real estate agent named George Naden with whom Pattullo was to form a long association.

As James predicted, Duff was even busier once he was elected to the city council. The first Prince Rupert council was immersed in the detail of getting basic city services underway. Pattullo was made chairman of the finance committee and he took a very active role in council business. The council met on four or five nights every week and additional committee meetings were often held during the day. Council work, along with his own office, kept Pattullo on the go from eight until midnight, but then, as he wrote to James, he liked to be busy.[43]

Pattullo thought that the way to encourage the development of Prince Rupert was to establish public services as quickly as possible in order to make the city an attractive place in which to live. He therefore advocated large-scale spending on municipal public works. When he tabled the city's first budget it provided for revenue and expenditure of nearly $150,000 and proposed a tax rate on property that many criticized for being too high. But Pattullo argued that a single tax of fifteen mills on the unimproved value of all city land was necessary if the city were to meet its expenses and carry out improvements.[44] 'Finance Minister Pattullo,' as he was billed in the local papers, also planned to borrow substantial amounts from the Bank of Montreal to finance particular projects. Both his general approach and his specific budget were approved by a majority of the council.

The problem was that the town was not autonomous and the city council's freedom to act was severely limited by powerful outside forces. When the builders of the Grand Trunk Pacific selected Kaien Island as the site for Prince Rupert they were more interested in the deep sea harbour than in the land on which the town would be built. The elevation and terrain of the townsite meant that city streets often had to be raised on trestles or blasted through rock. Grading and building the townsite was enormously expensive and the council needed large amounts of money. But the railway company was not willing to pay either for the cost of its decision to locate the town or for the fact that it owned much of the land and virtually all of the waterfront in Prince Rupert. The officers of the Grand Trunk Pacific were outraged when they learned of the city's intention to tax their substantial holdings at the rate of fifteen mills, and they were able to bring some heavy artillery to bear on the city council and its finance committee.

Once again the Grand Trunk Pacific enlisted the support of the provincial government. A few days after the council was elected the company suggested to McBride that he introduce a bill to exempt it completely from taxation by the municipality.[45] When the premier did not take up that idea, the company urged him to amend Prince Rupert's Act of Incorporation to establish the Grand Trunk Pacific's tax payment at a fixed rate for a period of, say, fifteen years. D'Arcy Tate, the company's solicitor on British Columbia matters, complained that the tax assessment in Prince Rupert was greater than that in Montreal and Toronto combined. He threatened the cessation of all work in Prince Rupert which, he said, would severely prejudice the government's holdings in the town. Tate concluded, however, that he was confident the government had the interests of the Grand Trunk Pacific at heart. Indeed, he informed the premier, his company looked 'upon your Government in the light of partners.'[46] McBride did not agree to the specific request to alter the city's Act of Incorporation, but he did intervene personally in the negotiations between the city council and the railway company. He travelled to Prince Rupert to urge the council to weigh carefully the consequences of its attitude toward the

Grand Trunk Pacific and to deal more generously with the company.[47]

But political pressure was not all. On 29 September 1910 the Prince Rupert council received a letter from the local branch of the Bank of Montreal indicating it would not advance any more money to the city until its 'difficulties' with the Grand Trunk Pacific were settled.[48] One week later the provincial government wired the council's finance committee that it was withholding a loan of $50,000 for electric lighting in Prince Rupert because the city had missed the deadline with its application.[49] The council tried to put on a bold front in the face of these threats. Pattullo, as he was often to do throughout his political career, blamed the situation on uninformed reports in the newspapers rather than insurmountable difficulties with the Grand Trunk Pacific. Another council member was quite confident that Pattullo could handle the situation. 'He understood that alderman Pattullo had been able on one memorable occasion to walk into the Bank of Montreal and borrow a million dollars right off. If he could do that with one bank he could do it with another.' The whole matter was referred to the finance committee for more serious consideration. Pattullo returned to the council with a proposal that it issue $540,000 worth of local improvement debentures and he introduced a by-law to create a further debt of $50,000 to cover the construction of a city lighting plant. At that point the Bank of Montreal relented and indicated it was prepared to advance the city up to $250,000.[50]

While it was conducting these financial manoeuvres, the council was also negotiating with the Grand Trunk Pacific on the tax question. The president of the railway company had offered to pay the city a fixed rate of $5000 a year for twenty years. Pattullo was determined that the company would not be exempted from taxation, and he argued that such a token gesture was tantamount to an exemption that would make it very difficult for the city to proceed with public works. Even the *Prince Rupert Optimist*, which had been critical of the council's handling of financial matters, thought that Charles Hays's offer of $5000 a year was a joke, although not a very funny one since it would mean that the citizens of Prince Rupert would have to carry almost the entire tax burden.[51] In the midst of the local debate on this question, Pattullo gave an early indication of his later willingness to contemplate government action when private economic interests operated contrary to what he perceived to be the public interest. 'If the Grand Trunk Pacific does not continue to serve the interests of Canada,' he told the Prince Rupert council, 'Canada may take over the Grand Trunk Pacific which would perhaps be the best thing that could happen.'[52] But whatever Pattullo's views on state intervention, the Prince Rupert council was engaged in a very unequal struggle with the powerful railway company. There were further threats from the Grand Trunk Pacific, but by the end of the year the council had reached a tentative compromise with the company's representative, D'Arcy Tate. The assessment of the company's land was to be reduced from $7 million to $2 million for ten years and the net amount of its taxes was not to exceed $25,000 in any year. In return, the company agreed to hand several pieces of land over to the city for public use.[53]

Finding the money to carry out local improvements was not the only matter that occupied Pattullo's attention during his first term on council. When he ran for alderman he publicly espoused the idea that, as far as finances permitted, the city should own its utilities. In this he represented a form of civic populism that advocated public ownership as a means of curbing big business. These opponents of monopoly had achieved some limited success, particularly in western Canada.[54] In the case of the Prince Rupert telephone system, Puttullo was already involved in a practical step to ensure that this policy became a reality. He was a leading member of a group of citizens who wanted to prevent the British Columbia Telephone Company from controlling the town's phone lines. Prior to incorporation there was no public body to work through, so they put up the money to establish a local company to install a telephone system. The whole operation was then sold to the city at cost after the first council was elected. When the names of those who had been involved in this scheme were recorded in the minutes of the Prince Rupert council as a vote of thanks, Pattullo's was at the head of the list. In later life he was proud of the fact that 'we made it so hot for outside interests' and, as a result of this action, Prince Rupert has its own telephone system to the present day.[55] The first council also took steps to ensure that the city owned its own water and power supply. It persuaded the provincial government to reserve water and power rights on Woodworth Lake to the city rather than upholding the claims of the Tsimpsean Power and Light Company. Pattullo was also involved in this effort both before and after he was elected alderman.[56]

Public ownership, or at least public control, of utilities was to be an important ingredient in Pattullo's political career. There was even a minor foreshadowing of his later interest in regulating coal and petroleum products during his first term in local government in Prince Rupert. Strolling down to the wharf one summer day, Pattullo climbed up on the scale used for weighing coal and found that it gave more weight than it should. The scale showed that he weighed 250 pounds when, in fact, he weighed only 175. Personal vanity aside, Pattullo reckoned that 30 per cent was an unreasonable margin of profit and, at the next council meeting, he introduced and had passed a by-law to regulate the measuring and weighing of fuel. Henceforth all coal, coke, or other fuel sold in Prince Rupert had to be weighed on tested and certified scales until city scales were installed, and then it would have to be weighed by the city weigh-master.[57]

Politics in Prince Rupert provided Pattullo with the opportunity to weigh other matters. Setting the hourly rate paid to labourers working on city projects occupied both the first and the second Prince Rupert council. When he first ran for election, Pattullo announced that he favoured the eight-hour day and was sympathetic to organized labour, though he would also represent the unorganized. Accordingly, as chairman of the finance committee, he raised the hourly wage in city contracts from 32 cents to 37½ cents, even though it brought criticism from some of his business colleagues.[58] Pattullo wanted to see a stable labouring population established in Prince Rupert that would spend its wages locally. While it might be cheaper to contract city work out without stipulating a minimum wage,

Pattullo believed that this approach would encourage a 'foreign' element that would work for lower wages but send the money out of town. To overcome the 'Montenegro problem,' city contracts included a clause providing for an eight-hour day at $3.00 per day.[59] During his second election campaign Pattullo claimed that he saw his position 'as being midway between the capitalist and the labourer ... The Middleman,' he said, 'saw fair play for both labour and capital.' He would oppose big business, such as the Grand Trunk Pacific, when it tried to strangle the development of the town but he would also, it turned out, object to the actions of organized labour when they led to public disorder. As Pattullo put it, 'he stood for individual freedom consistent with the public welfare.'[60] It was a statement that he was to repeat many times.

The mandate of the first Prince Rupert council was short and, before the end of 1910, the politicians of the town were embroiled in the campaign to elect a new council for 1911. Pattullo stood for re-election. The campaign, once again, took his time away from business and he also drew some of his election expenses against his company accounts, explaining to Radford that if he were elected his salary as alderman would go into the business.[61] As always, he enjoyed the public occasions of the election and he was a popular platform performer. He defended the work of his finance committee with great verve and clarity, arguing that the original arrangement to borrow from the Bank of Montreal was a good deal because, even though the interest rate was higher than on debentures, the city only paid interest on the amount actually used rather than paying on the total debenture issue whether or not the money was spent. His supporters were impressed, and Pattullo was introduced at public meetings as the 'Lloyd George' of the council.[62] But his vigorous election campaign was not sufficient to save his colleagues from defeat. Pattullo himself was the sole survivor from the 1910 council after the votes were counted. Mayor Stork was replaced by the man he had defeated a few months earlier, William Manson. The new mayor and Conservative member of the legislature had been described by the Liberal *Optimist* as 'McBride's Boy' on the Grand Trunk Pacific assessment. 'The machine,' Pattullo wrote to Radford, gave 'us a beautiful shake down.'[63]

After the election of the second council, tensions between capital and labour increased. Mayor Manson and his supporters on council had promised to increase the hourly wage on city contracts to 45 cents. The measure was passed by the new council but contractors with existing contracts claimed they could not pay the new rate and still make a profit. The council refused to renegotiate these contracts and a strike was called that brought street work to a halt. The council panicked and, at a secret meeting held in the offices of Foley, Welch and Stewart, called on Victoria to send either HMS *Rainbow* or a detachment of militia to suppress the strikers.[64] The contractors, in the meantime, were bringing in strike breakers and hostility eventually led to violence when strikers attacked a group working on a cut on 1st Avenue. In the midst of this situation Pattullo remained in 'hearty sympathy with the aspirations of the labour people'[65] and tried to play the role of mediator, detailing his proposals in a letter to council. He thought that the actions of the striking workers were ill-advised and yet, at the same time, the situation had to be faced. He suggested that the city pay 37½ cents on existing contracts and appoint a commission of inquiry to establish a fair wage in relation to what workers in other coastal towns received. This scheme, he argued, would protect the contractors and would give the workers a higher wage if the present one were found to be inadequate. The idea was a rudimentary form of the system of arbitration he would advocate in later years. Unfortunately, in 1911 Pattullo was a minority of one on a Conservative council and his proposals became entangled in political rivalries. His letter was duly received and filed, but not acted upon.[66]

By the spring of 1911 Pattullo was increasingly frustrated with both politics and business in Prince Rupert. Initially he savoured his role as the opposition on the 1911 council. He expected 'to get a lot of fun out of it' and he delighted in asking pointed and probing questions of Manson and his followers.[67] But gadflies irritate rather than influence and, as the lone opponent, Pattullo had little impact on the decisions that shaped the future of the city. He was still hopeful about the long-term prospects of Prince Rupert, but he realized that his real estate investments were not going to bring a big return quickly – certainly not before the railway arrived, and he could see it would not be completed for at least a year or two. Partly because of the slow development of Prince Rupert, the construction company continued to drain his finances. So he looked around for other possibilities.

He considered other offers before deciding to move to Victoria to take over the management of the real estate department of R.V. Winch and Co Ltd. He resigned from the city council, put a manager into his own real estate office, and moved his family down to Victoria to try his luck there. Family considerations probably played a part in the decision. Lillian, who suffered from rheumatism, disliked the damp climate of the northern coast. They rented a house on McLure Street and Duff began working in his new office in the Temple Building on Fort Street. Winch and Co was a well-established firm. R.V. Winch had come to the coast from Ontario in 1886 and become heavily involved in salmon canning. By 1911 his business was substantial and diversified. The real estate branch had originally been established largely to handle the company's own interests. Winch was also the Victoria agent for a number of insurance companies that Pattullo represented in the north. Although living in Victoria, Pattullo continued his connection with Prince Rupert. He maintained all his business interests there and regularly travelled up the coast to oversee his operations. Publicly he still proclaimed that, once the railway was completed, Prince Rupert would be a wonder to behold. Shortly after he left town he published a letter in the *Optimist* advising others to follow his example and hang on to their inside property. He also called on the citizens to 'cut out peanut politics' and get together to boost Prince Rupert. At the same time he wrote to Radford to remind him not to indicate to anyone that the immediate prospect was discouraging.[68] But in the short-term at least, Pattullo's hopes were pinned on Victoria.

Yet, once again, his expectations were unfulfilled. The boom that he had earlier witnessed in Vancouver had now subsided.

Prices were no longer going up and Pattullo could only look wistfully at the value of lots he could have bought two years ago. His starting salary at Winch and Co was $150 a month, increasing to $200 a month after six months, and he was also to receive half of the profits.[69] But Pattullo quickly figured out that 50 per cent of nothing is nothing. The market was dropping in Victoria and he foresaw only a 'whole lot of hard work, most of it devilishly disagreeable.' Already he was thinking that if things did not turn out he would return to 'the rough and ready back at Rupert.' Pattullo was himself a little rough and ready for Victoria and, with his free-wheeling frontier style of doing business, he was not very comfortable working for an old firm that was set in its ways. He confided in Radford that Victoria was 'strong on climate but a little weak on some old fossils who want things to stay as they are.'[70] He was too independent and headstrong to work for someone else, so perhaps it was inevitable that he should have a falling out with Winch. The break came over a selling trip that Pattullo took to the east. He had not sold any property and had drawn expenses that Winch claimed were not authorized. Pattullo replied that he had cleared the expenses with the director of the company.[71] Clearly this quarrel was only a symptom. He had had enough of Victoria and, rather than make an unsatisfactory situation worse, he resigned from Winch and Co. Just a little over a year after he left, he was back in Prince Rupert.

While it was no more a boom town than the provincial capital, Prince Rupert was more congenial than the restrictions of someone else's office in stuffy Victoria. It was summer on the northern coast. The air was free and clean, and as the sunsparkle danced on the water it was easy to feel lighthearted. Fall would follow, but back in town Pattullo was among friends and felt renewed. Still optimistic about the city's long-term prospects, he picked up his business and political interests once again. While he was away a heavy winter snowfall had collapsed the roof of the construction company plant and damaged machinery. The loss was perhaps as much as $3000.[72] Just as Pattullo's business was still going from bad to worse so was the financial condition of the city of Prince Rupert, and, partly as a consequence of these two factors, local politics was about to become very lively.

By the end of 1912 city finances were in a chaotic state, the basic problem being that the council was unable, in a declining economy, to raise enough capital to carry out improvements. The mayor in 1912 was Seville M. Newton, who was serving the first of a number of terms as head of the Prince Rupert council. Newton was a fiesty individual who, as editor of the *Evening Empire*, had already faced court charges for his forthright comments on other local politicians. Pattullo indicated early that he would oppose Newton for the mayoralty in 1913. He had told Radford privately that if business did not improve and there was no good man to run against 'the present absurd bunch,' then he would be a candidate.[73] His public campaign began in mid-November 1912, two months before election day on 16 January 1913. Given the state of his business, the $2000 mayoral salary undoubtedly had some attraction for Pattullo, but there were easier ways of earning that amount of money and political considerations were uppermost in his mind. He gathered around him a group of aldermanic candidates and other supporters, some of whom would play a prominent role in his later political career. George Naden had been his colleague on the first Prince Rupert council and in 1913 he ran for alderman as a Pattullo supporter. A.M. Manson, who was prominent in local Liberal circles and was the defeated candidate for Skeena in the 1912 provincial election, also stood on the public platform with Pattullo in 1913. Other Liberals such as F.G. Dawson and G.W. Nickerson were involved for the first of many times in a campaign to elect T.D. Pattullo to public office. Pattullo mounted a characteristically vigorous campaign, enjoying, once again, the cut and thrust of public debate. Newton evidently did not think much of his chances of re-election. He stood aloof and did not officially enter the race until the day before the election. Meanwhile Pattullo was expounding the need for sane, businesslike government, for regularizing city finances, and for finding the money to proceed with public works. Because of his emphasis on the business and financial side of city government, Pattullo anticipated that his opponents would attempt to portray him as opposed to the interests of the working man. In a public letter at the beginning of the campaign he told the electors that he wanted to bring prosperity to city workers. The way to establish that prosperity, said Pattullo, in a phrase that was to reverberate around the whole province twenty years later, was to find the money 'to provide plenty of work at good wages.'[74]

On election day Pattullo won by a handy margin of 505 votes to 383, and he lost no time in revealing his capacity for effective administration.[75] He reorganized the mayor's office and immediately set up the standing committees of council, appointing Naden as chairman of the finance committee. Pattullo presided over his first council meeting on 20 January 1913 and made it clear he would be a crisp and efficient chairman. No time was spent on unnecessary gossip, and business was well prepared before the meetings and put through expeditiously. His first meeting adjourned as early as 8:45[76] and, while Pattullo was mayor, meetings were usually held only once a week.

It became apparent, with equal rapidity, that the major problem facing the new council was lack of funds. It inherited a deficit from the previous year and began by having to borrow from the bank to meet current expenses. Pattullo argued that expenses should be covered by revenue and called a halt to development by the city in one section of town.[77] But these were only temporary expedients. Pattullo quickly decided that, if it were to continue with public works, the city would have to borrow heavily by selling long-term city debentures on outside money markets. Prince Rupert was a city of 'immense possibilities,' but without financial resources of its own it depended on outside money.[78] He urged local labour leaders to restrain their wage demands until the city's financial problems were solved. At the same time he used the threat of labour unrest if the city were unable to raise money when he tried to convince the Grand Trunk Pacific and the provincial government to guarantee a bond issue of $2.5 million. He told E.J. Chamberlain, the president of the Grand Trunk Pacific, that although the issue might seem large for a city the size of Prince Rupert, he expected that the population would increase by thousands when the railway and the Panama Canal were completed and, meanwhile, the city must have adequate utilities for the anticipated development.[79] The arguments were, however, to no avail.

Mayor Pattullo therefore decided he would have to travel personally to the financial centres of the world to sell Prince Rupert's debentures. He obtained authorization from the council 'to proceed to such points in Canada, the United States and Great Britain as he may deem desirable' with a free hand to do whatever was necessary to dispose of the city's securities.[80] The plan was to go first to cities in the United States and Canada and then, if necessary, to go on to London. The problem was that British Columbia faced an economic downturn and Prince Rupert was not the only municipality that needed to finance local improvements. As a result, loan proposals from western Canadian municipalities were being received with great scepticism, particularly on British money markets. While Pattullo was in Britain, a leading London financier, R.M. Horne-Payne, made disparaging and widely publicized remarks about the 'scramble for money by responsible municipal bodies' which, he claimed, had shaken investor confidence in Canada.[81] It was to be Pattullo's first, but not his last, experience of the difficulties of raising money in eastern and overseas financial centres during a depression.

Pattullo's trip east was heavily attacked in the opposition press. The Prince Rupert *Evening Empire* was surely the most scurrilous and unrestrained newspaper in British Columbia, and Newton had been flailing away at Pattullo and his 'lickspittles' on council from the moment they were elected. The former mayor had a field-day with Pattullo's trip to sell city bonds, lampooning the effort with daily 'reports.' Newton did pick up one substantial point when he printed an item from the Woodstock *Sentinel-Review* indicating that Pattullo was visiting his home town on the way to Toronto and Montreal and then London. Newton clearly implied that Pattullo had decided to go to England before he had tried to sell debentures in North America. But for the most part Newton indulged in sarcasm. He suggested that while Pattullo was in Europe he could 'take a run over to St. Petersburg' where 'he could see if there are any new wrinkles which might be picked up for the better carrying on of a despotic government.' When Pattullo left London, the *Evening Empire* reported 'a pall of gloom overhanging the world's metropolis.' There would, however, be a grand farewell. 'The King and Queen, all members of the Royal family, the members of the House of Lords and Commons, and the gold-laced military will take an active part, cannon will roar, the Bishop of London will pray for a safe arrival in Canada, and all the ships of the navy which are in home waters will escort the money-laden hero out to sea.'[82] For Pattullo the hard truth was that he was not returning laden with money at all. He had not been able to sell any of Prince Rupert's debentures. When that fact became public knowledge at home, Newton was, for once, at a loss for words.

Although he tried to make the best of it, Pattullo quickly paid the political price for returning unsuccessful from the east. It would have been difficult for anyone to sell Prince Rupert debentures in the depressed money markets of 1913, but his critics maintained he should have recognized that before he left. Given the inflated value of Prince Rupert real estate, even local institutions did not want to lend money to the city until some basis had been established for permanent growth.[83] Exhibiting that element of naîvety that was to be a factor in his later political career, Pattullo appealed once more to the provincial government to guarantee the city's bonds. Inevitably, McBride refused and Pattullo had nowhere else to turn. By the end of the year even his supporters could not generate much enthusiasm for his re-election. Pattullo was rejected by the voters of Prince Rupert and the new mayor in 1914 was his old rival and strongest critic, S.M. Newton. Pattullo would never hold a position in civic government again, and he turned his attention to his private interests and to the business of government at other levels.

The winter of 1913–14 was in many ways a trying one for Pattullo even though he said he 'was never in better physical and consequently mental shape.'[84] He had left his family in Europe during the summer; Lillian would be spared at least one Prince Rupert winter and Doris went to school in Switzerland. Duff was lonely without them and when he lost the mayoralty there was another gap in his life. Though he still had huge debts, he was not completely broke and he had always been better at spending money than earning it, even when prospects were dim. Economically things were very forlorn as his business continued to absorb time and money but failed to yield anything that might brighten the outlook.

Still betting on the town's future, Pattullo had accumulated a considerable pile of chips. During five years in Prince Rupert he had bought more land than he had sold. The assessment roll for 1914 showed forty-five town lots in his name, and more than half of them were in section one in the centre of the city. The total assessed value of his holdings was $270,000.[85] Yet, like chips that could not be cashed, the paper value of the land was meaningless unless his property could be sold at a profit and, even with the completion of the railway, there was little prospect of that.

The last spike was driven on the Grand Trunk Pacific Railway on 8 April 1914 and the first train arrived in Prince Rupert the following day. Thousands of cheering citizens turned out in the noonday sun to welcome the engine that was supposed to drive their town into prosperous times. But the euphoria was short-lived. When the first regular passenger train arrived in town in September the news was carried as a small item tucked away on the second page of the local paper. By the fall of 1914 the Prince Rupert *Daily News*, like all other newspapers in Canada, was full of information on the war in Europe. Yet, for Pattullo, the impact of the First World War was most keenly felt at the local level rather than through distant events. The growth he expected from the arrival of the railway never eventuated. By the time the first train finally got to the coast, British Columbia was in the grip of a depression and the outbreak of war a few months later ended for the duration any lingering vestiges of the dream that Prince Rupert would become the new Terminal City. Within a year the directors of the Grand Trunk Pacific were expressing great concern about the growing number of Prince Rupert property owners who were delinquent on their payments and they also noted with alarm that more than 500 contracts with the company had been cancelled by default.[86]

The directors of the railway company were not alone in their anxiety. Pattullo's fortunes also went down with those of the town.

The coming of the railway had been the last chance. Radford had already raised the possibility that he and Pattullo should dissolve their partnership. The Dawson office did not produce enough profit for one man to live on and Prince Rupert yielded even less. Radford was upset because Pattullo was making nothing in Prince Rupert and yet drawing on the very limited profits in Dawson.[87] They agreed to hang on in case something turned up. But it was an empty hope. Pattullo acknowledged that 'if things do not pick up when the road is through, heroic measures will have to be resorted to.'[88] By the summer of 1914 he was going deeper and deeper into debt in order to meet current expenses. He had already borrowed heavily from Jack Horne and felt he could no longer call on him. So he turned to his old Dawson partner Emil Stauf for some help 'to keep the pot boiling,' and he arranged for credit of $2500 at a local bank on condition that he did not have to submit a financial statement. He also borrowed a little against his life insurance policy. Yet even all this was not enough, and he was 'compelled to fly a signal of distress' in his brother's direction.[89] James was in the process of moving his law practice from Dawson to Vancouver and did not have much spare cash. He was able to offer more advice than money. As the debts continued to pile up, Pattullo began to consider the possibility of relinquishing his interests and leaving town. He resisted the temptation to abandon Prince Rupert largely because of political considerations.

All the while that Pattullo had been in Prince Rupert he had maintained an interest in provincial politics, even though the Conservative domination of that arena seemed to offer little encouragement to a Liberal. In 1909 Pattullo had placed bets on the outcome of the provincial election, but did so without allowing his sympathies to interfere with his judgment. He won $50 on the overwhelming Conservative victory.[90] The Liberals were decimated by Richard McBride's Conservative cohorts again in 1912. Without a single member in the provincial legislature, the party had a major job of rebuilding ahead of it. Pattullo had always been prominent in Liberal circles in Prince Rupert. As a member of the executive of the local Liberal Association he had attended innumerable meetings in back rooms and he was familiar with the details of party organization. Within a week of being defeated in the mayoralty election in January 1914, he took to the public platform as an advocate of Liberalism. According to Liberal sources at least, Pattullo was a great success, excelling himself as a public performer as he lambasted the profligacy and corruption of the McBride government. A month later, at the annual meeting of the Prince Rupert Liberal Association, Pattullo was elected president and also selected as a delegate to attend the provincial convention of the party. When they met in Victoria at the end of February, the British Columbia Liberals were beginning to feel that the Conservatives were vulnerable. After the convention the party leaders toured the province and, in Prince Rupert, it was Pattullo who introduced Harlan Brewster and John Oliver to the townspeople. Together they railed against the corrupt Conservatives under whom, as Pattullo put it, 'the public domain has been debauched.'[91] Over the next few months Pattullo spoke at several public meetings. He espoused Liberal policies such as votes for women, which, he said, would result in 'better, cleaner government.' Along with other party spokesmen he attacked the Conservatives for giving away the province's resources to speculators. He claimed that the government in Victoria had done nothing for Prince Rupert other than impose a rigid control over patronage. Under 'the machine' it was necessary to become a member of the Conservative Association even to get a pick and shovel job. According to Pattullo, the Liberals would foster the development of sectors such as fishing upon which Prince Rupert depended. He also appealed to local prejudice by strongly favouring the exclusion of Orientals from the industry. While he was expounding the issues at large meetings, he promised the boys behind the scenes in the smoky rooms that when the next election was called he would be a candidate.[92]

With these political commitments, both public and private, Pattullo was reluctant to cut and run from his business disasters. He rationalized that it would now hurt the party's interests as well as his own, but he could not deny the fact that his financial situation was grim. He had very few cards left to play and the deck was stacking up against him. He was finding it increasingly difficult to meet interest and tax payments on the land he held, and he was now $1000 behind on current expenses.[93] He used money borrowed against his insurance policies to pay the interest on his bank loans. When he was obliged to call again on James for help, his brother was staggered to learn that Duff owed Jack Horne over $30,000. James realized for the first time that Duff's enterprises were based largely on borrowed money. He pointed out that there could be little expectation of activity in northern British Columbia for several years and, although he disliked the idea, he too wondered whether Duff should close down his business. James touched a raw nerve when he reminded his brother he had skipped town once before because he was heavily in debt. Referring to Duff's New York gambit, James noted soberly that 'the necessity I should say is greater now than then.' In the end, however, James concluded that Duff could avoid financial ruin with care and economy.[94]

Presumably his elder brother knew better, for care and economy had never been a big part of Duff Pattullo's make up and he was too old to change now. He thought he saw a way out of the financial maze when, in March 1915, Premier McBride prorogued the legislature and called an election for 10 April. Once again James advised Duff to stay out of the political game because it would only cost more money, but he might just as well have kept his views to himself. 'The gambler's aspect of the political situation' still appealed to Duff. He admitted he 'would have been many thousands of dollars ahead if I had never monkeyed with politics,' but here was a chance to get somewhere. If the government were defeated and Pattullo won a seat, he thought he had a good chance of getting a cabinet position. It was not, he hastened to add, that he claimed 'any transcendent capacity in that direction.' It was just that if the north could send 'a reasonably fit representative to the house,' it would have to be recognized. If, however, he were defeated he would have to adopt 'heroic measures' to deal with his financial problems. Perhaps he could take charge of the *Daily News* on salary, as some of his political friends had suggested. He also considered other options. He observed that a 'good many of the boys have left here for the front because they are up against it,' but that 'aspect of patriotism does not appeal to me and should only be resorted to as the final plunge.'[95] All things considered, Pattullo reckoned that politics was his best bet.

So he was ready 'to throw the dice.'[96] At a packed meeting, on 12 March 1915, Thomas Dufferin Pattullo was nominated as the Liberal candidate for the riding of Prince Rupert. Although he was down in Bella Coola doing party work, his absence did not prevent a roar of cheers when his name was announced.[97] William Manson's Skeena riding had recently been divided into two. A.M. Manson, who had run against William Manson in the last election, was the Liberal nominee in Omineca and now Pattullo was off and running in Prince Rupert. He knew that once he was in the race he would have to see it through come what may, 'otherwise the boys would never forgive me.'[98] He had a huge riding to cover and he expected the Conservatives to carry on crooked work, especially in the outlying polls. So he was prepared for a rough and tumble campaign over a wide area. Yet he relished the prospect of getting out among the people of the northern communities. He could forget his financial worries, which were no fun at all, and get on with the much more enjoyable business of publicly ripping the Conservatives to shreds.

Perhaps he should have been forewarned by past experience that whenever fortune seemed to be going his way, a wild card always appeared. This time it was an announcement from Victoria. No sooner had Pattullo got the Liberal nomination in Prince Rupert than McBride, faced with scandal and division within his party, postponed the election indefinitely. Still Pattullo continued to campaign against his opponents. He went to the Queen Charlotte Islands and was appalled that the settlers there could hardly call their soul their own, dominated as they were by the road bosses and other members of the Conservative machine. The campaign was no longer merely a fight. According to Pattullo, it was 'a moral crusade against the most iniquitous forces of corruption that have cursed the Dominion.'[99] Duff

Pattullo's anti-Conservative rhetoric was reminiscent of that of his father in the Woodstock *Sentinel* forty years before and it seemed to apply just as well in British Columbia in 1915. Pattullo took a similar line when he wrote to the Liberal leader, Harlan Brewster. He cautioned that the party should not be pressured into taking extreme positions. Promises would not bring them to power. The thing that would was the desire of the people to get 'the bunch of grafters, crooks, incompetents and criminally negligents out of office.' While he would go as far as anyone with radical legislation on behalf of the people, he told Brewster that it was not always good politics to preach all they intended to practise. They should alienate as few as possible. He also thought that the postponement of the election would increase his chances of winning, since he would have more time to cover the ground.[100] He was less willing to admit that, with the election date now uncertain, other problems could not be ignored.

A protracted campaign would only increase the financial pressure. He told the Liberal organizers in Prince Rupert that his resources were limited, that all his previous campaigns had been a drain on his finances and this one would be no exception. James was able to help out by putting away $200 a month for Duff's use while impressing upon him that he must incur no new liabilities.[101] Horne was more than a little upset when Pattullo drew $1000 to pay taxes out of one of his Vancouver accounts without letting him know. Pattullo explained that he thought it would only worry Horne to no advantage and that things had to be seen through in Prince Rupert.[102] While Horne accepted the situation, Radford had reached the end of his tether and wanted to end his partnership with Pattullo. The relationship between the two had been strained for several months and now they took to addressing each other in letters as Pattullo and Radford, rather than Duff and Billy as they had formerly done. After some negotiation by mail, Radford eventually agreed to buy out Pattullo's interest in the Dawson office for $1200 to be paid over a year, but he was still very bitter about the whole business. He told Pattullo that if he had taken a $50 a month position he would have contributed as much to the firm as he had done so far. The Dawson partner saw little point in considering what they might have achieved, as Pattullo was inclined to do. Why not say that we could have made $1 million rather than merely $50,000, he sarcastically suggested, 'it enlarges the scope for reflection so much more.' In his exasperation Radford was very forthright about his former partner. 'Do you know, Duff, sometimes I cannot understand you. Everyone picks you for a winner in anything you tackle. You're clever as hell, unlimited nerve, full of aggressiveness, and I will venture to say that you would make a big success of any portfolio in the Provincial Government and yet you haven't made any money for yourself.' Radford was not implying that he could have done any better in Prince Rupert, but he did think that Pattullo ought to have.[103]

Pattullo simply replied that nothing was to be gained from prolonged discussion.[104] The partnership was over and he was now involved with other matters. A few months earlier he had been shocked to learn of the death of his old partner and friend, Emil Stauf. After some reflection, however, he realized that since 'in due course we shall be called away to join our old friend Stauf it seems foolish to let things worry one too much.'[105] Pattullo still had his Prince Rupert office to take care of, but he devoted more of his time to campaigning across his vast electorate.

He became very familiar with a good swath of northern territory as he campaigned through the summer of 1915. He was not unaware of broader issues, but in his first provincial election he ran largely as a local politician and addressed himself to local issues. The boundaries of the Prince Rupert riding stretched from Smith Inlet in the south to the Nass River in the north, and from the Queen Charlotte Islands to Kitwanga up the Skeena River. He met people in small groups and clasped hands in Namu and Ocean Falls. He loved the Queen Charlottes and later recalled that he knew 'of no other place where you can tell a man to go to hell with more freedom and abandon.'[106] He visited small communities inland on the Skeena and he addressed larger crowds in Prince Rupert. In November, when the Liberals opened a new headquarters, Pattullo told an enthusiastic audience that his party was bound to do better than the Conservatives, since they could hardly do worse. He put it to the assembled citizens that they were responsible for the government that they got. 'The man who knowingly votes for incompetence and crookedness is hardly less guilty than the man he votes for.' If elected, Pattullo promised that the Liberals would place timber lands in the hands of actual users rather than speculators. They would develop careful plans for agricultural settlement and they would encourage mining and fishing. The party platform advocated public ownership of utilities as well as various measures to improve conditions for labour: workers' compensation along with a minimum wage and an eight-hour day on government supported work. Pattullo was a little concerned about the possible effect of the working man's vote in Prince Rupert. He worried that there might be a labour candidate who would split the anti-Conservative vote. At the provincial level there was some co-operation between Socialists and Liberals, and Pattullo wrote to Brewster to suggest that the Socialist candidate in the adjacent Fort George riding be allowed to run unopposed by the Liberals as long as no labour representative contested any other northern riding. The Liberals, Pattullo reminded his leader, were going to put a good deal of radical legislation on the books in the next few years and, now contradicting his earlier position, he urged that they do all they could to secure the working-class vote of northern British Columbia.[107]

Pattullo's campaign was in the north amongst northerners, but early in 1916 he did make a foray to the south where the Liberals were fighting two by-elections. He spoke at meetings in Vancouver in support of M.A. Macdonald and in Victoria for Brewster, prefacing and concluding his remarks in each case with a chapter from the gospel according to Pattullo on northern development. His activities were naturally reported in Prince Rupert, and they were also noted as far away as Woodstock. Yet another Pattullo was becoming a prominent Liberal just as his father and his uncle had done before him.[108] The Liberals were successful in both by-elections and Pattullo would soon benefit from the public exposure and the private contacts. He returned north envigorated and hopeful.

Yet all the hard work and high hopes were of little consequence until the Conservatives called the election. In December 1915 McBride, who was tired and ill, finally recognized he had lost his grip on the political situation and resigned as premier in favour of the pugnacious, scrappy William Bowser. The new leader had none of McBride's charm and, for the Liberals, he personified the dictatorial and disreputable politics they were crusading against. They were beside themselves with moral outrage when Bowser put through legislation to extend the life of the legislature and thus postpone the election once again. It was the first, but not the last time that Pattullo would wait in frustration for the Conservatives to call a provincial election.

Waiting for Bowser to set the date, Pattullo was being drawn closer and closer to the brink financially. Just as it was important to the whole province to get rid of the Conservatives, Pattullo knew it was vital for him to stick it out until after the election. He was confident that if he could win the political fight it would place him 'in a position where I can handle the situation here to much greater advantage.'[109] But it would be touch and go. Horne was getting very edgy about the huge amount Pattullo owed him when there was no likelihood of any return from their investments in Prince Rupert. Pattullo was worried that Horne would call in his loans, in which case he would be ruined. He wanted nothing untoward to happen because of the political situation. So he called on James once more, writing that if 'you are unable to help me until after the elections then the jig is up.'[110] His brother provided some assistance, even though he was in the process of leaving for France. He had taken leave from his law practice and was to go to the front as a captain in the Seaforth Highlanders. On the eve of his departure, Duff wrote to him again in desperation. 'You will be going away very soon and it occurs to me that if my Yukon friend should turn up thereafter and I were not prepared to meet the situation, the cabinet that I would occupy would likely be of miniature dimensions.' This time James was able to come up with a promissory note for $986.63 from their brother George which Duff could use if absolutely necessary.[111] By now George was a successful writer in the United States, so they assumed he would have no trouble in meeting the payment when it came due in a few months. These were only delaying actions at best and, in the spring of 1916, Pattullo realized that the end was fast approaching. He wondered how much longer he could hold on. Yet he did not lose hope, for if 'the cut throats in Victoria ever go to the country we may be able to save the situation.'[112]

As well as financial worries there was illness in the family over that winter. There was an epidemic of measles in Prince Rupert and Doris went down with the malady. As children do, his daughter soon recovered but Lillian now seemed to be constantly ill. Her rheumatism had become chronic and she would struggle against it for the rest of her life. Once during the winter while Duff was out of town his wife, as he insensitively put it, 'nearly kicked the bucket.'[113] It was indicative of the state of their relationship that he heard about it from a friend rather than from Lillian. Duff seldom suffered from illness and, being so vigorous and active, he found it difficult to sympathize with his wife's condition. The death of his mother when he was young may have helped to deprive him of the ability to show deep affection. Whatever the reason, Duff and Lillian were growing apart as a couple. By now Lillian was forty-five and Duff two years younger, and it was clear that Doris would be the only child. Lillian stayed at home while he was constantly involved in business and political affairs that took him away. His wife had little interest in the concerns that were the vital force in Duff's life.

The winter was a dark one, but with the turning of the seasons summer inevitably arrived and with it came Bowser's election call. It would be hot and heavy, but Pattullo was more than ready for the campaign leading up to voting day on 14 September 1916. He spoke to large and enthusiastic meetings in Prince Rupert and travelled again to the small communities scattered around his riding. At one of the first of the public meetings Pattullo expressed western grievance at the assigning of munitions contracts and the extent to which they were concentrated in the east. 'We are really in the hollow of the hands of a few men back East,' he told the crowd, 'and I think we will have to get up a western party ... for our own protection.'[114] This early expression of western alienation did not characterize his whole campaign. There were plenty of targets closer to home. A few weeks later, when Brewster and M.A. Macdonald came to town, Pattullo appeared on the platform with the Liberal leaders from the south while the boys distributed pamphlets among the audience entitled 'What William Manson has done for Prince Rupert.' It was an old ruse: the inside pages were completely blank. The *Daily News* claimed that never before in the history of Prince Rupert had there been such enthusiasm at a meeting.[115] At a Friday night gathering in August when the crowd was large and the hall was hot, Pattullo was clearly in some discomfort towards the end of his speech and, before he could finish, he fainted to the floor. He rose to his feet to apologize for the abrupt conclusion to his discourse and, amid wild cheering, assured everyone that it was not to be taken as an indication of what would happen to him on election day.[116] It was capers such as these that earned Pattullo the nickname 'cock of the north' during the 1916 campaign.

When the election was finally called Pattullo was glad that he had covered the outlying communities the previous summer, but he retraced most of those steps again in 1916. His apparently triumphal progress was reported in exaggerated terms in Prince Rupert's Liberal newspaper. On Graham Island in the Queen Charlottes, Pattullo's party reached the Tlell River to find that the only boat was tied up on the other side. But it was no problem to a candidate who liked to tackle obstacles. Pattullo peeled off his clothes and swam the river to bring back the boat for the rest of the group. Perhaps a little more significant was the fact that Pattullo received some welcome support from socialist adherents. One of these, who chaired Pattullo's meeting in Port Clements, said that the Liberals and Socialists had a good deal in common, 'the chief difference being that Socialists wanted to reach their goal by a shorter route.' Some support even came from the other end of the political spectrum, since there were Conservatives who were said to be as anxious as the Liberals to see an end to 'Bowserism.'[117] There were shades of political opinion but in Prince Rupert, as in much of the province, the

1916 election was a straight battle between Liberals and Conservatives – between the bright new reformers and the dull old party that had been in office for too long. Pattullo was clear and unsubtle about what his opponent, William Manson, represented. 'He is a supporter of a government that is the most corrupt and inefficient that Canada has ever seen. He is an accessory both before and after the fact ... a weak, sycophantic follower, who doubtless does not realize the moral obliquity involved in the course which he has been pursuing.' It was time for a change, Pattullo asserted, and what was required was 'a strong, virile government.'[118]

The summer campaign went well and, by September, his supporters were confident of victory over the forces of evil. Even the weather seemed to be on his side. The *Daily News* reported the 'rather remarkable fact that, on every trip Mr. Pattullo has made throughout the constituency, he has been favoured with brilliant sunshine, no matter how the weather might be elsewhere, and, if there is anything in signs, it would appear that even providence is on the side of the people's candidate.'[119] The prospects were bright by election day on 14 September. The night before Pattullo had received a rousing reception at a meeting called by William Manson. He listened to the incumbent speak like a man already beaten and then he was invited up on to the platform to address the crowd for twenty minutes. When he went over time, a Manson supporter yelled 'Put him out.' Pattullo's people went wild with applause when he shot back, 'There is not a man in this house who can put me out.'[120]

This time Pattullo was right. It was not surprising that his plurality should be a little less than he anticipated during the euphoria of the campaign, but it was a comfortable win nevertheless. On election night he was 155 votes ahead of Manson in Prince Rupert itself and, when all the ballots were finally counted, Pattullo was still 116 ahead with 1062.[121] The soldiers' vote had closed the gap somewhat, but it could not be used to save Manson as it was to return Bowser in Vancouver. Liberal candidates were also successful in ridings adjacent to Prince Rupert. Alexander Manson won in Omineca and, in Atlin, Frank Moberly, who had served with Pattullo on the first Prince

Rupert council, was the new member. The Conservatives took Fort George, but that would be rectified in the next election. Pattullo was one of a coterie of new Liberal MLAS from the north and the turnaround there was just one ingredient in a major political shift in the province as a whole. The new Liberal broom had swept the dusty old Conservatives clean out of office. Thirty-six Liberals had been elected and the Conservatives were reduced to nine.[122] Supported by various groups advocating reform and by those who simply wanted the government out, the Liberals had been elected with a mandate for change. And yet still they had to wait. Using the excuse of the need to count the overseas vote, Bowser delayed for more than two months before resigning.

While the political manoeuvres went on in Victoria, in the north Pattullo began to attend local functions as the newly elected member of the legislature. At the close of the Prince Rupert Exhibition he presented cups and medals to the successful competitors.[123] At the same time he hoped to represent the constituency as more than just a member. The Prince Rupert Liberal Association pushed his claim to a cabinet post, and one member wrote to Brewster to explain that Duff was the proper man to represent the north, because 'Mr Pattullo is a Northman with a Northman's appreciation of and sympathy with the problems of the North.'[124] He was certainly the most capable of the northern members and, by the time he went down on a trip to Victoria in October, he was confident he would have a portfolio. He had been touted in the south as a possible minister of public works or of lands.[125] The premier-elect announced the make up of British Columbia's first Liberal cabinet before Bowser resigned on 23 November. When the names were revealed, Thomas Dufferin Pattullo was to be the new minister of lands.

His new status did nothing to relieve the pressure on the financial front. Horne remained very uneasy and wondered if they should off-load some of their Prince Rupert property. Pattullo now owed Horne $38,098.75 and his brother James another $4986.63. It was an incredible level of debt but now, for the first time since he had been in the government service in the Yukon, he had the prospect of a regular salary. In 1917 he would claim a total income of $7978.[126] So he told Horne to wait and see what he could do about the situation. The connections between Prince Rupert's interests and his own were as clear as ever and he was trying to get some Norwegian capital committed to building a pulp mill in the area. Once he was sworn in as a minister of the crown, he hoped he would be in a better position to bring such schemes to fruition.

He intended to foster Prince Rupert's interests in other ways as well and almost got himself into some political hot water when he spoke too freely about his plans. He referred to the fact that the Liberals would soon control the allocation of government positions and then had to backtrack because Brewster had declared he was opposed to patronage. In a letter to his leader, Pattullo explained that the word 'patronage' was a 'colloquialism I used for brevity's sake.' While he did not want to imply any retreat from Brewster's policy of eradicating the evils of patronage, 'it cannot hurt and it will surely help to do so with as little friction as possible.'[127] Clearly he intended to apply a little grease to the political wheels by providing jobs for some of the boys who had worked on his campaigns and, as he was to do throughout his political career, Pattullo responded to criticism by stoutly defending his position rather than reflecting upon whether it should be modified.

There were immediate importunings to begin dealing with other local problems. The mayor of Prince Rupert, M.P. McCaffery, wrote to the new member to ask him to use his influence to free up some waterfront land so the city could build a wharf and suggesting also that he look into the possibility of Prince Rupert's gaining control over the staking of water powers in the area. The mayor did not want Pattullo to miss a good 'bet' for doing something that the people of Prince Rupert would appreciate.[128]

Having been selected as minister of lands, Pattullo had to go back to the people of Prince Rupert in a by-election. Before the law was changed in 1929, newly appointed cabinet ministers were required by the Constitution Act to resign their seat to have their position confirmed by the people in their riding.[129] Duff Pattullo was duly re-elected two days before Christmas

1916 and, just before the new year, the city held a public reception for its representative. It was billed as a non-partisan gathering, but there was a long line-up of local Liberals who wanted to wish Pattullo well. Some were aware of the wider issues. Frank Moberly, the new member for Atlin, spoke of the problems that would face the minister with the influx of immigrants and returned soldiers after the war was over. But local matters were paramount in the speeches. The president of the Prince Rupert Trades and Labor Council drew Pattullo's attention to a political fact of life he would have to remember throughout his long career. S.D. Macdonald said that he had supported Pattullo in the election, not because he was a Liberal, but because he wanted the government out. He hoped that Pattullo and the Liberals would consider the cause of labour, because if they did not the workers of Prince Rupert would oppose them. In reply, Pattullo thanked Macdonald for reminding him of the problems of labour. He also told his audience that the north was represented in Victoria as never before and its importance must be constantly kept before the south. Whereas in the past, proposals brought before the Department of Lands were advocated according to their benefit to Vancouver and Victoria, now they would have to be shown to benefit Prince Rupert, Vancouver, and Victoria. He regretted he and his family had to move to Victoria, but promised the citizens of Prince Rupert that they would have ready access to his office and that his services were always at the disposal of the community. Naîvely, Pattullo also stated that all that was required to solve the problems of the day was 'sound common sense and hard work.'[130]

While in public Pattullo's remarks were appropriate and assured, his private thoughts were more complex. He had won election as a member of the legislature and was instantly a cabinet member in a new government. He seemed to have a promising political career ahead of him. Yet, he was no longer a young man and he was set in his ways. He had years of experience behind him, but he had not really made a success of anything. Although he assumed that his public office would enable him to improve his private means, he was still hard pressed financially. Certainly he hoped he would handle the public's business more successfully than he had managed his own. Earlier in the year he had written a letter to James mostly about his financial woes, but also expressing the wish that 'the permutations of time deal kindly with a well intentioned ill performer who would serve his country, let us hope, better than he has served himself.'[131]

He would sit as the member for Prince Rupert for nearly thirty years and, throughout that time, he would try to represent its interests. He frequently travelled up the coast to visit the constituency, to speak to the people, and to meet with the back-room boys who worked for his re-election time after time. There were the inevitable charges that he neglected Prince Rupert and, from the local perspective, perhaps sometimes they were true. But there was no doubt that the north had left an indelible imprint upon him, and the attitudes and ideas he developed on the northern frontier would inform his political career in the south. It was not until 1942 that he attended a session of the legislature in Victoria simply as the private member for Prince Rupert. First as minister of lands, then as leader of the opposition, and later as premier, he was involved in an ever wider world of politics. The 1916 election was both the first and the last he fought primarily within his own constituency. From now on provincial and later even national concerns were within his bailiwick. The move to Victoria was to be permanent, and it held implications he could not possibly know of at the time.

CHAPTER 4

Minister of Lands

'You cannot have a tree and cut it at the same time'

By 1917 Victoria was no longer the business and commercial metropolis of British Columbia, but the capital city was still centre stage for provincial politics. From the time he moved there at the beginning of the year, politics were to be the primary force in Duff Pattullo's life. Victoria suited him in many ways. It had the feel of a small town rather than a large city, and politics was the biggest industry. The few blocks around the shore of James Bay that included the legislative buildings and the Empress Hotel became the focal point of his life and work. It was very much a man's world and Pattullo was most at ease when he was working or socializing with the boys. He thrived on the routine of administrative work in his office, relished the repartee of debate during the session, and was the life of the party at social occasions over at the Empress. Generous and outgoing, he did not allow political differences to interfere with personal friendships. It seemed he had found a place where he really could fit in, and, while many would come and go at the 'Rattenbury caravanseri,' Duff Pattullo became almost a permanent fixture. He would serve in his first role, as minister of lands, for over a decade, until 1928.

When Pattullo arrived in Victoria early in 1917 he was anxious to get on with the job. He settled his family and put his business affairs on the back burner so he could concentrate on the task at hand. He rented a house on Clive Drive in Oak Bay while they got their bearings in a new town and later they moved to Fort Street. Doris, who turned twelve soon after they moved to Victoria, hated the Fort Street place and was much happier when her father bought a house at 912 Newport Street in 1921. The new home was a substantial one with relatively large grounds and they soon had a board tennis court put in. For Duff, this house was ideally located because Newport Street ran behind the Oak Bay golf course. He did not have far to go to put in his accustomed eighteen holes. Neither Lillian nor Doris shared Duff's enthusiasm for golf and they did not care for the political game either. As a teenager during her father's early career in provincial politics, Doris had other things on her mind. Lillian was even less interested in politics and disliked the social life that went with it. She much preferred musical afternoons or a long evening at home, smoking and playing bridge with her own circle of cronies. When Doris was older, Duff would take his daughter to political functions rather than impose on Lillian. For his part, Duff worked long hours and, more and more as time went on, he was out of town for extended periods. In many ways he enjoyed being away. If he wrote to Lillian while he was away from home, the letters have not survived. When he was in Victoria he did not bring the concerns of the office home in the evening. Lillian and Doris never offered political advice and Duff did not ask them for it. Though they did family things together, the three largely pursued their own separate interests outside the home, and Duff and Lillian particularly grew further and further apart. It would get to the point where there was so little understanding between husband and wife that Lillian would wonder aloud why he bothered with politics at all.[1]

By contrast, Duff's growing prominence in provincial politics was a source of great pleasure to his father in Woodstock. George Pattullo had always supported Duff, even in his worst moments, and now he was able to reap a parent's reward by savouring his son's success. Whenever Duff visited Burnside, his presence was duly reported in the Woodstock *Sentinel* and he would take the opportunity to extol the virtues of British Columbia. In the late summer of 1919 Pattullo senior came to the coast and, just as Duff had accompanied his father on his political travels when he was a boy, now George went with his son. As they toured up north, through the towns along the Grand Trunk Pacific, now part of the Canadian National system, George Pattullo saw at first hand the ease with which his son moved among the people and the popularity of the new minister. When he returned to the east he wrote to congratulate the newly elected leader of the national Liberal party, William Lyon Mackenzie King. He apologized that the letter was written three weeks after the Liberal convention, but he explained that he had been 'absent on a trip to B.C. to visit my two sons (Captain J.B. Pattullo, K.C. and the Honourable T.D. Pattullo Minister of Lands).'[2] The father's pride was very evident. Even James was coming around a little on the question of Duff's political career. When he returned from the war he practised law again in the Vancouver firm of Pattullo and Tobin. Some of the financial consequences of Duff's real estate dealings in Prince Rupert were still with them and, while James was not entirely convinced that Duff's political plunge had been a good thing, he kept his reservations to himself. The two did not see as much of each other as they had done in Dawson, but Duff was often in Vancouver and they would get together over a bottle of Scotch.

James was still a worrier, but Duff simply cast aside his financial cares. It was partly the excitement of a new challenge and partly because he could now afford to let go. For the first time since he had worked in the Gold Commissioner's Office in Dawson City he had a steady income. At least it was relatively assured until the next election. He would not become wealthy on his minister's salary of $6000, but over the next four years he always had money in the bank.[3] He maintained some of his interests in Prince Rupert. He held on to a few of his city lots on the assumption that if he could do things for the community his own land would appreciate in value, and he retained an interest in the Prince Rupert *Daily News* for political reasons. If he had money to spare he purchased bonds and, when that seemed too dull and he needed some excitement, he gambled on the stock market. But Duff spent too freely and gave too generously to ever accumulate a pile of assets. He enjoyed good food and drink and, whether he was at home or on the road, he entertained expansively. He placed endless orders for flowers and chocolates for women he met on political occasions or who had provided hospitality when he travelled. And for the men there was always plenty of Grant's best procurable on hand. He had come within an ace of bankruptcy in the last few months in Prince Rupert, but the experience had not made him tight-fisted. He enjoyed not having to worry about money and remained open handed in the easy-come-easy-go way of the frontier. His personal finances had certainly stabilized somewhat, though his material improvement only served to highlight the fact that politics would always be a volatile, uncertain business.

That bit of reality, however, was not at the forefront of his mind in the early weeks of 1917 as he joined his colleagues in the task of launching a new-fledged government. For Duff, this was a chance to fly higher than ever: to forget the crashing failures of the past and to prove to family and friends that his own high opinion of his abilities was not misplaced. At forty-three, he could not count on too many more big opportunities like this one. So he threw all his considerable drive and energy into pursuing the success he had failed to achieve in other areas. It was an exciting and challenging prospect and, most of all, Duff Pattullo reckoned that provincial politics in Victoria were going to be loads of fun.

Certainly Duff always looked as though he was enjoying himself, for displaying ruffled feathers in public was not his style. He seemed to work off most of his frustrations on the golf course where he was quite capable of a good temper tantrum. On one occasion he worked up such a rage about his game that he heaved a valuable set of golf clubs over the cliff where the Oak Bay golf course met the shoreline. Because he was lefthanded, a replacement set was not so easy to come by and he asked the course professional to keep his eye out for a good set of clubs. The professional climbed down the cliff and retrieved Pattullo's own set and sold them back to him. Not wanting to admit what he had done in anger, Duff pretended he had not seen the clubs before.[4]

About the precincts of the legislative buildings, however, he cut a smooth and dashing figure. He still looked boyish and he radiated good health and energy. Duff Pattullo's reputation as a fine and elegant dresser, for never having a hair out of place, and for always looking cool whatever the political temperature was to become legendary around Victoria. It was alleged on the floor of the house, by the independent member for Alberni, that the minister of lands parted his hair with a spirit level. Once, when the legislature was to be prorogued on a sunny Saturday afternoon, Duff arranged a golf game afterwards with some other members, and then he made his entrance into the chamber resplendent in a new suit of plus fours in gray tweed, the whole ensemble topped off with a flower from his garden in his lapel.[5]

While none may have matched Pattullo on the sartorial front, there was plenty of talent among the members of the Executive Council of the fourteenth parliament of British Columbia. Among the men that Pattullo was meeting as colleagues were individuals who would play important roles in his future political career. For the first couple of years the administration went through a shake-down period, in terms of personnel and policy. The premier, Harlan Brewster, who had fought for so long in opposition, would savour victory only briefly. He had scarcely got his government into gear when, returning from a trip to Ottawa, he caught pneumonia and died in Calgary on 1 March 1918. His place was taken by John Oliver, the 'dirt farmer' from Delta, who played the part of a country bumpkin but who, underneath his homespun surface, was an astute if not innovative politician. When Oliver became premier, his position as minister of agriculture was taken by Edward Dodsley Barrow. The provincial secretary was John Duncan MacLean who, while he would never set the world on fire, was solid and reliable. If one were looking for a future star, Malcolm Archibald Macdonald, the attorney-general, would have seemed a likely candidate. There was no doubt he was bright and articulate, but within the year he had to resign over allegations that the Canadian Pacific Railway had contributed heavily to his election campaign. His portfolio was taken by the Vancouver lawyer, John Wallace deBeque Farris, who was also made minister of labour when that department was established during the first session in 1917. The former federal member of parliament, Ralph Smith, was minister of finance, but his death before the first session began created yet another vacancy. Brewster served as finance minister through the first sitting of the legislature and then appointed John Hart to the position. Hart ran an accounting and financial firm, Gillespie and Hart, in Victoria and, except for the years 1924–33, he would be 'almost a perpetual finance minister' until 1949.[6] James Horace King served as minister of works for six years before moving to the federal cabinet. And Duff was particularly pleased that William Sloan, who he had known from his Yukon days, would be a cabinet colleague. The Nanaimo member was minister of mines. These were the men who would do much to define the nature of Liberalism in British Columbia over the next twenty-five years, and five of them – Brewster, Oliver, MacLean, Pattullo, and Hart – would be provincial premiers.

When the Liberals were elected to office in late 1916 they needed to call on every bit of their reformist enthusiasm, for they faced a host of problems as the disruptions of war were followed by the demands of reconstruction. When they took over the province's finances the total debt was more than $23 million, and it was likely to get worse before it got better. The balance sheet for the year ending March 1917 showed that receipts were $6,291,693 while expenditure was $10,422,206.[7] And with the federal government moving into the provincial preserve of income tax as a temporary wartime expedient, revenue would be severely reduced. British Columbia had not benefited to the same extent as central Canada from federal spending on production for war. By the end of 1918 agriculture, mining, and fishing were all in a bad way and in Vancouver manufacturers were laying off rather than hiring. There was perhaps more hope for employment in the growing lumber industry. Declining opportunities had led to a resurgence in trade-union membership, and strikes and work disruptions were becoming more frequent as workers resisted the pressures of the wartime economy. When the war was over, veterans returned to British Columbia to face a rapidly climbing cost of living and limited opportunities for well-paid work. Reintegrating these thousands of former soldiers into an invigorated peacetime economy would not be an easy task.

But the Liberals believed they were ready for change. They crusaded, like knights in shining armour, against the consequences of years of Conservative graft and corruption. They, of course, would introduce clean and open government. They believed in the need for government intervention, and they spoke in ringing tones about working in the interests of all members of society rather than just the privileged few. When the Liberal government's first throne speech contained a reference to the 'brotherhood of man,' it was the Honourable T.D. Pattullo who rose in the house to champion the notion before an apparently uncomprehending opposition. At this early stage in his career in the legislature, Duff Pattullo was not a polished orator. Words tumbled out in staccato style as if his mind moved more quickly than he could formulate the phrases. But, as always, what he lacked in finesse he made up in enthusiasm. On this occasion he berated his opponents for their inability to comprehend 'moral tenets,' and his spirited defence of the 'brotherhood of man' clause gave rise to the suspicion that he was its author.[8]

The Liberals' reformism was, however, not confined to rhetoric. During the first years of the government they passed progressive legislation that ran the gamut of reform issues. British Columbia became the first province in Canada to have a Department of Labour, and there was legislation to improve workmen's compensation, to establish new safety regulations in industry, to extend the application of the eight-hour day, and to provide a minimum wage for women and girls. Enacting women's suffrage was the most dramatic but not the only piece of legislation affecting women. The same act gave women the right to run for public office, while other legislation established mothers' pensions, maintenance for deserted wives, and made both parents the legal guardians of their children. A commission was created in 1919 which, although short-lived, was to supervise and regulate public utilities, and there was a good deal of legislative activity in the areas of public health and education.[9] But turning rhetoric into reality required more than merely passing legislation, as Duff Pattullo knew only too well when he took over the Department of Lands.

He firmly believed that effective policy demanded sound administration. Indeed, he was fond of saying that, in weighing up the relative importance of administration and legislation, he would assign 60 per cent to administration and 40 per cent to legislation. Or, to put it more bluntly, a poor law well administered was better than a good law that was badly administered.[10] The Department of Lands conducted the largest real estate business in the province and it was therefore particularly important that it be run efficiently. Not that running a government was the same as conducting a business. On the contrary, Pattullo was always most emphatic, especially when he spoke to businessmen, that there was a vast difference between business and government.[11] He pointed out that there were numerous examples of successful businessmen who were failures in government, trusting, no doubt, that the reverse would be so in his case. The one point at which he would concede a similarity between business and government was that those managing the public's interests should be at least as efficient as those in the private sector. Efficiency was important in all areas of government, but it was absolutely crucial in the British Columbia Department of Lands. Pattullo's department was the largest revenue producer for a government that had an expensive reform agenda. So in his early years in provincial politics he devoted much of his time to his own department: to reorganizing its operations and putting them, even if only in one sense, on a business-like footing. And, here too, there was a connection between public and private interest, for he was determined to manage the public's assets better than he had handled his own.

Driven by the need to prove himself, the minister set a cracking pace around the lands office. He rose early in the morning, often played a round of golf before breakfast, and was in to the office before eight o'clock, ahead of most others who worked in the parliament buildings. He immediately refurbished the ministerial office to suit his own taste and work habits. Pattullo loathed a cluttered desk and kept his office clean, trim, and ready for business. William Bowser, ever on the look-out for a substantial political issue, publicly criticized Pattullo for putting expensive oriental fittings and a private lavatory in his departmental offices.[12] In the case of the fixtures it was unclear whether Bowser's objections were fiscal or cultural, and it should be said that he was merely responding in kind. For Pattullo, needless to say, was absolutely scathing about the rank incompetence of the former Conservative minister of lands, W.R. Ross, and the chaos he had left in the departmental offices. Instead of letting paper accumulate, Pattullo dealt with it on the day it arrived. He firmly believed that brevity was a virtue in business or in any correspondence. He thought that, as a general though not an absolute rule, most matters could be covered in one page of single-spaced type. So his letters were terse, crisp, and to the point. He made day-to-day decisions instantly rather than pondering them at length. Other cabinet colleagues thought he was the most efficient administrator that the province had seen. Even some Conservatives, looking back on it, agreed that the Department of Lands was one of the best managed in the government.[13] His critics, however, claimed he moved too quickly and therefore that his judgments were not always the best. Pattullo worked on the assumption that it was best to deal with matters rapidly. That way, things got done, even if he made some mistakes. He intended to give the impression of a man on the move and his motto around the office was one that he followed in everyday life. We must, said Duff, 'be up and doing.'

As minister of lands, Pattullo was constantly on the move in another sense. In order to know the territory that he administered, he frequently travelled to the outlying areas of British Columbia. He looked forward to getting away from the office and leaving Victoria for the parts of the province where he felt most at home – the interior and particularly the north. He still believed that the tiny, tenuous resource towns tucked away in the inlets and valleys were the real and future British Columbia. These little islands of development were surrounded by a vast sea of mountains and forests, and, as with ocean and island, each defined the existence of the other. Pattullo recognized this relationship, and he revelled in the beauty and magnificence of the wilderness as much as he argued the need to exploit its resources. For it seemed to a northerner in 1917 that the land was as enduring and endless as the ocean. Most of all, Duff liked to get out amongst the people who were working to develop the hinterland – the ordinary people who were special to him. When he went north, he went not so much to make speeches as just to 'visit the folks.'[14] This was the place and these were the people that Pattullo loved.

He certainly became a BC booster as minister of lands, but his enthusiasm was genuine and heartfelt. When he gave speeches in the east he told audiences that he still had 'a deep affection and reverence for the Province of Ontario but I am bound to say that my heart is in British Columbia.' In 1922 he spent two days in an aircraft over the coast inspecting forest reserves. He was the first cabinet minister in British Columbia to do departmental business by air, but the trip was more significant in a personal way. Later, in a speech to the Canadian Club at the Château Laurier in Ottawa, he compared flying over the British Columbia coast with flying between London and Paris. The flight over France was enjoyable enough as he looked down on 'a very pretty panorama, but the air trip in British Columbia was one thrill after another of magnificence.'[15] He believed in the frontier and in the need to unlock its huge potential and thus assure the future of the province. He urged the people of Vancouver and Victoria to become more familiar with the rest of the province. In speech after speech he amended Horace Greeley's admonition by saying, 'Go north young man.' If he were 'broke' and out of work, he said, 'he would prefer to be on an undeveloped quarter in the north country than on a corner of a street in Vancouver.'[16] For Pattullo, these were not merely the romantic sentiments of a man who never left the city. Though he now lived in the capital, he went north as often as he could, and he always returned renewed, invigorated, and ready for the fray.

Back in Victoria at the Department of Lands, Pattullo gathered around him a group of men with whom he could work effectively and who would keep business moving while he was away. Within days of assuming office he unceremoniously dumped Robert Renwick, the deputy minister of lands, who had served for a number of years under the Conservatives. Opponents observed that it was not an auspicious start for a government determined to root out patronage, but Pattullo stoutly defended his action by saying that the public expected a thorough reorganization of the department and its work and he could not do the job if he had to rely solely on men from the old regime. Suspicions were not allayed, however, when, on the same day that Renwick was dismissed, a Prince Rupert newspaper announced that his successor would be George R. Naden, a prominent local Liberal and longtime friend of the new minister.[17] Naden had been in Prince Rupert even longer than Pattullo, and, like Duff, he was heavily involved in both real estate and the Liberal party. He was a member of the first Prince Rupert council in 1910 and, in 1913, when Duff was mayor, Naden was chairman of the finance committee. He had worked hard on Pattullo's election campaign in 1916, and now he would be the minister's right-hand man in Victoria. He could also acquit himself well, though one assumes not too well, on the golf course. Naden, in short, was one of the boys. Having lived in the Kootenays as well as Prince Rupert, he shared Pattullo's enthusiasm and understanding of the hinterland. Pattullo already knew he could work efficiently with Naden, and the two lost no time getting started in the lands office. Another friend from Prince Rupert, William Turnbull, was brought down as Naden's assistant and he became the department's trouble shooter. Not all the senior officials were newcomers from the north, since Pattullo retained some of the former heads of branches within the department.

Under Pattullo, the British Columbia Department of Lands was divided into five sections. The Lands Branch dealt largely with the preemption and sale of crown lands in association with the Survey Branch, which conducted survey and topographical work all over the province. The Grazing Branch was responsible for monitoring grassland resources, allocating public grazing land, and collecting fees. The Water Rights Branch likewise surveyed, assessed, and provided information on water resources. The fifth division of the department, the Forest Branch, was the largest single operation in the provincial government. Pattullo claimed in 1921 that at least one-third of the population of the province depended on the timber industry and it produced one-half of the province's revenue.[18] Directed by chief foresters, M.A. Grainger and, after 1920, P.Z. Caverhill, this branch was charged with inspecting and protecting forest resources, supervision of and liaison with the forestry industry, and developing markets. Though the number of civil servants would increase under Pattullo's leadership, the lands department, like the rest of the British Columbia government in 1917, was a pretty rudimentary organization given the magnitude of the task ahead.

There was a flurry of legislation from all five branches of his department during the first few years in which Pattullo was minister of lands. Much of it was technical and detailed. The Townsite Proportionate Allotment Act of 1918, for example, provided that purchasers of crown lots in townsites or suburbs who were in arrears on payments could, in lieu of completing payment, secure an allotment to the value of the amount already paid.[19] Clearly that enactment arose out of his own financial difficulties in Prince Rupert and would have enabled him to consolidate his interests there. But this kind of regulation also had a general application. The thrust of much of his early legislation was to simplify the process of getting people on the land by cutting both the cost and the red tape, and by ensuring that those who acquired crown land would develop it.

Because the land and its resources were essential to any postwar economic recovery, Pattullo was interested in lasting development rather than speculative bubbles that burst with the next economic downturn. There had already been too much of that sort of thing under the Tories. He was highly critical of the McBride government that had presided over the boom years of the first decade of the century. There had been far too many unrestrained give-always to big business by a government that was itself an 'arch-speculator.'[20] Now it was time to consolidate and encourage yet also control economic development. Pattullo knew very well, from bitter personal experience, how brittle a dependent economy based on the extraction of primary resources could be. As a local politician in Dawson City and

Prince Rupert he had advocated the need for government intervention when private enterprise, whether it was individual or corporate, seemed inadequate on its own. Now he brought this tradition of the western Canadian hinterland to policy making at the provincial level.[21] Particularly in the uncertain economic climate that followed the end of the First World War, Pattullo believed that the government would have to take an active role in economic development.

He did not think that the state could, or should, do everything. Individual enterprise would always be a driving force in regional development. 'I believe in the individual ownership of property and the opportunity to exercise individual initiative,' he once told representatives of the construction industry, 'but these must always be consistent with the general public welfare.' He believed that government should only intervene where co-operative effort could be brought to its highest point of efficiency. Of one thing he was certain, however – that government would play an important role and would be of great assistance to industrial and agrarian development.[22]

As well as these general views about the role of government, Duff Pattullo also came to the provincial cabinet with a great deal of practical experience in the nitty gritty of administering land policy at the local level. In the land registry office in Woodstock, the gold commissioner's office in Dawson, and city hall in Prince Rupert he had accumulated day-to-day knowledge that would stand him in good stead as the Liberal government translated its reform sentiment into detailed legislation. Within days of his appointment to the lands portfolio, Pattullo wrote to the premier and the minister of agriculture to suggest ways that the government could assist settlement. As well as opening up new areas, he saw the need to force development on alienated crown land, particularly when it was owned by large companies. He suggested the formation of a land settlement board to replace the agricultural credits commission, with wide powers to assist agricultural development. He also urged that the matter be taken up immediately with a view to passing legislation in the first session.[23] Pattullo was not alone in these views, but now he was in a position to see them implemented. Much of his advice was incorporated in the Land Settlement and Development Act of 1917 which created the Land Settlement Board and gave it the power to acquire land either from the crown or private owners, to improve it for agricultural purposes, and to advance loans to settlers.[24] Returned soldiers or the widows of servicemen who purchased land from the board were entitled to an abatement of $500 on the price. Under this legislation, several areas of the province were opened up to settlers for the first time.

Through his first years as minister, Pattullo continued to advise other members of the government on practical matters relating to lands. He outlined for the minister of agriculture, E.D. Barrow, a step-by-step procedure for using a section of the Land Settlement and Development Act to set up a commission to drain and dyke swamp land at Sumas in the Fraser Valley.[25] He expected colleagues to keep up with him, however, and was impatient with those who did not have his command of detail. Once the initial Land Settlement legislation was passed, the government saw the need to strengthen the powers of the board and asked A.M. Manson, the member for Omineca, to come up with an amendment. Instead of drafting actual wording, Manson merely made a series of general recommendations. Pattullo explained to the premier that, while a 'good lawyer like Alex ought to be able to lick this thing into shape in short order ... we must remember that he is still in his political teens.' Knowing him from the early days in Prince Rupert, Duff had always hoped that Manson would grow up politically, but, he wrote wearily, 'it seems that the less people know, the longer it takes them to find out.'[26]

He had a similar, no-nonsense approach with civil servants who seemed to be slow to put policy into effect on the ground. When an ex-private Cockayne appealed to the minister because he was not getting satisfaction from the Land Settlement Board, Pattullo wrote to the chairman of the board with biting sarcasm. 'You will recall,' he lectured, 'that I insisted that the Board should be called a "Land Settlement" Board, for the purpose of designating just what the Board is supposed to be, namely, a board that will induce land settlement.' The Department of

Lands could provide general information to prospective settlers, but that was not sufficient. The board would have to pursue such matters to their conclusion. And that conclusion, he reminded its chairman, was the settlement of ex-private Cockayne on the land.[27]

As much as he grappled with detail, Pattullo did not lose sight of long-range objectives. The immediate goal in 1917 and 1918 was to assist returning servicemen to reintegrate themselves into society. Along with Oliver and other members of the cabinet, he firmly and somewhat naïvely believed that settling soldiers on agricultural land would solve the problem. Not that he was as single-minded as Oliver was on the matter. Pattullo also arranged for the Land Settlement Board to purchase city lots and build houses for returning soldiers who did not share the government's enthusiasm for rustic virtues.[28] And, for Pattullo more than most other ministers, providing for returned servicemen was just a start. While it was important to assist its existing citizens, as far as he was concerned British Columbia also needed large numbers of new immigrants to generate growth. Through all the economic fluctuations of the late 1910s and early 1920s, and even during times of high unemployment, he was a constant and vocal advocate of attracting new population. According to Pattullo, every new immigrant was a potential market and a potential source of development. He did not think that full employment was a necessary prerequisite for immigration. It is well known, he said, 'that sometimes the stranger within the gates sees opportunity which the man right on the ground is overlooking.'[29] He constantly urged British Columbians to accept the need for immigrants and, in other parts of Canada, as well as in the United States and Great Britain, he extolled the opportunities offered by his province. His advocacy of increased immigration harkened back to the days of Laurier and the expansion of the west in which Pattullo had taken part.

The gates to British Columbia were not, however, to be held open to all strangers. While Pattullo was prepared to lead public opinion on the need to encourage immigration, he did nothing to stem the racist tide that flowed strongly in west-coast society.

He proposed to carry out 'an aggressive immigration policy with a view to securing the right kind of settlers'[30] Clearly, however, 'the right kind of settlers.' did not include Asians, since British Columbia was to be a white man's country. He had, he said, no objection to the oriental 'other than he belonged to the yellow race and could not be assimilated,' but such immigrants were not wanted because they would be 'detrimental to the progress of the Anglo-Saxon on the Pacific Coast.' Although he never pushed it as far as others did, Pattullo toyed with the notion of eugenics and suggested that, 'for its own protection,' society might someday require laws 'that will prevent the propagation of unfit human species.'[31] His view of the role of native people was no different from that of every government official responsible for crown land in British Columbia since Joseph Trutch in the 1860s. It was simple enough: Indians were to be moved aside to enable Europeans to develop resources. Pattullo added some new details to the rationalization of provincial policy, claiming, for example, that Indians were particularly responsible for setting forest fires, and he also perpetuated old nonsense, such as the assertion that native people had a great disregard for the laws of the province.[32] He was distressed when the federal government was slow to ratify the recommendations of the McKenna-McBride Commission of 1913–16 which had cut away a good deal of prime land from Indian reserves. In British Columbia, developmental optimism has always had its racist dark side, and Pattullo, as much as he epitomized the one element of the provincial psyche, was not immune from the other.

It was in the context of the Indian land question that he quickly learned another political lesson. Early in 1919 the British Columbia government passed the Indian Affairs Settlement Act which, among other things, indicated that the province would enter into negotiations with the Indians on the findings of the McKenna-McBride Commission. Federal officials took exception to what they saw as a provincial intrusion on the federal government's exclusive right to deal with native people.[33] Pattullo was authorized to go to Ottawa to discuss the question of Indian land with Arthur Meighen, who was then federal minister of the interior. Meighen evidently did not want to deal with the British Columbia representative on this vexed issue and what followed was an instructive lesson in the nature of dominion-provincial relations.

Pattullo left for Ottawa, telegraphing ahead for a meeting during the week of 10 November 1919. He arrived in the capital on Monday the 10th and on Tuesday arranged an appointment with Meighen for the afternoon. Arriving at the arranged time, he was told that Meighen was in a meeting but would see him on Wednesday. On Wednesday Meighen said he was leaving town, and suggested that Pattullo talk to the deputy superintendent of Indian affairs with a view to a meeting when he returned on Saturday. Pattullo drew up a memorandum with the deputy superintendent only to find on Saturday that Meighen was still away and could not be reached. Pattullo arranged an appointment for Monday, then on Monday he was asked to wait until Tuesday. On Tuesday, when Meighen was unavailable once again, Pattullo pointed out that he could not wait in Ottawa indefinitely. The deputy superintendent urged him to try one more time because the matter should be settled. So, having arranged a meeting for the following Monday, Pattullo left to attend to some business in Toronto. When he returned Meighen was not available on Monday and Pattullo was asked to wait in his hotel for a message on Tuesday morning. Next day he waited until 12:30 and when he returned to the hotel at 2 o'clock there was a message timed at 12:35 indicating that the minister had left for Toronto on the noon train. At that, Pattullo withdrew his memorandum and returned to the coast. He left a letter for Meighen detailing what had happened and sent it with a covering letter to the prime minister. He told Borden that, although he had heard around Ottawa that Meighen was becoming absent-minded, he thought 'it would require a very acute case of absent-mindedness to explain the Minister's action in this instance.' He added that 'I should very much regret to hear that the Minister is suffering from mental infirmity, but if he is, he should, in the meantime, be relieved of his duties in order that the public business may proceed.'[34] The experience had obviously rankled, and it was an Ottawa run-around that Pattullo never forgot.

Pattullo shared with many other British Columbians a healthy suspicion of the federal government. In Duff's case it was born of his northern experience and nurtured during his early years as a provincial minister. On soldier settlement, for example, the government of British Columbia felt it had to push Ottawa to assume its responsibility for what was a national problem. Oliver proposed that the prime minister call a conference and, after Robert Borden agreed, Pattullo attended his first dominion-provincial conference in November 1918. He and the other British Columbia delegates derived some satisfaction from the fact that the conference resulted in amendments to federal legislation on soldier settlement.[35]

Fortunately, he had much greater success in British Columbia dealing with matters that fell within provincial jurisdiction. Here he could do the follow-up on an initial policy without interference from other levels of government. A successful land settlement policy, he realized, required more than simply selecting a piece of land and dumping people on it. It has been argued that the Liberals' soldier settlement schemes were a failure: that sites were chosen without a careful evaluation of the quality of the land, that the locations were sometimes too isolated, and that not enough decision-making authority was given to the local community. In many cases these conclusions are valid and Pattullo, along with Oliver, must bear much of the responsibility.[36] But in some places he had more success. He was particularly proud of the work he did to assist settlement in the southern Okanagan. The town that grew up as a result was named after the premier, though Duff probably thought in retrospect that Oliver ought to have been called Pattullo. Yet it was perhaps appropriate that Pattullo's name was affixed to a dam rather than a town, even if it did lead to irreverent remarks in the house as opposition members made much of reversing the name of the Pattullo dam. It was once when he was driving south to inspect the country between Pentiction and the American border that Pattullo came to understand the problems faced by the dry-land orchardists who depended on irrigation to bring in a crop.[37]

When Pattullo took over as minister of lands the irrigation

systems of the Okanagan Valley were in a sorry state. Most of them were built during the boom years of the first decade of the twentieth century by land development companies. These companies amassed large amounts of land, built irrigation works to deliver water, and then sold the land in small blocks ready to be planted with trees. Constructing the dams and flumes was an expensive proposition. It was estimated that it cost at least $60 per acre to irrigate Okanagan benchland, and the land speculators required a great deal of up-front capital. They reduced costs by building temporary wooden flumes that delivered enough water to keep young trees going but not sufficient to produce high yields. Then they formed subsidiary irrigation companies so that, if the water systems broke down, the original land company could not be held responsible. Encouraged by company promoters who promised high returns from small acreages, individual orchardists often borrowed heavily to buy the land. Both the financial and the irrigation structures began to collapse in the recession of 1913 as the debt load was too heavy to support, and the wooden flumes deteriorated to the point where they could no longer deliver water.[38] By the end of the war, with returning soldiers creating the need for new development, many Okanagan fruit growers were faced with the prospect of having to abandon their orchards.

For Pattullo it was an obvious example of the failure of private enterprise and the need for government intervention. He told the people in the Okanagan that the companies were merely there to make money: 'that they had bought the land, installed an irrigation system sufficient to sell the land, and cared nothing for what happened afterwards.' He told the companies that their investors would have to take some losses because his primary concern was to protect the growers.[39] Then he put his staff on to studying the problem and formulated a policy to deal with it. He arranged for the government to buy out the deteriorating assets of the irrigation companies and passed legislation to set up locally run irrigation districts. A water conservation fund was established in the Department of Lands to advance loans to enable the districts to acquire and restore the irrigation systems. As the land was brought back into production, the loans would have to be repaid. In this way the water users themselves would own the water works and the government would provide the initial capital to make them viable. The success of this policy, Pattullo wrote to Oliver, 'will, of course, depend on its administration.'[40]

Duff Pattullo always thought of the Okanagan irrigation scheme as one of his most successful initiatives. He referred to it often in speeches, citing it as an example of effective government intervention to provide practical assistance to people. He strongly defended the policy against criticism from all quarters. There were contradictory cries of outrage from Conservative members from the Okanagan, first because Pattullo had spent so much money and later because he insisted that the conservation districts repay their loans. Pattullo, who was developing the habit of dismissing all opposition attacks as merely ill-informed political rhetoric, quickly brushed aside these objections to his irrigation policy. Then, in 1923, with the provincial economy in a downturn and the government increasingly concerned about its tenure, there were objections from a more substantial source.

John Oliver had begun to fidget about the cost of Pattullo's irrigation program. By the end of their first administration the Liberals had done a great deal in a short time, but they realized there were too many watertight compartments in the cabinet and not enough team play. Policies tended to be decided by ministers without much common discussion by the executive.[41] In the second administration, after the election of 1920, they made efforts to overcome this problem and the premier spent more time checking up on his ministers. So when Oliver asked for an account of spending on irrigation, Pattullo responded with a letter that, at three pages, was unusually long. He was at pains to emphasize the care with which the department evaluated each scheme before it advanced funds, and he detailed the fact that nearly all the irrigation districts were making the repayments on their loans on time.[42] Unfortunately Pattullo's first point was undercut when, almost immediately, the Vernon Irrigation District requested more money to repair a storage dam that had been poorly constructed. Oliver moved from mild questioning to raising serious objections. He feared that the government was to be saddled with a loss it could not afford and, furthermore, would be 'very unfair to the ordinary taxpayer who receives no advantage whatever from Government expenditures such as are herein referred to.' Indeed, he added loftily, 'it is also morally wrong.' He was, he wrote, 'fast coming to the conclusion that it is an entirely mistaken policy for the Government to advance or furnish money for any of these undertakings.'[43]

Pattullo refused to be intimidated, even in the face of such criticism from his leader. Instead, he vigorously defended his own position. He 'noted' the premier's comments on the particular expense of the Vernon dam but, as to Oliver's observations on the general policy, he totally disagreed. He was convinced that the policy was a good one and that without the intervention of the government several areas in the Okanagan would now be in the same position as the failing Walhachin settlement on the Thompson River west of Kamloops. There a hastily constructed and inadequate irrigation system was a major factor in the collapse of a group enterprize.[44] He did not see that there was any unfairness involved, let alone that the expenditure was morally wrong. He observed that 'almost every class of society, at some time or other, secures a special benefit that does not directly go to anyone else.' But Pattullo saw no problem with that since, 'in the aggregate it is not at all improbable that everyone finally ends up on a fairly even basis.' There were, no doubt, cases where government assistance should not have been given but, as far as he was concerned, the irrigation districts in the interior were not among them.[45]

Pattullo's Okanagan irrigation scheme was a successful if relatively straightforward policy. The companies kicked and complained when the irrigation works were taken over at prices that were too low to allow them to make good on their losses, and their representatives on the other side of the house gave Pattullo a rough time politically. But the vested interests were not powerful enough to undermine the policy. By 1923, after seven years as minister, Pattullo had enough confidence and muscle to defend the scheme against attacks from within the administration. He was not always so successful, however. Limited as it was to a single sector with few wider ramifications, his intervention to restore Okanagan irrigation was a finite operation. Asserting the government's right to regulate the vast and ubiquitous forest industry was altogether another matter, and Duff found that a much tougher nut to crack.

By the time Pattullo became minister of lands, forestry was the largest industry in British Columbia. It had surpassed mining as the biggest revenue producer during the period of free-wheeling development in the late nineteenth and early twentieth centuries. Rapid settlement on the prairies provided a new and ever-expanding market for British Columbia's forest products. But the government had failed to use its ownership of crown land to control development and protect the forest, or to capture a reasonable share of the revenue.[46] Huge tracts of forest land had been handed over to companies that frequently just sat on their assets in the hope they would appreciate in value. They were more interested in forest land as speculative property than as a source of lumber. Those who did cut timber merely exploited the resource for maximum profit. Forestry methods were wasteful and destructive, there was little concern for conservation or replanting, and too many raw logs were exported without further manufacturing within the province. The industry grew as if today were very short and tomorrow would never come.

Towards the end of the first decade of the twentieth century, as the boom began to fizzle out and timber prices collapsed, even the McBride Conservatives were persuaded of the need to establish a modicum of control over the industry. Much of the persuading was done by the industry itself, which began to appreciate that the rampant exploitation could not go on for ever. The government responded with an investigation into the state of forestry, followed by legislation designed to improve it. The Royal Commission on Timber and Forestry of 1909 and the subsequent Forest Act of 1912 were initial if halting steps in the direction of protecting the resource and regulating the harvest. Perhaps the most significant part of the legislation was the establishment of the British Columbia Forest Branch within the

Department of Lands. The branch was to administer all matters connected with forestry and it had wide powers, particularly in the areas of forest inspection and fire prevention.[47] The government had the will, at least for a moment, and now it had the mechanism to impose regulation, but these things meant little if it lacked the expertise. Before it could control exploitation of the resource, the government had to take inventory to establish its nature and extent. In 1912 H.R. MacMillan, a graduate in forestry from Yale who was working for the Dominion Forestry Branch, was appointed British Columbia's first chief forester. He hired a field staff to start the cruises and surveys and to gather the statistical information that was so essential if government policy were to be implemented in the woods. Thus, under Pattullo's predecessor W.R. Ross, the Department of Lands was already moving to assert the public interest in forestry. Duff, of course, would hardly admit to the fact. He did grudgingly allow that Ross had 'apparently made an attempt at reorganization, but, unfortunately for him, he had been travelling in bad company and he soon slid back.'[48]

Rhetoric aside, Pattullo knew when he became minister that it was up to him to continue a process that had already begun. Certainly the war had interrupted the work and the Forestry Branch was so depleted by 1917 that major rebuilding was necessary just to bring it back to its prewar footing. It was not only that the staff had been cut to the bone. The war also made other demands that had to be met without much reflection about the long-range consequences. In early 1918, when the lumber companies were slow to reach an agreement with the Imperial Munitions Board to make spruce available for making aeroplanes, Pattullo stepped in with an order in council giving him the right to appropriate any stands of Sitka spruce, whether in public or private hands, for war purposes.[49] He had a penchant for assuming arbitrary powers to meet what he judged to be crisis situations and, on this occasion, as on most others, he was not deterred when the opposition accused him of being a dictator. Once the wartime emergency was over, the minister would turn to more orthodox methods. It was remarkable how little had changed since 1912 and, just as the Conservatives had done, Pattullo was obliged to walk a fine line between encouraging the development of the forestry industry and ensuring that the public interest was protected.

The first task was to develop the department's expertise and knowledge. H.R. MacMillan had resigned as chief forester to go into the private sector just before the 1916 election, so Pattullo appointed M.A. Grainger, who had been the author of much of the 1912 Forest Act, to the position. The forestry staff expanded rapidly after the war was over. The process of taking an inventory of British Columbia's forests was reinstated so that policy could be based on reliable information. Departmental foresters carried out extensive cruises all over the province to assess the extent and quality of timber stands. While Pattullo was minister, the department experimented with aerial reconnaissance of forest lands. The number of forest rangers was increased and they were appointed on the basis of expertise rather than political affiliation. Firefighting technology was improved. There was greater mechanization, aircraft were used for patrols, and a radio network was established. The department conducted silvicultural research, looking into matters such as natural seed dispersal, forest regeneration, and the impact of controlled thinning. Setting up timber reserves in the form of provincial forests was another move in the direction of resource management.[50] If knowledge were the only basis for sound policy, then Pattullo had few excuses.

There were, however, other exigencies. The cost of research became increasingly difficult to defend within cabinet. In the December 1920 election many Liberals went down to defeat and the government retained only a slight majority in the house. The opposition, though divided, was more numerous and more vigorous. The political climate had changed and the economic outlook continued to be uncertain. A brief postwar upswing turned into a recession in the early 1920s. Under these circumstances the Liberals' bright reformism quickly dimmed. John Oliver responded to political and economic adversity by growing more and more cautious. In 1921 he insisted that ministers cut back their budget and then complained when Pattullo reduced his estimates by only $70,000. The premier particularly objected to the cost of survey work. 'I do not believe for a moment,' he wrote to Pattullo, 'that it is absolutely necessary to spend $155,000 this year in land surveys or that it is necessary to spend $30,000 in photo typrographical surveys.'[51] The following year the scaling fund was under attack. The department made a levy on the forestry industry that was used for scaling, or measuring the number of board feet in logs as the basis for assessing charges to the industry. Pattullo was annoyed when Oliver wanted the money to go into general revenue. He did not think that such monies should be thrown into the 'common jack pot,' thus obliging the department to defend the cost of scaling every year. But the premier was adamant that all expenditures were to be scrutinized by the legislature. Given the state of provincial finances, Pattullo was constantly having to make the point that 'we can move just as fast and no faster than economic conditions will permit.'[52]

Economic and political factors imposed even greater limitations outside the department than they did within. Pattullo's belief in the importance of expertise partly accounts for the continued development of professional, scientific forestry through the 1920s. At the same time, he learned that expertise was easier to develop that it was to apply. Gathering reliable information merely required enough money and a capable staff. Applying that knowledge in the form of policy demanded that Pattullo tangle with the forest companies, with the political and economic odds increasingly stacked against him. Consequently, the technical knowledge of foresters within the department ran ahead of the minister's ability to implement their ideas. While Pattullo began with the intention of imposing government control over the forest companies in the public interest, he achieved, at best, only mixed results. In the long run, political and economic pragmatism overrode reformist ideals and the companies regained control of the situation. Duff may have come in like a lion, but he went out like a lamb.

In a few cases he held out against unlimited exploitation. Perhaps the most notable example was the failed attempt by an eastern syndicate to grab a huge area of forest land in the Prince George area to feed a proposed pulp and paper mill. Because the newspaper was becoming the great mass media of North America, the continent had a voracious appetite for newsprint. Based on this market, pulp and paper manufacturing became the most important new Canadian staple industry of the 1920s.[53] In British Columbia, pulp and paper mills had the advantage of exploiting trees that were not necessarily suitable for lumber and they offered the possibility of major economic development in the interior where those species tended to predominate. So when, in 1920, a group of eastern interests calling themselves the Fraser River Syndicate approached Pattullo with a plan to build a pulp mill near Prince George, there seemed, on the face of it, to be every reason to encourage the scheme. But as negotiations dragged on, it became obvious that the syndicate was only interested in locating in British Columbia on its own terms.

Pattullo was prepared to meet some but, in the end, not all of the easterners' demands. The company wanted a pulp licence for 170 square miles of forest. A pulp licence was a form of tenure that enabled the government to gain revenue from forest land that was considered to be too poor to produce lumber. The problem was that the Fraser Syndicate expected to get a licence on terms that were much more favourable than allowed for by the existing legislation. Pattullo was initially encouraging, and replied that he would send a cruising party into the area to assess its potential and determine how much of the forest was suitable for lumber and how much for pulp wood. Almost any log could be used for pulp, but Pattullo wanted to be sure that large numbers of more valuable saw logs would not be turned to pulp. The company men took exception to the delay that the departmental cruise would cause and even argued that it was completely unnecessary. If they could raise the capital to go ahead, then that in itself would be sufficient evidence that there was enough pulp wood in the area to support the project. It was as if these capitalists had never heard the word 'speculation.' Pattullo curbed his annoyance and patiently pointed out that he could not accede to all of the company's terms merely on its request and that he had to justify what he did on the grounds of public policy.[54]

In the meantime he received expert advice from his chief forester. Caverhill reported that the spruce in the Prince George area was of a high quality and there was more than enough for a thirty-year supply. In contrast to the members of the syndicate who emphasized the difficulties of working in the interior, Caverhill believed that, because the required species were more concentrated in the Prince George area, logging there would be easier than it was for the pulp companies on the coast. He was confident that the land could be disposed of to others if this deal fell through, so he argued that the government should not lower the stumpage fees simply to force immediate development. It would be better to keep stumpage rates up and wait until conditions were more favourable than to sacrifice the raw material. At the same time, the minister received some political advice from his deputy which had to be weighed against the views of his experts. Naden wrote that it 'would mean everything to the people living in Prince George' if the project went ahead. 'You know this as well as I, and will appreciate the necessity of the Government doing everything in their power to try and get an industry of such magnitude established.'[55] Naden was indeed telling Pattullo what he already knew and, in the short run at least, political expediency prevailed over expertise.

Pattullo offered a number of concessions to encourage the Fraser Syndicate to locate in Prince George. He was prepared to guarantee a thirty-year supply of timber to be paid for only as cut, to set the ground rental at half that paid for timber licences, to fix stumpage at a relatively low rate for thirty years, and to levy royalties on the final product according to use rather than the department's designation of the trees. Thus, logs used for pulp would pay the pulp royalty and those used for timber the timber royalty, in spite of the chief forester's opinion that much of the spruce in the Prince George area was suitable for milling as lumber.[56] But all this was still not enough. The syndicate now wanted both the stumpage and the royalty rates to be fixed for thirty years. 'In our opinion,' one of its members wrote, 'greater inducements must be offered than anything yet proposed by your Department.'[57] But Pattullo had reached the end of his tether. Royalties represented the crown's interest in the resource and he was already engaged in crucial negotiations with the forestry industry to adjust timber royalties for the entire province. He would not consider a further special arrangement for one company.

There was sporadic discussion with the Fraser River Syndicate over several years. In 1926 Pattullo thought he had an agreement and made a public announcement that the project would go ahead.[58] But the company only raised new issues, complaining this time that it could not operate under the provision of the Forest Act that gave the minister the power to cancel a pulp lease.[59] Pattullo pointed out that other companies with large investments were operating under the provision. He felt this new objection was 'an excuse rather than a reason.' He was probably correct when he suggested that the truth of the matter was that the Syndicate could not raise the necessary capital under current market conditions.[60] He threatened again, as he had done before, to throw the forest land that was being held for the Syndicate open to others. By 1928, however, pulp and paper prices were declining and Pattullo never did make good on his threat.

The whole episode brought little glory to the minister. Perhaps the only positive side was that Caverhill's original advice – that the trees be left where they were until they could be cut more profitably – was inadvertently followed. The legislation that provided the Fraser River Syndicate with its final objection did facilitate the expansion of existing mills such as the Powell River Company and Pacific Mills at Ocean Falls. The act gave the minister the power to establish pulp districts adjacent to a mill or an existing pulp licence. The timber within the district was set aside for the operator's use and sold as required at the stumpage rates in place at the time of sale. Under the legislation, pulp district number one was designated near Pacific Mills in an effort to ensure a continuous supply of logs for thirty years. Though the Prince George deal never came to fruition, the production from other mills climbed slowly through the decade and pulp and paper continued to be a major source of income.[61]

The Fraser River affair demonstrated that Pattullo would not completely capitulate to the industry, but there is no doubt that the power of the forest companies was on the increase through the 1920s. Pulp and paper was the new expansion sector of the decade, but lumber production was still the mainstay of the forest industry, accounting for about half of forest industry production through the 1920s.[62] Here, too, Pattullo found it increasingly difficult to press the role of the Forest Branch. The establishment of an independent forestry bureaucracy did not necessarily lead to more sophisticated government intervention in the industry. That still required the political will to stand up to the most powerful economic interests in the province. And nowhere was the growing power of the industry more evident than in the negotiations that led up to the establishment of new royalty rates in 1924.

By the early 1920s most people involved in forestry, whether from government or industry, agreed that the royalty structure would have to be changed. The timber royalty was the amount that the government levied on trees as they were cut on timber licences and leases and crown land that had been granted after 1887. At the insistence of the industry, the royalty arrangement in the 1912 Forest Act was modified by the Timber Royalty Act of 1914.[63] This legislation gave licence-holders security of tenure and fixed royalties on a sliding scale for forty years, adjustable over five-year periods. The problem was that royalties were set for each five-year period on the basis of the wholesale price of lumber. This method did not allow for the possibility that if production costs rose faster than the selling price, then the margin of profit would decrease. And that was exactly what happened after 1914. Costs of production increased during the war and changes in the value of the Canadian dollar meant that, while lumbermen got better prices, they were paying higher royalties out of lower profits. At the beginning of the second five-year period, on 1 January 1920, royalties increased by 37 cents per thousand board feet, or from 43 to 74 per cent depending on the grade of lumber and the region where it was cut.[64] As inflation continued to push up the cost of production in the early 1920s, lumbermen insisted that the basis for calculating royalties that had seemed so desirable five years before would have to be altered again. If not, they said, the industry would be crippled. Pattullo calculated that, if the 1914 Timber Royalty Act remained in force, royalties would double on 1 January 1925 and that would certainly force many mills to close.[65] So the rates had to be changed. There was general agreement on the nature of the problem. The trick would be to find a solution in a situation where the battle lines between an invigorated forest industry and a weakened government were growing ever more apparent.

The voice of the forest industry became much more concerted with the formation of the Timber Industries Council of British Columbia in 1921. This umbrella organization was set up largely by Martin Grainger, Pattullo's former chief forester who, like H.R. MacMillan before him, left the Forest Branch for private enterprise. Having formed the council, Grainger did not stay long and in 1922 he was replaced by William McNeill, who had also earlier worked in the lands department. He now became the spokesman for the timberholders in negotiations with Pattullo. Hitherto the timbermen had influenced government policy from within by having individuals in the Forest Branch who were sympathetic to their interests. As it developed its expertise, the branch became more detached: its objectives were different from, or even opposed to those of the industry. Caverhill, who Pattullo had hired to replace Grainger in 1920, was much more independent from the forestry business than his predecessor had been. Consequently the industry now had to exert influence and effect policy from without. McNeill worked to bring as much political pressure as possible to bear on the government by publicizing the industry's position. Through its journal, the *British Columbia Lumberman*, and the provincial newspapers, the Timber Industries Council mounted an extensive propaganda campaign to convince the public that the forestry industry was in a bad way and needed fast relief from government interference.

These developments put Pattullo in an very uncomfortable position, for the industry was marshalling its forces against an increasingly vulnerable government. As the rhetorical volume rose by decibels, the Liberals' position became more problematic. Pattullo could not find a solution to the royalty issue that he thought the government, with its slim majority, could put through the house. At the same time he did not want to go into a difficult election with the forestry industry arrayed against the party, so he drew back from introducing legislation. And yet, after the 1924 election the Liberals were worse off than they had been before. They were now in a minority position in the house and a vigorous assertion of the government's role in forestry became even more unlikely. Though he did not realize it at the start, the minister of lands was playing a losing game.

The opening gambit came early in 1923. Naden, speaking for the department, proposed that the new royalty rate be tied to stumpage value rather than the wholesale price of lumber. That is to say, it would be based on an assessment of the selling value of the standing tree. Naden suggested that the department and the industry should decide together on the basis for the calculation and the proportion to go to the government. But even if agreement could be reached on that score, the assessment of stumpage value and the cost of production would have to be made by departmental foresters. Naden could make this proposition in the confidence that the Department of Lands now had the qualified staff to go into the woods and mills and make accurate surveys of values and costs. Indeed, the suggestion had been formulated by the department's forestry experts. For the industry, however, that was the problem. Such investigations, the timbermen vehemently argued, would be a completely unwarranted intrusion by government into their affairs. McNeill denounced the notion as 'utopian' and described it as the product of a bureaucracy 'whose chief function in all political life is to establish itself more and more in power, and for that purpose require larger and still larger amounts of money.' Other industry representatives predicted dire consequences if 'experts' and 'theorists' were allowed to override 'practical suggestions.'[66] Clearly, at one level, this was a struggle between Pattullo's government foresters and the private enterprisers of the forestry industry: of scientific expertise versus exploitation capitalism.

At a more fundamental level the debate was about the extent to which the public, through its government, was entitled to a share of the publicly owned resource. The government's foresters believed that, whatever the timberholder had paid for his licence on the speculative market, it only gave him the right to cut trees that were still owned by the crown. Accordingly, the payment to the owner of the resource should be related to its market value. The industry men, however, saw licensed forest land more as private property and rankled at the thought they should have to pay the government, in the form of a royalty, for timber they already regarded as theirs.[67] This basic philosophical difference was expressed in the continuing debate about how much the industry should pay – which, in 1923–4, came down to a squabble over how royalties should be calculated.

As negotiations dragged on, compromise seemed to be impossible. The industry accepted the idea that royalties should be based on stumpage value, but there was no agreement on the method of calculation and therefore on an actual figure for the payment. Pattullo explained they were 'looking to the working out of a formula that would be satisfactory to the timber industry and at the same time would properly protect the interests of the public at large and the timber resources of the Province.'[68] McNeill was more singleminded. He simply argued, right to the end, that any royalty rate higher than that recommended by the Timber Industries Council would be disastrous for the industry and therefore for the province.[69] Having decided not to introduce legislation during the last session of 1923, Pattullo was in an even more difficult position after the June 1924 election. Not only were the Liberals in a minority, but the 1925 deadline was staring him in the face. Everyone involved in the dispute agreed that the royalties scheduled under the existing legislation could not be permitted to go into effect and that the rates had to be changed before 1 January. With the combination of a tight deadline and an unstable political situation, Pattullo had little room to manoeuvre.

Finally, in the heat of the political day, he capitulated to the industry position. In December 1923 Pattullo introduced legislation establishing an arbitrary royalty rate over two five-year periods.[70] The industry did not get a fixed royalty over an extended period as it had hoped, but more importantly the departmental foresters did not get a rate that was tied to stumpage value as they had wanted. In order to encourage the utilization of poorer species, the royalty was made somewhat lower for the interior than it was on the coast. But, as Pattullo admitted, under this arrangement the public share in the resource did not change at all. Based on 1924 production levels, he reckoned that the 1925 royalty would yield about the same revenue to the government. He rather disingenuously claimed that the legislation was the product of long consideration by the forestry service.[71] The fact was that by forcing the issue at a political level, the industry had done an end run around the government's experts. Though the legislation went smoothly through the house, the minister responsible still faced a good deal of criticism from those who said that he had not done enough to protect the people's share. The cause was even taken up by that erstwhile champion of the proletariat and millionaire leader of the recently decimated Provincial party, General A.D. McRae. As in most of McRae's jousting with the government, this thrust against Pattullo's royalty policy was easily parried by the cut of self-interest. McRae was a founder of the Western Canadian Lumber Company, had vast timber holdings, and had been a strong member of the lumber lobby for many years. It was hardly convincing for him to argue that it was not 'good form' for the timberholders just elected to the legislature to participate in the debate on royalties when, but for a few votes in Vancouver City, he would have been there himself.[72] We can safely assume that he would not have remained silent on the matter. For Pattullo, who from constant practice was becoming ever more forthright in defence of his own views, McRae's tilting presented little challenge.

The minister of lands justified the new timber royalty in terms of the importance of maintaining stability in the industry. McRae, because he held extensive timberlands in the form of crown grants, gave Pattullo the opportunity to emphasize the point that the royalties only applied to those who held timber licences. It would be unreasonable to burden licenceholders with undue royalties and then expect them to compete in the marketplace with those who held crown-granted timber and did not pay the royalty.[73] At a more general level, Pattullo simply argued that, if the government used royalties to take a pound of flesh from the industry, then lumber operations would be put out of business and neither the government nor the industry could afford that. The policy was not evil and it was sufficient unto the day. As Duff put it when he spoke on the subject: 'There is only one day more important than tomorrow for you and me and that is today. We know not what the morrow will bring forth, but we know pretty well what today will do and in our anxiety for tomorrow we must not overlook the fact that we have to protect today.' In short, he wrote, 'we must keep this industry going.'[74]

Forestry policy had become 'a question of maintaining a proper balance,' and clearly the scales had tipped in favour of the industry.[75] The royalty struggle was indicative of the extent to which the timberholders could determine government policy by political pressure. Through the remainder of Pattullo's tenure as minister of lands, the department and the industry continued to co-operate only in areas that were obviously beneficial to the business side of forestry. Thus, in consultation with the industry, the department did a great deal of work on developing offshore markets for British Columbia forest products. Other areas of departmental activity were either curtailed or had little effect on the exploitation of the forests. Even measures for fire protection and fighting, particularly if they had real teeth or required increased spending, were difficult to put through the house. Efforts to ban smoking in the woods during the summer season and to empower fire wardens to call out men without compensation to fight fires went down to defeat.[76] At the same time it was clear that the government was paying an increased share of the fire protection bill, while the industry paid correspondingly less. Pattullo set up provincial forests and in 1927 he introduced legislation to establish Garibaldi Park as a public park. Scientific research towards forest management and sustained yield went on at government stations without having much impact in the woods. There was little notion of reforestation. Pattullo had apparently learned little from his trips to observe forestry practice in Scandinavia that he wanted to apply to British Columbia. He said that to talk of 'artificial planting in this province at the present time is absurd. It is not necessary in the first place and in the second place it would be altogether too costly.' Both the minister and the industry were happy to rely on what they called 'natural regeneration' as the means of replenishing the resource.[77]

Conservation was sometimes a political issue. The question of logging in Strathcona Park was hotly debated in the summer of 1926. Much of the heat was generated by Conservative newspapers, since both the *Colonist* and the *Province* began to cultivate a conservationist conscience.[78] Strathcona Park was created by the McBride government in 1911, but some forest land within the park boundaries was still in private hands. Pattullo thought it was unfortunate that the 'morning paper' had not been more wide awake when the Conservatives alienated the land in the first place.[79] Now that the issue was raised, he argued that private owners could not be prevented from cutting their own timber and the government could not afford to buy them out. He claimed that the logged-off areas would regenerate very quickly: that new growth would soon overcome the desolation created by the loggers. Besides, he cheerfully added, there were many other scenic areas within the province.[80] As the pressure of public opinion mounted, he backed off a little from this hard-line position on logging in the park. He made a much-publicized trip to the park with his chief forester and spent several days in the wilderness exploring for himself the beauty and resources of the area. He emerged to announce that the government would purchase some of the timber rights around Buttle Lake.[81] He had responded minimally on the particular case, but his general policy did not change. As Duff bluntly put it: 'You cannot have a tree and cut it at the same time.'[82] He was, of course, perfectly correct. The problem for the conservationists was that Pattullo was largely of the view that trees should be cut.

'Logging is no more destructive than the harvest of our wheat fields,' Pattullo claimed, 'and the climate and the fertility of the soil are not destroyed in the process.'[83] With the minister of lands increasingly expressing such views it was not surprising that, in spite of crown ownership of the resource and the growing expertise of forestry staff, the province did not move much beyond clear-cut logging by the end of the 1920s. In the early years as minister, Pattullo had instituted a thorough reorganization of his department and he then went on to introduce some effective policies. Increasingly, though, he had to respond to political exigencies. As minister he experienced some of the joys of power, but he soon came to appreciate the distinct limitations on the authority of the provincial government as he had to reckon with other interests and forces. By the end of his tenure as minister of lands there had developed a pattern of things not brought to fruition, of policies begun but not completed. In part at least, it was because Pattullo was now doing other things.

CHAPTER 5

Party Spokesman

'There are no pessimists in heaven'

From about 1924, Duff Pattullo became a more prominent public figure. For the first seven or eight years he was minister of lands, he commanded the detail of departmental administration and legislation. By the early 1920s he was on top of all that and the work had become somewhat routine. Given the changed circumstances of the Liberal government after 1920, there seemed to be less scope for innovative and costly ideas in cabinet. The burst of reform legislation during the 1910s would not be repeated in the following decade. While the government may have been marking time, Duff needed to move forward. He had to have some new direction in which to expend his energy. So he spent more time as a public proponent of policy and in trying to convince British Columbians that that they should still vote Liberal. Just as forestry policy became more political during the royalty debate of 1924, so did Pattullo's role within the government.

As the Liberal government of John Oliver grew older through the 1920s, it also became tired and worn out: its grip on power weaker after every election. The Liberals needed new policies, or, at the very least, new spokesmen to advocate old ones. Duff Pattullo was one of the cabinet members who assumed this function and his role became more public as the decade went on. As the government's energy drained away, Pattullo was increasingly vocal and vociferous in its defence. In speech after speech he explained the particular work of his own department, and also advocated the general program of the government. Pattullo was becoming as much a spokesman for the party as he was minister of lands. As he grew in confidence he obviously enjoyed this new role, especially when it meant taking the offensive against other politicians. As far as Duff was concerned, hectoring and bantering the opposition on the public platform was still loads of fun.

He was most at ease campaigning in his own riding of Prince Rupert where he knew the people. He continued to make frequent trips up the coast, particularly during election time. And yet the stretch between being minister of lands in Victoria and a local member in Prince Rupert was often a difficult one. By the early 1920s it was obvious that he would continue to live in Victoria at least as long as he remained in the cabinet, so he had to protect his political interests in the north at long distance. He therefore made sure that the city got its share of government spending. One example was the new provincial government building that he arranged for Prince Rupert. It was an substantial structure of brick and stone set in spacious grounds at the foot of 2nd Avenue, and when he opened it in January 1923 it was a tangible testimonial to his political influence. At the same time, the vote of $200,000 for the building had, naturally enough, attracted a good deal of partizan criticism in Victoria, while in Prince Rupert complaints from Liberals that he was not doing enough for the riding could still be heard even after the provincial building was opened.[1]

The annoyance of Pattullo's political opponents was not entirely misplaced, for the new building would signify the extent of his influence in ways that went beyond its imposing structure. All of the functions of the provincial government were centred in the new building and they were presided over by the government agent. That office was filled by Norman Watt, who had been a friend of Duff Pattullo's since they had worked together in the Gold Commissioner's Office in Dawson City. Watt had also served as Pattullo's private secretary in the lands department. As well as taking care of the province's business in Prince Rupert, Watt no doubt looked after the minister's political interests by seeing that those who supported him did not go unrewarded. Pattullo had a group of loyal Liberal party members in Prince Rupert who did the necessary organizational work, particularly around election time.

Yet throughout his career, Pattullo never took his re-election in Prince Rupert for granted. Some of his electoral battles would be hard fought to a close result. It was not so in 1920, however. After the voting was over in that election, Pattullo seemed safe enough when, on the final count, he had more than twice as many votes as the Conservative candidate, his old rival Seville Newton.[2] The victory was an expensive one, though. Prince Rupert was an extensive riding and Pattullo was always a big spender. His re-election had cost nearly $8000 – more than any other riding except Vancouver, which elected six members.[3]

Whatever money it had spent, the party as a whole was not nearly so secure. When they ran against the boodling Bowser and his Conservatives for a second time in the 1920 election, the Liberals really had nothing new to offer the people and they campaigned on their record of honest, effective government. But by now it was obvious they were not able to solve all of the problems of the postwar era. Veterans felt that measures to assist them were inadequate, there was widespread industrial unrest in 1919 as workers went out in sympathy with the Winnipeg General Strike, and the economic and political dissatisfaction of farmers was expressed in the formation of the United Farmers of British Columbia in 1917. Beset on all sides, the electoral sweep of 1916 was a distant memory by 1920.

The Liberals emerged from the election with a bare majority and there were immediate signs of disaffection within the party. David Whiteside from New Westminster and the troublesome Fort George member, Harry Perry, decided they would not attend caucus meetings. Perry complained that the caucus system stifled the intellect and made those who were not in the cabinet largely irrelevant.[4] Pattullo, who had experienced the disastrous consequences of party infighting in the Yukon, must have viewed these developments with great alarm. On a trip to the north he was deputized by Oliver to see if he could get Perry to toe the party line, or at least make it clear where he stood.

Perry agreed to change his ways and assured Duff of his loyal support of the government. But the Grand Trunk to Fort George was hardly the Damascus road, and Perry's conversion was prompted not so much by a blinding flash of light as a cheque for $500 from Duff Pattullo.[5] Though the price was right for now, Perry had only a temporary change of heart, and this was not the last time that Pattullo would have difficulty with his northern colleague.

Nor was the grumbling in Liberal ranks after 1920 confined to backbenchers who felt the caucus was powerless. It was also heard among some of the most prominent members of the cabinet. Though the entire Executive Council had been re-elected in 1920, ministers soon began to resign. The first to leave was Mary Ellen Smith, the first woman to serve in any Canadian cabinet, who now decided she had little influence within the government. There was further evidence of real dissatisfaction within the powerful Vancouver Liberal organization when J.W. deB. Farris, the attorney-general and minister of labour, departed at the beginning of 1922. In spite of Oliver's urgings not to deplete his cabinet further, the newly elected Liberal prime minister, William Lyon Mackenzie King, persuaded J.H. King to leave the Ministry of Public Works in British Columbia for the same position in Ottawa. By the time the British Columbia Liberal party met in convention in September 1922 the stresses and strains were obvious. The certainties that had carried the Liberals through their first four years in office evaporated away during the second administration. And if pressure from within were not enough, there was soon to be a new onslaught from without.

During the latter part of the Liberals' second term the most telling blows came not from the Tories but from the newly formed Provincial party. Made up of Conservatives who were frustrated with Bowser's continued leadership and members of the United Farmers of British Columbia who wanted to take more direct political action, the new party was launched at a convention in Vancouver in December 1922.[6] The leader, in fact if not in name, was Major-General A.D. McRae, a Shaughnessy millionaire who, at first glance, seemed an unlikely candidate to head a political reform movement. But, for some months, he had been leading the charge against the provincial Liberals in particular, extravagance and corruption in general, and the manifold evils of the party system. On the pages of *The Searchlight*, a broadsheet published by his supporters in Vancouver, McRae proposed to shed a harsh but pure light on the scandals of machine politics. Since the objective was to get Oliver out and not let Bowser in, McRae intended to illuminate the grafting of both the old parties. He alleged that the Pacific Great Eastern Railway had provided slush funds for electoral purposes, and he forced Oliver to set up a royal commission to investigate the company's finances.

For a moment it seemed that the Liberals were blinded in the harsh glare of adverse publicity. Internally divided, they were not in good shape to withstand this external attack, so it was fortunate that their opponent was not invulnerable. Indeed, the would-be governing general was soon hoist with his own petard. Oliver had his son do some checking in the New Westminster land registry office and he discovered that McRae had made huge profits in some dubious land dealings at Port Mann.[7] The Liberals maintained that this knight errant of provincial politics was in no position to pontificate on the probity of others. The commission into the Pacific Great Eastern exonerated the government though, needless to say, it did not satisfy the critics. The Provincial party was still a threat but it now seemed less menacing. Because Oliver hoped that in the next election the third party would take more votes from the Conservatives than the Liberals, he did not want to kill it off. He told supporters that it would be best to keep it 'alive but badly crippled.'[8]

In this context of political trench warfare leading up to the 1924 election, Duff Pattullo came to prominence as a frontline spokesman for the government and its policies. He was, of course, not new to the task of tangling with political opponents. He had always enjoyed the rough and tumble of debate, both in the house and on the hustings. Now he would speak more frequently to a variety of audiences throughout the province. He became an even more accomplished platform performer. He had always been a clear and forthright speaker who did not mince many matters. His newspaper work had taught him to be careful and sparing in the use of words. His crisp speaking style was doubtless a breath of fresh air compared to the windy perorations of his leader. Once as a newly elected member of the legislature Pattullo introduced Oliver to a Prince Rupert audience by telling the citizens he would have to be brief. He had to leave plenty of time for Oliver since it took the premier an hour to start, two hours to speak, and an hour to finish.[9] One suspects that Duff was only half joking. Certainly his own speaking style was very different. He liked to be concise and to the point.

Pattullo's speeches operated at a number of levels. At their most obvious, they were intended to create an aura of assurance. Amidst so much negative publicity, Pattullo was called upon to express the confidence that was so much a part of his own personality. Since the Liberals saw the fate of the province as bound up with their own, criticism of the government tended to be read as doubt about the future of British Columbia. Duff provided the antidote of optimism: optimism in the unlimited wealth of the Pacific province, and optimism in the Liberal party as the custodian of that wealth. He was now a booster for all British Columbia just as he had been for Prince Rupert in his early years on the coast. His speeches included paeans of praise to the province as the most wonderful place on earth. 'I doubt,' he told the Vancouver Board of Trade, 'whether, taking all factors into consideration, there is any more highly favoured part of the earth's surface than British Columbia.'[10] Unfortunately some people were questioning this ordinarily self-evident truth because a campaign of pessimism was being conducted for political purposes. In his secular sermons Duff had dire warnings for the purveyors of gloom that only 'saps the vitals of any individual or collection of individuals ... There are no pessimists in heaven,' he averred, 'it could not be heaven if there were. It follows therefore that all pessimists go to hell.'[11]

As far as Pattullo was concerned, as an optimist the best was always yet to come. He was fond of recalling how, as a boy, he had regretted that he lived in what appeared to be such a prosaic age. It seemed the past was full of romance, but not the present.

Then, suddenly, he found himself borne into the twentieth century: the most romantic and marvelous age of all time. Humankind was not without its faults, but he never lost faith, 'in spite of the moral turpitude which has come so plainly to the surface since the war.'[12] Not having fought overseas, or even taken great interest in the war to end all wars, he was perhaps less effected by the disillusionment that came from the failure of reform after the war. While it was nurtured in the naïve boomerism of the prewar years in British Columbia, Pattullo's outlook was first and foremost a personal one. He had always tried to see the bright side. By now the characteristic was engrained strongly enough to be maintained through the trials of the 1920s and, later, the tribulations of the 1930s.

Associated with this generalized optimism, Pattullo also spoke of his understanding of Liberalism. He expressed his notion of Liberalism firstly by contrasting it with Toryism which, he said, derived from the autocracy of chieftains and kings. Tories, Pattullo explained, 'believe in their divine right and if they could have their way they would abolish elections and conduct the business of the country primarily in the interests of themselves, with such slop-over benefit as might incidentally accrue to the great masses of our people. It has always been so and we can expect that it always will be so.' Liberalism was the natural sequel to Toryism, for 'it began as a protest against the usurpation and abuse of authority and power by the few over the many, for the benefit of the few at the expense of the many.' Here he drew on the Reform tradition that his father had represented in Ontario, to show that the Tory party was the same now as it had been in the days of the Family Compact. Since Confederation a few men had controlled the economic destiny of the nation and there were no lengths to which they would not go to maintain their grip. Fortunately, the Liberal party also remained 'true to its long cherished traditions' and continued steadfastly to stand 'for the development of the country for the great masses of the people.' Indeed, Pattullo once reminded the Vancouver Liberal Association, if the present-day Liberal party has no message for the masses of the people it has no reason to exist.[13]

Not surprisingly, some discrepancy between rhetoric and reality was apparent when Pattullo defended the policy of the British Columbia Liberal party in the 1920s. But explaining the government's program, in both general and specific terms, was the main point of most of his speeches. 'What this country wants,' he said, referring as he often did to the province as a country, is not the 'small, picayune, cheeseparing policy' offered by the opposition, 'but a broad, comprehensive, progressive, development policy.'[14] When he got down to the details of government initiatives, he spent most of his time defending the work of his own department. Pattullo was not involved in all areas of government policy in the early 1920s. The furore over the government's management of liquor distribution, the ever-present problem of what to do with the Pacific Great Eastern Railway, and the endless negotiations with the federal government over freight rates were all matters in which Pattullo played little personal part. When he spoke in public he liked to speak with the confidence that he knew what he was talking about from personal experience. So he constantly harkened back to the program of his own department and spoke about such things as soldier settlement, Okanagan irrigation, and forestry policy, and used them as examples to illustrate his general point about how well the government was serving the interests of the people. It was not because he could not see the forest for the trees, but as he said, 'Whenever I talk on public matters ... I find myself unconsciously inclined to talk timber.'[15]

These, then, were the themes Pattullo reiterated in speeches during the run up to the 1924 election. He also responded in detail to the charges made by McRae, especially when they involved lands department policy. In November 1923 he devoted a biting speech in the house to the latest issue of the *Searchlight* which had, among other things, made the accusation that, in his efforts to get a pulp mill established in Prince George, he had offered a fixed royalty to the Fraser Syndicate. He noted that this claim was typical of the misinformation McRae was disseminating. In fact it was his refusal to consider a fixed royalty that led to the collapse of the deal. McRae had apparently confused 'royalty' with 'stumpage' and Pattullo cited the error as evidence of the general's incompetence. Pattullo resented the suggestion that the leader of the Provincial party had a monopoly on honesty and referred to his followers as a bunch of 'has-beens' and 'never-wasers.'[16] But, for all of Pattullo's aggressiveness, when Oliver called the election for 20 June 1924, the Liberals knew they had a fight on their hands. In a bitter campaign, feisty speeches alone would not be sufficient to carry the day.

Organization would also be crucial, and here, too, Pattullo was called upon. He became increasingly involved in the detail of party work outside of his own constituency. He and Alex Manson were made responsible for eight ridings in the north and the interior and were instructed to 'arrange suitable conditions' and report back to Oliver. They wondered if Atlin might be difficult to win but reckoned that there would be no other problems in the north.[17] Results were, however, likely to be more mixed in the interior. Pattullo was also charged by the premier with putting together a series of campaign pamphlets that would describe the work of the various government departments. Other ministers were to feed the information to Pattullo and he was to publish a piece of party propaganda once every week during the two months before the election.[18] The minister of land's administrative ability and capacity for hard work were being put to more political purpose by the party leader.

While he was involved in provincial organization he did not, of course, forget his own riding. The backroom boys up in Prince Rupert would take care of the leg work, but Pattullo had to spend time in the north giving speeches and making promises. He had been working for some time to persuade the federal government to build a grain elevator in Prince Rupert and now, at last, it seemed he had been successful. A couple of weeks before the election, while he was campaigning in the north, he received a telegram from Oliver saying that he could announce that the project would go ahead. Much to his annoyance, however, as soon as he made the announcement the federal government had a different story. J.H. King, the federal minister of public works, informed him that, while he was confident the project would be approved, parliament had not yet voted the money so it would be better not to say anything in public.[19] By the time that message arrived it was too late, and Pattullo was left with a potential embarrassment. Still, even if he could place no reliance on the federal government, he was confident of his own efforts and telegrammed Oliver on the eve of the election that the north would be solidly Liberal.[20]

Duff was right about the north, but it was just as well he had not made a similar prediction for the rest of the province. The announcement of the possibility of a grain elevator had some effect and Pattullo was returned in Prince Rupert. He won by fewer than three hundred votes over Seville Newton, who ran as an Independent Conservative. Six of the eight ridings that Pattullo was responsible for organizing also went Liberal. Northerners still saw the Liberal party as the most likely to foster northern development, and so the north was as solid as Pattullo said it would be. But Cariboo went to the Provincial party and the Conservatives took the new riding of Mackenzie. And throughout the rest of the province there was little joy for the Liberals, who ended up with twenty-three supporters in a house of forty-eight.[21] The results were particularly bad in Victoria, where all four new members were Conservatives. John Hart, perhaps seeing the writing on the wall, had resigned as finance minister just before the election. Even the premier himself, who had won in two ridings (Delta and Victoria) in 1920, now could not carry one. Oliver's loss in Victoria was only slightly mitigated by the defeat of the other two party leaders, Bowser and McRae, in Vancouver. The 1924 election showed that the Liberal decline had not been stemmed. The government had gone from bad to worse and clearly there would have to be some serious soul searching.

For a moment, though, Pattullo paused to savour his re-election and to consider the thought he could make a long-term career in the uncertain business of provincial politics. He enjoyed the congratulations of friends and relatives. Family members in Ontario wrote to him with their best wishes. They must have realized it had been touch and go, both for the party and for Pattullo himself, so they were thrilled to hear he was still a minister of the crown in British Columbia. A niece wrote to say she had been on tenterhooks during the election and she had no idea she could become so excited over any mere man. Unlike Duff's father, she had to look up the spelling of 'hallelujah' in the dictionary after the results were announced. They were all acutely aware, and none more so than Duff, that this time his father was not there to enjoy his son's political success. George Robson Pattullo, who had been such a force in Duff's early life, died in 1922. After their mother was taken from them, it was their father who had raised the Pattullo children. It was a particularly sad loss for Duff that his father was gone, even if, as one of his sisters wrote, he still seemed particularly near at election time.[22] So much of Duff Pattullo came from being his father's son. Certainly George Pattullo senior would have agreed that political life must go on, and would have insisted that an ailing Liberal party find the remedy and revive itself.

The party was still alive, if not kicking, so it was a diagnosis rather than a post-mortem that was required. Oliver wrote to all Liberal candidates asking for their explanation for the dissatisfaction with the government. The replies included the usual local grievances: complaints that Liberals were not getting their fair share of patronage, for example. The candidate in Grand Forks-Greenwood claimed that he was defeated by George Naden, who had handed out too much timber land in the area to Doukhobors rather than to 'white men.'[23] In the end, though, Oliver decided that rather more significant factors were involved. He blamed the federal government for not having reached an agreement with British Columbia on equalization of freight rates, he allowed that Liberal organization had been weak in some areas, particularly Victoria, and he implied that he had miscalculated the effect of the Provincial party which he now thought had taken more votes from the Liberals than from the Conservatives. Oliver was initially very discouraged about his own future in public life, but he soon decided not to take his defeat in Victoria personally.[24]

After some debate, both with himself and with his colleagues, Oliver stayed on as party leader. He rejected the lure of federal politics and also the views of those who opposed his leadership. In a close-run contest, he won a by-election in Nelson and then returned to the helm in Victoria. But his hand was shaky and his direction uncertain. He was still disconcerted by the near defeat and had no clear idea of what to do next. Freight rates and the Pacific Great Eastern Railway still took up much of his time, but these were issues that had little direct relevance for many British Columbians. Two years later he wrote to Vancouver Liberal member of the legislature Victor Odlum that, 'while I cannot claim to have been doing anything spectacular, yet my time has been very fully occupied.' Evidently one of Oliver's political maxims was that 'there are times when it requires more courage to stand still than to go forward.'[25] At least one of his senior ministers strongly disagreed. Duff Pattullo still believed what he had earlier told the house: 'If you are not going ahead you are going behind. There is no such thing as standing still.'[26]

Though he must have recognized that Oliver was a spent force, there is no evidence that Pattullo was openly disloyal to his leader. He certainly became much more outspoken in his relations with the premier. His letters to Oliver after 1924 indicate he was prepared to take a much more independent line. There were changes in the Liberal cabinet after the election. With Hart gone, John D. MacLean moved from provincial secretary to finance. There were suggestions within the Executive Council that Pattullo be given more responsibilities, including the finance portfolio.[27] Though Oliver left him where he was in the meantime, there can be no doubt he was a more powerful presence at the cabinet table.

At the same time he was becoming even more prominent as a public advocate of policy. Now that they were in a minority position, the Liberals expected to have a difficult time in the legislature. When the first post-election session began on 3 November 1924, it quickly became apparent that the opposition was not as concerted as the Liberals had feared. With the support of independent and Labour members they could maintain a majority and, in the end, the three Provincial party members often voted with the government. Nevertheless, Pattullo believed that, with the government weaker, it needed to be defended much more vigorously. In the 1924 session he engaged in 'spirited bursts of verbal cross firing' with the opposition.[28] The following year, after MacLean had presented the budget, Pattullo was the first government speaker in the debate, jumping in with characteristic verve to argue his party's position and heap scorn on those sitting across the floor. Conservatives described his performance as 'boasting, bragging and egotistical,' yet they were sufficiently impressed to accuse him of having his eye on the Liberal leadership.[29] The position was not vacant in 1925, however, and if Pattullo was thinking along those lines he kept it to himself.

He continued to speak frequently and forcefully to various groups outside the legislature. While he still spent a good deal of time cataloguing the things he had done as minister of lands, more thoughtful listeners must have realized that most of the innovative moves had occurred during the first Liberal administration before 1920. And flailing away at Richard McBride after a decade of Liberal government presumably brought diminishing returns. Yet Pattullo was a popular speaker who was much in demand and he made sure he was never too far away from the spotlight. As long as the Liberals could hang on in the legislature there would be no provincial campaign in the offing, so he took to the road during the federal elections of 1925 and 1926.

Until now Pattullo had taken little part in federal politics. He was at the convention of western Liberals that met in Winnipeg in August 1917, though it was the only Liberal convention he would ever attend outside of British Columbia. Clifford Sifton, who had denied Duff advancement in the Yukon, wanted to use the meeting to mobilize western opposition to Wilfrid Laurier's stand against conscription and the Union government. Pattullo favoured conscription, but like most western Liberals he stood beside the old leader and voted against supporting the Union government.[30] He believed that Laurier was the greatest Canadian who had ever lived and, more importantly, he was too much a Liberal partisan to ever consider a union with the Conservatives. He rejected the coalition of 1917 as firmly as he would dismiss all attempts to join Liberals and Conservatives in marriages of inconvenience.

He was rather less enamoured with the new federal Liberal leader, William Lyon Mackenzie King, when he succeeded to the position in 1919. As far as Pattullo was concerned, King was simply not a Laurier. He congratulated King on his 'splendid victory' in the 1921 federal election,[31] even though he soon realized that having a Liberal leader in Ottawa would not necessarily make dealing with the federal government any easier. King also received felicitations from Duff's father, George Pattullo, in Woodstock. The elder Pattullo followed up a week later with a suggestion that he might be given a senate appointment.[32] King apparently did not take up the idea, perhaps because North Oxford, for once, did not elect a Liberal in 1921. Earlier King had told George Pattullo that no letters gave as much pleasure as those that referred 'to the dearly loved ones who have passed away.'[33] So once again Duff's father reminded King of the friendship between the two old Liberal families. But in many ways the two sons had moved very far apart. Duff had left southern Ontario for the small towns of frontier British Columbia, whereas King had come of age while attending university in the big cities of the east.

A year after he was elected Liberal leader, King came to Pattullo's world. At the beginning of October 1920, after visiting Victoria, he took the steamer *Prince George* up the coast. Following Pattullo's suggestion he went ashore at Ocean Falls, where he was more taken with the plant than the scenery, observing that the pulp mill was 'the finest factory I have ever been through.' In Prince Rupert he met with the local boys who managed Pattullo's riding. He was most happy to see L.W. Patmore, who had been a classmate at the University of Toronto. To King the resources of the northern coast seemed unlimited, but Prince Rupert Liberals told him that their city was being held back by the neglect of the federal government. The locals were keenly disappointed that the town was sidetracked because Laurier's Grand Trunk Pacific policy had never been fulfilled. Though King was moved by the 'courage and fortitude of men in a pioneer community,' he thought Prince Rupert 'is very crude, all rocky, no natural beauty save across the harbour.'[34] Next day, travelling by train to Prince George, the Liberal leader was more impressed by the massive beauty of the Skeena valley. While the man who would later take pleasure in erecting Gothic ruins on the gentle Gatineau hillsides around Kingsmere may have felt moments of awe in this wild land, he did not feel at home in the rough-hewn places that Duff knew. And though he spoke in public of the failure of Laurier's policies in British Columbia since 1911, he certainly did not understand the problems of underdevelopment in the first-hand way that Pattullo did. Each had inherited a part of the Laurier mantle: King the central Canadian emphasis on national unity and Pattullo the concerns of a new society in the west. Meeting the demands of both would become increasingly difficult. Nevertheless the two were Liberals and at this stage Pattullo and King wrote to each other in cordial terms. Duff told King his visit had done a lot of good in British Columbia, and King congratulated Pattullo on his re-election in Prince Rupert at the end of the year.

Goodwill did not necessarily translate into action. Prior to the 1921 federal election Pattullo received a vague statement from King about the need to look at the railway situation in all provinces but questioning 'the wisdom of being specific with regard to any particular road.' At the same time King was unequivocally opposed to setting up a royal commission on better terms for British Columbia.[35] When King became prime minister in 1921, Pattullo's congratulations were tempered with regrets that the election results on the coast were disappointing since British Columbia had elected only three Liberals.[36] The national leader continued to give the impression that provincial matters were of little concern to him, and the underlying tension between the two levels in the Liberal party was not assuaged. By 1924 even federal Liberal organizers in British Columbia recognized that, while Oliver still spoke positively about his relations with Ottawa and told the people what the federal government was doing for the province, 'his public speeches in this regard have not that ring of hopefulness which ought to characterise them.' The federal government was told by its own organizers that it should make some gestures towards British Columbia in the form of, among other things, a grain elevator in Prince Rupert.[37] James G. Turgeon, one of King's principal advisers on party matters in British Columbia, had suggested in 1922 setting up a western organization of the federal party based on an awareness of western conditions. But King did nothing with the idea until he faced a difficult federal election campaign in 1925.[38]

During the 1925 election Pattullo gave a number of speeches in support of the federal Liberals. It must have taken some effort to subsume his regionalism and speak in favour of a national government that had done little for British Columbia. He dismissed Arthur Meighen's forthright advocacy of protection, because it was an 'insular, selfish and monopolistic policy,' in favour of King's non-committal vacuity on the issue. Pattullo must have been listening very carefully for what he said was King's 'clear cut enunciation that the discrimination which has heretofore existed against the West is to be removed.' Yet he told westerners that it was important to vote for the Liberal party because it was the party that would protect the interests of the west. If Pattullo had his tongue stuck to his cheek, no one in the audience noticed. Evidently enunciating clearly, he went on to say that policy was more important than personality. Yet he chose an odd example to illustrate the point. He claimed that many people who did not care for the Liberal candidate in Vancouver, Gerry McGeer, as an individual would vote for him just the same because he was the most able advocate that the province had on the freight-rate issue. Yet McGeer, of all the provincial politicians in Pattullo's time, epitomized personality over policy.[39]

If Pattullo's speeches in 1925 were somewhat equivocal, the views of the British Columbia electorate were not. On election day, 29 October 1925, the results were bad enough for the Liberals in the rest of Canada and they were worse in British Columbia where, once again, they won only three of the province's fourteen seats.[40] The tensions between the two levels of the Liberal party remained as federal leaders blamed the unpopularity of the provincial government for the poor showing in British Columbia, just as local liberals tended to attribute their woes to Ottawa. As Mackenzie King put it to a west-coast Liberal, 'It is part of the inevitable fate of any party in office in the federal arena to be called upon to shoulder the aprobrium which provincial governments of like party complexion may have incurred.'[41] Provincial liberals in British Columbia believed the reverse was also true, though not equally so since the federal government had more power than they did. There was another federal election in less than a year, after the minority governments of both King and Meighen had been defeated in the House of Commons. In 1926 Pattullo again spoke in support of the federal party, describing the customs scandal as 'one of those things' and Meighen's effort to form a government as a prime example of the lengths to which the party of entrenched interest would go to take control.[42] Once again, however, his efforts seem to have had little effect. When the votes were counted, King had the majority that he was denied in 1925, but in British Columbia the party had lost even more ground. Only one lone Liberal was elected.[43] These federal results did not augur well for the provincial party which was now more than half way through its term.

The federal-provincial split within the Liberal party exacerbated tensions at the local level, particularly the division between Vancouver and the rest of the province. Anti-Vancouver sentiment was also a product of regionalism within the province. The Vancouver urban area grew rapidly during the 1920s. Much of the expansion was in the suburbs, as the automobile made it possible for more people to live further away from where they worked. By the end of the decade Vancouver had became the third largest city in Canada, and it was natural for people in the hinterland to be sensitive about the growing influence of the metropolitan centre. As a northerner, Pattullo had a healthy suspicion of the city he had not been able to break into as a businessman in 1908.

Among Liberals, resentment against Vancouver was also generated by the feeling that a cabal of cronies in the city ran things in the interest of the federal rather than the provincial party. One favourite explanation for the electoral ills of the party in British Columbia was that they were caused by the pernicious influence of the 'Vancouver machine.' Disaffected Liberals accused men like John Farris, Brenton Brown, W.T. McArthur, and Gordon Wismer of running a corrupt organization that had reduced Oliver to merely 'the titular head of the party,' while Farris was said to be the 'master of the situation.'[44] There was some truth to these allegations and there was also a good deal of exaggeration. In politics, though, perception is often more important than reality. For their part, many Vancouver Liberals felt that, far from controlling the situation, both their interests and those of the city were largely ignored by the Liberal administration in Victoria. As Pattullo became a force to be reckoned with in cabinet, part of the reckoning was to become subject to the hostility of disaffected Liberals. He engaged in a series of running battles with Vancouverites during 1925 and 1926.

The first furore blew up when, late in 1924, Pattullo decided to allow logging on 170 acres of provincial land on the Capilano watershed. Many people in Vancouver feared that cutting the trees would have a disastrous effect on the city's water supply. At least three of the city's members of the legislature, Charles Woodward, Christopher McRae, and Victor Odlum, all of whom were Liberals, said they were against the scheme. Strong objections were voiced by the Vancouver City Council. Some members of the council were also frustrated by the fact that their plan to build a dam on Seymour Lake had to be approved by the water-rights branch in the Department of Lands. They accused Pattullo of stalling development by insisting that city proposals be assessed by the experts in his department.[45] Pattullo's reaction to these issues was first to bluster, and then to compromise. 'It may just as well be understood clearly and definitely,' he told the citizens of Vancouver, 'that I personally, have no intention of being bluffed, browbeaten, bull-dozed nor calumniated into submission to the dictation of a few interested persons who know little of the real situation.'[46] Then he suggested that the question of logging the area be considered by a commission of six experts. More important than the logging issue for Pattullo was the fact that other municipalities besides Vancouver depended on the watershed and their interests also needed to be protected. In the end he backed down on the matter of logging on the watershed and agreed to the formation of the Greater Vancouver Water Board to manage the area. Pattullo's argument that the fire risk would be reduced by controlled logging was vindicated, at least in his own mind, when shortly after a fire wiped out much of the timber in the area.[47]

The minister had to do some political firefighting of his own around his efforts to establish the university endowment lands on Point Grey immediately to the west of the city. There was criticism, largely from Conservative members from outside Vancouver, that far too much money was being squandered on the University of British Columbia. Pattullo told the house that he disagreed with the argument that young people were getting too much education and being weaned away from rural virtues. The trouble, he said, was not too much education, but too little.[48] Still the objections continued, if not to education itself, then to the way in which Pattullo handled the development of residential property on the endowment lands. When he could not reach an agreement with the municipality of Point Grey over tax assessment, he removed the endowment lands from its jurisdiction and placed them under the control of his department. There were accusations of extravagance, and even malfeasance, from within his own party over the development of the university.[49] In November 1925 he was called before the Public Accounts Committee that was probing payments on the endowment lands. After an uncomfortable time before the committee, he instructed his staff to inform him in future before each individual piece of work was started. In due course Pattullo did receive some credit from the town planners at the University of British Columbia for the manner in which the endowment lands were developed.[50]

All of this was nothing compared to the fuss that arose when he announced that eighty acres adjacent to the endowment lands had been sold to the Valhalla Cemetery Company. This decision led to another row, this time with the representatives of the people of Point Grey who did not want a cemetery on their boundary. The going got so rough that the Point Grey Municipal Council called in the press for an apology 'from the Provincial Government for remarks of the Honourable T.D. Pattullo, which charged that the council was incompetent and was dominated by the C.P.R.'[51] Again a Pattullo plan was opposed by the Vancouver members of the legislature, particularly the

Liberal Ian Mackenzie, but also Woodward and McRae. At a meeting of Point Grey ratepayers Woodward publicly criticized Pattullo. Even the premier himself met with representatives of Point Grey to discuss the issue. It seemed to some observers that the cemetery proposal had got to 'the interesting place where an irresistable force collides with an immovable object.'[52] In the end, however, Pattullo backed down once again and the land was bought back from the cemetery company. He was perhaps persuaded by the fact that the municipality was proposing to build a golf course on the site. If Pattullo had ever considered the possibility of making some choice bits of Valhalla available to selected Liberal colleagues he kept the idea to himself. All he could do was concur with those who hoped that the issue was now buried.[53]

While particular disputes might be interred under a pile of compromises, the more general question of Vancouver's representation in Victoria remained very much alive. The minister of lands was seen as the prime protagonist in a cabinet that ignored Vancouver's interests. He was accused of being antagonistic and dictatorial towards the city even though, as often as not, he conceded to local demands. Pattullo's most vocal and consistent opponent was the Vancouver Liberal member of the legislature, Charles Woodward. Beginning the moment he was elected in 1924, Woodward constantly complained to the premier that Pattullo was riding rough-shod over the city. For Woodward, the minister's mishandling of every single issue – the Capilano watershed, the university endowment lands, and the Valhalla cemetery – added up to the general conclusion that he ought to be removed from the cabinet so that a Vancouver member could take his place. It was very poor politics, he told the premier, 'to have Cabinet Minister's located promiscuously,' by which he meant 'without any regard for Vancouver City's claim for cabinet representation.' Deliberately misspelling Duff's name, he advised that 'Mr Pattallow should be dropped' because he 'is the greatest political fool that we have.' With an assumption of supremacy that would not have endeared him to the rest of British Columbia, Woodward concluded that, after all, 'Vancouver is the king pin of the province.' Nor did Woodward confine his criticisms to private correspondence with the premier; he also attacked Pattullo and the issue that he represented in public, both inside and outside the legislature.[54]

Though Woodward expressed them intemperately, he was not alone in his views, and Vancouver Liberals certainly had a point. The controversies that swirled around Pattullo's decisions about specific pieces of land in the Vancouver area were symptomatic of a major problem for the Oliver government, and they reflected a perennial issue in British Columbia politics. Since Farris resigned as attorney-general at the beginning of 1922, Vancouver had been without representation in the provincial cabinet. Five of the six members from the city were Liberals and so Vancouver, which provided something like 20 per cent of the Liberal caucus, had no minister, while there were two (Pattullo and Manson) from Prince Rupert. Part of the problem was that Oliver could not find a Vancouver member who was willing and able to join the cabinet. Woodward himself quickly proved he was far too slippery a fish to be considered for the position. In the first session after he was elected he voted against important government measures, such as Pattullo's 1924 timber royalty legislation.[55] Other Vancouver Liberals were said to be too busy with their business interests and Mary Ellen Smith had already resigned from the cabinet once. Oliver could have been more vigorous and persuasive, but the problem was not entirely of his making. By the time some action was taken, with the appointment of Ian Mackenzie as provincial secretary and Dugald Donaghy to finance in June 1928, it was too late to convince many Vancouverites that their interests were taken seriously by the provincial government.

While Pattullo tried to gloss over the issue, the dissatisfaction in Vancouver was indicative of a general malaise within the provincial party. When he came to the metropolitan centre to discuss one or two 'tempests in a teapot,' he said there was no reason for the slightest ill-feeling between the government and Vancouver. He blamed his problems on the Vancouver media that 'misreported, misinterpreted, misrepresented, and deliberately falsified' his views and policies.[56] Once he suggested that if he did not get the nomination in Prince Rupert he might run in Vancouver in the next election.[57] It was just as well he still had the confidence of Liberals in the north, for the problems in Vancouver did not go away by pretending they did not exist. At a meeting of Liberals at the Hotel Vancouver just after the 1926 federal election, Oliver was thoroughly raked over the coals by those who thought his government was responsible for the weakness of the party. Again Pattullo tried to be sanguine, saying that it was impossible for any government to avoid giving offence. Considering the state of the party and the obvious need for change, even his eternal optimism must have been wearing thin. By the end of the year there were rumours of a major reorganization of the government, and some even suggested that Pattullo was intending to do the job.[58]

Such reports were premature, however. The old premier had one more burst of energy that briefly enlivened his government. The provincial economy had improved, and for the first time since they came to power in 1916 the Liberals offered a budget that projected a surplus. Oliver, who had never been a strong believer in social legislation, was persuaded by some of the more progressive members of the cabinet, including Pattullo, to return to reform. In early 1927 the British Columbia government was the first in Canada to pass an Old Age Pensions Act.[59] It was minimal legislation that had to await the enactment of a federal bill, but soon after its passage an Alberni man was the first Canadian to receive an old-age pension cheque. The Liberals also passed a Produce Marketing Act, but only after a long debate during which Ian Mackenzie expressed the view that it was 'communistic.'[60] The party convention in 1927 decided to work towards health insurance and maternity benefits, to spend more on public works, and to reform the education system. The party responded with loud praises and standing ovations for the leader, yet Oliver did not seem to have much spark. It terms of actual legislation this reform revival was merely the dying echo of the 1916 program. By now the party had a lot of fellow travellers and excess baggage. The opposition was naturally unimpressed, and spent most of its time in the legislature scrapping over old bones of contention.

The 1927 session was particularly fractious. Oliver was a

weary man and did not have the energy to cope, but his minister of lands was certainly up to it. Duff always got a charge out of the raucous, partisan debate of the British Columbia legislature and this year was no exception. He had the members in stitches with his reference to the house as a 'public asylum,' a phrase which he withdrew in favour of the term 'public forum,' though not before Tom Uphill, the Labour member from Fernie, had asked the speaker for a certificate of sanity.[61] It was all jolly good fun, and Duff was in his element.

By now the Pattullo style was also becoming familiar around the province. When he talked to people as a politician he did not believe in unnecessary palaver. His notion of efficiency was to cut the chatter and get down to business. He usually had definite and forthright views, and what to him was merely self-assurance, others saw as arrogance. His evident egotism was not universally admired. Charles Woodward took Pattullo to task on the front page of the conservative *Vancouver Province* for being an autocrat. 'This honourable minister at the head of the land department knows it all,' Woodward charged. 'I have had occasion to talk to this gentleman and you cannot get a word in edgeways. I find that this is his reputation all over the province.'[62] Duff often laughed off such criticism, saying a cabinet minister inevitably loses friends because of the necessity of refusing requests. Indeed, he joked that he had done pretty well on that score for, in contrast to the partisan Conservatives, he had antagonized 25,000 people in the last ten years. The Victoria reporter Bruce Hutchison later wrote of this period that Pattullo 'seemed to be the Big Bad Wolf of the government: the gruff trouble-shooter of the ministry, who seemed to revel in hot water and controversy.'[63]

Most, but not all, Liberal supporters found Pattullo's manner easier to take than did opponents. One party man wrote to the premier that he liked 'the splendid spirit of optimism of Pattullo,' and added facetiously that 'he never commits himself and, above all, never bubbles over.'[64] The opposition press could likewise wax satirical when it came to the subject of Duff Pattullo. In December 1926 the *Colonist* commented on his often self-congratulatory air by reporting that 'it is about 10 years since the Premier by lucky chance or directed by the mysterious influence of providence called Mr. Pattullo into his cabinet. The marvellous influence of the new minister almost immediately became apparent. The industries of the Province instantly began to grow like vegetables under glass and they have been growing with yearly increasing vigor ever since.'[65] But, the views of the *Colonist*'s editor notwithstanding, it seemed by 1927 that neither Pattullo nor providence could turn Liberal fortunes around.

Behind its pallid mask of reform the government was still very ill and, although few knew it as yet, its leader was dying. In the early summer, after Oliver left for a visit to the United States, it was learned that he had incurable cancer. An operation at the Mayo Clinic had failed to stem the disease. With Oliver and other ministers out of town, Duff Pattullo was holding the fort as acting provincial secretary. While the premier was convalescing with his son in Hamilton, Ontario, Pattullo wrote him a letter of loyalty, saying that he was sorry the premier would not be leading them in another electoral fight. 'I believe that under your leadership we could again overcome our friend, the Enemy. Under a new alignment, nobody can foresee what will happen.'[66] Pattullo was undoubtedly genuine in his expression of sympathy, but at the same time practical politics had to be considered. Without Oliver as leader, he expected major ructions within the party, so a week later he wrote to the premier's son to find out what his father's intentions were. If he wanted to stay in the east, then the cabinet should know so they could put the political house in order. If he planned to return, he should do so soon and end the uncertainty.[67] Like Pattullo, Oliver had become a British Columbian and, a shadow of his former self, he came back to the coast to die.

Oliver returned at the beginning of July and called a meeting of Liberals to discuss the situation. Though he wanted them to choose a new leader immediately, they refused to replace him while he was still alive. But the work of the government had to go on and, at Oliver's insistence, John D. MacLean was named acting premier and leader designate. Selected while the old leader was still among them, MacLean represented continuity with the past rather than any perceptible change of direction. More aggressive and ambitious members of the cabinet like Pattullo may have seen it as merely an interim appointment: a chance to reflect and rebuild. Certainly Duff knew the party was in bad shape and they would soon have to go to the people. It made good political sense for him to conclude that, if he were the leader, there would not be time for him to turn things around and put his stamp on the party before the next election. Certainly as long as Oliver was still present it seemed that the emphasis would be on past achievements rather than future possibilities. At the end of the month Pattullo sent greetings to his leader on the occasion of his seventy-first birthday. He wrote on behalf of his colleagues that 'we have been associated together for over a decade, during a most extraordinary and varying period, yet every question was determined in friendly compromise, and it is gratifying that there has always existed a spirit of cordiality.'[68] Amidst the plaudits of his party and feelings of nostalgia, Oliver lingered on for another few weeks before he passed away on 17 August 1927.

The new premier was a picture of poise: full of equanimity in the face of a host of major problems. John MacLean, who was exactly the same age as Pattullo, had come to British Columbia from Prince Edward Island as a school teacher. He became a principal in Rossland before he went to McGill University and graduated in 1905 as a medical doctor. He was practising in Greenwood when he was elected to the legislature in 1916. Since then he had held a number of portfolios, spending the longest time as provincial secretary but also serving as minister of education, finance, railways, and industries. MacLean was a team player. Long on experience in cabinet but short on new ideas, he was less than charismatic. Though he approved of the newfound reformism, he would not push it any further than it had already gone. There were some minor cabinet changes. Pattullo retained the lands portfolio and was also sworn in as provincial secretary, a job he had been doing for some time anyway. But nothing bold or imaginative was presented to the 1928 session of the legislature and the election manifesto that followed was more elaborate than innovative. When MacLean set the election for 18 July 1928, Pattullo must have known that continuity would not be enough to carry the day if the voters believed it was time for a change.

On the face of it, the Conservatives were offering a change in 1928. At least they had a new leader, if not new policies. After losing his third election and his own seat in Vancouver, Bowser had resigned as Conservative leader in 1924. The Liberals' old foe was gone but not forgotten. MacLean was warned by a supporter early in 1928 that, although 'Bovril Bill (Bowser) is somnolent,' he could always rise again. The same source suggested that, if the Conservatives were to win in British Columbia, then McRae '(the Remount General)' might ride once more into provincial politics.[69] But the leader that the Liberals actually had to contend with in 1928 was Simon Fraser Tolmie. The son of an old British Columbia fur-trade family, Tolmie was a veterinary doctor, a farmer, and a member of the House of Commons in Ottawa. After being elected as a Unionist in 1917 he had served as minister of agriculture in 1919–21 and again in 1926, and later he was national organizer for the conservatives. He turned down the leadership of the provincial party when he was first offered it in 1924, but was persuaded to accept the position as a compromise candidate by a deadlocked party convention in 1926. Yet he did not immediately relinquish his federal seat. Tolmie remained in Ottawa until the 1928 election was called and then he rushed back to British Columbia for three weeks of hard campaigning. Not a ball of fire, the Liberals' opponent was an amiable fellow, pleasant and sociable and hard to really dislike. He was not associated with any of the factions that had been fighting it out within the Conservative party in British Columbia and he seemed aloof from the intensely partisan politics of his own province. By the same token, the years he had spent in the rarefied political air of Ottawa had not prepared him for the gale-force winds of west-coast politics. Returning home for the 1928 election, perhaps Tolmie's most important asset was that he was not a Liberal.

As Duff Pattullo prepared for his fourth provincial election campaign, he knew that this time the Liberals were in big trouble. He and MacLean appeared on the platform together at

Duff's nominating meeting in Prince Rupert in early June. They sounded confident in public, but the backroom talk with the boys up north was more realistic. Some of Pattullo's supporters were not even certain he could win in his own constituency. It meant he had to work doubly hard, because this time round he would also be a major factor in the provincial campaign. Over the last twelve months he had given dozens of speeches to Liberal gatherings, service groups, and public meetings. His performance in the legislature during the spring session had been particularly strong. When he spoke in reply to the speech from the throne he began with a series of announcements on lands policy: that the annual lumber cut would be restricted to the annual increment, that orchardists would get relief on the costs of irrigation, that there would be aid for the reclamation of Sumas Lake, and so on. After these specifics, he went on to a wide-ranging address on many aspects of the social and economic life of the province. Even the *Vancouver Province* allowed it was 'one of the best speeches made in the Legislature in a number of years ... which never once descended to the plane of petty politics.'[70] Now that the election was on, his speeches would be less lofty, but party organizers particularly requested Duff Pattullo when they asked for cabinet ministers to come to the local ridings.[71]

Both Pattullo and the party tried to put the best face on the situation. They ran on their record, arguing that they should be returned so they could continue the good work. In April Duff had been in Ottawa representing the provincial government in discussions on the sale of the Pacific Great Eastern and the return of the Peace River block and the railway belt to British Columbia.[72] The Pacific Great Eastern railway had been a millstone around the provincial government's neck since Oliver took it over in 1918, the same year he first demanded that the dominion return the lands that British Columbia had conveyed to the Canadian Pacific Railway in the 1880s. Inevitably, neither issue was resolved in 1928, and the election claim that, if the Liberals were defeated, negotiations over railways and railway land would come to a halt was hardly persuasive. On matters closer to home, the party published a pamphlet called

What Liberalism Has Done for the Masses with a photograph of the first old-age pensioner in Canada on the cover.[73] Other than pensions, however, most of the information was old news. The pamphlet listed things the Liberals had done long ago, rather than offering good reasons for renewed confidence. Pattullo reminded the voters of the Liberal party's proposals on health insurance and maternity benefits, but a promise to merely look into these matters did not amount to much.[74] Duff also tried to mend his political fences in Vancouver, where he was still under attack from some Liberals. He said he had not been antagonistic towards Vancouver, but a minister was a minister for the whole province and had to take wider interests into account. None of this moved his critics, of course, but, after a forthright letter from MacLean on the matter of party loyalty, Charles Woodward decided not to run again.[75]

Going into an election with a divided party and little to offer the voter, the trick is to attack the opposition. Pattullo knew the political game and how to play it, so he took the offensive with gusto. He delighted in turning Tolmie's agricultural metaphors against him. Since the Conservative leader spoke horsey language much of the time, Pattullo thought he would be forgiven for saying that 'he was never built for speed. And as a matter of fact is he not just a bit of a plug?'[76] When the laughter died down, Pattullo went on to express fundamental disagreements with Tolmie's political philosophy. He had always rejected the notion that the business of government was just like any other business. Now Tolmie was pushing the idea in his campaign literature and running a bevy of businessmen in an effort to give it credence.[77] Pattullo dismissed other Conservative policies as vague and unclear. Tolmie announced that he 'will devise a reforestation policy,' which Pattullo thought was pretty amusing since, in his view, that was what his department had been doing for years. The Liberals had gathered reports from every government department which, they claimed, showed that virtually everything Tolmie promised to do was already being done. Pattullo carefully pulled apart all aspects of Tolmie's program and then concluded 'there is a beautiful nebulousness in all the Doctor's statements.'[78] The trouble was that the Liberal manifesto did not have much bite either. In many ways there was little to choose between the two parties in 1928, other than the fact that one of them had been in power for almost twelve years. Still, Pattullo persisted in pointing out Tory shortcomings and belabouring the benefits of Liberalism. Tolmie and his followers, he said, were 'sitting in the shades of Opposition' and so 'cannot see the sunshine enjoyed by the great masses of the people of British Columbia.'[79]

The election was in mid-July, but there seemed to be little other reason for Liberals to have a sunny outlook. Yet many of them were genuinely optimistic about their chances. Two days before the vote MacLean informed his candidates that he expected 'a sweeping victory for the Government.'[80] A gushing Gerry McGeer had already told Mackenzie King that the tide had turned in British Columbia.[81] Pattullo was somewhat more cautious in his predictions. He did not respond to MacLean's assertion that things never looked better for them in Vancouver and Victoria, though he did say that the north would be solidly Liberal once again.[82] Federal Liberals were even less sanguine. J.H. King thought the best that they could hope for was a slight majority.[83] Another party organizer wrote King that the provincial government had become a liability to the federal party, so the national leader would be well advised to stay out of the campaign in British Columbia. It cannot have been much comfort to MacLean when he received a copy of that letter.[84]

There was worse to follow. As the returns came in it was clear that the 1928 election was an unmitigated disaster for the Liberals. The only place where they had any joy at all was in the north. Pattullo surprised some of his supporters by hanging on in Prince Rupert, though he did so by fewer than one hundred votes.[85] Duff faced the outcome with some panache nonetheless: he pretended to be completely confident by leaving Prince Rupert on the Vancouver boat the evening before the final result was known.[86] The Liberals lost in Atlin, but otherwise, as Duff had predicted, they retained the northern seats. Everywhere else in the province they were decimated. They did not win one of the ten seats in Vancouver and Victoria, and wherever else they looked – Vancouver Island, the lower mainland, or the interior – the political landscape was very bleak. The Conservatives had taken thirty-five seats while the Liberals were reduced to a tiny group of twelve. Premier MacLean, who had given up his safe riding in Yale to run in Victoria, along with two other cabinet ministers, was among the losers. The turnover in seats was perhaps more dramatic than the shift in the popular vote. The Liberal share of the vote actually increased by nearly 9 per cent, but at the same time the Conservatives had raised their percentage by more than 20.[87] There was no disguising the fact that this was a decisive defeat.

The explanations began as soon as the election was over. MacLean was probably correct when he wrote to King that he had not been leader long enough to stem the Liberal decline, though it was also obvious he had provided little inspiration to his weary followers.[88] The party organization was pretty dozy at both the provincial and the constituency level. The Liberals had clearly run out of steam, so the Conservatives did not need to do much more than argue it was time for a change. That neither party had an innovative program to offer the voters was perhaps less important than the fact that the opposition to the Liberals was less divided than it had been in 1920 or 1924. With the disappearance of the Provincial party, the Conservatives had taken over the government, but they had got there less by the force of their own momentum than by the inertia of the party in power. At the same time, the situation looked pretty grim for the Liberals who were defeated and in disarray. Yet an experienced politician who was always optimistic, and who was thinking about the future rather than dwelling on the present, might well conclude that the position which had just been lost could, with a lot of hard work and some luck, also be regained.

Duff Pattullo was relegated to the opposition benches by the Conservative victory, but his career in provincial politics was already longer and more influential than most. Over the past twelve years he had presided over the postwar development of major sectors of the British Columbia economy. He had managed one of the government's most important departments during a period when bureaucracy and administration had become substantially more sophisticated. He had asserted the role of the public sector and recognized the power of private enterprise. More recently he had become a prominent spokesman for a government in decline. While others led the provincial Liberal party, he could not single-handedly revive it, and now he viewed with dismay its defeat at the hands of the Conservatives. Yet, with all this behind him, he was still an optimist, and so the best was yet to come.

CHAPTER 6

Leader of the Opposition

'How long is this serious burlesque to continue?'

For the moment, it did not look good for Pattullo or the Liberals. The post-election winter of 1928–9 was one of dreary discontent, with, it seemed, little hope of a glorious summer to follow. The provincial Liberal party had been deteriorating for years and many thought it would be an equally long process to bring it back to fighting form. And, while Liberal party fortunes were low, the provincial economy appeared to be on an upswing. After all of the uncertainties of the postwar decade, it finally looked as though British Columbia might boom again. Forestry production, which was indicative of the provincial economy generally, had climbed back up above 1920 levels by 1928.[1] Certainly businessmen were optimistic about the future, as were their representatives in government. In contrast to the Liberals, Tolmie and his party were pleased with themselves as they contemplated both the political and the economic situation in the early months of 1929. Had they been interested in listening, however, Duff Pattullo could have told them that, in British Columbia politics, nothing was more certain than change.

If 1928 seemed like a good time to win an election in British Columbia, the impression did not last for long. It would soon be obvious to all that both the Liberal fall and the economic rise were more apparent than real. The Liberals were down but not out, and with a new leader and a changed political climate they would soon regroup. The signs of economic strength were likewise largely superficial. The provincial economy had expanded and become somewhat more sophisticated during the 1920s, but its fundamental weakness still remained. It was still an economy based largely on the export of a limited range of primary products to outside markets and therefore vulnerable to economic forces that were beyond provincial control. Before the decade was out, one day of trading on the New York stock exchange would show British Columbians just how fragile their dependent economy was, and the reverberations would last through the decade to come.

For Pattullo and the Liberal caucus the more immediate issue after the 1928 election was the matter of leadership. MacLean had clearly had enough. Within days of the election he raised the possibility of a federal position with Mackenzie King.[2] He had not unduly rocked the boat with the federal government, so now he could look to his reward. After he ran unsuccessfully in a federal by-election in Victoria in December, King appointed him commissioner of the Canadian Farm Loan Board in Ottawa for a ten-year term beginning on 1 January 1929. With MacLean gone, the Liberals at least had to have a house leader for the first session of the new parliament. Duff was the senior member among the Liberals elected in 1928. He was the only member of the 1916 Brewster cabinet still in the house, he had served in two major portfolios, and he was the most prominent party spokesman. There was a laying on of hands of sorts by MacLean. In December 1928 there was a contretemps over who should have access to orders in council. The provincial secretary, S.L. Howe, said that the practice had been to make them available to the leader of the opposition or his designate. Pattullo insisted he was the senior Liberal and should not have to go through MacLean, who was not even an elected member. More importantly, he argued that, once signed by the lieutenant-governor, the orders were public documents and should all be laid before the house as the previous administration had done. The matter became a political issue of government secrecy, but in the meantime MacLean nominated Pattullo as the one who should see orders in council.[3]

Duff Pattullo was certainly the best, and perhaps the only

candidate to lead the Liberals in the legislature. There was a brief attempt by Vancouver Liberals to have Ian Mackenzie, who had been elected in North Vancouver, assume the leadership. Mary Ellen Smith tried to call a meeting of the provincial executive of the British Columbia Liberal Association in Vancouver for 21 January 1929 to discuss the leadership. Many Liberals from other parts of the province saw the proposed meeting as just another attempt by the Vancouver gang to grab control.[4] Pattullo wrote to Mary Ellen Smith to point out that the executive could not do much about the leadership since the Liberal caucus would elect a house leader and a permanent leader would have to be chosen by a party convention. Furthermore, the Vancouver meeting had been called for the day before the legislative session was to start in Victoria, which was hardly convenient for the members. He concluded with the blunt advice that she cool down. 'Dear Mrs Smith,' he wrote patronizingly, 'eschew foolish newspaper interviews, and tell the guys who are advising you to "cut the rough stuff." '[5] Pattullo was not going to allow a Vancouver coup, and he was already acting as though he were in charge.

When the session opened on 22 January, it was announced that Duff Pattullo had been appointed Liberal house leader by unanimous choice of the caucus.[6] He was constantly reminded by his opponents in both parties that being house leader did not mean he was party leader. It would be nearly eighteen months before his position was confirmed at a Liberal party convention. But Duff carried on as if the first decision were the final one and the position was permanent. During this interim period he wrote to the prominent Vancouver Liberal, Evlyn Farris, that he had always found that 'having used such measure of intelligence as is given to me, that whatever happens thereafter always turned out for the best. This may seem a childlike theory, but it is a very comforting practice.'[7] He took up the task of leading the little band of Liberals, 'the twelve apostles' as he called them, in the house. And he did so, not only with intelligence, but also with energy and drive. It was obvious that he assumed that the leadership was settled, unless perhaps he should change his mind.

The only thing that might have diverted him was a federal portfolio. There was a great deal of talk about that possibility, at least by others, in early 1930. In public Pattullo supported the federal party and its leader even though his private thoughts about both were more ambivalent. In November 1929 when King came to Vancouver Pattullo gave a speech in which included the necessary words. He proposed 'that Vancouver shall no longer live in the turgid backwaters of Toryism, but ... we shall not stop until the lifeblood of Liberalism, which, in essence, is the welfare of all the people, shall pulsate through every artery of public thought.'[8] The following month he was in Ottawa and there was newspaper speculation, both in British Columbia and the east, that Pattullo might be taken into the federal cabinet. When he returned to the coast he declined to comment, but others did not hesitate. Supporters wrote to tell him he was badly needed in British Columbia and they hoped there was nothing to the rumour. Charles Woodward, in contrast, warned King that taking Pattullo into the cabinet would be a serious mistake for 'he would be like a red rag to a bull' in Vancouver.[9] The speculation arose again in April and May the following year when it was widely assumed that J.H. King would go to the Senate and a new minister from British Columbia would have to be appointed to the federal cabinet. Many expected Pattullo to be the choice.

It is hard to tell exactly what Duff thought. He said little in public or in private. In letters to friends he said the papers were full of rumours, that he had been strongly urged to enter the federal field, but not that he intended to do so.[10] L.W. Patmore, writing to King about the political situation in Prince Rupert, claimed that Pattullo wanted to be in the federal cabinet. Even if Pattullo had said as much to Patmore, he may have been merely keeping his options open or using the federal possibility to maintain some leverage over the provincial party. What Pattullo did make absolutely clear was that, once he was confirmed as leader of the provincial party, there would be no question of moving to Ottawa. To desert the province at that point would, he felt, not be 'playing the game.'[11] Mackenzie King was considering Pattullo, among others, to represent British Columbia in his cabinet, but in the end his decision was made by delay. King had hoped that the provincial convention would be postponed until after the August federal election. In that way the provincial party could have whoever was left over after federal representation had been decided. The provincial party did not play along with that plan and called its convention for Kamloops on 30 and 31 May 1930. Pattullo, the only candidate for the leadership, was duly elected without dissent. Some days later King telegraphed his congratulations to Pattullo. He apologized for not communicating immediately, explaining that 'I have had to give my time exclusively to the many matters demanding concentrated attention at Ottawa.'[12] In the privacy of his diary King was more forthright. Now that Pattullo was ruled out of a federal post, King wrote that 'I never regarded him as strong.' Within a month Ian Mackenzie was called to Ottawa to represent British Columbia in the Liberal cabinet and King was 'glad that we got Mackenzie instead of Pattullo, he is a better stamp, likely to be pretty effective.'[13] Though he would never have admitted it, the subsequent careers of the two men proved King wrong. Mackenzie was not nearly as capable as Pattullo and he did not hold his liquor well. But he was more amenable and less likely to take an independent line. Pattullo also got what he wanted. For him, running his own show in British Columbia would be a lot more fun than serving as a yes-man under Mackenzie King in Ottawa.

And so the course was set. Duff Pattullo stayed in British Columbia as leader of the provincial Liberal party and his majesty's loyal opposition. As the congratulations rolled in from around the province he had little time to pause and reflect. There was so much to do. Liberals in British Columbia were more optimistic than they had been when Duff became interim leader. Many thought he had already done well as house leader. Some, who said that they would have enjoyed voting against him in January 1929, wrote to congratulate him for 'the able and clever way' he had led the party.[14] The provincial convention had given Liberals a much needed shot of adrenalin. There was a federal election two months after Duff was elected provincial leader and, once again, British Columbia went against the trend. Mackenzie King was defeated as the Liberals lost seats in every region of the country except the far west. In British Columbia they increased their representation from one to five.[15] But if there were some glimmers of political light for the Liberal party on the west coast, the economic outlook seemed uniformly black to the majority of British Columbians.

By the time he was confirmed as Liberal leader it was clear to most that the province was already in a bad way, and apparent to some that it was only going to get worse. The economic disaster that was heralded rather than caused by the stock market crash of 1929 was not a temporary affair as many continued to hope. As the world markets for British Columbia's limited range of primary products dried up, both production and income declined drastically. The drop was apparent by the middle of 1930 and by 1932 the estimated value of gross production in British Columbia would be less than half what it was in 1929.[16] In the forestry industry, Pattullo's old bailiwick, the value of production declined by nearly 42 per cent between 1929 and 1932.[17] British Columbia had no substantial secondary sector to fall back on, so there was no other source of income for either the private or the public sector.

As revenue fell off rapidly in both sectors, thousands of workers found themselves without any income at all when they lost their jobs. Unemployment figures were not collected as they are today, but the 1931 census showed that by the middle of that year more than 25 per cent of British Columbia wage earners were out of work.[18] As politicians from the Pacific province were fond of pointing out, they had to deal not only with the local unemployed but also with those who gravitated to the coast from other parts of Canada: the 'break beam and box car tourists' as Premier Tolmie called them.[19] Relief was initially a municipal responsibility and few cities could stand the cost. Municipalities such as Burnaby and North Vancouver that were bedroom suburbs with a limited and declining tax base went into receivership. Resource towns were also hard pressed. In Prince Rupert relief payments drained the city's coffers until, in 1933, a commissioner replaced the local government.[20] The provincial government faced the same squeeze of declining income and increased demand for expenditure. And the financial problems of governments were only those of individuals writ large. Many who were lucky enough to hold on to work had to make do on a smaller pay cheque. Yet the impact of the depression was not uniformly felt, and not every one was worse off in the 'dirty thirties.' Dropping prices meant that those who still had money found it often went further than it had in the previous decade. While some British Columbians had a higher real income, few escaped the depression of spirit that was caused by the economic disaster, widespread unemployment, and declining expectations.

Though there were those who still doggedly refused to accept the notion, there was a growing realization that people could not solve day-to-day economic and social problems on their own. The doctrine of individual responsibility, which had never helped to pay the rent, now failed even to sustain belief. People turned expectantly to governments for answers, hoping that political leaders could deal with the crisis in capitalism that had thrown so many lives into disarray. The 1930s was a particularly political decade and politicians were seen as potential agents of social reform.[21] In British Columbia, the provincial government was the focus of much of this hope. The municipalities clearly lacked the power and resources to deal with the situation and the federal government seemed distant and remote from everyday concerns. So people looked to Victoria for effective policies. But, as long as Tolmie was in office, they were to be disappointed. As the depression deepened, British Columbians watched, increasingly uncertain and afraid, as Conservatism's clever hopes expired. With such high expectations on the part of the people, it was doubtless easier to be leader of the opposition than of the government in power, but Duff Pattullo was certain of one thing: he could do better than Tolmie.

In order to prove that point, he would have to lead the Liberals back into office, and to do that there were at least three other things he would have to accomplish. First, the provincial Liberal party would have to be reorganized into an efficient political force. With the party machinery broken down and little money to hire mechanics, most of the repairs would have to be done by Pattullo himself. Second, he needed to formulate a policy to deal with the depression. With politics such a popular pastime it seemed that everyone had a solution to the problems of the day, so he needed to steer between the extremes and develop ideas that could actually be put into practice. The third task was to discredit and defeat the Conservatives. With the government growing weaker, Pattullo's job was made easier, but his opponents would not merely curl up and die. Since he could not count on Tolmie's defeating himself, he would have to be a winner. Any one of these tasks would tax the energy and skill of most politicians, and, taken together, all three constituted a formidable challenge.

With all of this work, Pattullo had little time for other things. His personal life still took a distant second place to his profession. By now he described himself as a professional politician and he believed his occupation was an important and honourable one.[22] Since politics would determine the future, he urged other people to take more time to study it, while, for him, his career consumed his life. Lillian remained completely uninterested in politics. According to Duff her nerves were gone and she now had arthritis that got progressively worse. She was sometimes doubled up with pain. After seeing a succession of doctors she was losing hope that her condition would ever improve. When Lillian had a particularly severe bout, Duff wrote to one of his sisters that it 'is too sad that everybody cannot be vulgarly healthy like I am.'[23] The two were a real contrast: Duff was always on the go and out in the world while his wife was often incapacitated and so preferred to stay at home.

Partly for that reason they bought a new house in 1932. In the early 1930s house prices were depressed along with all other sectors of the economy as people with financial problems were anxious to sell. For those who still had money there were some real bargains around. Duff found such a place at 951 Beach Drive: a large grey stone house standing on the rocky shore facing the Strait of Juan de Fuca. The former owner, a senior naval officer, had used a lot of fine wood from old ships in finishing the house. Duff paid $11,500 for the house which was assessed at $15,000, and soon after he took possession he bought two adjacent lots so he could not be built in.[24] Lillian loved the place. They furnished the house with antique furniture and Persian rugs. Her corner bedroom faced the sea from two directions. Often when Duff left for work she would be taking her morning coffee and watching the sunrise. Because of her poor health they could not have house guests as often as Duff, who always enjoyed company, would have liked. Still the new house did have its advantages for him too. He had his own den where he read and worked, with a picture of Wilfrid Laurier on one wall and a splendid photograph of his father with James and George on the opposite side. He enjoyed the mountains and the ocean every morning as he came down to breakfast. Moving from Newport Avenue to Beach Drive also meant he was moving from the back to the front of the Oak Bay golf course. 'How fortunate to be a woman,' he once wrote to a lady friend, 'and have nothing to do but play golf.'[25] The comment revealed a number of attitudes, and it was also somewhat disingenuous, for Duff could never have lived on golf alone. After his early morning round he left the house for work, usually whistling a tune from Harry Lauder.[26] He took great pleasure in tooling along Beach Drive in his brand new Nash sedan to his office in the legislative building, and his good nature lasted all day. Both the drive and the destination were among the joys of his life.

If he found little comfort in being a husband, Duff Pattullo loved being a grandfather. Doris had married Clifford Collison and the first grandchild, Anne, was born in 1927. Elizabeth, the second, was a year old when he became party leader and Clare would arrive in 1935. Duff got a great kick out of the times he spent with his grand-daughters, romping around in the huge attic of the new house or taking them to Beacon Hill Park to feed the ducks. There was a part of Duff that refused to grow up, and spending time with Anne and Beth after the day's work was done enabled him to be a boy again. In 1928 he had purchased a cottage at Saseenos on the Sooke basin. The family spent a good part of the summer there and Duff would drive out for the weekend. According to Duff, Lillian had nothing to do but loaf and there was plenty of room for the kids to play. Duff took the same delight in watching his growing grandchildren learn to swim as he had when Doris went through the same stage in Prince Rupert. It was a place to which he could escape and relax away from the fray, though Doris said her father still talked nothing but politics and golf.[27]

Duff also played an important role within the extended family. He had many acquaintances in the political world, but few close friends. Most of his friends were family. For that reason, the death of his brother James on 5 August 1930, just a little over two months after Duff had been elected provincial leader, was a great shock. Since the war James had practised law in Vancouver with the firm of Pattullo and Tobin. He had never entirely approved of Duff's political career, and continued to give his younger brother fatherly advice, most of which Duff ignored. Yet the two brothers remained buddies as they had been ever since they both came west more than twenty years before. When Duff was in Vancouver on political business he usually took time to play golf with James at the Shaughnessy golf club and then they drank some scotch together. A couple of years earlier, on James's fifty-seventh birthday, Duff had sent him a gift of Heinz's fifty-seven varieties. Now James was gone. He had been ill for six months, but still Duff was shattered by his brother's death.

It also left him the senior male member of the Pattullo family. His older sister, Ethelwyn Ballantyne, had always been the matriarch but Duff took his family responsibilities seriously because he enjoyed them so much. In 1929 he had made a nostalgic trip back to his great-grandfather's land in Caledon where the Pattullos had made a new start a century before. He visited his sisters, Ethelwyn, Pearl, Kate, and Mary, as often as he could when he was in Ontario, where they all lived. And he kept in touch by mail, though Ethelwyn said his letters were 'short and sweet' and rather far between.[28] Being a man's man, Duff saw more of George than he did of his other brothers and sisters. In December 1930, at the end of an eventful year, Duff spent time with George in New York. By now his younger brother was an extremely wealthy man. He had given up writing westerns and war stories, married the daughter of a Texas millionaire, and gone into the milling business with a cousin from Woodstock named Jeff Short. The business expanded through the 1920s and they patented a flour-bleaching process that produced enormous profits. The Short Milling company had plants in Canada and Chicago. When he was not travelling, George resided in an opulent apartment in the Carlyle Hotel in New York; he had a large private yacht in Florida and he rented a river for sport fishing in Norway. When Duff got together with George, he could live the high life for a while. Not all of the family had George's material success. Duff had never made much money and his other surviving brother, Andrew, represented the reverse side of the Pattullo character. He, too, lived in the United States, but was a ne'er-do-well who survived on his wits and handouts from George.

The changes in his family reminded Duff of 'the effluxion of time.' All of his mother and father's family had passed away and he was now in the position that they once were, taking 'daily and perennial pleasure out of my grandkids.'[29] Children arrived to take the place of those who were gone and the family, like politics, endured by renewal. Soon after he was made party leader in British Columbia, in the midst of a federal election campaign, Duff wrote to a cousin to congratulate him on the birth of a son. 'This is an event,' he noted, 'of transcendently more importance than the result of the political campaign.'[30] He knew that there was more to life than politics, and yet it was political life that took up most of his time.

The task of rebuilding the Liberal party in British Columbia and leading the opposition to the Conservative government was a massive one, but if anyone thought Duff Pattullo would be daunted, even for a moment, they reckoned without his endless energy and the immense pleasure he took in his work. He always enjoyed himself as Liberal leader and he certainly maintained his reputation for looking snappy on all occasions. In early 1928 R.H. Pooley, a political enemy with whom Duff was friendly, anticipating the Liberal defeat, predicted that Pattullo might end up as dominion immigration agent in London. 'I can see him in my mind's eye,' said Pooley, 'with his spats, top hat, his monocle and his cane swinging down Picadilly.'[31] Unfortunately for Pooley and the Conservatives, Duff stayed in Victoria and they continued to jest about his appearance. Tolmie was apparently the author of the often repeated remark that 'when Duff gets his plus-fours on and his blue stockings and his niblick, by gosh, he thinks he's the Duke of Kakiack.'[32] Such comments were all a part of the political game in Victoria but his opponents were sadly mistaken if they thought that, because Pattullo cut a dashing figure on the golf course, he did not play or fight hard. He enjoyed himself because he set a cracking pace at work. One morning, soon after he was elected house leader, some people came to the Hotel Vancouver to get an interview with Pattullo, only to discover he was nowhere to be found. At 11:45 he breezed into the lobby 'with his hat on one side, his cane aswing and a cheery smile on his face.' He had been up, he said, and busy doing things since well before 9AM.[33] One still had to be awake early in the morning to stay ahead of Duff Pattullo.

He seemed to flourish as leader of the opposition. He applied his formidable capacity for organization to rebuilding the Liberal party. He was tough but sporting in his attacks on the Conservatives, reminding some of a boxer who loves the game as he goes toe to toe with his opponents, trading massive blows with a smile on his face. As he wrote himself, though 'I fight hard, I feel no animosities, but quite the reverse.' And when the battle was over, even his opponents had to admit that he was 'perhaps the ablest opposition leader the Legislature had ever seen.'[34] Supporters thought he was at the height of his career. He enjoyed being away from the cares of ministerial office and having the freedom to criticize without the responsibility of power. It was not that he had little to do, but that he thrived on work. A friend who had worked with Pattullo in the lands department wrote of him shortly after he became Liberal leader that he would not listen to any talk of obstacles when he wanted something done, with the result that he accomplished things that looked impossible to others.[35]

Completely confident of himself, Pattullo began to remake the British Columbia Liberal party in his own image. He did not wait until his position was confirmed at the convention in 1930, but started the process as soon as he became house leader in

January 1929. He began at the centre and then worked outwards. The party headquarters was under his direct control and run out of Victoria. He rented offices on the sixth floor of the appropriately named Central Building at the corner of Broad and View streets and hired a skeletal staff. The office was managed by Major S.F.M. Moodie, the provincial organizer. Moodie was born in Golden, British Columbia, and had served overseas with the Irish Fusiliers during the First World War. He had a bachelor's degree from McGill University and a Master of Arts in sociology from the University of British Columbia, and he taught at King George high school in Vancouver as well as part time at the university before he became organizer for the provincial Liberal party in 1927.[36] Though he had worked on the disastrous 1928 election, Pattullo correctly felt that the defeat was not Moodie's fault and kept him on. The major was an amiable even frivolous man, good at glad-handing among the party troops, organizing meetings in the ridings, and, under Pattullo's disciplined direction, he also kept the office work moving. In addition to Moodie, there was one secretary at the central office and she was assisted by occasional temporary help. The function of this office was to encourage and guide party work throughout the province. Like every other organization in British Columbia, the Liberal party was strapped for funds, and so for the first couple of years Pattullo paid most of the rent and salaries out of his own pocket. The outlay of thousands of dollars was a financial strain for the leader, but it did mean that no one questioned his right to run the operation.[37]

From his headquarters in Victoria Pattullo also controlled all other aspects of party organization, both at the provincial and the local riding level. The principal Liberal body in the province was the British Columbia Liberal Association, but it consisted only of its executive officers and committees except when it met in convention. There were only two conventions while Pattullo was leader of the opposition: one in June 1930 when he was made leader, and another in October 1932 to adopt a party platform. As long as Pattullo had the support of the majority of the Executive Committee he effectively controlled the association and its related subcommittees.[38]

That is not to say he always got everything he wanted. He had his greatest difficulties with the finance committee. This committee was one of two offshoots of the provincial executive, the other being the organization committee. The finance committee was chaired by A.M. Manson from Prince Rupert, and the other two members were J.W. de B. Farris and Brenton Brown from Vancouver. Though it was obviously difficult to raise money for any purpose in the early 1930s, Pattullo became increasingly exasperated as the finance committee sent only excuses while he had to pay party expenses. There was the cost of the office in Victoria, the outlay for trips all over the province, and Pattullo even paid for air time when he spoke on the radio. He had to tell local Liberal associations there was no central fund they could draw on for work in the ridings.[39] By late 1931 he had been paying party expenses for months.

Earlier in the year he tried to convince his brother George to contribute to the British Columbia Liberal party. He explained he was trying to establish an independent provincial Liberal party that was not beholden to the few who usually controlled Liberal finances. They invariably wanted to run things in the interests of the federal wing of the party and some had written off the provincial party entirely after the defeat in 1928.[40] Badly in need of some help, Duff wrote to George, asking for a reply to his home address by registered mail. George felt it would be improper for an American citizen to give money to a Canadian political party and so declined the invitation to contribute to the British Columbia Liberals. George also thought that Duff was making a mistake by trying to finance the party on his own, and he wondered if there was not 'any honest Liberal money out there which won't expect the favours demanded by the big fellows with whom you are very properly declining to traffic?' When he replied to George's letter, Duff did not answer that question. Instead he argued that a contribution from George would not be read amiss by the public, but would merely be taken as evidence of 'fraternal feeling.'[41] But George remained adamant about political contributions, though he did send Duff the occasional modest 'Christmas present.' In later life, Duff recalled that many Liberals reckoned he could finance the party because he had a wealthy brother, so for him 'having a rich brother was a considerable handicap.'[42] In November 1931, during a crucial by-election battle in the Columbia riding, Moodie wrote from Golden to say he needed more money. Pattullo replied with a personal cheque for $100 and the comment that 'our Central [Finance] Committee is just exactly where it was – nowhere.'[43]

As far as Duff was concerned it was not good enough. He had already told Manson there should be no trouble raising money if they got into it wholeheartedly and it was up to him to whip the party finances into shape.[44] By mid-1932 he was expecting a provincial election at any moment and still the finance committee was not even covering half of the expenses. It was, he wrote, 'a pretty shabby piece of business.' He felt that the leader had quite enough on his shoulders without having to finance the party and he was coming over to Vancouver to deal with the matter. He made it clear he was not interested in discussion that merely pointed out the difficulty of getting funds, 'because the money has to be raised, and it is the duty of the Finance Committee to raise it, and I expect it to do so.'[45] The party's financial position improved after the convention in the fall of 1932, but Pattullo never received enough money to cover expenses.

He was much more successful, in spite of the financial problems, in organizing Liberals in the local ridings. This work was also directed from the Central Building in Victoria. The office was a clearing house for information and from it Pattullo and Moodie encouraged and guided the work at the local level.[46] Pattullo began organizing the party forces by appointing an agent in every locality. In polling divisions too small to have a Liberal association these persons would be designated 'keymen' or 'poll captain.' As he told Liberal members of the legislature, 'Such a person may rest assured that the Liberal party, when the opportunity occurs, will not be ungrateful for his efforts.'[47] These party workers were to be responsible for organization at the local level and, in particular, making sure that the voters' list was kept up to date.

The provincial voters' list was a constant preoccupation. In

British Columbia anyone who failed to vote in an election had their name struck off the list. Moreover, with such a mobile population, people were constantly moving into different ridings while others became eligible to vote for the first time. Pattullo moved his own vote to Victoria in 1931 because he felt he might be removed from the Prince Rupert list if someone questioned his residence. He would then be ineligible to stand as a candidate.[48] Both Pattullo and Moodie were concerned that in most ridings there were more voters on the federal list than the provincial one, which implied they were missing potential supporters. Apparently many people assumed that if their name were on the federal list they would also be able to vote provincially.[49] It was up to party workers, rather than official enumerators, to see that the names of supporters were added to the provincial list, so it became a partisan operation. Moodie told local workers to 'use their own judgement' about sending enrolment forms to those of doubtful party loyalty.[50] Every year, beginning in 1930, Pattullo anticipated the possibility of a provincial election and urged his workers to gather as many applications for enrolment as they could by the April deadline for the Court of Revision. He wanted the constituencies to compete with each other to see which one enrolled the most voters in proportion to its size.[51] This drive was very successful in many ridings. In Vancouver, for example, they added more than twenty thousand new names to the list by May 1932. Then the government cancelled the lists for Vancouver and Victoria and the work in those ridings had to begin all over again. Because Pattullo thought the cancellation might herald an early election, he wrote to the ridings once again to urge them to renewed efforts on the voters' lists.[52]

The work done out of the Central Building was fundamental to rebuilding the party, but Pattullo knew there were limits to what could be achieved by remote control from an office in Victoria. The ridings, particularly those in the outlying areas, had to be visited as often as possible. Beginning in 1929, he tried to visit the entire province every other year. He made shorter trips in the in-between years, so in 1930 and 1932 he spent more time on organization in Victoria. As with everything else, when he was on the road he set a gruelling pace. He would sometimes be away for weeks: visiting a new place, attending a different meeting, and making another speech every day. In September and October 1929, for example, his itinerary called for him to be in seventeen towns in the Kootenays and southern interior in seventeen days. In 1931 he held over seventy meetings throughout the province.[53] He even gave his speeches rapidly, as if he had a lot to get across and limited time in which to do it. Stenographers reckoned he spoke at 200 to 280 words a minute. Fortunately his speeches also had the merit of being short.[54]

Duff enjoyed these tours. He still liked to get out among the people, to rally the rank and file, and to relax with the local boys around the poker table when the day was done. Once, during a speech at Sooke, he took the attorney-general to task for recommending to Ottawa that the grand jury system be abolished. A man in the audience interjected that Pattullo had once advocated that very policy. Duff said he could not remember it, and agreed to a wager that he would put on a community dance if he were proved wrong. It turned out that fourteen years earlier Farris had introduced a recommendation to abolish grand juries, which Duff had supported on a division. So he paid for a dance at Sooke for three hundred people. Everyone had a great time and Pattullo felt that the event 'excited more comment than all the principles for which we have been fighting for years. I think they were delighted to catch my memory at fault.'[55] He also loved to get after opposing members of the legislature when he was in their own ridings. In August 1932 he wrote to a friend that he was looking forward to two weeks in the Okanagan. Since the area was represented by three Conservative ministers, and he intended to attack all three, he expected 'we will probably have some amusement.' A party press release added that 'it is understood that Mr. Pattullo will handle these gentlemen without gloves.'[56]

Whether he was on the road or in Victoria, he preferred to keep out of local squabbles, say, over the nomination of a candidate for the next election. He argued that if he attempted to interfere with every local situation the Liberals would soon be in the same state of disunity as the Conservatives. Of course, not every Liberal in British Columbia was thrilled with his leadership and he could not avoid running into some of the disaffected. In Qualicum, during the summer of 1931, he had to deal with a Liberal who objected to the party leader coming into 'his district' without letting him know in advance. Duff met him on the golf course and got an earful of how the local man had no use for him. Pattullo refused to get excited and the next day his critic apologized and said that, notwithstanding his feelings for the leader, he would do all he could for the party.[57] Mostly Pattullo tried to avoid such situations. When local disputes threatened the party's standing, he sent Moodie in as the troubleshooter from the central office. He was, however, clear that the functioning of party organization took precedence over the opinions of individual officers, and they would soon have to fight an election that would involve issues greater than the candidature of any one Liberal.

When he was unable to reach the people in person, he spoke to them through the press or on the radio. If the newspaper was the great mass media of the 1920s, radio was the new medium of the 1930s and Pattullo used both to good effect. He could usually count on the support of two of the four major dailies in Vancouver and Victoria. The *Victoria Times* was unflagging in its advocacy of the Liberal position, while the *Vancouver Sun*, under its forthright owner-editor Robert Cromie, was somewhat less dependable. The Conservatives had no such worries about the *Vancouver Province* and the *Victoria Colonist*. Pattullo told those British Columbia Liberals who thought that Cromie was unreliable, not to worry. He was convinced that, when it came to a provincial election campaign, the *Sun*'s editor would support the party.[58] And his expectation was not based on mere blind faith, it was rather the product of hard work. Pattullo kept pumping information and press releases onto the news desks of the province's newspapers. The unmistakable Pattullo touch was evident in the colourful language of these releases, particularly when they referred to the Tolmie administration under which 'the wild orgy of expenditure and the tinsel parade continues.' Once, in extreme frustration with the government, he wondered aloud: 'How long is this serious burlesque to continue?'[59] But he could not do all the writing, so in the case of the *Sun*, he had Norman Senior of the editorial department on retainer to write favourable articles. He also let Cromie know when he felt his statements were not being given sufficient prominence.[60] Pattullo had enough personal experience in newspaper work to know how to manipulate the established media.

He was also one of the first politicians in British Columbia to use radio, the new form of communication. Sometimes he broadcast as often as once a week. The 1931 session of the house ended, appropriately enough, on 1 April and Pattullo immediately began a series of radio addresses. Since he was not necessarily talking to the converted he tried to avoid partisan speeches. The first of these speeches was on the University of British Columbia and the importance of higher education. He argued the need to make the university open to as many as possible. He rejected the view that education equalled training students to make money and said its function was rather to build character and to teach young people to think lucidly. These talks produced more publicity when they were reported and commented upon in the press.[61] Evidently not all of these addresses were quite so benign towards the government as Pattullo thought. Bruce Hutchison described the talks as a barrage by air. 'Once a week at 7:00 p.m. Daddy Duff told harrowing bedtime stories over the radio about the Tolmie Government, in terms which seemed brutally designed to keep the electors awake all night.' Still, as far as Pattullo could tell, his radio addresses were favourably received.[62] But, just in case there were any misguided people who continued to support Tolmie, once they were over he then went forth into the province in person again.

Pattullo's pace was relentless, and by the end of 1931 there were signs that his efforts were beginning to pay off. The clearest indication of a turn in the tide was the Columbia by-election on 19 December. After the 1928 election there was the usual round of by-elections as newly appointed cabinet ministers resigned to have their position confirmed by their electorate. Since then all four other by-elections had gone Conservative. Three of the four were uncontested by the Liberals, but one resulted in the loss of a Liberal seat. When Ian Mackenzie resigned to go to Ottawa, a by-election was called in North Vancouver for 5 November 1930. It came soon after the Conservative victory in the federal election and at first Pattullo suggested they would not run a candidate. Inevitably the Liberal who was finally selected was much less prominent than Mackenzie. Under these circumstances a Liberal defeat was not surprising. Though he did not win the by-election, the organizational lesson was not lost on Pattullo. In his view they were beaten because the Conservatives had put six hundred new names on the voters' list while the Liberals had not added any.[63] With the departure of one, the apostles were down to eleven and Duff could not afford to lose another.

To eliminate any doubts about his leadership and his reorganization of the party, Pattullo would have to win the next by-election in a Liberal riding. The opportunity came with the death of the Liberal member for Columbia in October 1931. The contest was called for 19 December and Tolmie thought the Liberals might throw in the sponge once more.[64] Even some Liberals agreed, arguing they could not afford to lose again. But now Pattullo was ready, and determined to show that hard organizational work would bring political results. He sent Moodie back to his home town of Golden in early November to manage the operation. Moodie reported back that their candidate, Thomas King, was a good man but seemed to be overconfident. The outcome was by no means a foregone conclusion. The best that Moodie could say was that it would be 'a good dog fight.' They would have to overwhelm the opposition with meetings and he asked that Pattullo and several other prominent Liberals come up to speak.[65] Pattullo was in the riding for several days and fairly confident of the outcome. Yet it was still a relief, and a vindication, when the result came in and the Liberals had won. 'It was,' said Pattullo, 'a glorious victory' which looked to him like the beginning of the end of the Conservatives.[66] Tolmie admitted that 'we got Hell licked out of us at Golden' but still thought that a by-election score of four out of five was not too bad.[67] The premier perhaps had the last laugh when, six months later, he eliminated the Columbia riding altogether in a redistribution. Duff was very angry, and could hardly conceive how any government could take such despicable action.[68] The Columbia by-election nevertheless marked a significant turn in his political fortunes.

There was a further indication of renewed organizational vigour when Pattullo called a party convention for the first week of October 1932. This time it was held in Vancouver, which made it expensive for delegates from far-flung areas to attend. Pattullo was concerned that there would not be enough representation from the interior and the north and urged Liberals in all areas to send strong representatives.[69] He also had to deal with the scepticism of those like Alex Manson who thought that party conventions served little useful purpose other than as a safety valve for letting off steam. In the event the convention was a great success, and Manson later admitted he had been mistaken and regretted his absence.[70] According to Norman Senior, at least, its outstanding feature was the extraordinary attendance. The ballroom of the Hotel Georgia was packed with over five hundred enthusiastic delegates. As Pattullo put it after it was over, 'It was almost of a religious fervour.'[71] There were ringing endorsements of Pattullo's leadership as he promised to grapple with 'the forces of reaction.' Ian Mackenzie urged the party, which was clearly charged for the electoral battle, to stand by 'old Duff.' Amidst the wild applause, the Scottish-born Mackenzie exhorted Pattullo to 'Lay on old Duff, and damned be he who first cries hold enough.'[72]

Mackenzie's paraphrase of the last words of the doomed king perhaps gave some Liberals pause. In British Columbia it seemed that the forces of Liberalism were on the move, arrayed to triumph over tyranny, and to some observers this militancy was in marked contrast to the inertia in Ottawa. In the same issue of the *Vancouver Sun* where the excitement at the provincial convention was front-page news, Robert Cromie wrote an editorial headed 'Mackenzie King Is Through.' Cromie's assessment of King as national Liberal leader was scathing and hard, but not entirely inaccurate, and it was surely no accident that it was published on the day that five hundred party delegates began their meeting in Vancouver. According to the editor of the *Sun*, King's political usefulness had ended because he was too set and stodgy to respond to changing times. His 'inert policy of "do nothing" is utterly in conflict with the present temper of the Canadian people.' While Liberalism was surging forward all over the world, King was 'living in a groove as deep and narrow as a political grave.' Fortunately, as far as Cromie was concerned, the 'march of Liberalism cannot be hampered or hindered by the inertia of the isolated recluse of Kingsmere.'[73] Cromie was not alone among Liberals in his views, but such criticisms did not prompt King to think again. For King, the most important thing that happened at the British Columbia convention was the pro forma endorsement of his leadership of the national party.[74] The fact that there was now a renewed provincial party with a vigorous set of policies was of no consequence compared to King's overwhelming preoccupation: himself. Ideas, other than his own, were insignificant, and his critics were simply consigned to a growing list of permanent enemies. Thus, R.B. Bennett was 'the worst bounder' that King had ever come across, with 'the possible exception of Cromie of Vancouver.'[75] For his part, Pattullo rejected suggestions from within the party that he should respond to the *Sun* editorial, arguing that it would do no good and might be harmful. He was certainly following King's advice, given just after the 1930 federal election, that 'each province will have to work out its own salvation,' and perhaps he thought the national leader should do the same.[76]

The Vancouver convention of the British Columbia Liberal Association not only demonstrated the organizational vigour of the Pattullo party, it also indicated the policy directions he was taking. He did not believe that the policy adumbrated by the convention should be too specific, in a way that would tie the hands of the leader. He was bound to oppose any effort 'to build a platform of chimerical planks, which can only land us in trouble without accomplishing anything.'[77] He rather thought there should be a declaration of those overriding principles that the party stood for. Even if only in a general way, the convention endorsed the ideas Pattullo had been advocating since he became leader and, here too, the tenor of things was very different from Ottawa. For, in contrast to the cautious conservatism of Mackenzie King, Duff Pattullo was a reformist Liberal.

Pattullo's reformism was not, as some have suggested, conceived out of the chaos of the early 1930s.[78] His ideas and policies had deep roots that went back to his father's association with the Liberal government of Oliver Mowat in late nineteenth-century Ontario. They were nurtured in the small, dependent resource towns of the northern frontier and invigorated during the early years of British Columbia's first Liberal government. He frequently referred to the social legislation passed under Brewster and Oliver after 1916, and he indicated that he would continue in that reform tradition.

At the same time he was in no doubt that the depression called for extraordinary measures. Since becoming leader of the opposition, Pattullo had taken more time for reading and thinking, particularly on economic matters, than he had done when he was a minister. He subscribed to a number of economic journals and newspapers and was a keen observer of what was going on in other parts of the world. He was also fed information and ideas by those around him, though he drew selectively on this input. The ubiquitous Gerry McGeer is one who has been credited with too much influence on Pattullo.[79] McGeer favoured Pattullo, as he did Mackenzie King, with lengthy letters explaining his mystical monetary message. McGeer believed, with all the enthusiasm of the newly converted, in the notion that government should take absolute control of banking and credit. Pattullo may have sympathized with some of the general directions McGeer was taking, but, like John Maynard Keynes, he definitely did not think Gerry was correct in every particular. Indeed, Duff was sometimes irritated by these long lectures by letter, feeling, for instance, that he did not need a primer from McGeer on the distinction between money and credit. So, while the McGeer ego may have taken vaguely positive noises to mean blanket approval, it is an exaggeration to say that Duff 'had endorsed his theories.' On the contrary, he thought many of McGeer's proposals were quite unrealistic.[80] Pattullo's own ideas, though not unique, were his own, and he certainly knew the difference between righteous nonsense, even when it was forcefully argued, and practical politics.

Duff Pattullo firmly believed many of the problems of the day could be solved by an active, interventionist state. In an increasingly complex society there had to be some influence that could reconcile conflicting interests in the general good. Such reconciliation could only be achieved 'through collective authority and that authority is the state.'[81] Liberalism, broadly defined, was in the best position to use the power of the state in the interests of the greatest number of people because, in Pattullo's mind, it would preserve the greatest measure of individual freedom and initiative while meeting the requirements of organized society. According to Duff, the old adage of 'Every man for himself and the devil take the hindmost simply means that the devil is going to get everybody.' Clearly, in the context of the depression, someone had to take action to help people who could not help themselves, and Pattullo believed only the state had the power to act effectively. 'Governments,' he said, 'must take the initiative, and have the courage to do it.'[82]

By using the power of the state to achieve reform, Pattullo intended to walk a middle path between the extremes of the right and the left. On the one hand, the Tolmie Tories continued to represent the self-interest of the few. Concerned primarily, according to Pattullo, for the welfare of the business class, they 'hope to maintain the status-quo for a few people that have, while everyone else has to tighten his belt.' They refused to adapt old institutions to new needs and, though they sometimes described their policies as innovative, they were, in fact, 'as old as ... the methods of the cave man.' The government of British Columbia should now offer something more than a policy of 'to the victors belong the spoils.'[83] It should mediate between the various classes rather than serving the interests of one. Partly for that reason, he also rejected socialist solutions, though he was never as alarmed by the radical left as he was by the reactionary right. Liberal reform, he believed, would prevent people, frustrated with the unresponsiveness of the Conservatives, from advocating revolutionary change. Society had been drifting more in the direction of communal effort, but that did not mean that communism would work, for while the community might control the people's bodies, it could only affect, and not control, the soul. Human nature would still be human nature, he argued, and individuals would still be acquisitive. Thus, when the Co-operative Commonwealth Federation came upon the political scene, he dismissed its policies as 'undiluted Socialism, that is, Government ownership of all resources and all activities.' He was clear and definite on the point that 'we cannot tolerate or permit starvation in our midst.' At the same time, he was equally adamant that socialism did not provide the answer.[84]

He did not propose any radical upheaval of the system, but rather asserted that there had to be a thoroughgoing reform of capitalism in order to ensure its continued survival. Increasingly through 1932 and 1933 he talked about 'socialised capitalism,' by which he meant that capital would have to 'recognize both the duty and the desirability of giving larger consideration to the needs and welfare of society generally.' As he explained to Robert Cromie: 'If we are to continue to enjoy the individualism which is now ours, we must be prepared to carry not only our own burden, but the burden of others unable to carry the load.'[85] Like many economists of the day, Pattullo believed that capitalism could only be preserved by a redistribution of wealth, though his conclusions were based on wide experience rather than deep learning.[86] He once responded to one of McGeer's superficially erudite letters on the state of the economy with a brief analogy that he, along with many other people, could understand. 'In the old national game of poker,' he wrote, 'when one man got all the chips, the game stopped, unless there was a redistribution of the chips, or a new medium substituted. I have seen the boys play for beans. In this great economic poker game, both currency and credit have gravitated to limited sources, and the people have lost purchasing power.'[87] Thus, as he was fond of saying, his objective was not to change the game but to redistribute the chips.

Many of these general ideas that Pattullo had been developing found more specific expression in the resolutions passed at the Liberal convention in October 1932. The party called for a thorough review of the whole financial structure of the province and suggested that 'national credit' should be used to put purchasing power back in the hands of the people and reduce unemployment. Pattullo also favoured the formation of an economic council to examine the provincial economy and to advise government on policy. The whole area of municipal taxation and revenue should be investigated with a view to establishing a more equitable distribution between the municipalities and the province. The various levels of government were urged to co-operate in a program of public works to stimulate the economy. The province should build and improve highways and make every effort to expand the tourist trade. Given the high level of unemployment, consideration should be given to shorter hours of work, and the Department of Labour should work with industry to find ways to extend employment to more people. Every encouragement should be given to agriculture, particularly by establishing marketing boards. At the time, Pattullo was also advocating a back-to-the-land movement. State health insurance should be introduced as soon as possible. And it was resolved that the federal government be requested to appoint a royal commission to investigate the extent to which British Columbia had been disadvantaged within Confederation. Here, in rough outline, was the plan of action that Pattullo would take to the people of British Columbia.[88]

The convention resolutions were, necessarily in Pattullo's view, somewhat less than precise, but he continued to elaborate and expound upon them in the twelve months that led up to the next provincial election. If any of his program were to go into effect, then he had to get into power, and that meant not offending or frightening voters unnecessarily. He also needed some flexibility to move with the rapidly changing times. As he took his political medicine show on the road he wanted to be sure he would have the right remedy for whatever the malady. What he was offering at this stage was not 'Pattullo's Pink Pills for Pale Persons' but rather 'Pattullo's Palatable Pills for Poor People.'[89]

He also knew that winning the next election would depend, not so much on the credibility of his policies, as on discrediting the opposition. He did not agree with some advisers who said he did not need a constructive program because governments usually defeat themselves rather than being beaten by the opposition.[90] He did, however, clearly understand that the best form of defence was attack. And mounting devastating assaults on his political opponents was very much Pattullo's forte. Indeed, many at the time thought it was what he did best when he was leader of the opposition.

There was no doubt he was assisted by the government itself, which presented an easy if shifting target. Tolmie cannot be blamed for lacking the gift of prophecy and, as it turned out, he probably inherited an impossible situation. But he had few political skills other than an amiable disposition and he only succeeded in making a bad situation worse. He spent his term as premier blundering about looking for solutions to problems that would defeat many a politician more capable than he before the decade was out. Before the magnitude of the depression was apparent he said he would increase spending, then in the early 1930s he applied retrenchment across the board. In addition to being contradictory, neither approach worked, and Tolmie grew more and more desperate.

Meanwhile Pattullo never let up. There was nothing subtle in his approach, no adroit manoeuvres or tricky tactics. It was just a straightforward, all out, frontal assault. He was particularly effective in the house, where his speeches were forceful, trenchant, and scathing. He improved immeasurably as an orator while he was in opposition. He gave clear notice of his intentions in his first speech after being made house leader. His reply to the address from the throne was one of the best he had made, according to Bruce Hutchison. He began in a gentle, low-key way by offering congratulations all around to those in the new parliament. He then ascended in easy stages 'from a tone of courteous skepticism' towards the government 'to an effective crescendo of denunciation.'[91] Tolmie was away ill when Pattullo spoke, but Duff had discovered that the minister of finance, W.C. Shelly, had secretly handed the exclusive right to sell provincial bonds over to a private company, and so he used that piece of folly for the climax of his speech. He moved a resolution deploring the move which was, of course, voted down, yet it made the point effectively. Several times, in a deliberate slip of the tongue, he referred to the government as the opposition – just out of habit, he said with a smile. It was, by all accounts, a command performance. Even members opposite were impressed.[92] And they now knew what they were in for.

From the day of that first speech as Liberal leader, members looked forward to his harangues with either fear or favour, and whenever Pattullo rose once more to berate the Tolmie administration the galleries were full. If his speeches were assaults on the government position, then words were his weapons, and he took particular joy in them. He liked to dredge the dictionary for a new words or phrases, which he kept as arrows in a quiver ready to fire across the floor of the house at the appropriate moment. He spoke of the 'oleaginous saponicity' of the government. Or, in the same vein, he claimed that, whereas under the Liberals the people's economic bread was 'spread with good political butter,' now we 'see the economic bread of our people oleomargarined with the grease of the party machine.' The 1932 Conservative budget speech was delivered in a great hurry as if the minister wanted to get it off his chest. And little wonder, said Pattullo, for how could he possibly hold down 'a so unctuous and pharisaical homily.' In another mood he referred to the 'financial Pegasus driven by Tolmie' being in a wild, unstoppable flight.[93] He always had great fun reading from the election speeches of cabinet ministers and when he came to an especially incongruous section he would intone it out while waving the pages aloft in mock heroics. He was particularly fond of the remark made by the minister of labour, William McKenzie, that under the Conservatives 'the trees will be filled with fruit and the streams with fish.'[94] Members on the other side quickly learned not to tangle with Pattullo in banter across the floor unless their wits were as nimble as his. Certainly the ponderous Tolmie was no match for him. During the first session under the Conservatives, as Pattullo was in full flight, Tolmie asked what he expected of the government after only six months. The opening was a mile wide. We expected nothing, shot back Pattullo, 'and we are getting nothing.'[95]

Pattullo was well armed to strike telling blows against the

government. Only a handful of members had been in the house as long as he had and none could equal his mastery of parliamentary procedure. With their big majority, the Conservatives could always outvote him but Pattullo was seldom outmanoeuvred by tactics in the legislature. Nor could he be tired out, any more than he could be talked down. During the first session the government members tried to teach Pattullo a lesson by keeping the house up past midnight. But next morning he was there looking fresher than they were, and as sharp and critical as ever.[96] After twelve years in government he had more detail at his fingertips than most of the Conservative cabinet. He thought he was particularly well placed to comment on the government's policy in the first couple of years since it simply followed the Liberal example. All the new cabinet had done, he said, was 'hang up their hats in our old offices and carry out our policies.'[97] Through the growing Liberal party organization he had people at the local level provide him with information about alleged Conservative mismanagement: political ammunition that was stored away for future use. He could use heavy artillery against the government's major initiatives, while peppering away with small arms fire on minor issues.

One such issue that was usually minor, but sometimes became major, was patronage. Political payoffs in the form of government appointments were an enduring feature of provincial politics, and one that was all the more keenly watched in a time of high unemployment. Much to the annoyance of many members of his own party, Tolmie took the view that there ought not to be a wholesale turnover in government positions when he came to power.[98] Yet, at the same time, he managed to undermine this high-minded approach with a few well-publicized firings of Liberal appointees. The biggest furore came when W.C. Shelly dismissed Norman Watt, the government agent in Prince Rupert. Watt was, of course, relieved of his position largely because of his close association with Pattullo and he was certainly not politically neutral. There was hurried correspondence between Pattullo and Watt to make sure that certain letters did not fall into government hands. Duff assured his friend that he destroyed 'letters that came to me from time to time from various sources' as a matter of course and there had been a 'general cleaning out' when he left the lands department.[99] Publicly, however, he was outraged by the dismissal and the accompanying slur on Watt's reputation. And he turned the specific case into a general issue, saying that the Conservatives had always looked on the control of government as 'a potlatch for the benefit of supporters.' Pattullo kept the matter alive in the house. He forced Shelly into shifting his ground, or in plain language 'lying,' and, to get out of the situation, the government set up an inquiry into the matter. Pattullo planned to use the investigation to put Shelly on trial. There had been a lot of scrappy, low-level debate, and, sitting on the government side of the House, Pat Maitland wrote that if the whole issue 'never comes up again it will be too soon.'[100] But it came back sooner than that. During the next session Pattullo continued to press the issue, until finally Tolmie made a statement in the house that reflected the findings of the board of inquiry and completely exonerated Watt.

Pattullo could catch the government napping on particular cases, but naturally he could not convince Tolmie to change his mind on major policies. In fact, as he wrote to an acquaintance in 1931, the government usually did the opposite of what he recommended, and that, he added, 'is the reason it is in so much trouble.'[101] The budget speech, along with the speech from the throne, were the major opportunities during the session for Pattullo to make 'recommendations' to Tolmie. Here too, he was assisted by the government's uncertainty about what financial course to follow.

Initially the Conservatives seemed to want to do very little in the area of fiscal policy. Tolmie's first minister of finance was W.C. Shelly, who was living proof of the Pattullo adage that a successful businessman did not necessarily make a successful politician. Shelly brought in two do-nothing budgets that failed to offer any relief to the people facing economic crisis. According to Pattullo, the only new expenditure was on studies of the province's financial situation. He thought these innumerable commissions were completely unnecessary since the government had said it 'knew all about everything' before it came into office.[102] Just as there was no new spending there was no relief from taxation in either budget. After Shelly's second effort during the 1930 session, even some Conservatives were unimpressed. Maitland observed that if 'finances were automobile collisions,' then Shelly 'would be an expert on accidents.'[103] Pattullo did not expect Shelly to present another budget, though politically it would have been better for the Liberals had he stayed on. Before the end of the year Tolmie had another finance minister, and he was made of sterner stuff.

Shelly's replacement was J.W. Jones, the Okanagan member who gave the impression he had learned his economics at a roadside fruit stall. He believed he could balance the province's books by opening for fewer hours, firing staff, and charging customers another 1 per cent. After a quick assessment of the provincial finances, Jones concluded it was 'imperative that economy must be exercised until it hurts.'[104] True to his word, his first budget was extremely painful. Jones's 1931 economic blueprint proposed to cut spending severely and to raise taxes as well. As he delivered the budget speech, his colleagues were 'about as cheerful as a hold up gang closely watched.' Rolf Bruhn, the minister of public works, sent a note up to Maitland which read, 'this looks like a funeral.' To which Maitland replied, 'It is.'[105] For many British Columbians, the most pernicious part of Jones's first budget was a 1 per cent surtax on all income over a basic minimum. Employers were compelled to take the amount out of wages which, as Pattullo put it, turned every employer into a tax collector. The finance minister was thereafter known as 'one percent Jones,' while Duff developed a new formula for attacking Conservative economic policy. He pointed out that it would, for example, take the contributions of 3000 working women under the new surtax to pay the recent increase in the salary of the three-man liquor board. Or, alternatively, it would require the 1 per cent tax on the wages of 1200 girls to pay the salary and expenses of the new agent-general in London. As Pattullo saw it, Jones was putting the burden of government profligacy on the poor people.[106]

Since his cabinet seemed unable to come up with a satisfactory economic policy, Tolmie turned to advisers from the private sector. When a delegation of high-powered businessmen presented themselves in Victoria as willing and able to advise his government on financial and other matters, Tolmie accepted their offer. The leader of the group seemed to be H.R. MacMillan, another successful businessman who was politically naïve, but it was George Kidd, a director of a Vancouver investment firm and former president of the British Columbia Power Corporation, who became chairman of the inquiry. The Kidd Commission was established in April 1932. It planned to work fast and was given 'every assistance' by the government, including complete access to its records. Fortunately for him, Tolmie did reserve the right to reject any of the commission's recommendations.[107] The commission's first mandate was to investigate provincial finances, and then, arising out of its critique of economic policy, it made suggestions for a thorough overhaul of the political system.

On financial matters the commissioners were Robin Hoods in reverse: they wanted to steal from the poor and give to the rich. Since the provincial deficit was still climbing and there was no more room for increased taxation, the Kidd Commission advocated ruthless cutting of government services and programs. It started at the top, by suggesting that the number of members in the legislature be reduced from forty-eight to twenty-eight, and wanted the government to cut more deeply from there on down. The salaries and number of civil servants would be reduced and certain government departments amalgamated. The report recommended an end to free education after the age of fourteen, savage cuts in teachers' salaries, withholding the grant to the University of British Columbia altogether, wholesale reductions in welfare services, repeal of the minimum wage, replacing the provincial police in most areas by the Royal Canadian Mounted Police which was funded by the federal government, selling the Pacific Great Eastern railway, and the cessation of all public works except road maintenance.[108] The recommended economies were too much even for Tolmie to swallow and the government rejected most of Kidd's suggestions. The problem was that, while the commissioners may have been naïve, they were not kidding.[109] Tolmie offended big business by rejecting the commission's suggestions at the same time as he outraged other social groups by appearing to consider them.

The Kidd Commission did not confine itself to economic matters and offered political advice which Tolmie found more to his taste. According to the commissioners, the economic woes of the province were a consequence of the extravagance of the party system. Political parties run by professional politicians competed with each other for support by spending ever larger amounts of money on government programs and patronage. Parties, therefore, so the argument went, by definition precluded the application of sound business principles to public finance. Cutting the size of the legislature was supposed to reduce the influence of local interest. The report proposed to undermine another fundamental principle of responsible government by advocating that the federally appointed lieutenant-governor be given the power to withhold consent to expenditure. The Kidd Commissioners also favoured the idea of a coalition government. The notion was that by bringing the best available talent, regardless of party, into government there would be a much greater chance of developing solutions to the province's problems.

Pattullo was annoyed as the commission deliberated because he was not given access to their findings, then his irritation turned to anger when he did hear what it had to say. In July 1932 the government was leaking results of the commission's work to the press and Pattullo tried, without success, to obtain the report. Tolmie finally sent him a copy on 30 August, the day it was made public.[110] Duff read the document and concluded that a number of the commissioners' recommendations 'were weird, and showed their entire ignorance of governmental problems.'[111] He would have agreed with University of British Columbia professor Henry Angus, who commented that the report showed that 'businessman are not economists,' and Pattullo would have added that they are not politicians either.[112] As far as he was concerned it was just another ploy by the business interests who had supported the Conservatives to take power by another means. The reactionary and autocratic tendencies he had always seen within big business must have been confirmed when the *British Columbia Financial Times* suggested replacing the present system of government with a dictatorship.[113] There are always those, he observed, 'who think that a benevolent autocracy would be more efficient than our present democratic institutions, and doubtless there may be some who would prefer the autocracy without benevolence,' but that did not mean the people should be denied representation simply because the province faced a crisis.[114] The crisis was, after all, partly created by the very businessmen who now wanted to run things, for they too had overextended themselves during the years before the crash.

Few publicly expressed views as extreme as those of the *Financial Times*, but there was plenty of noisy clamour for a coalition government in 1932 and 1933. The notion that government should be formed out of a coalition of interests rather than competition among parties continued to be widely held in British Columbia. For more than thirty years after British Columbia became a province there were no parties in the traditional sense in the legislature, and even after party lines were established in 1903 the possibility of returning to some form of non-party government still flowed as a strong undercurrent in provincial politics. Now it surfaced and became a part of the mainstream. Advocates of the idea pointed out that a coalition government in the national interest had been formed in Britain in 1931. So why not in British Columbia? There were calls from all over the province for an end to party politics. The Rotary Club of Prince Rupert resolved that 'party government has got to be discarded sooner or later: and in the case of B.C., the sooner the better.' Tolmie was well aware of the strong support 'on the part of many of our substantial people' for some form of union government.[115] But the loudest and most public cries for an end to political parties came from the Conservative press.

While the Kidd Commission was still deliberating, the *Vancouver Province* began a vigorous editorial campaign in support of a coalition. The newspaper could no longer support the Tolmie government and it could not, of course, favour the Liberals. So the editor argued that neither party, nor for that matter the party system itself, was acceptable. There was little difference between the two parties, the *Province* asserted, except that one was in and the other was out, and there had to be something better than this 'scrummage of "ins" and "outs." ' The fact that the Tolmie government was ineffective was no reason to bring in 'Mr. Pattullo and his unregenerate lot.'[116] The way out of this political impasse that the right wing had manufactured in its own mind was to bring an end to party politics by the formation of a coalition government. In other words, now that the Conservatives were losing the game, they wanted to change the rules.

Under such pressure, Tolmie was persuaded to pursue the coalition idea. The concept was not new to him since he had served in a Union government when he first went to Ottawa in 1917. He canvassed opinion in his own party, and in the business community, both on the west coast and in the east, and then announced he would try to form a union government. For a while he must have thought he had found the solution to his political problems as letters and messages supporting his decision flooded in.[117] He twice invited Pattullo to join him in a coalition government: first in September 1932 and again in March 1933. There were behind-the-scenes efforts to convince other Liberals to climb aboard. The debate became very intense and the attacks on Pattullo in the *Province* grew more strident. For Pattullo, there were great political dangers in these developments. If the idea of forming a coalition really took hold, and particularly if there was much support for it among Liberals, he could be made to appear as a narrow partizan defending the interests of his own party rather than those of the people of British Columbia.

Characteristically, though, Pattullo spent very little time cogitating on the intricacies of the political situation. At one level it was simply a matter of True Grit: a Liberal he was born and a Liberal he would die. His position was clear from the start and he did not waver. He flatly rejected any suggestion he might join a coalition, and he made it clear that any other Liberal who joined with Tolmie was no longer a Liberal as far as the provincial party was concerned. In the midst of the coalition battle, at the Liberal convention, Ian Mackenzie had urged both

Pattullo and the party on to victory with a reference to Macbeth. Duff himself was partial to some lines from the ancient days of Caledon:

> Come one, come all! this rock shall fly
> From its firm base as soon as I.[118]

For Pattullo, there was neither rhyme nor reason to joining with the Conservatives. He was convinced that the idea of coalition came almost entirely from business interests who, realizing that the Tolmie government was thoroughly discredited, now wanted to dominate a new administration. 'What they want is control, regardless of the name of the administration.'[119] He quickly dismissed the comparison with Great Britain as irrelevant to British Columbia. In the old country the call for coalition had arisen out of a political stalemate where no party had a clear majority. In British Columbia, as Pattullo constantly pointed out, the government had a three-to-one majority in the legislature. At least in terms of control of the house, there was nothing stopping the Conservatives from passing any measure they wanted to introduce. What, he wondered, would be the point of coalescing with a party that 'having the power, so obviously lacks the capacity to intelligently exercise it?'[120] Even more important for Pattullo was his view that the incompetence of the Tolmie government had brought political parties, and even government itself, into disrepute. The party system was not flawless, but it was certainly better than having a 'number of men running around with personal axes to grind.'[121] While there was all manner of currents and cross-currents running through provincial politics, to Pattullo the situation seemed clear: the Liberal party had to stand firm as an organization and continue to advance progressive policies 'that make for the benefit of all people, but are at the same time safe and sane.' When he had taken over as leader, the Liberal party had had no reason to think it would be in the dominant position it had since achieved, and so it 'would be recreant to its duty to now take any course of action that would largely nullify its usefulness.'[122] His final, largely unstated, but probably most important reason for rejecting the notion of a union government was that he was perfectly confident he could win the next election. There was no point in boarding a sinking ship when his own was sailing into battle with guns ablaze. He could see no logic whatever in the notion that he should join forces with Tolmie.

So Pattullo's replies to the premier's invitations were polite but firm. Tolmie first asked Pattullo to join him in a union government by letter dated 9 September 1932. The missive was brief, and vague except on the point that Tolmie would lead the proposed administration. Pattullo noted that Tolmie had given him no idea of what policies and measures he had in mind that he could not already put through with his large majority. Tolmie had also said nothing about the composition of the house under a union government. In any event, replied Pattullo, Tolmie and he had been at total variance over policy and administration for several years and it did not seem 'reasonable to suppose that these differences could be suddenly reconciled.'[123] Tolmie renewed the invitation in March 1933 and this time Pattullo was rather more pointed in his reply. 'At your time of life and in your condition of health,' he wrote to Tolmie, 'I do not like to speak harshly, yet it seems that this is a time when one should speak bluntly and frankly.' Since this letter came while the house was in session, he reiterated the point that if Tolmie had measures to deal with the current crisis, he should introduce them. 'Instead of dealing with the immediate present, you appear to be mostly concerned as to the possible outcome of the approaching election. I do not share your alarm. In any event,' he continued, 'it is the business of the people to express their wishes.' So the best service Tolmie could do for British Columbia was to call an election and have the issue settled. For some time, Duff had been advising the premier to 'hurry off to the Lieutenant-Governor and resign.'[124]

Sound arguments were only part of Pattullo's defence against coalition. If his views were to have political force, then his party had to be solidly behind him. At this point all the hard work to reorganize the Liberal party and to establish his personal control over it paid off. As the pressure for a coalition began to build, he warned the presidents of all Liberal riding associations that the government's forces were making bold attempts to create dissatisfaction within the Liberal party. These efforts had to be resisted for, as he put it in a radio address, 'if a Party does not follow some sound principles, it becomes a rabble.' Like a general on the eve of battle, he had stirring words for the troops. No doubt there would be disagreements among Liberals and he anticipated that, but he also expected everyone to stand fast, 'both to resist and to refute all designing argument. This is the time to show our mettle. When the conflict is over, let it not be said that there was a single defection from our ranks.'[125] Yet some Liberals were taken in with the idea of union government. In Prince Rupert even some of Pattullo's long-time supporters were 'bubbling over' with the idea and there were whispers that Manson would join the new group. Years later Pattullo claimed that John Hart, George Pearson, and both J.W. de B. and his brother Wendell Farris all privately favoured a coalition.[126] But, in the end, there were few public desertions and the ranks held firm. Many wrote to congratulate their leader on the stand he was taking. The fact that most party members were behind him showed that the provincial party had become Pattullo's party. His control over the party that was so clearly evident by the end of 1932 was to be a crucial factor in the political developments of the next twelve months.

Though 1933 would be a tumultuous and eventful year for Duff Pattullo, it began quietly enough. In January there was a lull before the political storm as he waited for Tolmie to call either an election or a session of the legislature. He celebrated his sixtieth birthday on 19th of the month. He perhaps gave thought during the day to the last sixty years, all that he had done and all he had achieved, and to what the next year might hold in store. Otherwise it seemed like just another day in the life of a politician: it began early on the golf course, he spent the morning at Liberal headquarters greeting callers, the afternoon at the Provincial Seed, Bulb and Potato Show, and the evening at a youth rally in the suburbs.[127] And his outward appearance was not deceiving. Inwardly Pattullo was poised and at ease, at the peak of health, and ready for whatever might follow. Columnist Bruce Hutchison commented, perhaps thinking of Tolmie, that those who feel that the burdens of public life are too great should follow Pattullo's recipe: 'golf before breakfast, a flagon of buttermilk before golf, plenty of work, a good row now and then an unquestioning, childlike faith in the future.'[128] Somewhat to his annoyance, his golf game would deteriorate over the next few months from lack of practice, but not so his political gamesmanship.

The two protagonists, Pattullo and Tolmie, Liberal and Conservative, confident and confused, clashed once more in the legislature during the session of 1933. In January Tolmie decided that, rather than call an election, he would summon the house again on 23 February. Privately, Duff claimed that he could not find the words to describe his disgust with the ineptitude of the government; publicly he was never at a loss for words, so he issued a press statement to tell people 'the truth is that this decrepit and palsied administration is hanging on in desperation, hoping that something may transpire that will save it from burial under an avalanche of public sentiment.'[129] He said the Tolmie government no longer had the moral authority to introduce any measure of importance, and he announced before the session started that he would not be bound in the future by any legislation passed by the Conservatives.

When the session began, Duff was at his best. He knew he had to remain on the offensive. He had been warned that, with the government so weak, the spotlight was on him in the way it is ordinarily on the party in power. He therefore had one of the chief disadvantages of office without any of the advantages.[130] He had to be forthright in opposition, and positive, if not detailed, about what he would do differently. Tolmie, by contrast, was absent because of illness much of the time and he left R.H. Pooley to stage-manage the session. When the premier did speak he seemed to generate as little enthusiasm, even on his own side of the house, as 'cold porridge.'[131] Pattullo felt he should not be too critical of the government since it would be 'too much like flogging a dead horse.' The throne speech merely presented a 'superfluity of words and a paucity of ideas.' Duff thought it was the weakest address from the throne he had heard in seventeen years in the house 'and that is saying something for Addresses.'[132]

The budget was no better. The provincial government was under a lot of political and financial pressure to produce a balanced budget. Sir Thomas White, who was minister of finance when Tolmie first went to Ottawa and was now at the Canadian Imperial Bank of Commerce, sent the premier Christmas greetings, dated 14 January 1933, and then followed up with a jolly little lecture on the need for provincial governments to balance their budgets. In the midst of the session, just days before the budget, R.B. Bennett informed Tolmie that he would not consider any more financial requests from British Columbia until the budget was balanced.[133] Pattullo was increasingly voicing his opinion that British Columbia's budgets were being formulated in the east. Certainly Jones duly produced estimates that balanced, but as far as Pattullo was concerned the balancing act was based on an illusion. He was convinced that, once again, the estimates were padded and, by the minister's own admission, they made no provision for forest protection or unemployment relief. 'The Government,' Duff told the honourable members using an image that some would understand, 'having gone on a prolonged financial jag, is now staggering along before its final fall into the gutter of oblivion.'[134]

Pattullo's speeches in the house were not just negative anti-government tirades. He spoke as well of his own ideas and what he would do if he were in power. During the 1933 budget debate he made it clear that he preferred the example of the New Deal in the United States to the British model of union government. He had been very impressed with Franklin D. Roosevelt's inaugural address a few weeks before in which the new American president had outlined his course of action. Indeed, he thought while listening to the speech that Roosevelt 'must have been reading the platform of the Liberal Party of British Columbia and speeches of leaders of Liberal thought in this Province. The truth is, of course, that it is a coincidence of Liberal thought.' Duff said that, prior to his election, Roosevelt had frequently used the word 'liberal' and it was accepted as it was intended. It was not interpreted, as it was by his opponents in British Columbia, to mean something personal or partisan. He supposed that he, Pattullo, might use some other word. 'I do not exactly care for the word "Democratic" – it sounds harsh, and the word "Progressive" is not sufficiently embracing. The word "Liberal" is broad and spacious. There is harmony of sound and sense in it.' Pattullo also admired Roosevelt because he seemed to be a man of action. There was no union government in the United States and yet the president was getting on with the job of trying to deal with the problems of the depression. And Duff would do the same. 'If I were sitting on the Treasury Benches at this moment, with a three-to-one majority behind me, does anyone imagine that I would either be begging or trying to bludgeon the Opposition to join me in order that I could carry out what I had in mind?'[135]

Tolmie was not in the house for Pattullo's reply to the budget speech, nor was he listening to what he had to say. The premier's second formal offer to join a coalition was made to the leader of the opposition eleven days later and Pattullo rejected it immediately. The week after that Tolmie appeared briefly in the legislature and the pressure showed. The premier was only there because the opposition had refused to grant supply without an indication of the government's policies. He quickly became very irritated and lashed out at Pattullo with uncharacteristic vigour. As Duff told it, the 'Doctor ... said that he had no use for me, that he might go to a dog fight with me, that he did not think that I was a vote-getter, and that the only reason that he had asked me to join his Government was that I was head of the Liberal Party, and he wanted to get the Party's support.' Pattullo replied that last week's invitation to join a union government could only have been a trap that would have resulted in his carrying Tolmie – a leader who could not even control his own government.[136] The members on the floor and those in the galleries watched, fascinated, as the two Titans went at it. The clash was short but brutal and when it was over Tolmie had achieved nothing except clarifying the impossibility of coalition with Pattullo, which suited Duff just fine. As the session ended,

Pat Maitland described his leader as a 'sad man – in a sad plight' while 'Duff as usual finished with a flourish.'[137]

Pattullo had already taken the opportunity of his reply to the budget speech to wish all the members well in the future, as if it were already all over for this government and he would lead the next one. He was quite right, though few shared his confidence at the time and there were to be many twists and turns in the political plot before the next election was over. Tolmie procrastinated as developments moved further and further beyond his grasp. The session ended on 7 April without any indication of an election date. The legislature was dissolved on 1 August and still the writs had not been served. Pattullo waited in frustration, just as he had done in 1916, for the Conservatives to name the day. He proposed a constitutional change to end this dubious practice of governments hanging on to power after the legislature had legally expired. Technically it meant that the people were without elected representatives.[138] The suggestion was to no immediate avail. Tolmie waited until mid-September before setting 2 November 1933 as polling day.

The endless delay made Tolmie appear desperate, as indeed he was for his party was disintegrating around him. The premier persisted with the idea of a union government even though the Conservative party refused to endorse the plan. The Conservative Association decided that the party would not campaign officially and advised each local riding organization to act on its own. Confused Conservatives scattered in all directions. The old warhorse, William Bowser, returned to the fray to lead anti-Tolmie Conservatives under the 'Non-Partisan' label. Others, including a number of Tolmie's cabinet ministers, who wished to follow neither leader, ran as independents. Tolmie himself campaigned half-heartedly as a Unionist, and in the end he had few prominent supporters besides his faithful lieutenant R.H. Pooley of Esquimalt.

To some observers, both then and now, the election result in 1933 is largely explained by the collapse of the Conservative party.[139] Yet that was less than half the story. Though it is true that governments often defeat themselves, this was not an election that went by default. The break up of the party may account for the Conservative defeat, but it is only the beginning of an explanation of the Liberal victory. While the Conservatives were coming apart at the seams, Pattullo remained in firm control of the party he had stitched back together. There were defections. The former Liberal finance minister, Dugald Donaghy, joined up with the Bowser group and Duff's cranky adversary from Vancouver, Charles Woodward, also went his own way. Pattullo observed publicly that, in the army, Donaghy would be called a 'deserter' and he made it plain that anyone who ran as an 'independent Liberal' had no standing whatever in the party.[140] Without wanting to intervene in local situations, he exercised some influence over nominations. He diverted Mary Ellen Smith's interest in running again by cloaking his fear that she would be an unreliable colleague with concern that he did not want to see her run and lose.[141] At the same time he encouraged others in Vancouver to stand for the first time. Perhaps his most prominent new recruit was George Weir from the Department of Education at the University of British Columbia. Weir was bright, and as impassioned in his commitment to reform as he had been in his public opposition to the Kidd report. Former colleagues in government such as John Hart, E.D. Barrow, Harry Perry, and K.C. MacDonald ran again with Pattullo's blessing. He was less enthusiastic about the candidacy of Gerry McGeer, who was constrained to write his leader, even before the election began, to deny newspaper reports that he had demanded an assurance that he would be attorney-general in a new Liberal government.[142] One measure of Pattullo's control over his party was that he could make it clear to all potential candidates that he was not making any advance commitments on cabinet positions.[143] This election was going to be Pattullo's show, and he was not far wrong when he said that his party was the only coherent force with a clearly defined policy.[144]

Liberal party unity under Pattullo was, by the time the election was called, not very important in the fight against the Conservatives. In a sense they had already been beaten when the Liberals held firm behind Pattullo's stand against a coalition. The real battle of the election campaign was not with the Conservatives, who by then scarcely presented an identifiable target, but instead with a quite different party that had only just entered the field: the Co-operative Commonwealth Federation (CCF). The new force in British Columbia politics was acknowledged by the fact that the Liberals directed much of their fire against the left, rather than the right, in the final weeks before polling day.

In 1933 the British Columbia Co-operative Commonwealth Federation was a collection of disparate and fractious groups that had been cobbled together at the last minute. Many its leaders were rather more interested in bickering among themselves about fine points of doctrine than in speaking with a clear voice to the masses. There were obvious lines of division between hard-line socialists, like the father and son team of Ernest and Harold Winch, and gradualists such as Bill Pritchard or the Reverend Robert Connell, who became house leader after the election. Then there was Dr Lyle Telford, who moved so fast that no one knew where he stood, though, as the party's most ardent campaigner, he blazed like a comet in the electoral firmament. Rather than coming to terms with these conflicting amibitions, the CCF campaigned without a leader. And when the party met in September to build an election platform it was a makeshift job founded on compromise which, in terms specific reforms, was little different from the one that the Liberals had constructed.[145]

For all that it was deeply divided and had little time to organize, the CCF ran or backed candidates in all ridings, attracted a good deal of support, and certainly put the fear of godless socialism into the capitalist class. Tolmie thought that if the suggestions of the CCF were followed, 'it will shake this country to its foundations,' which, of course, was pretty much what the radicals in the party intended. Jimmy Jones could only explain the growing support for the CCF in the Okanagan 'by saying that people's minds are so befuddled with their losses in fruit growing.'[146] The apparent attraction of the CCF for many voters was one of the reasons Pattullo received an invitation to dine with members of the business community at the home of H.R. MacMillan.[147] And, since some things in British Columbia politics always stay the same no matter how much they change, the advent of the new party prompted another refrain from the coalition chorus. Pattullo received suggestions he should form alliances against or even with the CCF. Many Liberals felt that the reorganized left would take votes away from them. Pattullo's party workers in Prince Rupert were always concerned about losing the working-class vote and some thought this would be the hardest fight he had ever had in his own riding. Manson came back from a trip north and told Pattullo that some of his best friends supported the CCF.[148] Duff, needless to say, was unperturbed by any of these developments. He told party members not to worry, that if they simply pressed on regardless, all would be well. As far as he was concerned, Conservative businessman who were fearful of the CCF 'have the remedy in their own hands. Personally, I am not alarmed by the C.C.F. Movement.'[149] Few others had Pattullo's clarity of foresight in that election year.

In the midst of the 1933 campaign, the columnist P.W. Luce told the eastern readers of *Saturday Night* what they liked to hear. Under the headline 'political bedlam in British Columbia,' he claimed that 'British Columbia is in the throes of the maddest election campaign Canada has ever seen.' Exaggerating somewhat, Luce noted that there were 225 candidates representing twelve distinct political groups and 'only the most rabid politician would be so rash as to predict what the result will be when the votes are cast.'[150] One easterner had already accepted this interpretation of west-coast politics. Mackenzie King decided to leave British Columbia out of his western tour in the summer of 1933 because a provincial election was in the offing 'and matters are very unsettled there.' So Pattullo got no help from that quarter. He publicly explained King's absence by saying that the federal leader did not want to interfere in local issues; privately, no doubt, he wished that it were true.[151]

While many were confused, Duff Pattullo, who knew British Columbia better than most, was confident of the outcome. As the election was called, Pattullo, who did not think of himself as either rabid or rash, was certain the Liberals would be elected with a good majority. While others might listen to the clamour created by what he called 'noisy and militant minorities,' Pattullo had faith in the organization and program of his own party.[152]

He was also completely unimpressed with those arrayed against him. He largely ignored Tolmie and his group, for by now the premier was a spent force. He hardly even campaigned, which was the reasonable thing to do since he had nothing to offer British Columbians. Tolmie believed that people had lost sight of the work ethic in the prosperity of the 1920s and now 'nothing but a little slack at the waistline will bring them back to common sense.' His assertion, during his one campaign speech in Vancouver, that he should be re-elected because his was 'the only group with depression experience' was hardly persuasive.[153] The other Conservative fragment, the non-partisans, did not cause Duff to lose much sleep either. When he ran into William Bowser during a summer speaking tour in the Okanagan, he was 'greatly shocked' by what he saw. Instead of the feisty political scrapper of old, Bowser now looked terrible – 'only the shadow of his former self.' Pattullo wrote to one of the Prince Rupert boys that he hoped Bowser would tour the north 'in order that his supporters may be disillusioned.'[154] But in the end it did not matter, for Bowser died just a week before election day. As for the CCF, it had created a bit of a stir at the start, but Duff was convinced it had shot its bolt before the official campaign began.[155] A reaction against the new party had already set in and it was bound to send votes in his direction.

In the final analysis, however, Pattullo's certainty about the outcome of the election was based on his own self-confidence rather than the limitations of others. He had given speeches all over British Columbia during the summer, making, as the *Vancouver Province* put it, 'a regular sentimental journey ... round the great open spaces.' He reiterated the Liberal party's policies as they had been outlined at the convention the previous year and he always added a personal touch to what he had to say. In Barkerville he claimed a special attachment to the Cariboo because his Uncle Thomas was buried there. The *Province* noted that his uncle was 'the original scion of that stock who put the Duff into Pattullo' whereas, in fact, he had provided the Tom that Duff eschewed![156] By now the editor of the *Province* had fallen back on the lowest form of humour, having been so consistently wrong in his political analysis. Rather than supporting one of the non-party parties, the people of the province, Pattullo felt sure, were responding to his Liberal party and its message.

After the election was announced in mid-September, Pattullo simply retraced his steps and reiterated his policies during the six-week campaign. On 14 September, the day after the writs were issued, he took the boat to Vancouver. He spent a day there with his family – Lillian, Doris, and his two grand-daughters who called him 'TD.' Then he left for the north where he began his campaign. His opening address in Stewart was a forty-five minute, rapid-fire review of Liberal policy.[157] He spoke in the short staccato sentences he reverted to when he was keyed up with wanting to get on with the job. Later in Vancouver he warmed up an audience of 3500 with the 'direct simplicity' of his approach. His notion of 'socialized capitalism' and the need 'to establish the necessary credit to carry out a broad program of constructive and useful wage-distributing public enterprise' translated into the simple election slogan of 'work and wages.' He indicated the middle-of-the-road nature of his reformism by declaring that his platform was progressive enough to appeal to radicals and stable enough to appeal to conservatives. He was not, he said, appealing to Liberals so much as to liberal thought.[158] The campaign was the culmination of five years' work and preparation, and it went smoothly to the end. At a loss for a substantive issue, the *Province*'s editor tried to cast the aspersion that the liquor interests were financing his campaign.[159] But the unsubstantiated charge had as little effect as the hecklers at Pattullo's campaign meetings.

As politicians do, Pattullo got all kinds of advice about how he should conduct his campaign, most of which he ignored. Perhaps the most unusual suggestion came from his brother George, who was freer with his advice than he was with his money. In the thick of the electoral fray Duff received a letter from George wishing him good luck in the campaign. His brother then went on with 'an interesting scientific fact' he got from a friend who had attended a cockfight in Mexico. 'In America,'

George claimed, 'when a cock gets a numbing wallop, his handlers revive him by sticking his head into a pan of water. The technique is better in Mexico; there the handlers fill their mouths with water, up-end the cock's tail feathers and spray his testicles. And that rooster gets up on his hind legs, shakes his head and just wades into the fight again to beat hell. I mention this,' George concluded, 'as a friendly gesture, to the end that you may always carry along with you a short length of rubber hose.'[160] With such advice, Duff could hardly lose, and indeed he did not.

When the dust settled on election day, the result was as clear and unequivocal as Pattullo expected it would be. He had won an absolute victory, both in Prince Rupert and in the province as a whole. In his own riding he had trounced his CCF opponent. He had received nearly 65 per cent of the ballot and was more than a thousand votes ahead of the CCF candidate. Province-wide, the Liberals had attracted nearly 42 per cent of the votes cast. It was less than a majority, but then the Liberals had not had 50 per cent of the popular vote since 1916. What was important was that the votes had translated into 34 of the 47 seats in the legislature. Pattullo and the Liberals were clearly the winners and they would form the government. To the surprise of many, the CCF became the opposition. The new party had done well, particularly in the Vancouver suburbs. It had got more than 31 per cent of the provincial vote, but, because a couple of candidates piled up huge majorities, that popular vote produced only seven seats.[161] The CCF would also be supported by the perennial, independent Labour member, Tom Uphill of Fernie. The ragged remnants of the party that had formed the government at dissolution were reduced to virtual non-existence. The so-called Non-Partisans elected two members, and only one lonely Unionist, R.H. Pooley, who had been in the house even longer that Pattullo, was returned. In Saanich, Tolmie was beaten by a Liberal, as he was in the province as a whole.

The triumph belonged to Duff Pattullo. Over the last twelve months he had been steadfast and clear-sighted through the fire and smoke of a rapidly changing political situation, and now the victory was his. Even those Liberals who did not care much for his leadership had to acknowledge 'that the election was won by the courage and accepted honesty of Mr. Pattullo rather than by the Liberal Party as such.'[162] The party organization had held firm during the coalition crisis and had delivered the vote on election day. But even that was very much Pattullo's achievement. He had financed and built up the provincial Liberal organization during the dark days after 1928. It became his party, under his control, and, now that the strife was over and the triumph won, Pattullo was entitled to the praise.

Other politicians began to lick their wounds and, along with the pundits, to interpret the results. No doubt many defeated Conservatives were correct when they concluded that many who would have normally supported them voted instead for the Liberals as the best chance to defeat the CCF. At the same time they had to admit that running without a leader, without a party, and without a policy had also been a drawback.[163] The *Province* initially had the grace to acknowledge Pattullo's victory in a straightforward way, but after taking a few days to reflect its editor was back to the same old nonsense. He argued that, to the extent that many Conservatives had voted Liberal, Pattullo was really a unionist premier at the head of a unionist government.[164] Other Conservatives quickly gave credit where credit was due. Within a day of the election, Pat Maitland wrote to Duff to say he deserved the win because he had been consistent and loyal to his party and his principles.[165] And if its editor chose to be obtuse about the election result, the *Province* columnist, Bruce Hutchison, was sharp enough to see the point. The 1933 election marked one of the most remarkable comebacks in the history of British Columbia politics.[166] Pattullo had been elected leader of the opposition without great enthusiasm by a party that expected to be out of power for at least two terms. But he had taken his team by the scruff of the neck and dragged it back onto the field where, as captain, he had set the example by his relentless pursuit of the opposing players. When the game was called the score was hardly a matter of interpretation.

For his part, Duff ignored most of the sideline chatter. As far as he was concerned, the election result was simply the logical outcome of the course he had taken over the last five years. He heard the first results come in at his office in the legislative buildings. Then he drove home to Beach Drive where, with his family and a few close friends, he stayed up until midnight listening to the returns on the radio. He accepted the result quietly, without great excitement or jubilation. While much was wrong with the universe in 1933, at least the world of British Columbia politics was unfolding as it should.

Pattullo would have been less than human had he not taken some pleasure from the congratulations that flowed in from family, friends, and colleagues over the next few days. His relatives and friends in the east wrote of their excitement that Duff was premier of British Columbia. The election result had, of course, been widely reported in eastern newspapers, not least of which was the Woodstock *Sentinel-Review* which took great pride in the success of a native son.[167] George spoke for the rest of the family when he wrote to congratulate his brother, and for himself when he added that 'it gives me a special glow that you have always played the game on your own and have arrived entirely through your own efforts. And that is priceless to men of your temperament.'[168] The family's only regret was that Duff's father was not alive to enjoy this day. As George put it to his older sister, 'What a pity Bops could not have lived to see Duff Premier of British Columbia! He did love political and public honours so ardently – this triumph would have crowned his life with happiness. Can't you just see him with his back to the sitting room fire, rolling on his tongue "The Premier"? Why, we would never have heard him refer again to our brother as just "Duff." I would give *anything* if he could only be back with us now.'[169]

Politicians also sent their felicitations, though their sentiments were often less straightforward. For some, like Gerry McGeer, the goodwill would be shortlived.[170] Perhaps the most ironic and disingenuous greetings came from Mackenzie King, who had 'been thinking a good deal of how pleased your mother and father, and mine, would have been to see us both at the head of the Liberal party in our respective spheres of action.'

But his assurance to Pattullo that 'you can always rely on my complete understanding of anything which may be taken for granted' was ironic in light of future developments and disingenuous because his advice to federal Liberals at the same time was to distance themselves from Pattullo in case he became a liability.[171] King's empty words were, however, balanced by those that were genuine and heartfelt. Perhaps the most touching and effusive message came from an old Yukoner the day after the election. 'Congratulations Sourdough! The sun is shining gloriously this morning indicating the glorious victory of yesterday.'[172]

CHAPTER 7

The Politics of Reform

'We must be up and doing'

Duff Pattullo was more subdued when, the morning after, he awoke to the fact that he was premier of British Columbia. Not that he thought the outcome was of no consequence. On the contrary, it was a tremendous event. He had been working towards this end in a direct way for the last five years, just as, in another sense, he had been preparing for it all his life. Now he had reached the top of his chosen profession and become leader of his chosen province all in one day. And these two, his profession and his province, were the most important things in his life. He liked to refer to himself as a 'professional politician,' though 'in the right sense of the term. Politics is the science of Government. A professional is an expert. After my years of experience I think I am entitled to call myself an expert in the science of Government.'[1] And indeed he was, since politics had been an integral part of his life since he was a child. As a young man he had left his birthplace and came to the province which, since it was where his heart was, he soon called home. Now the voters had called upon him to apply his expertise to the problems of his province.

That was one reason why he accepted the verdict of the people of British Columbia without outward excitement. He who had once been the prodigal son now faced a prodigious task. Pattullo was only too well aware that winning an election was a simple matter compared to the task of solving the problems and healing the wounds of a depression-torn province. Another reason for his apparent calm was that, for Duff Pattullo, the fight was really much more important, and enjoyable, than the victory. Once he had won, it was time to move on to other battles. He had no time to savour his success and no interest in gloating over it in public. And though he would never have admitted it, the election campaign had also drained a great deal of his energy. It had been a protracted affair and he had been on the go without a break for months. Now it was over, the pace was telling even on his robust constitution. Over the next few months, as he worked his way into his new job, he would suffer from a number of minor and, particularly for one of Pattullo's temperament, irritating illnesses.

So while the day after the election was a momentous one for Duff Pattullo, it was also a day of quiet reflection upon the fact that many things had not changed. He was at his desk in the legislative building as usual before nine in the morning 'as if nothing had happened.' He read the congratulatory telegrams that had already arrived and looked over the list of possible cabinet ministers, though he made no final decisions. He spoke briefly to newsmen, saying this was not time to talk, rather it was time to start thinking and working. 'I am going over the Bay now to pay my respects to my old friend, Dr. Tolmie, and that will be all for today. What's the use of talking about the poll? The result is clear enough and now we have to get down to business.'[2]

And there was certainly plenty of business for a new government to take care of. British Columbia still faced a massive economic crisis. The agency that Pattullo later set up to gather economic information estimated that the value of both primary and total production in the province increased fractionally from 1932 to 1933. Yet the levels for 1933 remained at 50 per cent or less of what they had been in 1929, so the province's economic engine was still running at half power.[3] In numbers of dollars, the average per capita income in British Columbia had dropped by nearly 50 per cent.[4] The level of unemployment had only got worse since the 1931 census had shown that more than one in four British Columbian workers was out of a job.[5] The cold statistics were one clear measure of the problem, but it was not numbers on a page that evoked emotions. The scenes associated with unemployment in the 'dirty thirties' had much more immediate impact – the lines of dour-faced men waiting at soup kitchens or the ramshakle, unsanitary 'jungles' around False Creek in Vancouver where the homeless went to exist. In the fall of 1932 the federal government had taken over relief camps for single unemployed men and they were being run by the Department of National Defence. For single men the camps were no more than a temporary and debilitating expedient. They were not even an option for married men or unemployed women. The effort to provide relief for these people placed an impossible strain on the resources of the municipal and provincial governments since, particularly in the cities, the number applying relief and the cost of providing it continued to climb.

The hard economic times were manifested in social upheaval throughout the province. As Pattullo and the Liberals came to power, there were strikes and closures in the resource sector. Men in the relief camps were taking action to express their growing sense of hopelessness. In the Okanagan Valley, not normally a hot-bed of radicalism, orchardists were organizing vigilance committees in an effort to control the marketing of fruit and were rallying to the cry of 'a cent a pound or on the ground.'[6] In the cities, people were forced to postpone major lifetime decisions such as getting married and having children.[7] Many who had little or no income were excluded from the housing market and lived in substandard conditions. Under these circumstances the social pressure for effective government action was building, and it continued to mount even after the economy hit rock bottom in 1933.

Yet the 1930s were not simply years of great depression. Along with hardship and suffering, there was also progress and improvement, even if only in measurable material terms. Those who had incomes still spent money, and though they may have had fewer dollars they often were worth more. In terms of consumer durables, Canadians were statistically better off by the end of the decade. They owned more cars, radios, and refrigerators in 1939 than they had in 1929.[8] Duff Pattullo understood this sense of progress, or at least change, in the midst of depression. He was fond of telling people how, as a boy, he 'lamented the fact that we were living in a too prosaic age. Nothing seemed to be happening. But now suddenly the scene changed. Scientific invention and discovery brought about tremendous alterations in our viewpoint. Surprise after surprise met us until we have become so sophisticated that nothing would surprise us.' He totally disagreed with those who argued that education and science had moved the world too far too fast. Rather, he said, society was at a stage where a 'little knowledge is a dangerous thing.' In any event, 'you cannot stop the urge of the human mind.' Discovery and invention had made possible a higher standard of living and so it is 'useless to say that we must get back to the old days of the simple life.' Rather it should be made possible 'for an ever increasing percentage of our people to rise to these standards, not for the purpose of over indulgence but for greater enjoyment of daily pursuit, for leisure and for cultural development.'[9] For Pattullo, then, it was not sufficient, or even possible, to bring things back to where they were in 1929 by solving immediate problems. The positive forces in society had to be harnessed so that the individual lives of British Columbians could be enriched.

Pattullo had always believed that in government, as in life, one could neither go back nor sit still, the only choice was to move forward. As he took over as premier of British Columbia, he understood the need for action. He certainly did not intend to 'sit quietly and watch the world topple over the precipice' as the Tolmie government had done. 'We must,' said Duff, 'be up and doing.'[10] Both the need and the demand for decisive measures was clear enough. Exactly what the government should do to take hold of the situation continued to be a matter of conflicting interpretation. But Pattullo was still thinking in a straight line. Now that the election was won, it was first things first and then on to the next matter. First he would select a cabinet, then he would examine the state of government finances, then he would bring a legislative program to the first session of the new parliament.

The political Pattullo was already well known to British

Columbians. He had mellowed somewhat since the days when he was minister of lands and seemed to be scrapping with everyone who presumed to question his views. He had truly enjoyed being leader of the opposition, building up his own political organization and fighting the good fight with the Conservatives. Those five years had been a change that was as good as a holiday to him. As he took over as premier it was clear that he intended to be master of his government. Duff Pattullo still had immense confidence in his own ability and that self-assurance was both good and bad. It meant he was vigorous and decisive, he could act when action was called for. At the same time, because he valued his own opinion more highly than that of others, he tended to be intolerant and to overreact to criticism, especially when he was beset on all sides. All of these Pattullo characteristics were by now a matter of public record.

And yet, as a particular personality, their new premier was in many ways an unknown quantity to most British Columbians. Even though Pattullo had been in the Legislative Assembly for seventeen years and had never been just a private member, in spite of the fact that he spent more time out among the people than any other provincial politician, and while he could hardly be described as introverted or reticent, the fact remained that few really knew him well. As premier, he continued, at a certain level, to be very sociable. He hosted dozens of dinners at the Empress and receptions at Beach Drive, often inviting fifty or sixty people including politicians of all parties. On these occasions he was an affable and convivial, generous and outgoing host – in short, the life of the party. He could be similarly congenial at work. Allon Peebles, who was brought in to work on the health insurance scheme in 1935, had a knock at his office door soon after he arrived and opened it to find Pattullo standing there. Whereas most premiers would have sent instructions through a secretary, Duff took the time to ask the new arrival if he were comfortable and getting the necessary assistance. Peebles later recalled that the visit 'left me with a feeling of personal loyalty' towards his boss 'which I have always retained.'[11] At the same time, part of Pattullo's complexity was that he also maintained a certain amount of reserve and distance from others. His friends called him Duff, but only his closest, and he did not like the familiar form of his name used in print. Around the legislature his persona was such that Liberal members and senior bureaucrats most frequently referred to him as 'the chief.'[12]

Keeping up appearances remained very important to him and he was still mindful of his outward presentation, perhaps as a means of self-containment. A year after he became premier he made some revealing remarks when wrote to his tailor, ostensibly on the subject of the construction of trousers. 'There are any number of people who unhesitatingly expound their views on the construction of the Ship of State which they know as little as I do about the building of clothes, but the people most difficult to satisfy are those who think they know most about everything but who know least about anything. Consequently I feel that I may approach the subject of clothes building without diffidence.' Accordingly, he went on, 'I notice from snapshots taken that my clothes give me the appearance of what I am not, namely old. The kind of clothes that should be built are those which will make one appear as young as one's contemporaries think they are. This may be an impossible objective, and I presume that in the final analysis in this, as in other matters, we must strive for moderation.'[13] Pattullo turned sixty-one on 19 January 1934, two months after he became premier, and to mark the occasion the Liberal newspaper, the *Victoria Times*, published an account that showed that a certain amount of mythology was developing around his long career: misinformation that no doubt added to his aura if not to the accuracy of people's knowledge of him. The *Times* claimed, for example, that he had entered provincial politics in 1916 in spite of 'a flourishing brokerage and financial business.'[14] Other newspaper writers would turn his Yukon experience into almost heroic proportions. While they were probably inevitable, such tales were unfortunate, for the truth about his early career was vivid enough. It was as though he were being made larger than life.

But then, after four years of the worst depression in the province's history, perhaps British Columbians needed to believe their premier was superhuman. The problems were massive and as yet no government really seemed to know what to do about them. It was clear that the people expected much of the new government they had given such a large mandate. There was more than a dash of naïvety about these hopes as more was expected of the Pattullo government than it could possibly deliver. But Pattullo himself was partly responsible for the creation of these great expectations. He had used the snappy slogan 'work and wages' and now was the time of reckoning. Such thoughts must have given the new premier pause, though not for long.

For Pattullo believed in an interventionist state and his government would be arguably the most active in Canada during the 1930s. It was certainly very different from the cautious, moderate Liberalism of the Oliver government during the 1920s. Pattullo intended to rise above the often petty issues of provincial politics in the past, to move beyond the frontier concerns of roads, bridges, and patronage, to develop the role of the provincial state and elevate it to another level. As the minister primarily responsible for the resource economy in the previous decade he had presided over the expansion of the economic power of British Columbia. Now, faced with the constraints of the 1930s, he advocated a further extension of influence of the provincial government in the social and economic spheres. And with increased activity in new areas, the power of the provincial government would have to be enhanced.

Pattullo was an individualist who believed in private property, but he believed equally strongly that the state had to act as the mediator among individuals. Amid the growing complexities of modern society, and given the fact that no two people were exactly alike, there had to be 'a correlating influence to reconcile conflicting interests for the general good. This can only be done through collective authority and that authority is the state.' A more vigorous state did not mean socialism, it meant 'socialized capitalism.' That is to say, 'capital must be used to the benefit and not to the detriment of the people as a whole.' Or, as Pattullo put it now, just as he had done when he spoke in support of the first Liberal throne speech in 1916, retaining individual liberty 'is to recognize that we are truly our brother's keeper.'[15]

His particular policies were founded in a general philosophy but, as he took over the reins of power in 1933, Pattullo did not have time to ruminate about things he had made up his mind on long ago. He was always more inclined to action than to reflection, and now was the time to get on with it. He certainly created the impression that things were happening very quickly. One veteran reporter claimed that the whole atmosphere had changed in Victoria. Whereas for the past year the government 'was seized with a slow paralysis,' now 'everybody is on the move. Something is happening all the time.'[16]

Pattullo's particular policies also constituted a break with the past. Just after he was elected premier of British Columbia, he indicated his intent to the national leader of the Liberal party. 'We will have to be prepared to adopt radical measures. We are in the midst of a most extraordinary evolution and we must be prepared to create precedent to meet the new conditions.'[17] Such a statement no doubt only caused further anxiety in the querulous heart of Mackenzie King, but Pattullo was far more impressed with the national leadership in the United States than he was with anything happening in Ottawa. It was in the activism of Franklin Roosevelt's New Deal that he saw the best model for both his general approach and his particular measures. The difference was that the American president had all the power and resources of the federal government at his command, whereas Pattullo was premier of a Canadian province that had no money. Establishing even a 'little new deal' in British Columbia would not be an easy matter and it was just as well that Pattullo never made much of obstacles.[18]

Pattullo's first task as premier, appointing a cabinet, was potentially fraught with difficulty. One drawback of his large majority was that he had many candidates to choose from, so that balancing the various ambitions, regions, and interests could become a delicate matter. He contemplated his options for a few days and made a trip to Vancouver to consult with other Liberals. But when the new Executive Council was announced it was clear that Pattullo had made his own decisions for his own reasons. Whereas Tolmie's cabinet had been the largest ever in British Columbia, Pattullo reduced it to eight members. His executive was intended to be a tight-knit team that could work together under his decisive leadership.

Pattullo's cabinet was clearly to be his cabinet. Like Oliver and MacLean, he was president of the council as well as premier. The only member other than himself with lengthy ministerial experience was John Hart. Like Pattullo, Hart had been first elected in the Liberal sweep of 1916. As minister of finance in the Pattullo government, he was back in the position he had held from 1917 to 1924. Hart had also worked with Pattullo on Liberal party finances during the period in opposition. He was no duffer on the golf course and he won competitions that, according to Duff, demanded 'classy golf.'[19] Because of their long association, Pattullo was probably closer to John Hart on a personal level than to any other member of the cabinet, but that did not mean they would agree on all things. Hart was known and respected in financial circles and he would bring an element of stability, and even conservatism, to the government's fiscal management.

There were others with parliamentary, if not cabinet experience. Arthur Wellesley Gray, who had been a member of the legislature and mayor of New Westminster, was given lands and municipal affairs, Frank MacPherson of Cranbrook was minister of public works, and Kenneth Cattanach MacDonald from the Okanagan was put in charge of agriculture. These men were solid and reliable, if somewhat unimaginative. Any fireworks around the cabinet table were likely to come from those at the other end of the Liberal party's ideological spectrum. George Pearson had taken over William Sloan's Nanaimo seat in the 1928 election and had proven to be a forceful debater in the house. Now, like Sloan before him, he had charge of the Ministry of Mines and, in addition, he was to run the Department of Labour. Pearson was the keenest exponent of social and labour legislation in the cabinet. Also very committed to reform, but without experience in government, was George Weir, who Pattullo had convinced to leave the University of British Columbia for the uncertain world of politics. As provincial secretary, Weir ranked second to the premier and he also held the education portfolio. In many ways Pattullo's choice as attorney-general was the most controversial of all his cabinet appointments. Ignoring the presumed claims of others, he selected Gordon Sloan, who was a junior partner in the Farris law firm, had just been elected to the legislature for the first time, and now became the youngest member of the cabinet. He was the son of William Sloan, Pattullo's old Yukon friend and cabinet colleague. That connection was not insignificant, but Gordon Sloan was also bright and able and he represented Vancouver. These, then, were the men that the premier gathered around him to govern the province through difficult times.

The break with the past and the fact that Pattullo intended to run his own show was made clear as much by those who he left out of the cabinet as it was by the men he put in. The most vociferous exclusion was Gerry McGeer who, in spite of his pre-election denials, assumed he should be in the provincial cabinet, perhaps by divine right. Pattullo knew that McGeer's overblown ego would prevent him from being a team player and he also thought his particular monetary crusade would be better pursued at the federal level.[20] As soon as it was clear he was not in the cabinet, McGeer went on a rampage against Pattullo and his government. He favoured Mackenzie King with long letters on the matter. On 1 November 1933 he had written to King that it 'is impossible to give to our leader, Mr. Pattullo, too much credit for the splendid work he has done.' Two weeks later, having been told he would not be a minister in the new government, McGeer felt the need 'to be perfectly frank ... Pattullo's conduct since the election indicates that a widely prevalent suspicion of his leadership was more than justified.'[21] He likewise lambasted the three-week-old government in speeches during the election campaign in Vancouver where the vote was postponed to 27 November because of the death of William Bowser. During a radio broadcast he asserted his right to decide not only his own cabinet position, but that of others as well. He would not, he said, have accepted the attorney-generalship even if it were offered to him unless 'certain members now in the cabinet had been excluded.'[22] Pattullo was quite unmoved by McGeer's performance. In a letter to Mackenzie King he merely stated the obvious when he observed that, 'There is some satisfaction in having one's judgement so speedily confirmed.'[23]

In fact, as Pattullo noted, there were other distinguished men excluded from the cabinet who had more claim and less presumption than McGeer. Alex Manson was not made attorney-general either, even though, and also partly because, he had served in that position for nearly seven years under Oliver and Maclean. Pattullo had, of course, known and worked with Manson since their Prince Rupert days, but he had never been overwhelmed by the energy and ability of his fellow northener. So Manson was also passed over. Nor was he the only former minister left out of the new Liberal cabinet. E.D. Barrow, former minister of agriculture, and William Sutherland, formerly head of public works, were both re-elected in 1933 but did not return to the cabinet. These older man were left out partly to make room for some new blood, for this was a new Liberal government, and Pattullo intended to make a new start.

Those who were in the cabinet met in Pattullo's old office as leader of the opposition on 15 November and then went out to Government House to be sworn into their new role. Given the mood of the province, it was not a time for pomp and ceremony and the proceedings were brief and casual. The ministers wore ordinary business suits, though Pattullo himself, more a stickler for form, wore a black coat and grey trousers. At the official ceremony they were sworn in according to their order of precedence: Pattullo first, then Weir, followed by Sloan, Gray, Hart, MacDonald, Pearson, and MacPherson.[24] Seniority within the executive had more to do with the history of the evolution of the cabinet in British Columbia than it did with political reality in 1933. Those who put their faith in omens rather than history might have noted with interest that the new cabinet went to Government House in two cars, one driven by Pattullo and the other by Hart. But whatever the future may have held, Pattullo was the leader now and there was no doubt about who was in charge. The force and will with which he had selected his cabinet was a foretaste of his style as premier.

Pattullo and his ministers moved into their new offices and got down to business the day after they were sworn in. Because any new policies to deal with the depression would require the government to spend money, Pattullo and Hart began by looking into the state of the province's finances. They were not encouraged by what they saw. They had each department prepare a set of estimates for the coming year and, when they had figured it all out, they calculated that for 1933–4 there would be a deficit of $2,232,002 on expenditure of $22,729,593, and that was without making any provision for unemployment relief. The total provincial debt was something like $165 million.[25] The general fiscal situation was bad enough, but even as they took the time to establish the detail of that point, there were instant financial crises to be handled. Pattullo found as soon as he came to power that the province's credit had been cut off and yet he needed money right away to met the next month's payment on the debt. He turned to the east for help, but the response was full of forboding.

Having been in power for less than a month, Pattullo began to grapple with the issue that would dominate his premiership until the end: the extent to which British Columbia could reasonably expect help from the federal government. He turned first to the province's bank, the Canadian Bank of Commerce in Toronto, for help to meet the debt payments. He told the bank's manager, S.H. Logan, that he needed $1.5 million to tide the province over the next few weeks and suggested that he come to Victoria to discuss the situation in detail. Logan was concerned that the province already owed the bank more than $4 million and he did not want to lose any more if British Columbia were to default on its obligations. He replied that he was unable to do anything, other than suggesting that Pattullo ask Prime Minister Bennett for a government guarantee on a loan, and that there was no point in his coming west.[26]

So Pattullo redirected his request from Toronto to Ottawa, trusting that his hopes, rather than his expectations, would be realized. He knew he might well get a frosty reception from the federal government. R.B. Bennett had been prime minister since 1930 and Pattullo had assessed him as 'reactionary to a degree.'

He allowed that many thought that Bennett was a 'hard worker, and has the courage to shoot ahead, although I myself have some reservations that this courage is rather inspired by not knowing any better.'[27] Pattullo also knew that only a month earlier, when the prime minister had been out west, there were reports that Bennett believed British Columbia should be allowed to default and go into the hands of a receiver.[28] This worst-case scenario did not, however, eventuate. Bennett delayed responding to Pattullo's request by demanding more detailed information on the financial state of the province. Pattullo replied that he was hardly in a position to provide a full accounting in such a short time and, in any event, the details of British Columbia's position would be irrelevant if the immediate crisis were not met.[29] He had already told the province's bank manager that, since the Canadian Bank of Commerce had been British Columbia's bank for years, he should know as well as anyone that provincial finances were in a mess. Pattullo also reminded Logan that he had been pointing out for the last five years that the provincial government had submitted fraudulent estimates.[30] If the bank's officers took no notice, it was hardly his fault. In the end, the financial storm was weathered, but it was not an auspicious start for the new provincial government.

It was very clear by his first Christmas as premier that wise men from the east would not come to British Columbia bearing gifts of any substance. It was largely with advice, and seldom with money, that easterners found it better to give than to receive, and the new premier of British Columbia heard plenty of sermons from the centres of power beyond the Rockies about how to govern his province. In addition to Logan and Bennett, Mackenzie King wrote, in his case to explain how he had proceeded when he first got into power in 1921. In matters of self-interest King had great clarity of vision. He wanted Pattullo to continue exposing the scandals of the Tolmie government so that, when it came to the next federal election, Bennett and the Conservatives would be discredited by association.[31] Exactly what good this approach would do for unemployed British Columbians remained unclear. Sir Thomas White, a vice-president at the Canadian Bank of Commerce, was non-partisan about dispensing advice and he wrote to Pattullo, as he had done to Tolmie, about how 'Canadians are a rather steady people, not easily stampeded' and advocating the 'national' virtues of caution and stability. 'If it is in the national interest,' his homily went on, 'that unemployment relief be provided (and of course it must be) then the Government of Canada and not the banks should, in co-operation with the Provincial Governments, meet the emergency financing necessary.'[32] Pattullo was reminded of what he had always known, that there was little reciprocity between east and west. As he wrote to R.B. Bennett: 'I have an idea that the West understands the East better than the East understands the West, for the simple reason that most Westerners were born in the East and have kept in touch with conditions there.'[33]

In the exchange of letters surrounding his initial request for financial assistance, Pattullo indicated those issues that would be fundamental to his government. He assured the Canadian Bank of Commerce that if, after he and his ministers had reviewed British Columbia's finances, 'we find that we are indulging in any economic frills or furbelows ... we will act accordingly.' At the same time, it would not be possible to balance the provincial budget, either this year or next. Pattullo was adamant and clear that he had bottom lines that were more important than the figures at the end of the provincial estimates. He had absolutely no intention of abandoning what British Columbia had already achieved through social legislation by revoking mothers' or old-age pensions, or by closing institutions for the infirm or the sick. Such moves would only place these people in another category: on relief. Thus the institutions of health and education had to be reasonably maintained 'in order that the last condition may not be worse than the first.' He told the eastern bankers that 'if we have to choose between chaotic conditions through the closing of necessary public institutions and services and default on certain payments, we will choose the lesser of two evils, namely that of defaulting, and thereafter do the best we can.'[34]

Pattullo wrote to Bennett to arrange a meeting early in the

new year and listing the matters he felt had to be discussed. The first was the need for governmental initiative on the problem of unemployment. Related to funding relief and public works was the need to restructure British Columbia's debt at lower rates of interest. On that issue British Columbia was not asking any favours, for once the current financial crisis had passed the province would be able to pull its own weight. As British Columbia's leaders have always done, Pattullo extolled the virtues of the far west. 'We are an empire in ourselves and our hills and valleys are stored with potential wealth which make us one of the greatest assets of our Dominion.' Like most other Premiers of British Columbia, Pattullo believed his province was not getting a fair deal out of Confederation.[35] He realized this was an old subject, but he told Bennett that British Columbia needed an adjustment of terms, though at this stage all he asked for was an independent investigation into the matter. Then there was the Pacific Great Eastern. The investment in this railway was in large measure responsible for the provincial debt and Pattullo wanted to present the case, once again, for it to be absorbed into the national system. Taken together, these issues all added up to a thoroughgoing overhaul of the national fiscal system and Pattullo was predicting in public speeches that, as a scheme for division of powers, the British North America Act would have to be reconsidered.[36]

Pattullo constantly emphasized that he wished to co-operate with the federal government and the other provinces. He chaired a meeting with the other three western premiers in Victoria in the first week of December 1933. They discussed common problems and called for an early meeting with the federal government. They urged Ottawa to take full responsibility for single unemployed men, to use the national credit to finance extensive public works, and to refinance provincial debt at lower rates of interest. They also agreed that British Columbia would be included in any future meetings of the western provinces.[37] Pattullo felt that such meetings had some value, but he also understood their limitations. He told easterners that he had no sympathy with the notion of the western provinces uniting against the centre, but rather thought that all governments had to work together.[38] Any significant measures to deal with the depression would have to be thrashed out with the federal government. The western provinces had some common problems. Like the prairie provinces, British Columbia argued that it too suffered under a national tariff that protected the central Canadian market. But 'the west' was not a region, and Pattullo represented British Columbia. The coast province had its own historic grievances and unique interests. So when Bennett called a conference with all the provincial premiers in January 1934, Pattullo went armed with two newly prepared briefs: one on British Columbia's claim for better terms and a second arguing for federal takeover of the Pacific Great Eastern.

The claim for better terms was based on an examination of British Columbia's entry into Confederation in 1871 and its treatment by the federal government since then. There was some resonance for Pattullo in the fact that his province had become a part of Canada in the first place when, heavily in debt and facing an economic slump, it had turned to the federal government. The brief correctly argued that British Columbia came into Confederation under such terms as were acceptable in Ottawa and, in particular, the formula for establishing per capita payments to the new province was unfair. The fictitious population figure that would have put British Columbia on the same footing as other provinces was arbitrarily cut in half by Ottawa. That initial inequity had never been redressed, and the brief provided figures to show that, of all the provinces, only Prince Edward Island had received less than British Columbia from the federal government since 1867. Pattullo claimed that in the five years ending in 1931 the dominion had collected $20 million more than it spent in the province.[39] Federal payments also failed to take into account the vast area and particular topography of the westernmost province where the terrain made administrative costs much higher than in other parts of the country. Furthermore, the people of British Columbia had been suffering a double hardship since Ottawa had 'invaded' the formerly provincial preserve of direct taxation. The same Thomas White who was now urging Pattullo to be cautious about spending had, as minister of finance, introduced federal income tax as a temporary wartime expedient in 1917. This federal tax grab had severely limited the provincial government's ability to raise revenue. Finally, the brief argued that when the railway lands in the Peace River block were returned in 1930 no commission was established, as in the case of the prairie provinces, to determine compensation to British Columbia for having been deprived of the land.[40]

These historic grievances were particularly relevant, Pattullo argued, under the current conditions. Bennett had called the meeting with provincial premiers mostly to discuss unemployment, relief, and the dangerous level of provincial debt in the west. Pattullo's main objective when he went to Ottawa was to get federal help to set up a program of public works. He hoped that an examination of the old issues would give him leverage in the discussions on new problems. A re-examination of the national tax structure, for example, was particularly urgent given the province's need for money to provide work for the unemployed. So far the Bennett government had provided ad hoc help to the provinces for unemployment relief without assuming responsibility for the problem. Pattullo had always maintained that the primary responsibility for relief lay with the federal authority and he predicated any works program on the use of national credit.[41] In short, he insisted on co-operation between Ottawa and the provinces for a war on the depression. He understood the financial difficulties facing the dominion and he hoped there would be a similar recognition of the views of his government. In the event, however, there was precious little co-operation or understanding, either in the east generally or from R.B. Bennett in particular.

Pattullo's first dominion-provincial conference was a trying time for him. Illness delayed his departure and in the end he made the trip east before he had recovered. A nasal infection spread to his neck and then through his whole system. He spent much of his time in Ottawa in a hospital bed and his neck had to be lanced every day.[42] Yet he struggled up to attend the conference and made a strong and effective presentation. What he described as the 'sneering references' to British Columbia's position in eastern newspapers did little to raise his spirits. He and his province were characterized as a spendthrift relation coming to Ottawa to beg for money.[43] *Saturday Night* had run a commentary on Pattullo's views written in supercilious tones under the headline 'Regretting Confederation,' which Duff thought was a particularly outrageous misrepresentation. And, while Pattullo tried to put the best face upon it when it was over, the conference itself achieved nothing concrete as far as British Columbia was concerned. Instead of mutual negotiations, the western provinces were treated to a diatribe from the prime minister about their wasteful extravagance and the need to balance their budgets. Pattullo was pleased that the federal government proposed to spend money on public works rather than relief, but, instead of increasing aid to the provinces, Bennett made it clear that he intended to cut back severely. He even threatened to stop federal payments for unemployment relief altogether. Finally Bennett insisted that grants to provinces would be based on 'need' as determined by the federal cabinet. In the end, federal support was cut by an average of 20 per cent and Liberal governments like that of British Columbia were treated particularly harshly. Later Bennett did agree to a consideration of British Columbia's claim for better terms, although only by a cabinet committee and not by a royal commission as Pattullo had hoped.[44] Editorial writers in British Columbia may have been correct when they claimed that the new premier had increased the province's prestige in the east, but the meetings in Ottawa had not solved any of Pattullo's immediate problems.[45]

Having laid his cards on the federal table, Pattullo returned to British Columbia to do what he could about a new deal within his own jurisdiction. Having determined the province's financial position, he and Hart knew how many chips they had and now it was time for some redistribution. The first session of British Columbia's eighteenth parliament opened on 20 February 1934. Premier Pattullo tried to reduce the rancour that had characterized debate in the legislature over recent years. He personally welcomed all the members with a warm anecdote for each one.[46] He had the confidence of a big majority and hoped to bring some charm to the proceedings. After the opening he held a reception at the Empress. The opposition CCF members were in no mood for enjoyment, however: they took matters, and themselves, too seriously for that. After Pattullo's first substantive speech of the session they introduced the usual futile vote of non-confidence.[47] The gambit reflected their disparagement of Pattullo's middle-of-the-road reformism. They saw no point in even giving it a chance, and in that they were supported by Gerry McGeer. Once these opening pleasantries, and unpleasantness, were over, the Pattullo government got down to legislative business.

The six-week session produced a flurry of reformist measures that seemed to touch every area of provincial jurisdiction.[48] Laws were passed that were designed to spread work and wages around more evenly and fairly. Parallel acts established higher minimum wages for men and women in all occupations except farm labourers and domestic servants, and a third measure set a maximum eight-hour day and forty-eight hour week. Provision was made for the establishment of a Board of Industrial Relations to enforce this legislation, and with the power to fix wages for any group of workers and to investigate working conditions.[49] Financial assistance was provided to key economic sectors such as the mining and fishing industry. The forest protection fund was recreated at $300,000 annually. A Natural Products Marketing Act, designed to dovetail with proposed federal legislation and to regulate the marketing of natural products within provincial jurisdiction, was also passed.[50] All of these measures were to provide immediate relief for the British Columbia economy and the province's workers, but a lasting cure would require a more thorough diagnosis. So an act was passed to establish an Economic Council that was to gather information on the state of the economy and make policy recommendations to government.[51]

There were reformist measures in the social as well as the economic sphere. Pattullo firmly believed in the importance of education to the future of the province and had strongly objected to the cuts made by the previous government. An amendment to the Public Schools Act increased funding to schools and raised teachers' salaries.[52] The grant to the University of British Columbia was also restored. A committee was then struck to investigate the whole issue of financing provincial education with a view to a complete overhaul of the system. Another committee was set up to investigate the question of state health insurance. In an effort to enable hard-pressed homeowners to keep their property, a Mortgager's Relief Act created a new mortgage adjustment scheme and gave the courts authority to adjust agreements between borrowers and lenders.[53] A Department of Municipal Affairs was established and given the immediate responsibility of studying municipal taxation and making recommendations for the next session.[54] In the meantime loans were made to the cities to cover the cost of unemployment relief for the coming year.

All of this activity was predicated on a budget that projected a deficit of more than $2 million on the current account.[55] And the estimated deficit did not include either expenditure on unemployment relief or provision for the sinking fund. Nevertheless there was tax relief, particularly for those on low incomes. There were provisions for personal and other exemptions on provincial income tax, lower wages were exempted from the 1 per cent tax brought in by Jones in 1931, and the meal tax was repealed. Hart's first budget under the Pattullo government also proposed a massive restructuring of the provincial debt. The idea was to issue a new set of provincial securities at a lower rate of interest than the current bonds. The whole scheme depended on co-operation from the federal government which, among other things, was being asked to guarantee the new loans. The rub was that, so far, Bennett had refused to accede to this request.

Pattullo's view that it was necessary to deal decisively with Ottawa produced the most controversial legislation of the session. A few days before the house was due to be prorogued the premier received a telegram from Bennett informing him that the federal government was introducing legislation to set up a marketing board and urging that the province put through a statute to establish a board of its own to work along with the federal agency. Pattullo replied that a telegram was hardly a sufficient basis for formulating legislation and he asked for more detail. He did rush an act through in the last hours of the session, but he was proven correct when it was later declared ultra vires and had to be revised. Pattullo told the prime minister and the people of the province that having to respond quickly to such federal initiatives in a fast-breaking situation justified his acquisition of extraordinary, sweeping powers.[56]

Pattullo introduced a Special Powers Act that conferred all the authority of the legislature on to the government when the house was not sitting. Like much of the legislation passed during the 1934 sitting, this act was brief and to the point. 'Owing to the extraordinary conditions' within the province, the preamble stated, the government needed to be able 'to act promptly and effectively.' So the lieutenant-governor-in-council was given the power to pass ordinances that would have all the force of law without calling the legislature to debate and vote on them. The government could act in this way on a wide array of matters: anything to do with natural resources, the borrowing and lending of money by the province, public works, municipal institutions, the establishment and maintenance of hospitals and schools, and 'generally all matters of a merely local or private nature in the Province.' Property and civil rights also came under the Special Powers Act. There were some minimal safeguards in the legislation. All ordinances were to be published in the *Gazette*, they remained in force only until the beginning of the next sitting of the legislature, at which time everything done under the statute had to be reported to the house.[57] Many compared this legislation with the powers given President Roosevelt under the National Recovery Act. It was a bold move made at a time when many were calling for decisive action by government, but in the end it proved ill-advised for all it produced was an arid electrical storm of controversy: all thunder and lightning without any nourishing rain.

Duff Pattullo had risen calmly in the house at 10:10 on a Friday evening to announce what some thought was the most startling piece of legislation in Canadian history, with the possible exception of the federal government's 1914 War Measures Act.[58] The members of the legislature and the public were given the weekend to reflect upon the move and, by the time debate began on Monday, all hell had broken loose. Amidst the yelling and screaming, the accusation that was most frequently hurled about was 'dictator.' The premier of British Columbia, charged those opposed to the legislation, was assuming sinister and dictatorial powers. R.H. Pooley claimed that, at last, Duff's dream had come true and he proposed to make himself 'the great "I AM" and POO-BA of British Columbia ... We'll have to collect a few plumes, such as peacock feathers, to wear in his bonnet as he goes along the street, and then cultivate a special salute, such as "Hail Duff!" '[59] Independent member Tom Uphill brandished a placard with a swastika on it in the legislature. The CCF rented the Chamber of Commerce auditorium in Victoria and held a public meeting to denounce the act.[60] On the floor of the house Gerry McGeer generated so much high-voltage fury that he nearly blew a fuse. This 'Supreme Provincial Asininity' bill, he raged, was 'dangerous experimental hysteria, madness, a monstrosity, and utter nonsense.'[61] It was also contrary to the true gospel of Liberalism according to Mackenzie King as preached by the apostle McGeer. Even the normally supportive *Victoria Times* editorialized that 'if the government were a committee of archangels we would still object to the delegation to it by the Legislature of the power to pass any ordinance affecting civil rights and property.' The trouble with giving arbitrary powers to a well-intentioned government, the editorial went on, was that there was then nothing to stop ill-intentioned governments from assuming such powers.[62] It was a point that required little elaboration in the context of the 1930s.

Opposition to Pattullo's Special Powers Act was not confined to British Columbia. In the centres of power the bill was read as an attack on the federal government. Many eastern newspapers carried objections to the proposal that were quoted approvingly by the Conservative press in the province.[63] Even before he had seen the bill, Bennett wired Pattullo that it had 'the effect of destroying the relations between the Federal and provincial authorities' and he now presumed that British Columbia would solve its financial problems without reference to Ottawa. The telegram was merely a political ploy, however. Bennett admitted to the British Columbia member of his cabinet, H.H. Stevens, that he really could not see how Special Powers could be used 'as a club against the Federal Government.'[64] Perhaps more significant for Pattullo in the long run was the fact that Mackenzie King adamantly opposed the bill because it undermined the role of parliament. The national Liberal leader thought Pattullo 'has gone mad and will I think rue the day he assumed autocratic powers and tried the role of a dictator.' Publicly he said that the unfortunate act was a consequence of Bennett's unwillingness to deal adequately with the province's financial problems, but in private the problem was that Pattullo was 'imitating Bennett, but has not Bennett's experience, or constitution, or gall, and may break under the load he is placing on his own shoulders, with disaster to himself and his government.'[65]

Far from collapsing under the strain, amidst all this sound and fury the premier of British Columbia remained cool and collected. As well as strident opposition there was also a good deal of support for the bill. Some pointed out that assuming the powers meant little in itself. Much more important would be the measures that he passed under the new provisions.[66] Duff wrote to Ian Mackenzie that they were having quite a time in British Columbia. In a studied understatement he observed that a 'great deal of interest is being manifested in our "Special Powers Act."'[67] On other occasions he laughed off all the fuss. He wrote to the governor general to express appreciation for his visit to the province, 'on behalf of the people of British Columbia, whose servant (not Dictator) I am.'[68] In the house the Pattullo of old came to the fore when he gave a feisty speech defending the bill. He was, he said, opposed to the idea that the four western provinces combine against Ottawa, but if in British Columbia 'we have our backs to the wall, we are going to fight.'[69] Mostly, however, he sat patiently as the waves of opposition crashed about him, and when it was over the bill was passed. It had, nevertheless, been a damaging exercise. Pattullo claimed that he needed the power to respond instantly to federal initiatives in a fast-breaking situation, but that was not a sufficient justification to usurp the authority of the people's elected representatives. He only succeeded in stirring up a great deal of acrimony over an act that was so controversial it was never invoked. And, to the end of his premiership, he never entirely shook off the epithet of 'dictator.' Later that summer, when he spoke during a by-election in North Vancouver, he was greeted with cries of 'Heil Hitler' and 'Hello Mussolini.'[70]

In six weeks of legislative activity Pattullo had done what he immediately could within provincial jurisdiction. Any more thoroughgoing solution to the depression, or as Pattullo would have put it a 'broad guage policy,' would require substantial financial assistance from the federal government. And therein lay the fatal flaw in Pattullo's reformism: Ottawa was not forthcoming. Negotiations by letter and telegram had continued while the legislature was in session. In March 1934 Pattullo was summoned, in stentorian tones, to come to Ottawa at once. Bennett suggested that he adjourn the provincial legislature immediately in order to come to the federal capital to discuss British Columbia's financial position. This 'invitation' was extended 'notwithstanding the attitude of your government as indicated by the telegrams from your Minister of Finance and as reflected in the legislation which you have recently brought down.' Pattullo replied that he had 'no intention of attending any conference in Ottawa couched in such language.' He was not even sure, after the prime minister's telegram, that he could prorogue the house on the appointed date.[71] When the session was over, however, Pattullo and Hart prepared for the trip east. Since the dominion-provincial meeting with Bennett in January, Duff knew that it would be tough going in Ottawa, so he was hardly confident of success. Influential members of the federal cabinet, as well as Bennett himself, had taken exception to what they saw as British Columbia's 'stand and deliver attitude' even before they understood the real magnitude of Pattullo's plans.[72]

He was now on record as wanting three forms of financial assistance from Ottawa: immediate advances to enable the province to service its debt and pay for unemployment relief; a substantial infusion of funds to start job-creating public works; and a financial settlement based on British Columbia's case for a readjustment of the Terms of Union. Pattullo pushed hard on all three fronts during the spring and summer of 1934, while the provincial government continued to live from hand to mouth. Default on its interest payments at the beginning of April was only averted when the Bank of Commerce agreed to an advance on treasury bills at the last minute. Hart had written to the federal minister of finance, Edgar Rhodes, outlining the provincial budget and explaining that British Columbia needed in excess of $4 million just to meet exigencies to 1 July.[73] That amount was just stop-gap funding. Larger sums spent on public works would get people off the dole and generate real economic activity. After the meeting in Ottawa in January, Pattullo had observed in the press that Bennett was contemplating a total works program of $50 million. He wrote to the prime minister that something more like $200 million would be needed to produce substantial results. Ideally, Pattullo wanted the federal government to make large, interest-free loans available to the provinces for public projects which would be paid off during the period that the works were underway. And, finally, Pattullo was still pressing Bennett for a royal commission to examine his brief on British Columbia's claim for better terms. He arranged to go to Ottawa to discuss all these matters once more.

The meeting was in the last week of April, a time when spring has arrived on the coast but it can still be pretty chilly in Ottawa. If nothing else, Bennett certainly gave Pattullo plenty of time to take the air around Parliament Hill. When he arrived in Ottawa on 23 April, Pattullo was besieged by reporters who wanted his reaction to the suggestion that he was going to ask Bennett for $8 million. Duff replied with a laugh, 'Is that all they think I want.'[74] From then on, his sojourn in the east became less and less amusing. He met with Bennett and members of the cabinet the following day and reiterated what he had already explained many times by letter. The response was curt. The secretary of state, Charles Cahan, said that Pattullo's policies were tantamount to communism, and Bennett abruptly led his officials out of the meeting saying that he needed more time to consider British Columbia's requests.[75] Pattullo waited while Bennett made up his mind. Clearly the Conservative prime minister was not enthusiastic about financing the election promises of a Liberal premier. At the same time, Pattullo and his policies had by now attracted some attention in the east. The *Vancouver Sun* claimed his brand of activist Liberalism was being favourably compared to the caution of political leaders in Ottawa.[76] But in the end Bennett was unmoved. The British Columbia delegation waited in Ottawa for ten days before they heard, by letter from Bennett, that the answer was no. The preemptory rejection of British Columbia's position was also made public right away, before the provincial representatives had time to consider it. Pattullo wrote back immediately, but the prime minister had left town and the acting prime minister, Sir George Perley, could add nothing at all to Bennett's response.[77] For Duff it seemed that Ottawa did not change much, especially when Conservatives were in power. The whole exercise must have been reminiscent of his efforts to hold talks with Arthur Meighen fifteen years earlier.

Nor was the substance of Bennett's edict any more palatable than the manner in which it was handed down. Bennett wrote that he had considered British Columbia's request for assistance and, while he claimed he wanted to be helpful, he felt Pattullo and Hart had not been tough enough about reducing the deficit. He told them to submit a revised budget which showed 'something approaching a balance on current account.' He would not give British Columbia any more help as long as it had a deficit of more than $2 million, and he wished to have revised estimates within four or five weeks at the outside.[78] Pattullo's immediate response hinted that, in the event, the provincial deficit might be less than projected, but he had to be realistic. Then he restated his own view of the matter. With that, he took his leave from the capital, though Hart stayed behind to try to work out some details with Rhodes. But there was no change in the federal position and, the more he thought about it, the more angry Pattullo became. As he saw it, the federal government now wanted to control the provincial budget and he was adamant that 'under no circumstances will British Columbia consent to Dominion control over Provincial expenditure.'[79]

Having reached an impasse with Bennett, Pattullo tried other means. He left Ottawa for Montreal, New York, and Toronto to see if he could raise any funds on the money markets of the east. In Washington he saw Roosevelt briefly and expressed his admiration for the New Deal, but mostly he talked to financiers. He used all his charm and persuasion, and joked around with the financial boys on these occasions. Once, he later recalled, he had Logan call a meeting of those who often handled British Columbia's bonds. About seventy-five were present, but after he had addressed them and asked if there were any questions, no one had anything to say. So the premier of the ninth province told them a parable. A man died leaving nine sons, and on his deathbed called them all together and said that only the youngest was born in lawful wedlock. After a long silence the young fellow got up and said, 'Havn't you b____s got anything to say.' Laughter broke the silence of the meeting and all the financiers came forward ready to talk.[80] The story went the rounds of financial Canada, but in 1934 Pattullo failed to raise any money. Given the well-publicized possibility that British Columbia might default on its existing debt payments, Pattullo was hardly likely to raise more money on the open market.

Whenever he was in Ottawa Pattullo also met with Mackenzie King in the hope that, should there be a change of government, his views would be better understood at the federal level. After one such visit, Pattullo wrote to King of how enchanting he had found the setting at Kingsmere. He was writing from his own house which stood alone on the rocks overlooking the coast. Here on Canada's western shore, Pattullo continued, perhaps by way of making a point, the sea at this 'moment merely murmurs its message though at times it rises to thunderous eloquence.' He went on to summarize the position he had put before the federal government, his idea of interest-free loans for provincial works, and the need to improve the standard of living of all Canadians.[81] As he wrote, he probably did not know that he was already persona non grata in King's politics of personality. When Duff saw King in January 1934 the national Liberal leader was impressed by the way in which 'office had added to his solidity.' Indeed, King paid Pattullo an ultimate compliment when he wrote in his diary that 'in appearance he reminded me very much of grandfather's portrait.'[82] But this goodwill was only superficial and it dissipated when Pattullo uttered the two words, special powers, in the British Columbia legislature. For King the Special Powers Act was an assault on the rights of parliament that he, like his grandfather, William Lyon Mackenzie, was ordained to preserve. Next time Pattullo and King saw each other, King thought the premier was 'shockingly egotistical, conceited beyond words,' and, besides, he broke another of King's precepts by drinking both cocktails and whiskey at a social function. A few months later he was unimpressed when Pattullo told him 'what he thought all people were entitled to in the way of radios, automobiles, frigidaires etc. etc. – all through that state.[83] Pattullo no doubt explained his views with his usual vigour but in this case his enthusiasm was not infectious. King was studiously non-committal in reaction to Pattullo's ideas.

Meanwhile the 'negotiations' with Bennett continued. The nub of the problem was that Ottawa did not want to advance money to British Columbia without fiscal control over the province. For Pattullo the issue went right to the heart of Canadian federalism. He did not believe the framers of the British North America Act contemplated the possibility that the provinces would find themselves in debt to the federal government in order to carry out functions within provincial jurisdiction. Centralized control in such a far-flung country as Canada would, he argued, only lead to constant friction.[84] In June 1934 Rhodes telegraphed to Hart that the federal government still would not help British Columbia as long as the provincial government was running a deficit of $2 million. Though by now he should have known better, Pattullo was incredulous. He thought there must have been some mistake since this ultimatum put things back before his last meeting in Ottawa. If federal assistance was only forthcoming under the Rhodes's formula, then British Columbia would just have to do the best it could on its own, which would mean, of course, that the province would have to 'defer' some obligations.[85] The bottom line for Bennett was that he did not want any one province to default on loan payments since that would drive down the national credit rating. In the end, the crisis was averted by compromise. Pattullo was able to report a slightly improved financial position by July. Spending was down by about $500,000 and income was up by the same amount, therefore the actual deficit was about $1 million less than projected. On that basis British Columbia received, in Bennett's words, 'the same generous treatment as other western provinces.' That is to say, it was loaned enough money to meet immediate interest and relief payments.[86] Pattullo attended another dominion-provincial meeting, his third of the year, in late July, but again his arguments were dismissed. Ottawa gave enough help to enable his government to apply band aids to superficial sores, but not enough to cure the chronic ills that the depression had caused in British Columbia.

While these unsatisfactory dealings with Ottawa went on, it appears that Pattullo was seriously considering the possibility of moving to establish a semi-autonomous provincial economy. The plan was never announced as government policy so it is impossible to be certain about the details. Perhaps there were no details, but the general idea was that, if the federal government continued to be unresponsive, then British Columbia would 'go it alone.' Though he was not specific, Pattullo certainly threw out enough broad hints. He told the dominion government that if it 'feels that British Columbia is a burden I believe that British Columbia would be glad to remove the doubt.'[87] And, after his frustrating meetings in Ottawa in April, he said enough to reporters for the idea of a separate British Columbia economy to be the subject of newspaper discussion. The *Vancouver Sun* ran a front-page editorial headed in bold type, 'A Dominion of British Columbia.'[88] Such a scheme was clearly consistent with Pattullo's view that British Columbia was an empire unto itself. The veteran reporter Bruce Hutchison, who was one observer in a position to know, thought this was the real and secret purpose of the sweeping power to intervene in the provincial economy that the government granted itself under the Special Powers Act. It theoretically gave Pattullo the authority to do at the provincial level what he was trying to persuade Ottawa to carry out on a national basis: that is, to use British Columbia's resources and credit to finance a provincial recovery.[89]

However well formulated this 'go it alone' plan was, it was certainly never implemented. Pattullo was concerned that any move towards greater economic self-sufficiency would lead to secession talk in British Columbia and so he did not want any scheme to go off half-cocked. The explosiveness of the idea explained, for some, Pattullo's repeated protests of his loyalty to Canada and willingness to co-operate with the federal government.[90] John Hart likely played a large part in convincing him that as long as they were still trying to get help from the federal government they should not further antagonize Ottawa by striking out on their own. Prime Minister Bennett's instant and uninformed response to the Special Powers Act had shown just how touchy such an initiative could be. And besides, with the Conservatives already four years into their mandate, there was always the possibility that there would soon be a new and more sympathetic government in Ottawa.

But Pattullo could serve neither his people nor himself by simply standing and waiting. In British Columbia the pressure for action was building. He often warned the federal government of the dire consequences of inaction and made dark threats about the sinister forces that would benefit from mounting social unrest. 'Democracy is being endangered,' he said, 'because of the fatuous futility of proceeding along worn out lines.'[91] He was also concerned that, for the first time in the province's history, this depression was producing a large population of permanently unemployed: people who would never find work. Like most British Columbians, Pattullo knew all about economic cycles and had lived through downturns before. But both he and the province had always bounced back: immigration had always continued and economic expansion soon began again. This time it seemed that the effects of the disaster would be permanent, unless something were done soon. So Pattullo built on the legislation passed in the spring of 1934 and did what he could within the limits of his provincial jurisdiction.

By the end of the year he had several commissions and committees investigating numerous policy areas. The Economic Council was set to work immediately. As part of his new liberalism, Pattullo believed in employing experts to help achieve reforms. The obvious comparison was with Roosevelt's 'brain trust' in the United States, but in Canada too, intellectuals were advising and prodding governments to be more positive and active.[92] In British Columbia Pattullo appointed as chairman of the Economic Council a man who was to play a crucial role in advising his government on economic matters. He had tried to persuade Professor W.A. Carrothers of the Department of Economics at the University of British Columbia to run as a Liberal candidate in the 1933 election. Carrothers did not want to leave the university for the uncertainties of political life, but Pattullo was clearly impressed with his credentials and ability. Carrothers had a BA from the University of Manitoba and a PHD in economics from the University of Edinburgh. After post-graduate work at the London School of Economics and lecturing in political economy at Edinburgh, he returned to Canada to take up an appointment at the University of Saskatchewan. He moved to British Columbia in 1930 and now accepted Pattullo's urging to head up the Economic Council.[93] Carrothers subsequently wrote scores of reports and memoranda for the provincial government as well as publishing on a variety of aspects of British Columbia's economy and society. Under its able chairman, the staff of the Economic Council examined a host of questions: from the potential for the marketing the pelts of angora rabbits to the state of the province's major resource industries.

One major economic problem the Economic Council immediately put its finger on was the state of the coal industry. The coal companies, particularly on Vancouver Island, were suffering along with the other resource industries from the generally depressed economic conditions. Their sales were also falling off because of competition from an aggressively marketed new fuel. Coal was in many ways yesterday's source of energy and around the world it was being replaced by fuel oil. The problem in British Columbia was that all the fuel oil sold in the province was imported, largely from California. There was the suspicion that the multinational oil companies were unfairly undercutting the price of local coal and dumping surplus production in British Columbia. The Economic Council did not have time to investigate the complexities of the situation and so, probably on Carrothers's advice, Pattullo set up another commission to investigate that particular problem. In November 1934 his old colleague and attorney-general in the 1916 Liberal government, Mr Justice M.A. Macdonald, was appointed the sole commissioner of the Coal and Petroleum Products Commission. Macdonald was instructed to inquire into the methods and cost of production and distribution in both the coal and oil industries as well as the profits made in both sectors. Upon that basis he was asked to assess the comparative value of coal and oil as sources of energy, the contribution of each to the economy of the province, and, finally, whether or not the prices charged for coal and petroleum products were 'unjust or unreasonable.'[94]

Another area where Pattullo was making use of the best expertise was an investigation into state health insurance.[95] The problem of providing medical care for those who could not afford it had become a major issue through the early 1930s but Pattullo's was the only government in Canada to attempt to introduce a public plan during the decade. Doctors' incomes were declining, though probably less rapidly than most, and they were increasingly vexed about providing services to indigents without payment.[96] There was growing pressure on governments, from both doctors and patients, to step in and deal with the problem. In June 1933 Winnipeg doctors went on strike for seven months, denying all but emergency services to relief recipients, and in Vancouver doctors refused to work at the outpatient department of the Vancouver General Hospital because it was a major source of unpaid work.[97] State health insurance was widely discussed and the British example was frequently cited. In British Columbia the idea already had a long history. The Oliver government had appointed a royal commission to study health insurance along with other welfare issues in 1919.[98] Pattullo was personally highly committed to health insurance, though within his government the ball was carried by George Weir. The provincial secretary believed in the concept with a fervour that tended to obscure political reality. Weir did realize that 'the New Jerusalem' could not be built overnight. While there would always be 'survival of the fittest,' the function of government, he argued, was 'to fit the greatest number to survive.' Like Pattullo, Weir wanted to achieve a just balance between 'individual initiative and social control.'[99] At a less lofty level, Weir told caucus members that, if the Liberals did not introduce health insurance, they would 'be swept into the discard and a more radical party will assume power.' As he put it to his colleagues, only a 'purblind reactionary could fail to see the gravity of the situation.'[100] Unfortunately, many fell into Weir's categorization, both inside and outside the caucus.

Unaware of the opposition he would face, Weir began by canvassing medical opinion. He sent out a questionnaire to British Columbia doctors and, on the face of it, the returns showed strong support for health insurance. Of those who responded, 93 per cent were in favour of a medical plan. But only 65 per cent replied, and those who favoured the idea did so on the proviso that a mutually satisfactory scheme could be agreed upon.[101] It was not much of a survey, but on the strength of it the minister proceeded.

Weir persuaded Pattullo to hire one of Canada's most able and energetic scholars in the nascent area of social welfare. Harry Cassidy arrived in Victoria in September 1934 to take up the newly created position of director of social welfare. Cassidy was a native of the province whose first degree was from the University of British Columbia. He had a PHD from the Robert Brookings Graduate School in Washington, DC, and since 1929 he had been assistant professor of social work at the University of Toronto. He already had a considerable reputation as a result of his investigations into unemployment, housing, and labour conditions, he had close connections with the intellectuals of the League for Social Reconstruction, and he had taken a hand in drafting parts of the Regina Manifesto. The appointment of Cassidy, and of those who worked around him, showed that for the moment British Columbia led the way in the professionalization of social policy. 'Cassidy was one of the first of a new breed in Canada: the academically trained social policy expert.'[102] He had his own agenda for economic and social reform: that policy makers had to move beyond the notion of individual responsibility and embrace the concept that the state should provide support for the disadvantaged. Given these views, he was excited by the prospect of building up social services in British Columbia under the reformist Pattullo government.[103] Many areas of public health came under his jurisdiction but his major task was to establish health insurance. He immediately set about drafting a provincial health insurance bill.

The objective was to have legislation ready for the 1935 session. Weir and Cassidy worked on the scheme in consultation with British Columbia doctors and with actuaries and financial experts in the east. They also kept in close touch with Pattullo. When he was in Toronto, Weir wrote to the premier to report on his talks about health insurance. He also added some editorial comment. 'Toronto,' he noted, 'still has its transcendental smugness arising from long and almost exclusive contact with the Deity.'[104] While the boys from British Columbia could joke about the east, they could not escape its influence, even in areas that appeared to be within the purview of the province. British Columbia's health insurance bill was drafted by the beginning of 1935 when, once again, Ottawa threw a spanner in the works. In a series of radio talks, beginning on 2 January, Bennett announced to astonished Canadians that he planned to embark on a bold new program of reform. Included among his potpourri of proposals was health insurance. When it came to the legislative point, Bennett's announcements proved to be a largely bogus, pre-election ploy, and in particular he had no health insurance bill ready to present to the house. Nevertheless, Pattullo was forced to wait and see what the federal intentions really were.[105]

Rather than passing health insurance legislation, Weir tabled the draft bill along with an explanatory memorandum on 22 March 1935 with a view to facilitating wider discussion of the measure.[106] Cassidy continued to meet with doctors and a Hearings Committee was established to tour the province and listen to the public's reaction to the bill. Allon Peebles, another British Columbian with outside expertise, was appointed chairman of the committee. Peebles had a doctorate in economics from Columbia University and had worked as a researcher for the American Committee on the Cost of Health Care before returning to Canada as a life insurance executive.[107] Along with Cassidy, he was to pilot the bill through the deliberation phase so that Weir could pass it into law. The trouble with this approach was that the extended discussion of the health insurance proposal invigorated the opposition. Pattullo was confident that the measure was worthwhile, and that it 'should be able to run the gamut of any criticism.'[108] But in hindsight, it would have been better had he gritted his teeth and put the measure through without delay. Had he done so, British Columbia would have become the first jurisdiction in North America to bring in state health insurance. As it was, the impetus was lost in the swirl of conflicting opinion.

There were two major sources of opposition to the bill. The first was within Pattullo's own cabinet and caucus where there was serious disagreement on the issue. Ministers such as Gray and MacDonald had objections on principle while Hart fretted about the cost of such a measure. The more public and vocal opposition came from the medical profession. As Cassidy put it after the draft legislation was introduced: 'The doctors have begun to howl.'[109] The fundamental problem was that the government and the doctors had divergent views about the function of medical insurance. For Pattullo and Weir it was a relief measure, designed to help those who could not help themselves. The doctors, in contrast, saw the scheme as a means whereby the government would supplement their declining incomes. So while both government and the medical profession were in favour of health insurance in the abstract, when it came to the details of this particular scheme they were miles apart. Business interests also came out against the plan in the later stages of the debate.

Amidst growing controversy, a second and much watered down version of the bill was formulated and brought before the house in 1936. The wage ceiling for those to be insured was dropped, as were contributions by employers and employees. At the same time the doctors were to be paid more. The revenue gap created by these contradictory provisions was narrowed by eliminating government contributions to coverage for indigents. On the final vote, seven members of the Liberal caucus were among the nays, but the cabinet was whipped into line and the Health Insurance Act was passed with the additional support of most the CCF.[110] Peebles was then given the task of setting up the organization that would put the act into effect.

While these longer-term economic and social initiatives were important, the most pressing immediate task facing the Pattullo government was to turn the rhetoric of 'work and wages' into the reality of employment for British Columbians. The long suit in Pattullo's deck of policies to deal with the depression was still government spending on public works. He wanted to start projects that would provide employment, develop the province's infrastructure, and prime the economic pump. There would be other spin-off benefits as well: the development of roads, for example, would open up new parts of the province and encourage more tourists to come to British Columbia. In theory the scheme was based to some extent on Roosevelt's National Recovery Administration; in practice Pattullo had to do what he could with limited resources. Ottawa had provided money for a few specific projects early in 1934, but it had shown no interest in the idea of using the national credit to finance an extensive program of public works.[111] So Pattullo was reduced to instigating particular provincial projects and even then facing the obstructionism of the federal government.

Today the Pattullo name is better known to British Columbians as a bridge than as a premier, but few remember the controversy surrounding that bridge across the Fraser River. Though it was built primarily to provide jobs for British Columbians, that was not the only motivation. The bridge arose in part out of the settling of an old political score. After he had dissolved the legislature, but before the election in 1933, Tolmie had entered into an agreement with a company to build a bridge across the Fraser at Ladner. Pattullo immediately stated that, if elected, he would not be bound by any last-minute contracts signed by the Tolmie government. After the election he quickly cancelled the Ladner bridge contract and announced that the whole question of road links to Vancouver would have to be re-examined.[112] There were good reasons for building a bridge further up the Fraser at New Westminster: that location was closer to the Fraser Valley and a bridge would be easier to construct there than on the flat lands of Delta. There was already a combined railway and highway bridge across the Fraser at New Westminster but it had become completely inadequate. When, by the fall of 1934, it was clear that Bennett would do little for British Columbia, Pattullo announced that the provincial government would issue bonds to finance the construction of a new bridge adjacent to the old one at New Westminster.[113]

It was yet another Pattullo policy that produced a great hue and cry, and, once again, the controversy only made him more determined. There were, of course, local political considerations. Critics said, not without justification, that the Ladner bridge was scuttled because the Delta riding returned a CCF member while New Westminster was represented by Wells Gray, Pattullo's minister of lands. Vancouverites were upset because they would still have to drive to New Westminster to cross the Fraser River. It seemed to many that the old Pattullo, who ignored the interests of Vancouver, was resurrected. The *Sun* reminded people of past imbroglios such as the Valhalla cemetery and Capilano timber allocation.[114] Others objected to the plan to build a toll bridge, and still others simply argued that the provincial government could not afford such a project under current economic conditions. Prominent among this last group was R.B. Bennett, for whom it was merely another example of provincial extravagance. He refused to provide any financial help for the project and, when Pattullo decided to go ahead on his own, Bennett tried to sabotage the scheme by using the federal jurisdiction over navigable waterways. Bennett even took time to consult with the engineer who had built the existing bridge who, not surprisingly, was confident his structure could be safely modified to carry increased capacity. The prime minister passed the information on to the federal Department of Public Works, which conducted a public hearing on British Columbia's application for approval to build the bridge under the Navigable Waterways Protection Act.[115]

If, as the *Vancouver Sun* accused, Pattullo was obstinate and pig-headed about building this bridge, it was partly because he had to be. It was necessary to be singleminded to get even this comparatively straightforward proposal through the welter of local interests and federal-provincial complications. When the Liberal member for Dewdney, David Strachan, explained the depth of opposition to the bridge in the lower Fraser Valley he reckoned that it would be 'political suicide' to go ahead with the plan. Typically, Duff shrugged off the warning. 'I do not think,' he replied, 'that we should allow a temporary and evanescent opinion to prevent us carrying out measures which we know to be essentially for the public good.'[116] The bridge proposal was yet another measure he had to muscle through the legislature, and there were even suggestions in mainland newspapers that he had threatened to resign if Liberals did not get into line behind the project. The CCF made unsubstantiated allegations that the bridge scheme was part of a deal for campaign funds.[117] Amidst bitter debate, the legislation to enable construction of the bridge went through just before the end of the 1935 session. Five Liberals broke ranks on the issue.[118] After tenders were called, the contract was awarded to the Dominion Bridge Company. At the same time, Pattullo also announced a $2 million public works program to provide work in other parts of the province.[119]

At the local level he had been put on the defensive over the Fraser River bridge proposal while the federal government had yet to approve the scheme. Within the province, Pattullo particularly resented what he saw as misinformed criticism from Vancouver newspapers and he took to the air waves to counter the editorial views. These attacks served to revive his feeling that opposition to his policies came largely from the urban centres while in the north the people appreciated his efforts.[120] In Ottawa, the prime minister continued to drag his feet by refusing to approve the project. Now he wanted the province to put a lift span on the old dual-purpose bridge so that it could still be used by the railways and yet allow ocean-going vessels to go underneath. One of the problems with the existing bridge was that the swing span was slow to operate and the delay created traffic jams. But Pattullo responded that British Columbia could not afford the extra quarter of a million dollars estimated on these improvements. He threatened to cancel the contract with the railway companies, which he was entitled to do on three-years' notice, and then they would have to dismantle the old bridge and build their own across the Fraser. In the end he announced to British Columbians he could wait no longer. He would go ahead with building the new bridge even though the federal government had not given its approval.[121]

The skirmish with Bennett over the new Fraser River bridge was only one of many in an ongoing war with Ottawa. Through late 1934 and early 1935 Pattullo continued the struggle without much hope of making headway. The bottom line for Bennett was that he did not want the provinces to default and he continued to give British Columbia just enough to keep going. In August 1934 Pattullo got an additional $1 million to spend on public works. He noted that, while every little bit helped, the amount was hopelessly inadequate to deal with unemployment in the province.[122] At the end of the year Bennett acknowledged that British Columbia's claim for better terms had some validity and he granted the province an interim increase of $750,000 in federal payments. But these were only stop-gap measures. There was no fundamental overhaul of the federal-provincial relationship of the kind that Pattullo advocated. At one point Bennett indicated that he was toying with the idea of calling yet another conference with the provinces to look at matters such as duplicate taxation and jurisdiction over social legislation, health, and agriculture, with a view to making amendments to the British North America Act.[123] The suggestion was only tentative and the prime minister quickly dropped the idea. The born-again reformism that Bennett preached in his radio broadcasts in January 1935 also proved to be a superficial exercise in public relations. Communications between Pattullo and Bennett became terse, as if each recognized there was not much point in trying to convince the other. In February Bennett wrote to Pattullo that he had received complaints that the state of the road from Kingsgate on the American border south of Cranbrook was so bad it was reducing tourist traffic. Pattullo simply replied that he was aware of the problem and would be glad to turn that stretch of road over to the dominion.[124] He knew nothing would change as long as Bennett was prime minister.

Yet pressure for action continued to build in British Columbia, and Pattullo faced mounting criticism for his inability to produce work and wages. There was growing tension between the municipalities and the provincial government. The relationship between the cities and the province was analogous to that between Victoria and Ottawa. The local governments felt they were bearing the brunt of relief and the province was not doing enough to assist them. In October 1934 Pattullo refused to meet at short notice with the Union of British Columbia Municipalities on the question of the division of relief costs. His statement that he would not stand for delegations 'gate crashing like a mob from the street' was not calculated to win many friends. At the beginning of January 1935 the ubiquitous Gerry McGeer was sworn in as the new mayor of Vancouver and he immediately proposed to reduce interest payments on city bonds by 50 per cent. Pattullo did not want the major cities reneging on their financial obligations for much the same reason that Bennett did not want the provinces to default: it would drive down the credit rating of the senior level of government. Pattullo opposed McGeer's unilateral move to avoid interest obligations but did finally agree to legislation that would allow Vancouver to defer, but not cancel, payments. Pattullo did not reiterate McGeer's line that 'if the national government will not issue money it will probably have to issue bullets,' but with this pressure from the cities he repeatedly tried, in more temperate language, to persuade Bennett to provide additional money for relief.[125]

McGeer's remark was not entirely alarmist. The clearest signs of growing anger were among the men who had been consigned to the relief camps. A concerted campaign was developing against the appalling conditions and the futile work in the camps. The Relief Camp Workers' Union was organizing strikes and men were gathering on the streets of Vancouver. Pattullo warned Bennett that something should be done to deal with the grievances before the 'agitators' attracted more public support. The prime minister had little to add to his already stated view that the provincial government was responsible for law and order within the province. It is clear to me, he had written earlier in the year, 'that your government has not yet exhausted the means within its power to control conditions.'[126] The only other suggestion he now had to make was that the provincial government could visit the camps and investigate conditions. Pattullo replied that such an investigation would hardly meet the situation. In British Columbia the whole relief camp system was being condemned in the court of public opinion. By late March Pattullo saw no point in carrying on a futile conversation by letter and telegram with a federal government that failed to comprehend what was going on in British Columbia. He warned Acting Prime Minister George Perley that if he were under the impression 'that every ukase issued by your Government is accepted by public opinion generally your Government is labouring under a grave delusion.'[127]

The camp workers had also reached the end of their tether. In April 1935 there was a mass exodus from the camps and a series of large demonstrations in Vancouver. Pattullo continued to maintain that both the relief camps and the problem of unemployment were federal responsibilities and by June the strikers seemed to agree. The 'On-to-Ottawa' trek was organized in an attempt to convince the federal government that something had to be done.[128] But the leaders of the trek got no further when they met with Bennett in Ottawa than Pattullo had done, while the rank and file were savagely attacked by the police on the streets of Regina. Many workers in British Columbia who did have jobs were not much happier than those who had left the camps. Throughout the spring and summer of 1935 there was a series of strikes in mines in the interior as well as a major walkout on the Vancouver waterfront.

Amidst this growing social discontent some commentators felt that Pattullo was spending too much time negotiating with Ottawa. There was no doubt he was under great pressure and some feared it had 'caused an Ottawa or B.N.A. obsession' that prevented him from seeing the things that could be done within the province.[129] People were growing weary of being asked to be patient 'until that far off divine event' of an agreement with the federal government occurs.[130] Pattullo responded that there was no point in playing around with lesser issues while the fundamental problem remained. As far as he was concerned the increased centralization of Canadian government was preventing him from implementing effective reform. Given federal control over taxation, money, and banking, British Columbia could not float a bond issue or build a bridge, let alone provide work and wages for the unemployed, without a debilitating row with Ottawa. 'Whether we like it or whether we do not like it,' he explained to a Prince Rupert Liberal, 'our problem has got to be fought out with the Dominion.'[131]

In the meantime he was biding his time until there was, perhaps, a new government at the centre. Not that the prospect was fraught with promise. Pattullo had, once again, tried to convince Mackenzie King to be 'definite and concrete' on such matters as finance, social welfare, and public works. The Liberal leader's reply was as bland and non-committal as ever: when the right moment came the public would be left in no doubt about his position on any question.[132] Unfortunately the right moment did not come before the next election. By October 1935 Bennett's government was so unpopular that Mackenzie King won a sweeping victory without having to commit himself to doing anything much at all about the depression. British Columbia was somewhat more ambivalent than the rest of the country about King's policy of having no policy. The Liberals did well in all regions east of the Rockies in the 1935 federal election, whereas on the west coast they got only six of the province's sixteen seats. The Conservatives still had five seats and H.H. Stevens, Bennett's former minister of trade and commerce, had been re-elected under the Reconstruction banner. More ominous, perhaps, was the fact that the CCF had attracted a larger share of the popular vote than the Liberals, even if they had only three members of parliament to show for it.[133] Some British Columbia Liberals, particularly in Vancouver where the CCF had done well, saw the federal results as more of a comment on Pattullo's government than on King's campaign.

Still, the autocratic, dogmatic Bennett was gone, and Mackenzie King was back at the head of a Liberal government. There was little doubt that King was a smoother manager than Bennett, but, if anything, the Liberal leader was even more conservative than his predecessor on financial matters. He immediately signaled that direction by appointing the fiscally orthodox Charles Dunning as minister of finance. Though he was less open about saying so than Bennett, King had already dismissed the idea of government expenditure as a way out of the depression. Deficit spending would definitely not be an item on the King government's ledger. In the final analysis, Bennett the businessman had always believed that the provinces should not default on their loan payments. King, in contrast, could certainly contemplate, if not quite with equanimity, stepping over that financial brink. So King's election did not offer premiers like Duff Pattullo, who had expensive, reformist ideas, much to be optimistic about. The prime minister was a Liberal and so was Pattullo, but the two were a continent apart on what Liberalism meant.

Yet at some level Pattullo was still hoping against hope that King would not live up to expectations. He wrote the new prime minister a long, self-justificatory letter soon after the federal election. He claimed that, while some of the enthusiasts in the provincial party may have run away with the idea of work and wages, he had always 'predicated a works programme upon the co-operation of the Dominion Government.'[134] King could hardly disagree with need for collaboration, but within Canadian Confederation it is much easier for the prime minister to appear co-operative if he does not intend to do anything very energetic. Pattullo was certainly forewarned and therefore should have been forearmed. In his forthright way, Robert Cromie, the editor of the *Vancouver Sun*, had put it most clearly when he asked rhetorically, 'You think you will get a lot of action from Mackenzie King,' and then provided the answer, 'you will get nothing except evasions and promises and procrastinations. So, if the whole Pattullo programme is tied to the time we will get action from Mackenzie King, we are sunk.'[135] The tone of Pattullo's letter to King indicated a weariness of spirit arising from the fact that deep down he recognized that, although there was a new federal government, many things would not change in Ottawa. When King was in Victoria during the election campaign he thought Pattullo looked strained and dour, and he also had the feeling the welcome was somewhat perfunctory.[136] While the second reaction may have indicated more about King than Pattullo, Duff did realize that, even when it ceased to be entertaining, the political show must go on.

Like a jaded carnival man who has seen it all before but can still put a false smile on his face, Mackenzie King cranked up the dominion-provincial merry-go-round once more. The first conference under the new prime minister was in early December 1935. Pattullo left Victoria hoping for action in three areas of nationwide concern: a redistribution of taxing authority, effective action to relieve unemployment, and reduction of debt charges. Like most premiers he also had agenda items that were particular to his province. He was still trying to convince the federal government to take over the Pacific Great Eastern, for example.[137] As the conference began it looked as though at least the tone would be different under King's chairmanship. He sounded conciliatory and seemed to be willing to listen, so Pattullo gave a strong speech outlining the points he had made in Ottawa so many times before. But then, as the discussion droned on, it became apparent that, while the tones were softer, the substance of the meeting was very similar to those under Bennett. Though King talked a good game, he was not prepared to do anything along the lines Pattullo proposed. The federal government did agree to increase the supply of band aids a little by raising federal grants to the provinces for relief. There was plenty of facile rhetoric about collaboration and laying the groundwork for future progress. Yet all of this superficial chatter could not conceal the fact that nothing concrete had been achieved. It was perhaps significant that Pattullo was absent when King called the other premiers together so they could put on a smile for the camera.[138]

Some ideas outlined at the conference were then the subject of further discussion. The most significant was raised by Dunning with a committee of the conference. He suggested the federal government would assist the provinces with borrowing at lower rates of interest if they would agree to his plan to form a Loan Council to oversee such financial arrangements. Dunning was vague on detail, but Pattullo and the British Columbia delegation made it clear from the start they would have nothing to do with the proposed Loan Council if it meant any reduction in provincial autonomy.[139] Meaningless consultations continued through the spring of 1936. Some members of the federal cabinet had been disposed to making larger payments to hard-pressed provinces, but King had disabused them of any such ideas even while the December conference with the premiers was in session. He told his colleagues that now was the time to get 'down to rock bottom,' and the provinces would get no more grants without increased federal supervision.[140] Pattullo was three times in Ottawa in early 1936, once in January and twice in April, attempting to clarify the situation. Though he was never told in as many words, he soon realized that the Loan Council scheme simply meant federal control by another name. In March 1936 King allowed Alberta to default on loan payments when Premier William Aberhart would not agree to the Loan Council plan. That left Pattullo as the major hold-out against the proposal and fortunately British Columbia was able to meet its debt repayments from its own revenue.[141] Pattullo argued that the dominion already had too much control over provincial finances and further centralization would only increase the friction between the two levels of government. British Columbians would not be relegated to 'mere hewers of wood and drawers of water' with little control over their own affairs. King, however, thought that Pattullo 'entertains the most absurd ideas about the extent to which public monies should be spent at this time.'[142]

By early 1936 it was as clear to many observers as it was to the two protagonists that Pattullo and King had diametrically opposed views on how to deal with the depression. Pattullo wrote to King on Valentine's Day to point out that under the current circumstances it was impossible for governments to balance their budgets and also carry out essential measures. He suggested, yet again, that past debts be refinanced at lower rates and that public works be funded with non-interest-bearing, publicly created credit that would be repaid during the life of the project.[143] There was no Valentine's sentiment in King's response. He was horrified by Pattullo's ideas. He firmly believed in the dogma of the balanced budget and therefore that governments should spend less, not more, during a depression. He feared for the future of his country if men like Pattullo were to control public affairs. Why, he confided to his diary, these men want to 'use the public treasury as if it was something to be given away rather than guarded.'[144] Pattullo and King represented two separate strands of Canadian Liberalism: King retained the old laissez faire Liberalism of a bygone age while Pattullo had absorbed the newer Liberalism that called for a more active state. Pattullo's ideas about government spending to stimulate economic activity arose as much out of his early experience on the underdeveloped British Columbia frontier as it did out of his reading on economics in the 1930s. Perhaps remembering his Prince Rupert days, Pattullo told King that 'there comes a time when businesses in difficulties require fresh capital to push them to success and that is the position governmentally in Canada today.' From Pattullo's perspective, King's policy of 'heroic deflation' would only make things worse.[145] Each of them had come to his point of view through long experience and the two Liberals were now set in views that were, it seemed, irreconcilable.

As much as they disagreed on policy, there was also a clash of personalities between the two leaders. Pattullo, it sometimes seemed, had all those characteristics that King abhorred. The prime minister described the premier of British Columbia as vain and egotistical.[146] Part of the problem between them was that, in his own way, King was also utterly self-absorbed. In contrast to the tight, introspective King, Pattullo was gregarious and outgoing. He enjoyed socializing with other premiers and politicians when he was in Ottawa. Such behaviour did little to endear him to a prime minister who believed that 'it is the social life that destroys' and wanted to exclude all drinkers from his cabinet. King was alarmed when he saw Pattullo drinking heavily at a dinner party and wondered if he would 'blow up' one of these days.[147] Pattullo was not an alcoholic, but he was an accomplished social drinker of some capacity. He enjoyed the company of Mitchell Hepburn, the premier of Ontario, and later Maurice Duplessis of Quebec, when they were in Ottawa. On one occasion, after a function at Rideau Hall, he took a bunch of provincial premiers back to his rooms at the Château Laurier and he and Duplessis sat up drinking until after four in the morning.[148] He did not always see eye to eye with these men on political matters, but, unlike King, Pattullo believed in being affable on a social level towards those with whom he had political disagreements. With only one or two exceptions, he did not hold personal grudges with political opponents, while King could scarcely separate politics and personality.

So Pattullo's reformist Liberalism had smashed into a brick wall of fiscal conservatism maintained by a prime minister who disliked him. Though he would keep on trying, he knew that it would be next to impossible to convince King to restructure Canada's economic system and that the federal government would not finance work and wages in British Columbia. Even the higher relief payments to the provinces that were established at the dominion-provincial conference in December 1935 were decreased below their original level the following spring.[149] King did manage to see his way clear to giving federal approval to the Fraser River bridge, a project that by now was well under way and could not be stopped. In October 1936 British Columbia was given a $500,000 loan for public works, but it was only a drop in the bucket of Pattullo's expansive policies.[150] If the fuel were to come from the federal government, then Pattullo's plans to get his province out of the depression were running on empty.

Having got little or nothing out of Ottawa, he turned to his own people. The winter of 1935–6 was the low point of his first government as the patience of British Columbians wore very thin. Pattullo continued to argue that his province was like a wealthy man with plenty of assets but a temporary shortage of cash. Many of his growing number of critics in British Columbia thought the premier was rather more like Mr Micawber making unrealistic plans 'in case anything turned up.'[151] His speeches in the house during the spring session in 1936 were very defensive, as he tried to emphasize the positive achievements and explain away the failures. He was also becoming irritated with criticism in the press and in his worst moments he hinted darkly about imposing restraints on what he saw as the dissemination of misinformation.[152] Duff Pattullo was not his usual buoyant self.

His despondency and touchiness extended to personal matters. Early in 1936 he was haunted by a ghost of his family's past. He received a letter from his youngest brother Andrew in California who said he might visit Victoria that year. Andrew was the black sheep of the family. He lived in the United States, supported most of the time by George as he moved from place to place and in and out of relationships. He had taken the family tendency to drinking to excess, and was by now an alcoholic. So Duff wrote to George to ask him to use his influence to prevent Andrew from coming to Victoria. He expected one of the hardest summers since he entered politics and he did not want any embarrassment.[153] Then, in July 1936, Andrew shot himself. Duff was the first to get the news from California. He wrote to George who took care of the arrangements, just as he had done for his uncle Andrew more than thirty years ago.[154] When he explained what had happened to George, Duff was terse and unforthcoming as if he were keeping a tight rein on his feelings.

Duff and George kept in touch though it was perhaps fortunate that George was too busy with his business affairs to come to Victoria and visit his brother. He had become a bitter and strident opponent of Roosevelt and the New Deal in the United States. In an article published in the *Saturday Evening Post* later in the year, he denounced what he saw as New Deal giveaways which he believed were sapping the true spirit of the nation. The remedy for America's problems was not to be found in handing the 'management of finance and industry over to the Government.' As far as George was concerned, 'history has yet to record that driving out one crowd merely to install a greedier has ever improved a situation.' And so it was that, under the New Deal, 'campaigns which started out with the laudable objective of affording relief to the stricken presently developed into wholesale raids on the national purse.' To the end of his days, George Pattullo would remain an opponent of the 'prodigal spending and waste' of the New Deal because he believed it led to the 'destruction of the self-reliance of our people.'[155] Both were strong personalities with strong views, so it was just as well that Duff and George had agreed to differ in their political opinions and still remained affectionate as brothers.[156] George told anti-Roosevelt jokes in his letters to Duff, such as when an applicant at the pearly gates was told by St Peter they were having trouble in heaven because God had overreached himself and was strutting up and down pretending he was Franklin Roosevelt![157] It would not have helped Duff if George were to express such views in British Columbia at the wrong political moment. And the summer of 1936 would definitely have been the wrong moment.

Had there been opinion polls in those days they would have undoubtedly shown the popularity of the Pattullo government very much in the mid-term doldrums. And, like Roosevelt, Pattullo would have to go to the people before long, though he could be more flexible than the American president about the timing. In the 1930s by-elections were, in many ways, the equivalent of polls. They provided political leaders with an opportunity to demonstrate they still had popular support between general elections. In Pattullo's case they were also a chance to put his political woes and the wrangling with Ottawa behind him and to enjoy himself once more, out among the people of British Columbia.

Two by-elections were due in 1936, in Omineca and Vancouver-Burrard. They were made necessary by the resignations of Alex Manson and Gerry McGeer to run, unsuccessfully as it turned out, as Liberal candidates in the federal election in October 1935. He was not sorry to loose either of them as provincial members, but he was worried about the outcome of the by-elections. He delayed setting the dates in case something came of his negotiations with the new regime in Ottawa, but by the summer constitutionally he could wait no longer. There were many signs that the provincial Liberal party was beginning to fray around the edges. Pattullo could never count on all Liberal members to support him on major policy initiatives, but during the session at the beginning of 1936 two of them had voted against him on a motion of confidence.[158] There were calls for a provincial convention by those who wanted to ask questions about Pattullo's leadership. And the surest sign of insecurity within the party was that coalition chatter could be heard around the clubs where Vancouver's elite gathered to discuss how they should run the province. Some prominent Liberals were advocating an arrangement with the Conservatives to ensure the defeat of the CCF in the coming by-elections. Pattullo would have none of it. He knew that such an agreement would only drive Liberals away to the CCF, and that was likely to be the thin end of the wedge for a union government.[159] It was time for the leader to reassert his control over his fractious party and Pattullo's only tactic in such circumstances was full steam ahead into the fray.

He began where he thought he had the best chance of success, in the north among his own kind. He called the by-election in Omineca for 22 June and then threw himself into the campaign with characteristic energy. He did not confine himself to Omineca, but travelled throughout the province as he had done when he was leader of the opposition. In Victoria he waded into a federal by-election campaign without obvious support from his ministers and used it as a vote of confidence on his government.[160] He went to the Cariboo, to the farthest reaches of the Peace River country, and on to Dawson City, as well as to his old haunts in Omineca north of Prince Rupert. He became the first flying premier of the province as the trip was made by airplane. The Pattullo of old was on the go again and it seemed he had not lost his appeal, at least in the outlying parts of the province. The candidate in Omineca was a newcomer, obviously not as prominent or well-known as Manson, so it was likely the party's majority would be reduced. But the important thing was that, when the count was made, the Liberal was in front of the CCF candidate by more than two hundred votes and the Conservative was a distant third.[161] The party had retained the seat and much of the steam was taken out of the opposition to Pattullo's leadership. The dissidents had not been eliminated, but they at least ran for cover. A meeting of the Liberal executive a week after the victory in Omineca was much less troublesome than it would have been if the by-election had been lost.[162]

The win in the north renewed Pattullo's confidence and his leadership, but both could be undermined again if the Vancouver-Burrard by-election went the other way. When polling day was set for 2 September 1936 Pattullo knew that this one would not be so easy. He was not as comfortable and his leadership was not so sure in Vancouver. Once again the new Liberal candidate would not be as prominent as the former member, and the by-election turned into a real test of party strength when the two other parties nominated major candidates. The Conservative was the new party leader, Dr F.P. Patterson, while the CCF nominee was Lyle Telford. The co-operators of the CCF had been squabbling among themselves again and the moderate Robert Connell was ousted from the party leadership.[163] Telford was party president and was hoping to use the by-election as the way to become the CCF house leader. Pattullo bore the brunt of what was a long and intense campaign in which the Liberals fully exploited the divisions within the CCF. The vote was a close one, but the result was the one Pattullo wanted. The Liberal, John Forester, was more than four hundred votes ahead of Telford, and the Conservatives ran third.[164]

The political situation had swung Pattullo's way and by the fall of 1936 it was clear that the province's finances were also in better shape. During the summer John Hart had surprised many financiers by meeting the government's debt payments out of a special fund he had conserved for the purpose. Then, during the fall sitting of the legislature, he produced a budget that had some very positive signs. Revenues were up to the highest in the history of the province and so expenditure could be increased in some areas. There was more assistance to the municipalities, the amount spent on roads was increased, and grants for the university and health services were also raised. Even with this spending, the debt was reduced a little and Hart budgeted for a slight surplus on his operating account, though it still did not include unemployment relief or the sinking fund.[165] British Columbia was not booming as it once had, but clearly Hart's careful financial management had paid off. The provincial government had weathered the worst of the financial storm and survived. Now even observers in the east were beginning to take notice. The *Monetary Times* pronounced that Hart's budget speech was 'one of the most encouraging pieces of financial literature that has been issued in recent years' and *Maclean's Magazine* ran an article entitled 'Recovery in B.C.'[166] Pattullo and Hart were now able to go to Toronto and negotiate the sale of British Columbia bonds.[167]

By the beginning of 1937 Pattullo was a great deal more pleased with himself than he had been a year earlier. The summer campaigning had revived his spirits and his province was in a healthier financial position. He wrote to George sounding much more like his former self. He noted that the year had been a hectic one, but then he had not had a holiday, in the usual sense of the word, since 1908 when he left Dawson. At the same time his twenty years in politics had all been a holiday.[168] He was accustomed to having a check up with a doctor in the east at the end of every year. This year his doctor reported that, physically, he was fit enough to 'rule British Columbia for twenty more years.' There was some minor evidence he was getting older and he should lose some weight. He was advised to limit 'drinking to two scotches a day, avoid desserts except fruit, avoid soups and potatoes' and he would lose a pound or two a week. Follow this 'not terribly strenuous regime ... the ten commandments; the liberal policies, and,' his doctor concluded, 'they will have to shoot you on Judgment Day.'[169]

At the beginning of 1937 Duff Pattullo celebrated his sixty-fourth birthday. His changed political fortunes were indicated by the fact that George Miller, who had replaced McGeer as mayor of Vancouver, arranged a dinner party with the city's leading Liberals. It was a time to look back on past achievements and as well as to contemplate future possibilities. In a press statement released that day he reflected on his first years in the legislature and how the problems of returned servicemen were similar to those of the unemployed today. He recalled how the Liberal government was able to implement effective policies after the First World War because it could be done without reference to outside authority.[170] The contrast with the present was obvious. On the brighter side, he was, by the beginning of 1937, once more the master of his own party. And, largely as a result of his efforts, the party's prospects were also much improved.

For that, among other reasons, it was time to think about an election. He had until 1938, but he did not want to follow the example of the Conservatives and overrun his mandate. The CCF was still split apart by ideological disputes and the ouster of Connell, while the new leaders of both of the other parties had just been defeated in a by-election. The provincial economy had picked up and so had the financial position of the government. Right now things looked reasonably good and, in the uncertain economic and political climate of the day, Pattullo could not be sure how long they would last. He had the legislature dissolved on 12 April 1937 and called a general election for 1 June. He was attempting what no other government leader in Canada had succeeded in doing since 1930: to be re-elected with a solid majority.[171] He knew this election was not a foregone conclusion. There were two specific issues on which the government faced opposition. One was long-standing and the other had just developed.

The first of these was health insurance. The revised Health Insurance Act had become law at the beginning of 1936 and Weir and his officials were working towards implementing the scheme in early 1937. The opposition to state health insurance did not, however, quieten down with the passing of legislation. Before the bill was passed, Harry Cassidy accepted the fact that 'a good many of our bright ideas are being cut out of it as the politicians and the various conflicting interests paw over it.' Yet even he was not prepared for the persistent and noisy objections after the act went through. 'It is hard for one who was not here,' he wrote to a friend, 'to realize the intensity of the controversy engendered by so mild a measure.'[172] Less than a month before the 1 March 1937 deadline for putting the plan in place, Weir was still optimistic. He argued that the doctors had simply given the government a splendid fighting issue for the election: the protection of the people's health against an avaricious medical monopoly.[173] Others in the cabinet were getting very cold feet. When the crisis point came later in the month, Pattullo was in Ottawa talking to the federal government. There was a hurried exchange of letters between Victoria and Ottawa. Pattullo still wanted to go ahead with the scheme, but Hart convened a hasty cabinet meeting that recommended deferring the plan. Weir was not at the meeting but he, too, was changing his mind.

Even Allon Peebles, the chairman of the Health Insurance Commission, recommended delay. So there were simultaneous announcements by Pattullo in Ottawa and Weir in Victoria that health insurance would be postponed.[174] When the election was called it was also revealed there would be a referendum on the issue at the same time. Cassidy, not unnaturally, felt there was nothing wrong with the technical side of the insurance plan. Rather, the problem was with 'the way in which the political side of the whole thing has been handled.' Nevertheless, he hoped that health insurance was not dead.[175]

The second contentious election issue was a scheme Pattullo had recently instigated to add the Yukon Territory to the Province of British Columbia. He had renewed his acquaintance with the far north during the summer of 1936 when he flew over the land he had walked as a younger man. He was reminded of both its grandeur and its potential. He had already raised the possibility that British Columbia might take over the administration of the Yukon with Mackenzie King. Now he wanted to bring the idea to fruition before the election, so he pressed the federal government to discuss the plan. By March 1937 he had reached a tentative agreement on the conditions under which Ottawa would transfer the government of the Yukon Territory to Victoria.[176] With the election a little over a month away, Pattullo, perhaps prematurely, made the agreement public and then he was surprised at the opposition it stirred up. British Columbians were concerned about the possible cost to the provincial taxpayer and Yukoners seemed to be unanimously opposed to being governed from Victoria. Yukon mining interests lobbied against the imposition of British Columbia's mining laws, and the transfer of jurisdiction also promised to raise the vexed question of separate schools.[177] Once again Pattullo had gone ahead on a matter that seemed simple enough on the face of it, yet turned out to contain all sorts of complications. The acquisition of the Yukon looked like an election winner to him, but then it had to be explained and defended during the campaign.

Apart from addressing these divisive issues, Pattullo ran for re-election largely on the record of his government. So the campaign was somewhat subdued in comparison with the fervour of 1933. Still, as in the by-elections the previous year, Pattullo was the most vigorous and active campaigner. He spoke to meetings in Victoria and Vancouver, made several radio broadcasts, and, as usual, he toured large parts of the province. He flew up the coast to Prince Rupert to accept the nomination that would enable him to complete a quarter of a century as representative of the riding. He travelled the length of the Fraser Valley and about Vancouver Island. He admitted that the Liberals had not achieved all they had hoped for. For example, a public utilities commission had not been established as promised in 1933.[178] Even though the government's financial position was much improved it was obvious that many British Columbians were still without work and wages. Yet Pattullo argued that his government had done its best in very difficult circumstances, that the most crucial matter still before it was the province's relationship with the dominion, and that only his team had the experience to deal with the federal government. What, then, he asked, would be the point of changing now? He made much of the divisions within the CCF, though it was in that context he made a major gaff. He had a line in his speeches about how the CCF was dictatorial because it drummed dissenters out of the party. In response to a heckler in Prince Rupert who said there was someone who was trying to dictate right now, Pattullo quipped: 'Well, if there's going to be a dictator, I want to be dictator.' He was at least half joking, but the Conservative press was not amused and the comment was constantly thrown back at him. Characteristically, though, he did not back off the point. He later replied to a female heckler in Sidney, 'If I had to live with you I'd sure want to be a dictator,' then he quickly added, 'but I wouldn't want to take the chance.'[179]

Most of his speeches were less controversial and well received. When he came to the Terminal City, the Crystal Ballroom of the Hotel Vancouver was full to overflowing an hour before he began. Duff stood on his own, put his thumbs in the armholes of his waistcoat, and outlined his policies. The speech was described by the editor of the *Sun* as like the man himself: plain, solid, and sensible. Pattullo was not a magician, or even a politician, Cromie went on. 'He has no gift for handshaking or kissing babies. He sometimes makes bad friends by his plain, blunt, honest talk.' Voters were reminded of his reputation as an able administrator in the Oliver government when he 'just took off his coat and got things done.'[180] Pattullo would have absolutely disagreed with the idea that he was not a politician in every sense of the word, but clearly this time round he was being portrayed as an able manager rather than a zealous reformer. Towards the close of the campaign he emphasized the importance of the continuing negotiations with Ottawa, and how much stronger the provincial position would be if the will of the people were close to unanimous.[181]

The results, while not unanimous, did amount to an overwhelming victory for Pattullo and the Liberals. Pattullo himself was safe in Prince Rupert, though his critics would note that this time he had received just a shade less than 50 per cent of the votes.[182] Province-wide, the Liberals won thirty-one of forty-eight seats, leaving them with only four fewer members than at dissolution. The CCF made no progress at all. It declined in popular support and ended up with exactly the same number of seats as it had after the last election. The Conservatives showed signs of recovering from the devastation of 1933. They attracted 28 per cent of the popular vote, the same as the CCF, yet won one more seat than the socialists and so returned to the house as the official opposition.[183] The salient point of the election was, however, the extent to which British Columbians had supported their premier. Such a strong mandate in the midst of the depression was an astounding achievement. Commentators both then and now have suggested that the Liberal victory was largely a result of divisions within the CCF, but that would be to deny the role of the premier's personal force and energy.[184] This triumph was Pattullo's own.

CHAPTER 8

The Decline of Reform

'We do not want to be hogtied and hamstrung'

In the months after the 1937 election Duff Pattullo was flying high, as the proud often do before the fall. Yet the fatal flaw was still there. The fundamental nature of Pattullo's disagreement with the federal government in Ottawa had not changed. Yet within himself he was in command, within his party his word was law, and within his province he was unquestionably premier. He was said to have remarked that, 'even if it sounds egotistical, I tell you this; what I say goes in this province.'[1] In the east his re-election was described as 'an achievement never seen since the depression set in.'[2] And in Ottawa his main antagonist had admitted that Pattullo 'has got things pretty much his own way.' Though, with his customary generosity towards the British Columbian premier, Mackenzie King added that Duff's changed political fortunes were a consequence of 'improved conditions which he was unable to foresee at the time.'[3] In fact, Pattullo celebrated the coming to fruition of some of his own initiatives in the early months of his second term.

At the same time, if one were to search beyond the superficial sizzle for substantive new policies, it was apparent that much of the reformist heat had gone out of the Pattullo government. The second administration would be a good deal more cautious than the first. From the beginning the reform program had been predicated on the assumption of co-operative federalism: that Ottawa would be willing and able to provide the funding to enable him to carry out his schemes. By now it was clear that these expectations were very naîve. As he became increasingly frustrated with the lack of co-operation from Ottawa, Pattullo became more convinced that, instead of a new deal to end the depression, British Columbia was getting a raw deal out of Confederation. Thoroughgoing reform was impossible unless the province had more financial power and so Pattullo's vigorous assertion of provincial rights was the logical consequence his reformism. Much of the energy of his second administration would be absorbed in struggles with the federal government rather than bringing about fundamental reform in British Columbia.

Though the election was over, Pattullo continued to renew his bond with the people of British Columbia. He toured the interior in July 1937 and, beginning in late August, travelled up the coast and through the north. At this moment there was little doubt of his pre-eminence among the province's politicians. He knew well enough how quickly it all could change, but for now it seemed that even the gods smiled on him. In October he went east and he was scheduled to return from Toronto by United Airlines when a last-minute call to Ottawa resulted in a change of plans. The plane he would have taken crashed near Salt Lake City killing all the passengers. Duff himself put his escape down to 'Pattullo luck' rather than divine intervention. It is axiomatic that good luck is essential to success in politics, and one of the commonplaces around the legislature in Victoria was that 'Duff is hung with horseshoes.'[4]

However fortune was to favour him on trips to the east, his prestige ran very high in British Columbia and his authority among the people was matched by his demeanour in the house. When the first session of the new parliament convened on 26 October 1937 even opposition members admitted that Pattullo 'looks well and reflects his long experience' as he addressed them, as Maitland put it, on the subject of 'My Life – and its great influence on the building of a Province.'[5] Experienced commentators described the face and manner of Duff Pattullo in the legislature as reflecting the changes in British Columbia over the last generation. In the beginning his was the face of the boom years and his speeches were full of wild energy and impatience. With the depression of the early 1930s he became more controlled: an able critic and a prophet of reform. Now much of that enthusiasm had waned and he had few illusions, so he lectured the house like a patriarch. As the only member of the legislature to have won in every election since the first Liberal deliverance of 1916, Duff Pattullo was the senior politician.[6] Whatever else about him had changed, politics was still his life. It continued to be 'an interesting life if you have a sense of humor and do not allow it to worry you.' And, he added, 'it will not worry you if you are not vindictive and are ready to make allowance for original sin.'[7] Pattullo must have been making many allowances, for he seemed to have no worries as he took part in public occasions that celebrated his longevity in provincial politics.

In October 1937 the University of British Columbia paid tribute to the premier by conferring on him an honourary Doctor of Law. Earlier in the year Gordon Sloan had resigned as attorney-general and Pattullo assumed the portfolio until the election. After some discussion among legal experts it was decided he was entitled to add the letters KC to his name, and now he could also append LLD. In his congregation address he spoke of the importance of training 'whether in institutions especially designed for the purpose or in the wider and, may I say, harder university of life.' He went on to observe that 'a university is not an information factory, rather is it an institution where the mind can be trained and disciplined to think, to study, to differentiate, to separate the wheat from the chaff, the false from the true.' The statement was fine as far as it went but, as he was soon to rediscover, truth, like beauty, is in the eye of the beholder. As well as discussing the nature of a university the premier also talked about the limitations of government. 'The ship of a state is the largest and most difficult ship in the world to navigate. Everybody wants to be captain, the crew is sometimes mutinous, while the passengers, to whom governmental navigation is a simple process, want to go everywhere all at the same time.'[8]

One policy that Pattullo had navigated through the stormiest of political waters was the Fraser River bridge. On 15 November 1937, a month after he received his honourary doctorate, he officially opened the new bridge. Billed as the largest single construction project ever undertaken by the government of British Columbia, it had provided employment for hundreds of workers. The new span towered above the old railway bridge that was built almost forty years before and it represented the growing importance of road transportation and tourism to the provincial economy. For Pattullo it was a monument to the spirit of progress that characterized British Columbia and an example of what could be done through government spending. He took the occasion to argue, once again, that 'private expenditure should be supplemented by public endeavour.'[9] The bridge across the Fraser was built, in spite of constant criticism from all sides, because of Duff's singleminded determination, and so it was entirely appropriate that it should be named the Pattullo Bridge. As he cut through the chain with an acetylene torch to allow traffic to move across the span, he felt satisfaction in the fact that here was a policy that had been brought to a very tangible completion by employing the resources and workers of British Columbia.

The opening-day parade was, however, slightly marred by two constants of west-coast life: rain and the federal government. That Mackenzie King would reject all requests for a financial contribution to the Pattullo Bridge was by now as predictable as rain in the middle of November. This time there was some support in Ottawa for giving the British Columbia government a million dollars so that the bridge could operate toll free. A cabinet committee reported in favour of the grant and Ian Mackenzie, the British Columbia minister, supported the idea largely because there was soon to be a federal by-election in Victoria. When the matter came before the full cabinet, King insisted it was still his business 'to defend the Treasury' and with the support of a majority he 'closed the matter summarily.' Though he later had bad dreams about the decision, he felt vindicated when the Liberals won the by-election anyway. Once again King had responded to Pattullo's appeal for a broad-guage approach by 'holding steadily to the narrow and straight course all the way.'[10]

Pattullo had recently had occasion to reflect on the reasons why most of his little new deal had failed to come about. Late in the summer of 1937 he had visited the Coulee Dam in Washington State. This outstanding example of New Deal spending in the American west reminded Pattullo of the conservation and reclamation work that was done in the Okanagan Valley when he was minister of lands under John Oliver.[11] Yet, as he stood on the Coulee Dam and, a month later, welcomed the author of the New Deal to Victoria, he must have been struck by the contrast between the federal money that Roosevelt poured into the American west and the parsimony with which his province was treated by Ottawa. New Deal spending in the western United States fueled an economic takeoff of the kind that Pattullo wanted for British Columbia, but there would be no 'planned promised land' in the Canadian west in the 1930s.[12] There, the reform impulse was starved to death by a tight-fisted federal government.

Still, there were other things to celebrate. Duff turned sixty-five at the beginning of 1938 and there was an even bigger birthday party than the year before. This time it was a triple anniversary. In addition to his birthday on 19 January, the new year also marked forty years since he first came to the west coast and twenty-one years of continuous service in the British Columbia legislature. Mayor George Miller hosted a banquet in the crystal ballroom of the Hotel Vancouver and many of the province's leading Liberals were there. Dr Alfred Thompson, with whom Pattullo had fought against Frederick Congdon in the Yukon, spoke about the early days in Dawson and the beginning of Duff's political career. Toasts to the guest were proposed by Pat Maitland, who later in the year would be elected leader of the provincial Conservative party, and Senator J.W.deB. Farris, the *éminence grise* among Vancouver Liberals. John Hart presented Pattullo with a silver tea service on behalf of the three hundred people in the room. Telegrams were read from those such as Mackenzie King, R.B. Bennett, and Ian Mackenzie who could not attend. It was a moment when personal friends and political opponents alike joined to acknowledge Pattullo's long years of public service and his many contributions to British Columbia. Appropriately, Duff Pattullo's birthday cake was a huge replica of the legislative buildings. Even the editor of the *Vancouver Province* admitted that Pattullo was entitled to the compliments paid to him on this occasion.[13] Liberal newspapers were, of course, more fulsome. Leslie Fox, writing in the *Victoria Times*, quoted a Pattullo remark from the last sitting of the legislature: 'We do not apologise, we simply give reasons for our actions.'[14] This, apparently, was the philosophy that had taken him to the top. It was also the attitude that would play a large part in his downfall.

In the meantime, 'dauntless Duff' was certainly 'undisputed boss' of his party.[15] To underline the point he took a seat away from the opposition in May 1938 when the sudden death of Conservative leader Frank Patterson necessitated a by-election in Dewdney. At the end of the summer the provincial Liberal party held a convention at Kelowna and it was very much Duff Pattullo's show. The acrimony that had divided the party during his first term of office had subsided. He kept a tight rein on the proceedings, sitting beside the chairman the whole time with 'his eye on the delegates, his mouth at the microphone and his foot near the lid.' As one observer put it, he talked to his followers 'like a Dutch Uncle.' There was no polished oratory or ringing phrases: he simply told the members what was good for them in clear, blunt phrases. There were still a few malcontents. George Nickerson from Prince Rupert stormed out when his resolution criticizing growing government control in some sectors of the economy was rejected. Otherwise the convention was a ringing, if well-orchestrated, endorsement of Pattullo's leadership that concluded with the delegates expressing their appreciation of the leader by giving him a life-sized portrait of himself.[16]

Pattullo's pre-eminence in provincial politics was partly a consequence of the fact that the other two parties were in the midst of a rebuilding process. When the Conservatives lost both their leader and the Dewdney by-election they were left with the same number of seats as the CCF, so their role as official opposition was in jeopardy. Their position was salvaged when Rolf Bruhn, who had been an independent since the Tolmie collapse, returned to the Conservative fold. The Conservative party held its convention a month after the Liberals and Royal Lethington (Pat) Maitland was elected the new leader. He had served as minister without portfolio under Tolmie but stayed out of the 1933 election. He was re-elected in 1937 and now faced Pattullo in the house as leader of the opposition. As he watched the power and strength of the Liberals he reflected on how foolish Conservatives had been in 1933 to build up the union cause to the detriment of the Conservative party. He reckoned they would have to 'work for a generation to restore that which was lost.'[17]

Pattullo and Maitland had always sparred with each other in debate and also by exchanging caustic little notes across the floor of the house. Both had a sense of humour with a well-honed edge. Maitland kept a private log in which he commented on individuals and proceedings when the legislature was in session as a way of passing the tedious times. He expressed admiration for Pattullo, whom he thought to be 'a mile ahead of any other Liberal,' but he was scathing about other honourable members. Of Weir, for example, he once noted, simply 'add a "d." ' Maitland further referred to the humourless provincial secretary as that 'chuckling light hearted lad.' Duff, by contrast, could give as good as he got.[18] When Pat Maitland had a car accident, Pattullo wrote he was 'sorry to hear of your accident, but glad that you were not killed. It would have been a great loss to the Liberal Party.' Maitland thanked him for his kind letter of sympathy and retorted, 'I suppose my death would have deprived the Liberal Party of all inspiration.'[19] While these two men enjoyed such cheerful yet pointed jousting between themselves, neither got much joy out of the leadership of the third party.

The CCF was still dealing with the fallout that followed from the removal of Robert Connell and the rivalry between Lyle Telford and Harold Winch to succeed Connell. Telford fell from grace within the party after the 1937 election. He looked particularly bad when he had to withdraw ill-founded charges of corruption in the construction costs of the Pattullo Bridge. Telford removed himself from the running for leadership when he became mayor of Vancouver in early 1939 and Winch was elected party leader by a big majority at a convention in June. Still in his early thirties, Harold Winch was young and zealous and he found little cause for amusement in the plight of the unemployed and what he saw as the government's inaction. He had no time for the kind of repartee that went on between Pattullo and Maitland. The Conservative leader wrote of Winch that, 'We disagree – he thinks he is another Ramsay MacDonald – I don't.'[20] Pattullo was more charitable. He thought of Winch as a young man with a lot to learn, and he did not view his party with the same alarm as Maitland. These feelings were not mutual, however. Winch looked across the legislature and saw Pattullo as 'that fat epitome of capitalism,' and even years later remembered him as a brutal dictator.[21]

During the early months of his second mandate it certainly seemed as though Pattullo was very much in command of provincial politics. He had complete control over his own party and had little to fear, at least in the short term, from either opposition party. He flatly denied the wispy rumours floating around that he might retire or perhaps take up the office of agent general in London, a traditional resting place of British Columbia politicians. He said he intended to be premier for several years to come. After all, he told reporters, 'my cup is overflowing.'[22] Yet, outside the realms of the provincial legislature, party politics, and ceremonial occasions, there were signs of dissent and the gathering forces. Within the province many were still suffering the ill-effects of the depression and their discontent could quickly boil to the surface. And while it was far away in Ottawa, the federal government was always present, as impervious and parsimonious as ever.

British Columbia still faced serious economic and social problems. There had been signs of economic improvement in 1937, but the depression was not over and things were to get worse again before they got better. The group most visibly bearing the brunt of the hard times was still the single unemployed. Pattullo had constantly argued that the federal government, with its control over finance and banking, should first provide loans for public works to employ the employable unemployed and then bring in unemployment insurance for those who remained out of work. He had repeatedly warned that, if his advice were not followed, there could be a major social upheaval in British Columbia, and during the summer of 1938 it seemed that his prophecy might come true.[23] Drought and recession on the prairies in 1937–8 drove more men towards the coast in search of jobs. When the temporary winter work camps in British Columbia closed down in the spring, the unemployed drifted into Vancouver looking for work or relief. The provincial government had reduced its loans to municipalities and then announced there would be no relief for those from outside the province. The men protested against the reduction in relief payments by occupying selected public buildings in Vancouver. One group in the downtown Post Office proclaimed they were merely waiting for 'work and wages.'

So Pattullo made another trip to Ottawa. By now there was a current of thought within the federal government that the purse strings should be loosened a little and some money spent on public works. British Columbia would get a share of this money, but there were to be no special concessions to the province's particular problems. On his return, Pattullo announced the federal spending along with some new provincial projects. He advised the 'sit downers' to leave the buildings they had occupied, saying they would not be discriminated against if they applied for work.[24] When a delegation of the unemployed planned to go to Victoria to present claims for assistance, Pattullo told them not to bother. Instead, he would come to Vancouver on 20 June to meet with them. In the meantime, believing that subversive influences were at work and that the situation could no longer be tolerated, he arranged with the federal government to have the men forcibly evicted from the public buildings. On Sunday, 19 June, in the early morning when few people were on the streets, the police arrived with tear gas and baton and, particularly outside the Post Office, there were ugly and violent scenes as the men were forced out. The strike leader, Steve Brodie, was beaten senseless. That day was remembered as 'bloody Sunday,' and the atmosphere of anger was hardly conducive to reasonable discussion when Pattullo met a delegation of the single unemployed the following day.

The meeting was between two opposing points of view, each of which made no impression on the other. The single unemployed wanted food and relief right now and the prospect of jobs in the longer term. Pattullo reiterated the point that the two governments would spend more on works projects but absolutely refused to provide any more immediate relief. He now believed that able-bodied single men could take care of themselves during the summer, though he admitted to King that 'the public does not view sympathetically the bald advice that they should get out and rustle.'[25] At one level the provincial government seemed more interested in disposing of the problem than in solving it. Pattullo made much of the number of unemployed who were from other provinces, and he told the federal government that 'it is not our responsibility to provide for every penniless person who may come here from the rest of Canada, nor can we do so.'[26] He offered these men transportation back to the places they had come from and arranged for the federal authorities to do more to prevent men from illegally riding the trains through the mountains to the coast.[27] Removing the transients, he said, would make the situation easier for 'legitimate British Columbians.' At another, more fundamental level Pattullo urged the unemployed and their advocates to exercise greater individual initiative rather than relying on government. He claimed there had been a change in the mental attitude of the people and now 'everybody looks to government.' He warned British Columbians, in a radio address on the question of unemployment, that a 'general policy of sole dependence upon the Government would simply lead to moral decrepitude of the individual and the physical decrepitude of our industrial life.'[28] Such talk was a far cry from his vibrant advocacy of state intervention in 1933.

His counsel to the unemployed in the summer of 1938 was an extreme example in what Pattullo saw as an extreme situation, yet it also revealed a major shift in his thinking. He clearly recognized the limitations of provincial power and he realized the federal government would not give him much room to manoeuvre. There was no point in making promises he could not keep. So the words 'work and wages' were scarcely uttered by anyone in the Pattullo government after 1937. Most reform initiatives, and certainly any that encroached on federal jurisdiction, were on hold.

The changed tone of the government was apparent in its fiscal management and, as a consequence, in the growing prestige of the minister of finance. In November 1937 John Hart delivered, in a 'quiet monotone,' the new government's financial statement.[29] Because he expected income to rise to a record level, relief costs and part of the province's debt repayment could be met out of current revenue with no increase in taxation. Both the public debt and government spending were also higher, but the budget was approaching balance. Hart insisted that ministers stay within their estimates and that any extraordinary expenditure be closely investigated by his department. He was not at all superstitious about presenting his thirteenth provincial budget the following year, and with good reason. It was even more positive than the last. He was able to announce that the provincial debt was reduced for the first time since 1933. The province's improved credit rating was reflected in the fact that Hart was now able to raise loans on the New York money markets. He had enough sense of humour to announce the new loan on 1 April 1939, but it was his serious and cautious approach to the government's finances that was largely credited with bringing British Columbia back to solvency.[30] The influence of high spending, reformist ministers like George Weir was on the wane as Hart became, in effect, second in command within cabinet.

The clearest example of the decline of reform was the fate of health insurance. The question of state health insurance had been put to the people during the 1937 election. Nearly 59 per cent of those who expressed an opinion in the plebiscite favoured 'a comprehensive Health Insurance plan.'[31] The doctors had not changed their minds, however, and there was still opposition in cabinet. Once again, the scheme was held in abeyance, this time pending the outcome of the Royal Commission on Dominion-Provincial Relations. Weir was very upset and threatened to resign, though in the end he stayed on in the hope he might regain his influence in cabinet. Cassidy was also frustrated with the 'business of flattering, cajoling, persuading with dubious argument or even deceiving the politicians who are my masters, even in the interests of a good cause.' So he left the 'foul political air' to return to the 'free atmosphere' of academe at Berkeley. He later bitterly observed that the government had 'sheltered for more than five years in a funkhole ... lacking the courage either to go forward or retreat' and thus British Columbia ingloriously lost the chance to be the first government in North America to put state health insurance on the books.[32] After the party lost a by-election in Vancouver Centre in 1939, Weir informed Pattullo that many Liberals had refused to vote because they felt the government had developed a paralysis or, as some apparently put it, 'Tolmietized.'[33]

Pattullo was hardly pleased with the comparison with Tolmie and naturally he denied that his government was paralyzed. In a crisp reply to Weir he said he was merely keeping the ship on an even keel.[34] In fact he had helped to wreck the health insurance scheme by following a similar tack to one he had taken as minister of lands in the 1920s – namely, bringing in experts to formulate and administer a sound policy but failing to maintain a steady course when the political storms blew against the plan. And so the reform ideals foundered against the public pressure brought to bear by what appeared to be a powerful interest group. Pattullo would no doubt have argued that, as a politician, he could only achieve what was politically possible, and there would have been some validity to the point. Yet he, too, was frustrated by that fact. He firmly believed in the need for state health insurance and, to the end of his days, was very disappointed that he had not been able to bring it to pass in British Columbia.

Odd vestiges of the former reformism still remained even after 1937. During the second session of the new parliament in the fall of 1938, faint echoes of reform Liberalism could be heard in the halls of the legislature. Amendments were made to earlier legislation to provide for higher widows' pensions and increased benefits under the Workmen's Compensation Act.[35] Pattullo fulfilled a longstanding promise to bring in legislation to provide for government regulation of public utilities, and an act was passed to allow for the establishment of credit unions.[36] There were promises to spend more money on forest conservation. Other measures were more controversial and had a rough passage. The previous year the government had passed an Industrial Conciliation and Arbitration Act based on a New Zealand law that had been in effect for decades. Strikes were banned during the arbitration process and the British Columbia Act also restricted collective bargaining to employees rather than union representatives. After a nasty and bitter strike against the Pacific Lime Company in Blubber Bay in which workers defied the legislation, in 1938 the government amended the law to allow representatives who were not employees to negotiate, but only in the case of unions that were established by the end of the year. The CCF fought this amendment tooth and nail because it discriminated against new unions.[37] Union leaders felt the legislation meant too much government control over their affairs, a view that was only strengthened when, a year later, officers of the International Union of Mine, Mill and Smelter Workers were prosecuted for a strike at Pioneer Mines in Bridge River that was contrary to the provisions of the act.[38] It was just as well that organized labour and the CCF members did not realize that, in Pattullo's mind, industrial conciliation and arbitration was a prelude to outlawing strikes altogether. Such measures were just the tattered remnants of what five years earlier had been a seamless program of reform.

The one item from the old reform agenda that Pattullo did vigorously pursue after 1937 involved government regulation of business rather than labour. Since his appointment as coal and petroleum products commissioner in 1934, M.A. Macdonald had conducted a full and detailed investigation into the two industries. He reported to the government over a two-year period: the third and final volume came out in December 1938. Macdonald felt that the coal industry was unable to compete with the new and aggressive marketing of petroleum products partly because of its own internal problems. Accordingly he recommended changes to the financial structure of the Vancouver Island coal companies, to mining techniques, to marketing and distribution, and to the retail price of coal.[39] While Macdonald saw room for improvement in the coal industry, he reserved his harshest and most thoroughgoing criticism for the oil companies.

Though the companies were not very co-operative, Macdonald and his staff gradually established some salient facts about the oil industry in British Columbia. First, the industry was dominated by a few largely American companies and most of the crude oil was imported from California. Unlike the coal industry, the oil industry was integrated from top to bottom. That is, the oil companies controlled production and marketing from the arrival of the crude oil in the province to the sale of the final product to the consumer. British Columbia had become a dumping ground for surplus production and refineries were largely geared up to produce fuel oil that competed with local coal rather than gasoline that did not. The commissioner also concluded that the consumer was being charged too much for gasoline. The excess revenues from gasoline were partly concealed by creative accounting and partly funnelled into a wasteful distribution system. In reaching these basic conclusions the commission generated a vast amount of complicated information on the oil industry, but the bottom line of the report was simple. The 'outstanding fact established in this Inquiry' was that the oil companies were using the profits garnered from excessive gas prices to subsidize the cost of producing fuel oil, which was then sold at a loss and thereby competed unfairly with coal.[40] Or, to put it another way, the British Columbia motorist was financing the United States Oil companies' attack on the provincial coal industry. Macdonald therefore urged Pattullo to impose price controls on the oil industry.[41]

After some deliberation, Pattullo decided to follow Macdonald's advice. He introduced legislation to establish a Coal and Petroleum Control Board and appointed W.A. Carrothers from the Economic Council as chairman.[42] Carrothers did not agree with all of the detail in Macdonald's reports and he was cautious enough to gather his own information. In the end he found no fundamental fault with Macdonald's conclusions and so he formulated a set of regulations to control the industry. When the board moved to limit the price of gasoline, there was a furore in the oil industry that triggered a battle with the Pattullo government that lasted for two years.

The multinational oil companies in British Columbia argued that the effort to control their prices was a totally unwarranted government intervention into private enterprise. They managed to convince Pattullo's former colleague, now Mr Justice M.A. Manson, to grant an injunction against the order of the Control Board. The case went to the Supreme Court of Canada which finally decided, in April 1940, that the province had the constitutional right to control gasoline prices. At that, the oil companies, as Pattullo put it, 'went on strike.'[43] They stopped all sales of gasoline, except for what they determined to be essential services. Apart from anything else, Pattullo thought the oil company strike 'was a very bad example to labour.'[44] After a seven-day strike, the oil men and Carrothers got together and worked out a compromise price structure, and the companies then agreed to abide by the Control Board's rules. Pattullo nevertheless called a special session of the legislature and put through legislation to empower the Control Board to take over gas distribution in the event that the supply was cut off again, and giving the lieutenant-governor-in-council the power to enter the petroleum business.[45]

In the midst of this battle the Pattullo of old reappeared. He made some fighting speeches and reiterated his earlier arguments about the need for government intervention. When it got to the point that big business became so powerful as to behave as a law unto itself, he told British Columbians the government must move to protect the people's interests. He did not believe that his province should be 'dependent upon foreign gasoline in the hands of insolent companies.'[46] So this was the one reform measure he pushed to the limit during his second term. It was an area in which even the Supreme Court admitted the province had jurisdiction and, consequently, there was no interference from the federal level. The province of British Columbia therefore became the first government in Canada to make a sustained effort to control the multinational oil companies. But this particular case was the exception that proved the rule that the Pattullo government was much less progressive and activist the second time around.

As he retreated from reform, Pattullo took refuge in his northern vision. For him, the north was still the place of possibilities and so it was natural he should turn to the limitless land when he was beset on all sides by political exigencies. He still believed the north offered opportunities for British Columbians who were out of work. Just as he had done as a young man, they could find a place to fit in if they left the cities of the south for the wide open spaces. And he intended to facilitate that process. The plan to incorporate the Yukon into British Columbia had fallen apart. By the end of 1937 both the federal and the provincial governments had agreed to shelve the matter.[47] But Pattullo had other schemes to promote northern development. Since the early 1920s he had been interested in the prospect of oil in the Peace River country and he had tried to persuade oil companies to investigate the area. Now he announced that the provincial government would explore for oil. As Pattullo had recognized when he first went to the Yukon, opening up the north depended on establishing lines of communication and transportation. By the 1930s the railway age had passed and cars, trucks, and aeroplanes were becoming the means of moving people and goods across the sea of mountains. While discussing the acquisition of the Yukon, Pattullo had also raised the idea of building a highway to the north with Mackenzie King.[48] Just as the Pattullo Bridge had been the major public works enterprise of his first administration, the Alaska Highway was to be the biggest project of his second.

The notion of building a highway through northern British Columbia to Alaska was not a new one. Tolmie had advocated such a road in the early 1930s. As leader of the opposition when the depression took hold, Pattullo had dismissed the idea as 'simply foolish.'[49] Now he thought better of it. It was true he needed a new project to capture the public imagination, but he also pushed for this particular highway for many of the same reasons he had argued for government spending on public works generally. It would provide work for the unemployed, it would prime the economic pump, and it would open up new parts of the province such as the Peace River country for development. Pattullo also hoped that this particular route would bring large numbers of American tourists to British Columbia. This project, like many others, depended on federal support, but Ottawa was not persuaded by any of these arguments. It would be an expensive road to build and, as usual, Mackenzie King worried about the cost. After a meeting in Ottawa on the matter King noted in his diary that Pattullo wanted to build the Alaska Highway with 'no thought of the cost to the people.' Reflecting on that point, he added revealingly: 'I sometimes wish I could take my public duties with the free & easy assurance some of these men do. But I cannot be lighthearted.'[50] Once again it seemed that a Pattullo project had been blocked in Ottawa.

This time, however, Duff had another game plan. Since the Canadian government would not finance a road from British Columbia to Alaska, he turned to the American government. Pattullo and Roosevelt had agreed on the importance of the Alaska highway, as they did on many other things, when they met in Victoria in September 1937. The following month Pattullo visited Roosevelt at Hyde Park and they continued to discuss the matter by letter. By early 1938 Pattullo had an informal agreement that congressional authorization would be given to the American president to loan or expend up to $15 million on the highway.[51]

At that, Ottawa raised another set of objections. The fact that a provincial premier seemed to be conducting negotiations in Washington ruffled some feathers in the Canadian capital, especially in the Department of External Affairs. Pattullo was aware of the criticism and was at pains to reassure King his talks were entirely informal. In any event, he wrote in a characteristic statement, 'one need not be deflected from a sound proposal by a news voracious press, an irresponsible opposition, or other frailties of human nature.' King replied smoothly by letter that he was not aware that any exception had been taken to his actions, while writing in his diary that Pattullo 'like a fool, has been telling the Americans what to do to get under way with public works in Canada in connection with the Alaska Highway.'[52] The federal cabinet was also opposed to the idea of the Canadian part of the highway being built largely with money provided by a foreign government because it feared that Canadian sovereignty would be compromised by such an arrangement. These reservations were, however, still secondary.

The main concern was cost. An interdepartmental committee established by King to investigate the matter decided, before it moved on to consider the strategic question, that the American proposal was unacceptable even 'when judged solely from the financial angle.'[53] Though it was clear by the summer of 1938 that the federal government intended to stall the highway plan, Pattullo still pressed the matter. In the context of the crisis over unemployment in June, he pointed out to King that the construction of the road would absorb many of the single unemployed and relieve what he called 'congestion' in the cities.[54] Yet it was all to no avail. Later in the year Pattullo did convince King to match an American move and establish a Canadian commission to investigate the feasibility of an Alaska highway. But the prime minister made it clear that the appointment of the commission implied no commitment to the plan. Indeed, it had the advantage for King of producing further delay. Later the highway would be built as a military road rather than a depression panacea. What was possible in wartime was not in peace and so, once again, King had prevented one of Pattullo's plans from coming to fruition.[55]

The lesson that had been made so patently clear during his first term in office was only reiterated in the second. While policies like regulating the oil companies that were entirely within provincial jurisdiction could be carried through, anything that involved the federal government, such as building an Alaska highway, would at least be very difficult, and probably impossible to get underway. Particularly after 1937 Pattullo left many of the details of provincial policy and the running of particular departments to his ministers. His own preoccupation was the province's relations with the federal government. Much of what he wanted to achieve still depended the central authority and so he made countless trips, usually three or four times a year, back and forth to Ottawa trying to make British Columbia's case on a host of issues. He strongly believed that Canadian federalism could only work if there were co-operation and goodwill between the dominion and the provinces. He therefore became more and more exasperated with every failure in the east. Pattullo could win battles within British Columbia but not in Ottawa.

He had gone to the people in 1937 to get a strong mandate to represent British Columbia in negotiations with the dominion, knowing that matters were likely to come to a head during his next mandate. Soon after his re-election he told King that, 'We in British Columbia are getting pretty tired of eastern domination,' especially when that domination seemed to be based on misunderstanding. He was sick of hearing arguments in the east 'regarding western conditions and alleged western importunities' that 'suggest that we are at once spendthrifts and mendicants.' Hundreds of millions of dollars had been spent on canals and railways in central Canada and now he noted, in the context of arguing for the Alaska highway, that the St Lawrence Seaway project then being considered would 'doubtless take scores of millions.' He offered no objection to the scheme but he did suggest that undertakings of similar benefit to other parts of the country should also receive sympathetic consideration. British Columbia, he wrote, wanted to work to iron out misunderstandings, 'and in this process, Canada can only be strong in so far as the Provinces are strong and satisfied.'[56]

Because he still believed in energetic provinces within a cooperative confederation, he did not confront King publicly or openly break off relations with the prime minister as other premiers did. When William Aberhart suggested that the provinces should hold a conference without the federal government, Pattullo responded that Alberta had made a grave error in not co-operating more fully with Ottawa and that such a conference of the provinces would only create new dissension and solve nothing. When Mitchell Hepburn wrote in July 1937 to explain his break with Mackenzie King, Pattullo refused to become involved.[57] In fact, later that fall Pattullo happened to be in

Ottawa on election day in Ontario and, after a quiet dinner together, he and Mackenzie King went to the prime minister's office to listen to the returns.[58] Duff must have realized how ambivalent King was when Hepburn's government was returned to power. Unlike Aberhart, Hepburn, or Duplessis of Quebec, Pattullo did not fight with King out in the open, and, in contrast to many powerful men, he believed in being pleasant and amiable on a social level even with those he completely disagreed with on political issues. Pattullo did, however, constantly and consistently represent British Columbia's position that it deserved a fair deal from Confederation. As a consequence, King, followed by those historians who cannot see beyond the Ottawa sources, tended to lump Pattullo in 'with all the demagogues working together to overthrow the federal administration.'[59]

By now all of Pattullo's specific disagreements with the federal government had crystallized around the issue of financial relations. British Columbia, he constantly asserted, had to have the money to enable it to carry out the functions that were legitimately within its jurisdiction. Beyond that, 'it is very obvious that in a growing province such as British Columbia, just as in a growing business, we must have new money on Capital Account each year.' The dominion 'invasion' of the provincial income-tax field had placed his government in the dependent position of having to borrow from Ottawa just to retrieve some of the money that would otherwise have been collected within the province. Pattullo claimed that British Columbia, which had levied income tax longer than any other province, would not have had to borrow a single dollar from the dominion if Ottawa had not entered the field. 'It seems to me,' he wrote to King, 'that herein there lies upon the Dominion Government special responsibility to enable this Province to meet its obligations.' He was, in essence, arguing for an early form of transfer payments. British Columbia was 'neither pleading poverty nor asking for favours,' nor had his government been irresponsible as he often heard easterners say. On the contrary, 'we have worked this Province from almost an impossible situation to one of stability.' But if British Columbians were not to be mere hewers of wood and drawers of water for the rest of Canada there had to be some adjustment of dominion-provincial financial relations. For these reasons Pattullo placed a lot of hope in the recently appointed Royal Commission on Dominion-Provincial Relations. He assumed that, after the commission had done its work and the political deliberations were over, the provinces 'will be placed in a position where they will be able to function upon a sound financial basis, within the ambit of their own jurisdictions as finally determined.'[60] As with most of Pattullo's dealings with the federal government, however, his hopes ultimately proved to be naïve.

The Royal Commission on Dominion-Provincial Relations, the Rowell-Sirois Commission as it became known, was announced by Mackenzie King in February 1937. The commission was initially the brain-child of Ottawa bureaucrats who were concerned that federal-provincial tensions had produced a paralysis of government in Canada. Their solution was centralization. They wanted to reverse those centrifugal forces that had been spinning power out to the provinces ever since the assertion of provincial rights by Oliver Mowat in the 1880s. If authority, particularly over financial matters, were returned to the federal government, then, instead of constant wrangling between various levels of government, the fundamental problems of the depression could be solved in Ottawa.[61] In its way, this panacea was even more naïve than Pattullo's assertion of provincial rights, but for many its simplicity was its attraction. The bureaucrats who advocated the idea were not responsible to any electorate and did not have to operate in the disparate dominion of national, as distinct from Ottawa, politics.

Mackenzie King, who did know the real world of political compromise, was cool towards the commission idea at first, but he eventually warmed to it as a way of delaying rather than taking action. Though he announced the commission in February 1937, he waited until August before he made any appointments. Newton Rowell, formerly the representative from the Pattullo riding of North Oxford to the Ontario legislature and now chief justice of Ontario, and J.W. Dafoe, the editor of the Winnipeg *Free Press*, were chosen as commissioners. Thibaudeau Rinfret of the Supreme Court was also appointed, but when illness forced him to retire there was further delay before Joseph Sirois, a law professor from Quebec City, was selected as a replacement. Though they both had earlier connections with North Oxford, Pattullo was not heartened by the appointment of Rowell. He had earlier commented that he had 'a very high regard for Mr. Rowell personally, but not so high regard for his political sagacity.'[62] He immediately telegraphed King to urge the appointment of a British Columbian. The objections of Pattullo and others resulted in the addition of the economist Henry Angus from the University of British Columbia to the commission, while similar complaints from the Maritimes led to the selection of R.A. Mackay of Dalhousie University. Pattullo found little joy in the appointment of Angus, who was thought to be predisposed against the provincial-rights position of the British Columbia government.[63] The Rowell-Sirois Commission was to be an important and detailed investigation into the nature of Canadian federalism, and particularly the social responsibilities and fiscal powers of the dominion and provincial governments. Yet it was clear from the start that the commission was both the creation and the creature of the central government. It was unlikely that such a body would be receptive to the views of the periphery.

For his part, Pattullo armed himself for what he expected to be the most important struggle of his political career. He still placed some faith in this commission as he set to work preparing his government's case. Because British Columbia had its own peculiar concerns he rejected suggestions that the western provinces put together a joint presentation.[64] In fact, he would have preferred a separate inquiry into his province's particular claims, but Ottawa had set the agenda with this wide-ranging investigation and he had to respond to the process by making the strongest possible pitch to the commissioners in the hope he would be taken seriously. J.W.deB. Farris was the hired gun: as chief counsel for the province he would present the government's arguments. The details of the provincial brief were prepared by the various government departments and co-ordinated by Carrothers as chairman of the Economic Council. A massive amount of work went into British Columbia's brief, and by the time the commission began its hearings in Victoria in March 1938 it was ready.

Pattullo introduced the provincial case with his customary directness. He wasted little time with opening pleasantries before getting down to the substance of his argument. He had made most of the component points to the federal government many times before. He repeated British Columbia's claim to a reconsideration of the terms by which it had entered Confederation. He reminded the commissioners of the hardship imposed on the province when Ottawa began collecting income tax. The tax 'invasion' hit British Columbia particularly hard because the federal government took more money out of the province than it spent within it and, at the same time, made it difficult for the provincial government to increase its taxes. Moreover, Pattullo pointed out that British Columbia's topography meant that the per capita cost of providing many services was particularly high. For all these reasons he continued to maintain that his province was entitled to special consideration from the federal government. He also took the opportunity to raise old British Columbia issues, such as the argument that the federal government take over the Pacific Great Eastern, and even others, such as the exclusion of Orientals, that lay outside the commission's mandate.

But the side issues should not obscure the simplicity and, from Pattullo's point of view, the self-evidence of his main argument. The conditions of the depression decade had both raised people's expectations and increased government's responsibilities. These changes had worked with special severity on the governments of provinces such as British Columbia. He therefore assumed that, after this exercise in restructuring the dominion-provincial relationship was over, the provinces would be placed in a position where they would be able to function within their jurisdiction without having to go cap-in-hand to Ottawa for financial help. In short, Pattullo wanted British Columbia to be autonomous within its own sphere. To assist the commission in its task, his government had prepared a submission that was in large part 'a study of the economic anatomy of the Province as part of the Canadian Confederation.'[65] Having outlined the general argument, Pattullo left it to Farris to expound the detail.

While on paper the provincial case seemed clear and substantial, in the theatrical atmosphere of the commission's hearings the tone of the presentation was probably more important than the substance. Farris was particularly aggressive and adversarial, as if he were in a courtroom. The Vancouver lawyer had always played a prominent role in the federal Liberal party and had recently been rewarded with an appointment to the Senate. His commitment in principle to the provincial position can perhaps be measured by his later concern about the size of his fee. In any event, his high-powered style during the hearings played into the commissioners' hands rather than advancing the provincial cause.[66] When it came to presentations that 'lacked the National point of view' the commissioners were there to argue rather than to listen.[67] They were more interested in scoring minor points off the silly provincials than in putting their minds to the fact that the Pattullo government was proposing an alternative view of Confederation that acknowledged Canada's regional realities.

The commissioners were much happier with later submissions from other British Columbia groups that told them what they wanted to hear and emphasized the need for greater centralization. There were certainly some well-argued briefs that expressed the national point of view. But it also became clear that preposterous nonsense from those who took the federal line would be treated with more courtesy than the provincial government's detailed presentation. When H.R. MacMillan sallied forth claiming to represent the Associated Boards of Trade of British Columbia, he favoured the commissioners with some quotations from the Kidd Commission report.[68] He advocated a strong central government and his most startling suggestion was that plebiscites should be held to see if the people wanted their provinces governed by an elected legislature or a legislative council appointed by the dominion. The notion was ludicrous, but Rowell merely observed that some of MacMillan's ideas were 'rather impractical' as he nevertheless promised to give them full consideration.[69] Pattullo was extremely annoyed to hear the Kidd Commission foolishness regurgitated before this federal body.

Yet it was clear from the hearings in Victoria that the fix was in. The Rowell-Sirois Commission was not a device to negotiate with the government of British Columbia but rather a means of imposing the federal point of view. Pattullo had arranged some social occasions for the commissioners while they were on the west coast and when Rowell left he thanked the premier for his kindness. As a result of their informal talks the chairman of the commission was reminded of Duff's father and the great interest that Pattullo senior taken in his early public career.[70] Unfortunately for the son, Rowell would not reciprocate beyond such bland pleasantries. His commission would not provide a conduit by which Pattullo's view of the nature of Confederation could be made clear to the federal government.

As the commissioners went on to hear from other provinces and then to write their report, Pattullo knew he would have to promote his ideas himself. He also realized he was being backed into a corner. His presentation to the commission was being roundly criticized, even in the local press, as narrow and parochial which, in a sense, it was bound to be since it expressed the particular viewpoint of the British Columbia government. 'The centralisers,' Pattullo explained, 'almost force one to appear in the light of a provincialist.'[71] So he took every possible opportunity to restate his position that, while he stood for a strong British Columbia, he also believed in the need to cooperate with the dominion government. British Columbia made a supplementary submission to the Rowell-Sirois Commission in Ottawa on its claim for better terms. Publicly at least, Pattullo continued to maintain that the inquiry into dominion-provincial relations was a valuable exercise, as he was bound to do since he had postponed so much pending its outcome. Privately his feelings had to be more mixed. Though as yet he may not have appreciated the extent to which the commission was a set up, given the history of his dealings with Ottawa he was hardly entitled to expect much. Nevertheless, ever the optimist, he continued to hope against hope that, this time, the views of his government might be given a reasonable hearing.

As he waited for the commissioners' report, Pattullo tried to appear reasonable in spite of the slings and arrows that were directed against him. Perhaps the most outrageous of these came from George McCullagh, the businessman and publisher of the Toronto *Globe and Mail*. In the midst of a crusade in early 1939 to form his so-called leadership league, McCullagh had advocated, among many other things, the abolition of provincial governments. Pattullo issued a press statement regretting that McCullagh should pronounce so dogmatically on a subject about which he obviously knew so little.[72] At that, the easterner responded with a scurrilous personal attack on Pattullo and was quoted on the west coast as expressing the view that 'British Columbia has a governmental mad house which beats that of Alberta all to hell.'[73] The onslaught was so unreasonable that even the *Vancouver Province* came out in support of Pattullo, noting he was entitled to receive the same courtesy as he always gave in public debate, while other commentators concluded that such remarks said more about McCullagh than they did about Pattullo.[74]

Fortunately not all his political adversaries were so belligerent. There was even a rapprochement of sorts between the premier and the prime minister in the summer of 1939. Mackenzie King made a great play of accompanying King George VI and his wife Elizabeth as they travelled across Canada. Victoria was the westernmost stop on the royal tour and everything seemed to go off perfectly. After a dinner at Government House, King and Pattullo explained to King George that, although the dominion and the nine provinces scrapped with each other a great deal, they were really united at heart. The following day the premier and his wife received the royal visitors on the steps of the provincial legislative buildings. Lillian was suffering from arthritis and found standing particularly painful, so King took her on his arm throughout much of the day which freed Duff to converse with the King and Queen. After lunch at the Empress, while their majesties toured other parts of Victoria, Duff drove King out to his house on Beach Drive. Doris and two of the grandchildren were there and they all enjoyed a pleasant afternoon. Pattullo appreciated King's thoughtfulness towards Lillian during the day, and King was glad to have an old personal friendship that had worn pretty thin in recent years 'fully restored.' Pattullo referred publicly to the old family friendship between himself and the prime minister when he attended an anniversary dinner in honour of Mackenzie King in Toronto that August.[75] All of this personal good will was fine while it lasted, but it was merely the calm before the storm, as was the summer of 1939 for millions of people around the world.

The international upheaval that began in September 1939 seemed to change everything. Duff was in Alaska, in the midst of an extensive tour of the north, when war was declared. He created a stir when, during a speech at Fairbanks, he asserted that 'when Canada is at war, the United States is also at war.' He then added that the reverse was also true: 'that when the United States is at war, Canada is at war.' But it was the first remark that drew the response. President Roosevelt immediately restated the United States' position of neutrality and Duff received a flood of letters from Americans who objected to his presumption. Not least of them was from his brother George, who firmly believed that America should stay out of what he saw as a European conflict. George wrote that it was too bad if Duff had got some nasty letters, but 'when a man leads with his chin, somebody is bound to take a crack at it.' Duff was unperturbed, however. He made two predictions: one, that the United States would be in the war and, two, that Roosevelt would be elected for a third term.[76] In due course he would be proven correct on both.

The Second World War also changed the whole tenor of Canadian politics. Even a year earlier Pattullo had noted that the 'threat of war has dwarfed all other considerations. Yet,' he said, 'we must carry on.' As a provincial leader he argued that domestic issues should not be forgotten in the midst of the world war. Unlike other premiers, such as Duplessis of Quebec and Hepburn of Ontario, he did not oppose the federal government and its war effort. During the federal election campaign in March 1940 he declined invitations to speak in other parts of the country but he did support the federal Liberals on the hustings in British Columbia. As in the 1930 campaign, Mackenzie King did not visit the west coast. This time he sent his Quebec lieutenant, Ernest Lapointe, instead. Pattullo introduced Lapointe to a Vancouver audience with the comment that, next to waging the war, the Royal Commission on Dominion-Provincial Relations was the second most important matter facing Canada and it should not be allowed to die.[77] On that, Pattullo had his wish since the commission did not become a casualty of the war. But what had been established as a depression panacea was turned into a wartime expedient. It soon became clear that the position of the federal government was, to coin a phrase, federalism if necessary but not necessarily federalism.

When the commission finally brought down its recommendations, they confirmed all of Pattullo's worst fears. It was an extremely centralist document. The report might as well have been written in 1937 when the commission was first established as, in a sense, it was. It was one of those research exercises in which the researchers found what they were looking for. The findings of the Rowell-Sirois Commission were a clear expression of the views of the Ottawa bureaucrats who instigated the process and drafted the report.[78] The document was delivered to the federal government in February 1940, but King was not game enough to make it public until after the election was over. The report was tabled at the opening of parliament on 16 May 1940. Pattullo had slight forewarning of the commission's proposals when Ian Mackenzie sent him a crude but basically accurate summary a few days before the official version was available.[79] It did nothing to soften the blow.

The Rowell-Sirois Commission proposed a new and very different confederation. The essence of the recommendations were in plan 1, which advocated to a major shift of power from the provinces to the federal government. There was also a plan 2 that recommended a continuation of the present financial arrangements between the two levels of government with Ottawa assuming responsibility for the unemployed, but it was not seriously considered. Under plan 1 the federal government would assume provincial debts and responsibility for relief for the employable unemployed. Providing for those who were not employable would still be up to the provinces and health insurance would also remain a provincial matter. In return for assuming some new responsibilities, the federal government would be given formidable financial powers. The provinces would hand over the gathering of income and corporate tax and succession duties entirely to Ottawa. Then the dominion would generously 'recognise an obligation to respect the remaining revenue sources of the provinces.' The existing system of subsidies to the provinces would be replaced with new measures. The federal government would, first, pay the provinces an amount equal to 10 per cent of the net income earned by mining and oil-producing companies in the province. Ottawa would also pay, according to the commission, emergency grants in emergency situations. Pattullo knew only too well what the chances of getting one of those would be. The main form of federal assistance to the provinces would be national adjustment grants, but these too would be based on financial need as determined by Ottawa. The provinces would still be allowed to float loans, but if they were not approved by Ottawa the debt charges could not be counted as part of financial need when applying for an adjustment grant. This last point was, however, hypothetical as far as British Columbia was concerned, for under the recommended formula for setting adjustment grants it would get exactly nothing.[80] What all this amounted to was that, in return for assuming some very specific and limited responsibilities, the federal government would get almost total financial control over the provinces. Plan I was the antithesis of all that Pattullo's career in British Columbia had meant and a contradiction of everything he had stood for.

Nor did British Columbia get anywhere with its special claim for 'better terms.' The commission argued that, having freely signed the Terms of Union in 1871, the province could not now argue that the terms be adjusted. It could not accept that British Columbia had any claim based on the high cost of governing such a vast and difficult terrain. The commissioners did allow that the westernmost province was entitled to some adjustment in federal payments because there had been no revision of per capita subsidies and debt allowances such as the prairie provinces had received prior to 1930. At the same time any claim that could be reasonably made by British Columbia had already been taken care of by the special interim subsidy of $750,000 that was granted in 1934. They did, therefore, recommend that that grant should be made permanent. The Rowell-Sirois commissioners were similarly unimpressed with Pattullo's claim that the federal government should take over the Pacific Great Eastern railway, arguing that, if their recommendation that Ottawa take over provincial debt were followed, then that aspect of the problem would be solved anyway. The central and fundamental conclusions of the Rowell-Sirois Commission were quite the contrary to what Pattullo had hoped for, and there was no consolation to be found on the smaller issues.

Pattullo took his time to respond to the commission's conclusions, as if he knew the moment of reckoning was at hand. He issued a bland statement that premature comment would be a mistake and that the report would require careful study. He was not pressed to make his views known immediately. Mackenzie King recognized that the report would be unacceptable to many provinces and he wanted to delay any discussion of it. But there was a good deal of newspaper support for the report and the Ottawa bureaucrats wanted it implemented so the federal government could finance the war effort. By the fall the pressure for action was mounting. The federal minister of finance, James Ilsley, was trying to convince King and the rest of the cabinet to hold a dominion-provincial conference to approve plan 1. Ilsley phoned Pattullo to say that he, or a representative of the provincial government, should come to Ottawa immediately to discuss the commission's suggestions. With the provincial legislature soon to open, Pattullo, for once, refused to hurry off to Ottawa at federal bidding. He told King he would not be rushed on such a crucial matter. 'Some eastern interests,' he noted, 'such as the "Financial Post" of Toronto, seem desirous of pushing this matter to an immediate conclusion. Any time that the "Financial Post" of Toronto makes a recommendation, suspicion is at once created.'[81]

But if Pattullo would not be stampeded, delay would not deal with the issue. King was persuaded, much against his better judgment, to call a conference with the provinces. The invitation to Pattullo and the other premiers was sent on 2 November 1940 and tabled in the House of Commons on 7 November. King reminded the premiers that the Rowell-Sirois Commission had been established because of the inability of the Canadian political system to respond effectively to the problems of the depression, and he foresaw the need for major social and economic adjustments during the process of postwar reconstruction. But his strongest argument for adopting the commission's recommendations was the need for a united, national war effort. Winning the war demanded 'nothing less than the most effective organization of all our resources and a real equality of sacrifice,' and this goal was not attainable as long as the provinces and the dominion competed with each other for revenue. He therefore proposed that the premiers should meet with him to discuss the Rowell-Sirois proposals sometime in mid-January 1941.[82] King was still not convinced that the conference would be successful, but at least if he called the meeting the onus for failure could be placed on the provincial premiers. It was altogether too sophisticated a political manoeuvre for Pattullo who, in any event, had no choice but to accept the invitation.

On the day that King's letter was made public in Ottawa, Pattullo responded to it in the British Columbia legislature. He reiterated, without conceding the prime minister's central point, that 'the adoption of the Commission's recommendations is necessary to put our country in a position to pursue a policy which will achieve the maximum war effort.' He also said that the work of the commission had provided a valuable basis for discussion. He did not, however, agree with all of its conclusions and, in any event, the basis upon which they had been reached had already substantially changed. British Columbians were prepared to make any sacrifice to win the war, but his government would not agree to making permanent changes to Canadian federalism that were unlikely to work in peacetime under the pretext of the war effort. He acknowledged there were those who advocated placing 'plenary powers' in the hands of the federal authority, but he was firmly convinced that in 'peace time such authority could only lead to disruption and disunity.'[83]

A week later he spoke more fully on the subject during a major speech in the house. Opposition was already building in the press to Pattullo's stand and, as usual, he responded by being more forthright and aggressive. He still maintained he was determined to co-operate fully with Ottawa in an endeavour to reach a mutually satisfactory adjustment of dominion-provincial arrangements. At the same time the provinces had to have the power to function within their jurisdictions without having to borrow from Ottawa. Nor did he agree that acceptance of the Rowell-Sirois report was necessary to the war effort. The dominion government already had all the power and authority under the War Measures Act to do anything it considered necessary to win the war. 'I know this,' he concluded, 'that there are certain interests antagonistic to this Province who would like to tie the hands of Provincial authority so that for everything we require here, we would have to go to Ottawa, hat in hand, begging; they would like to see this province so that it cannot move of its own accord, but must have the sanction of Ottawa authority. Remote control would jeopardize the unity of Canada and would certainly be injurious to this great Province of British Columbia.' He then departed from his prepared script to speak directly and from conviction. He would not, he declared forcefully, 'permit British Columbia to be hog-tied and hamstrung by Ottawa.'[84]

Even at this stage Pattullo probably did not realize that the conference was merely a tactical manoeuvre by the federal government. As he waited for final word on the date and format of the meeting, he perhaps took heart from a second letter the prime minister wrote on 2 November indicating he agreed with Pattullo that 'premature efforts in the matter of the Commission's recommendations will only serve to work injury in the end.' So Pattullo cheerily arranged with King to arrive in Ottawa a few days before the conference to discuss matters informally.[85] He also spoke to Mitchell Hepburn of Ontario on the phone and the two exchanged letters saying how they were looking forward to the momentous discussions in January. Pattullo also sent Hepburn a copy of his 7 November statement to the British Columbia legislature. But there is no evidence that the two premiers co-ordinated their views as they prepared for the conference. And Pattullo had no contact at all with William Aberhart, which is not surprising since he had never approved of the Alberta premier's ideas.[86] He prepared his own statements for the conference for his own and, as he would have put it, British Columbian reasons. His state of mind had less to do with Hepburn of Ontario, Aberhart of Alberta, or even King in Ottawa than it did with the fact that Duff Pattullo of British Columbia had crossed the Chilkoot Pass to a new region more than forty years ago.

Confronting King and the federal government did not, like scaling the Chilkoot, demand mere energy and endurance, which Pattullo had; it also required power and subtlety, which he lacked. The nature of the federal strategy became alarmingly clear when he received the agenda for the dominion-provincial conference. Mackenzie King wrote to the premiers outlining the program and the committee structure for the meeting on 28 December 1940. Pattullo received his copy in Victoria on 2 January 1941, just six days before he was due to meet with King in Ottawa. In spite of the prime minister's reassurance that ample opportunity would be afforded 'to consider all relevant issues,' there was really only one item on the agenda. The conference had been set up to discuss only the implementation of the Rowell-Sirois Commission recommendations.[87] The provincial premiers were placed in the position of saying 'yes' or 'no' to plan 1. For Pattullo it was no choice. With the help of Carrothers and other senior officials, he had been drafting his statement on behalf of British Columbia for weeks.[88] Even if he had wanted to, it was too late to change his tack now. At one level the conference was to be a preordained clash between two diametrically opposed views of Canadian Confederation. At another level, Duff Pattullo was simply off to Ottawa for yet another one-way conversation with the federal government.

The conference opened in the Canadian House of Commons at 10:30 on the morning of 14 January 1941. With the agenda already fixed, King could afford to sound conciliatory at the start. In his opening speech he emphasized the need for the conference in wartime. He reiterated his November letter of invitation by saying 'the report commends itself strongly to our judgement' but added he did not regard it 'as the last word.' Sitting down the table to the prime minister's left, however, Pattullo could hardly have been persuaded of King's commitment to open discussion when he went on to say that while modifications in details 'may prove desirable,' the 'financial plan must be considered as a whole.' Nor was he comforted by King's bland reassurance that he was not proposing 'to rebuild the structure of confederation.' And he must have been incredulous when the prime minister continued that, far from bringing about greater centralization, the intent of the exercise was 'to safeguard the autonomy of the provinces.'[89]

In a sense the conference was over when Mitchell Hepburn rose to speak immediately after King. In his forthright way, the premier of Ontario declared his absolute opposition to the commission's report: a document that was not just inappropriate, but had been rendered irrelevant by the changed circumstances of wartime. The premiers who followed were rather more equivocal than Hepburn. Adélard Godbout of Quebec, A.S. MacMillan of Nova Scotia, and J.B. McNair of New Brunswick were neither wholly in favour nor wholly opposed to the report. They were followed by John Bracken of Manitoba who, in a long, detailed, and tedious speech that went on well into the afternoon session, defended plan 1 to the hilt and argued that its implementation was essential to national unity.

Pattullo followed Bracken and his address was a contrast in every way. It was short, crisp, and direct. He was not as abrasive as Hepburn, but he clearly and firmly expressed his opposition to the Rowell-Sirois proposals. Though he began by congratulating Mackenzie King for the high tone of his opening remarks, his next sentence made it perfectly clear he was 'at complete variance' with the federal government 'in respect of the report of the royal commission.' Implementation of plan 1, he argued, would lead to an ever-increasing centralization that, rather than creating harmony, 'would only aggravate disharmony.' He repeated his belief that in a country like Canada that was made up of five distinctive regions, 'there is nothing to be gained and much to be lost in attempting to bring them to a common level.

Everyone desires to see Canada strong and united, but this object cannot be achieved by way of a mechanization to establish a general Canadian average.' Certainly, he asserted, in a phrase that would come back to haunt him, 'British Columbia is in a category by itself.' Though, like the other provinces and the dominion, it had faced severe problems, it had pulled itself back to a sound economic situation 'after an arduous struggle up the hill of public economy.' His province did not want to be pushed down again 'there to turn the treadmill of mediocrity in perpetuity.' Pattullo's other major argument was that wartime was no time to make radical changes to Confederation. He regretted that winning the war was being used as an argument to impose a plan that would be both permanent and harmful. The federal government could take, and indeed was taking, temporary war measures every day. It did not need implementation of plan 1 to win the war. Addressing Mackenzie King, Pattullo concluded by saying he made 'these general observations ... with deep respect and grave concern.'[90] With that he sat down and gave the floor to others.

Pattullo was followed by Thane Campbell of Prince Edward Island and W.J. Patterson of Saskatchewan, both of whom were more or less in favour of the report. The last speaker was William Aberhart, who was flatly opposed. With these general statements completed, King's plan was that the delegates would meet the following morning to form committees to discuss various aspects of the report. The three opponents – Pattullo, Hepburn, and Aberhart – refused to join the process as long as plan 1 was, in effect, the only item on the agenda. When the plenary session was reconvened in the afternoon it was clear that the meeting had failed. The federal minister of finance stepped into the breach and read a prepared statement that indicated some of the implications of the collapse of the conference. Ilsley warned the premiers that the federal government would undoubtedly have to 'invade provincial tax fields' like succession duties and increase rates of income tax anyway. Nor could it guarantee to continue paying the present 40 per cent contribution to unemployment relief or to assist the provinces to pay their debts. Moreover, he warned that if gasoline rationing became necessary provincial revenues would decline even further. He made these threats, he said, 'at the risk of some misinterpretation,' but to Pattullo the point was perfectly clear.[91] Ilsley's statement simply confirmed what he had said all along: that the federal government did not need the implementation of plan I to do what it wanted in wartime.

There was then another round of commentary from the premiers as the conference dragged to its close. Pattullo, once again, asserted British Columbia's desire for autonomy within its sphere. We who 'are beyond the Rocky Mountains,' he said again, 'want to be left free to act ... we do not want to be hogtied and hamstrung, and that is exactly what will happen if this report is implemented.'[92] A foretaste of the division of opinion among British Columbians was given by Ian Mackenzie, now federal minister of pensions and national health, who said he was very disappointed in the stand his friend and premier of his province had taken. The prime minister finally closed the proceedings with the comment that, at least, it could not be said that, when the federal government took action, it did so without discussion. The conference ended with the singing of the national anthem and then King and the provincial premiers, with the exception of Hepburn, went out to dinner. King thought it was as 'happy and congenial' a dinner as any they had shared.[93]

King did not reckon the conference to have been a failure and Pattullo tried to put the best face on it. King believed he could not be criticized for lack of consultation and he had, as planned, placed responsibility for the rejection of plan I in the hands of three provincial premiers.[94] His government was now free to go ahead with the fiscal measures it considered necessary to meet the needs of the war. For his part, Duff Pattullo still assumed that, while politicians could fundamentally disagree with one another on policy, they could remain convivial on the personal level. He also tried to maintain a sense of humour about it all. A few days after the conference was over he sent the prime minister the rather unusual gift of a Schick magazine safety razor with his name engraved on it. In his lugubrious way, King replied that he and Duff had had 'many "close shaves" in the course of public life. I shall always regard the Schick Magazine Safety Razor as "a symbol of security," both physically and politically. May it prove such for each of us in these most uncertain and dangerous times.'[95] Perhaps Pattullo should have taken more heed of the prime minister's sombre tone, for many Canadians, including many British Columbians, were not at all amused by the failure of the dominion-provincial conference. Those two days in Ottawa were to determine the course of the rest of his political career.

Pattullo's performance at the conference has not received good press, either at the time or since. In the days after the meeting editorial writers from coast to coast portrayed him as one of a terrible trio of willful wreckers. In British Columbia newspapers the reaction was virtually unanimous. It could be taken for granted that the Vancouver *Province* and the Victoria *Colonist* would object to Pattullo's stand, just as they opposed everything he did. Thus the *Province* carried an editorial item entitled 'The Three Saboteurs' that went on to note that the emblem of the three premiers 'is the parish pump, rampant. Their motto is "each for none and none for each." '[96] But the denunciations were not confined to the conservative press. On the day the meeting ended the editor of the Vancouver *Sun* wrote that: 'The spectacle of the interprovincial conference in Ottawa is almost beyond belief. It will amaze, disappoint and disgust every thinking Canadian.' Even the Victoria *Times*, usually a mouthpiece for the Pattullo government, simply reprinted the *Sun* editorial without comment.[97] Some reporters thought Pattullo's performance was particularly disappointing. While little better could be expected of Hepburn and Aberhart, they had hoped the premier of British Columbia would be more flexible.[98]

While it is the function of newspapers to provide quick reactions to today's news, one might expect a more balanced assessment from historians who have the advantage of hindsight. By and large, however, they have simply joined the hue and cry. Having made the point that King called a conference he knew could not succeed, historians immersed in the Ottawa sources then move quickly and illogically on to blame three provincial premiers for the failure.[99] The comment of Alexander Skelton, the Ottawa bureaucrat who instigated the commission and wrote much of its report, that the session on the second morning when the three premiers refused to accept the federal agenda was 'the god-damndest exhibition and circus you can imagine' is constantly repeated as if it were the gospel truth rather than just jaundiced comment.[100] There is a tendency to assume that, led by Hepburn, the opponents acted in concert.[101] And, perhaps most importantly, Pattullo's critics ignore the fact that, while at a moment of wartime crisis, some provincial premiers accepted the federal proposal, in the long run, plan I was political nonsense. It would never have been accepted by Ontario or, as subsequent history would show, by the western provinces, to say nothing of Quebec. Pattullo was absolutely correct when he said that degree of centralization would only lead to trouble within Confederation. This view was not just a consequence of being 'securely anchored in his blinkered provincial stance,' but rather a realistic and, as it turned out, perspicacious view of Canadian federalism.[102] Nevertheless, the centralizers in Ottawa had their conference and, just as King had planned it, the commentators, then and now, blame the 'provincials' for its failure.

Pattullo did make the political error of not taking the objections to his position seriously enough. His initial reaction to criticism had always been to brush it aside, and in the days immediately after the conference he either underestimated the extent of opposition to his stand in British Columbia or overestimated his facility to overcome it. Instead of returning immediately to British Columbia to face his critics and explain what had happened in Ottawa, he stayed in the east for two more weeks. He remained in Ottawa for a few days, then he went to New York, partly to check out the financial markets and partly to have some new suits fitted by George's tailor. While there he responded to reports of the bad press he was getting on the west coast by issuing a statement that the criticism was extreme and inaccurate. Many British Columbians, however, were offended by hearing their premier speak to them from New York. 'After strolling down Wall St.,' suggested the editor of the *Vancouver Sun*, 'why doesn't Mr Pattullo stroll down Granville Street.'[103]

Sensing that Pattullo might be seriously wounded, the political vultures began to circle. Ian Mackenzie, who had once cried 'Lay on old Duff,' now wanted Pattullo to lay off. The rift between the two Liberals created quite a stir in British Columbia. Taking their cue from Mackenzie, other federal Liberals also spoke out against Pattullo. Mackenzie King confidant and member for the Cariboo, J.G. Turgeon, publicly criticized Pattullo, as did Tom Reid of New Westminster. Turgeon also called for a Liberal convention to define 'our policies and our loyalties.'[104] Former provincial member Byron Johnson wrote to Mackenzie to express his regret at the collapse of the conference.[105] In Prince Rupert one of Pattullo's political cronies from the early days, G.W. Nickerson, was so upset that he planned to run against Pattullo for the Liberal nomination in the next election. Duff was advised by one of the boys up north that, if he still intended to represent Prince Rupert, it would be a good idea to pay the town a visit and head off the movement against him.[106]

It was even rumoured that many members of his own cabinet were opposed to the hard-line position Pattullo had taken in Ottawa.[107] Much of this speculation centred on John Hart though, so far, he had been completely loyal in public. At the beginning of the month Hart had issued a new-year message to the people of British Columbia that was strong on the point that no sacrifice was too great to win the war. He was therefore saying the right things and, perhaps fortuitously, placing himself in a good position should the leadership of the provincial Liberal party become an issue. At the same time, in Pattullo's absence, it was Hart who explained the premier's position to British Columbians and also kept Duff informed of developments. When he issued a public statement defending Pattullo's refusal to accept the federal agenda, some commentators felt that Hart had failed to convince even himself.[108] Though the political waters in British Columbia were becoming muddied, one thing was crystal clear: as long as Pattullo stayed away the undercurrents would continue to boil.

The premier finally returned home at the end of January. The political situation demanded some finesse and dexterity, but instead he followed his usual procedure when he was beset on all sides: full steam ahead regardless. He issued a press release as soon as he got back which was mostly a brief reiteration of his arguments at the conference. He naïvely believed that anyone who examined his statement in Ottawa would 'understand why we took the position which we did take.' His only new point was that, when the premiers met with two federal ministers on the second morning of the conference to discuss the agenda, they had suggested a new one be prepared. The dominion representatives refused this suggestion and would not agree to any basis of discussion other than that laid down by Ottawa.[109] One statement would not, of course, clear the air, so in the weeks that followed Pattullo and his ministers made a number of radio speeches in an effort to convince people that acceptance of the Rowell-Sirois recommendations would have been a disaster for British Columbia. Pattullo held an impromptu forum on the sidewalk in front of the Vancouver courthouse that began with three cab drivers and an hour later had attracted a large crowd.

Then he went north to Prince Rupert to speak to his constituents. He told them there were 'powerful influences in the east who would like to see centralization of authority' and curb the activities of provincial governments. He, by contrast, had to maintain the interests of the periphery. In this northern town, where his career in provincial politics had begun a quarter of a century ago, he reminded his audience that 'no one knows better than you people in Prince Rupert the difficulty of long distance contact.'[110] Once again, at a time of crisis, Duff Pattullo returned to his frontier roots. Yet through the 1920s and 1930s, and particularly now with the nation at war, localism had become less of a factor within British Columbia politics.

These efforts to explain himself were made in the midst of the widespread expectation that an election would be called soon. The government's mandate would be four years old by the summer and, although technically he had until the fall of 1942, Pattullo could not wait so long without seeming as desperate as Tolmie in 1933. Yet he did not want to go to the people in the current climate. Apart from the racket of angry and self-righteous opponents, the Rowell-Sirois report had left his government in a real bind. He had hoped that the commission and the conference would clarify the nature of Canadian federalism and define provincial jurisdiction, particularly over financial matters. Now it seemed to him that the federal government, instead of describing the boundaries between jurisdictions, wanted to take over everything. And, as Pattullo knew only too well, you cannot have an activist government without money. So while he said he would welcome an electoral contest, he indicated it might come later than many expected. Nor would he summon the legislature to deal with the aftermath of the dominion-provincial conference. He was still operating on the belief that 'people in due time will understand all the implications of the Commission's report and just what happened in Ottawa.'[111] It was not at all clear, however, that he had the amount of time it would take for people to come around to his way of thinking. His defence of provincial rights was applauded by British Columbians during the depression, but was far less acceptable in the context of the patriotism and nationalism of wartime. And for a politician facing a major conflict, delay is always problematic: it gives one time to persuade voters, but it also allows opponents to mobilize.

Certainly the objections to Pattullo's stand in Ottawa did not fade away with the passing weeks. Some British Columbians applauded the position he took, but his opponents were strong and influential and they were able to make effective use of the issue of patriotism. Newspaper editors, both inside and outside the province, continued to argue that the notion that British Columbia was in a category by itself was an outrageous suggestion at a time when national unity was the paramount concern. The provincial conservative leader, Pat Maitland, who had vacillated on the value of the Rowell-Sirois Commission during the process, now found himself strongly in support of its recommendations as vital to the war effort. Behind these more public opponents was arrayed the power of big business. All of Pattullo's old enemies came out of the woodwork. Charles Woodward held a meeting of Vancouver's business leaders at the

Jericho Club to form an organization that would advocate the importance of the war effort and the need for a constitutional settlement that would make Ottawa 'supreme in all matters of national concern.' It seemed that all the old Vancouver names were on the list of those present – H.R. MacMillan, George Kidd, George Martin, and R. Bell-Irving – along with some newer ones like J.V. Clyne. Needless to say, as they themselves pointed out, the organization would be 'strictly non-partisan.' And in a sense, perhaps, it was true. Maitland certainly supported their efforts and they were also encouraged by Ian Mackenzie.[112] Pattullo was convinced that these business leaders were opposed to him for reasons other than his performance at the Ottawa conference.

His persistence in pressing his policy of imposing price control on the oil companies had also raised the ire of big business. Capitalists, both inside and outside the oil industry, objected to the particular effort to control gasoline prices and, now that they thought it had gone too far, to the general notion of government intervention. It had become a highly charged political issue in the summer of 1940 when Pattullo called a special session of the legislature to impose his will on the oil companies. Maitland described the move as 'a studied bid for more power' and hurled words like 'dictatorship' and 'communism' across the floor of the house.[113] And it was yet another issue that divided Pattullo's caucus. The Liberal opponents were led by Harry Perry, the fractious member from Prince George, who attacked Pattullo's measures against the oil companies as a violation of 'historic Liberalism.'[114] By early 1941 the immediate crisis over regulating the oil companies had passed, but the annoyance of big business had not. Pattullo knew that 'not only did our action alienate powerful oil interests, but also allied financial interests which are opposed to that kind of legislation.[115] He expected that big business would use every opportunity to take revenge.

There were signs that Pattullo was becoming thin-skinned in the face of the constant barrage of criticism. He felt any indication of weakness on his part would be played up in the press 'with constant misrepresentation and the usual lying.'[116] He engaged in a vitriolic exchange with John Dafoe, Rowell-Sirois commissioner and editor of the Winnipeg *Free Press*, in which he complained about 'error, misconstruction, misinterpretation, misrepresentation, falsification, lying and libel.'[117] A month later, when the *Province* published some forthright remarks about Pattullo's dealings with the federal government which, according to the premier, included quoted statements he had not made, he asked Wendell Farris to look into the possibility of bringing libel charges. Farris agreed with Pattullo's contention that the purpose of the article was to bring him 'personally within the contempt and contumely of the people of this province,' but advised that the item still did not constitute a legal libel.[118] The *Province* was, after all, simply continuing to do what it had been trying to do for years. Duff could still joke about such things in private. He told his brother George, the old newspaper man, that he had never experienced such vitriolic criticism. 'It is no longer liberty of the press but license; in fact, so much license that it is now licentious. I mentioned the other day that they are now nothing less than lice on the body politic, which of course keeps us scratching somewhat.'[119] It seemed, however, that Pattullo was not getting the fun he once did out of being the centre of controversy.

Nor was there much point in further skirmishing with the federal government. No more political mileage could be gained out of Ottawa-bashing, and Pattullo seemed to have lost the energy for it. He merely registered some perfunctory objections as Ottawa began to close in on the province's fiscal autonomy. In February British Columbia was informed that federal relief payments would be severely reduced and, the following month, Ottawa demanded repayment of some of the loans it had advanced during the depression. Pattullo started to object by writing to King that such measures would 'be interpreted as "putting the screws" on us.'[120] But the prime minister was not in the mood either. Much to Pattullo's annoyance, he brought the issue out into the open by tabling the correspondence between the two governments in the House of Commons. Pattullo then faced another sharp round of criticism in the provincial press. Even the *Times* suggested that 'supporters of the

Liberal Party in British Columbia should lose no time in taking stock of their position.'[121] And there was more to come.

The federal government went on to consider its taxation policy after the failure of the Rowell-Sirois recommendations. The plan was that Ottawa would levy taxes needed for the war effort and promised to compensate any province that surrendered its income, corporate, and succession taxes to the senior level of government. Provinces that failed to agree with the proposal would be left imposing heavy double taxation on their citizens. Pattullo was in the House of Commons in Ottawa when Ilsley announced these measures as a 'temporary wartime expedient' in his budget speech on 29 April 1941.[122] Pattullo had, of course, heard that phrase before, yet there was now little he could do but announce that he would co-operate with the federal minister of finance. On his return to British Columbia he issued the statement that, while he was prepared to accept these federal policies as war measures, he would not 'surrender our right to levy income tax but leave the matter to be adjusted at the conclusion of the war.' It seemed on the surface that the breach was healed. King expressed his appreciation for the provisional acceptance of the federal proposals and later that summer the prime minister spent an enjoyable evening in Pattullo's home.[123] But Duff surely knew that politically he was left with very little room for manoeuvre.

Realizing there was nothing to be gained from further delay, and hoping that some of the edge had been taken off the opposition, he called a provincial election for the fall. He first took a summer constitutional to the north and the interior. The two-week trip was partly relaxation and partly political. At a nomination meeting in Prince Rupert, Liberals unanimously selected him to be their candidate again.[124] He then travelled inland to Prince George and down through the Cariboo. In late July he also made a tour of the Kootenays. On 22 July he announced that the legislature was dissolved and, without specifying an exact date, that there would be a provincial election in October.[125] Later the polling day was set for 21 October 1941.

Contested during a world war when many people were overseas and those who remained had other things on their minds, the 1941 election was a relatively quiet one. Some even thought it was quite unnecessary. Pattullo justified going to the polls largely in terms of the need for a renewed mandate to co-ordinate the provincial income tax with the federal proposals. For him the tax issue remained paramount, though he also talked about the importance of the war effort and the need to be mindful of postwar reconstruction.[126] As ever, Duff Pattullo appeared to be confident of the outcome and cheerily predicted that his government would be returned with a good majority. Talking about an election earlier in the year he had said that, when it came, his motto would be the same as it always was: in the words of Walter Scott, 'Come one, come all.' In the face of personal criticism he was also reminded, he said, of a rather more mundane rhyme from his boyhood: 'Sticks and stones will break your bones, / But names will never hurt you.'[127]

Underneath the bravado, Pattullo was more uncertain. As he checked around the ridings he found there were many soft spots in Liberal support. And he would not benefit from the weakness of the other two parties as he had done in 1937. Both were more united and Pat Maitland and Harold Winch were now well established as leaders. Pattullo's concern about the outcome was reflected in an exchange of letters with J.L. Ralston, the minister of national defence, in which he raised the possibility of not polling the soldiers overseas.[128] In the event these British Columbians were not disenfranchised, but the notion was hardly an expression of complete confidence. For the many soldiers stationed in his own riding he provided generous quantities of what one of his organizers referred to as 'refreshments' in an effort to lubricate their loyalty.[129] Though he told party workers the general feeling throughout the province was that the government would be returned, he also urged them to 'take nothing for granted' because local situations could have an important bearing on the province-wide result.[130] He certainly knew this election was not a sure thing, yet he still expected to win. In his determination that he had been right, he probably still did not appreciate the depth of the opposition to his role in the Ottawa conference and he thus somewhat misread the mood of the people during the election. Still, as he had written a few years earlier, 'I have had the Sword of Damocles hanging over my head all my life; in fact, with social and economic conditions becoming ever more complex, one can never tell what the final outcome may be.'[131]

The campaign was low key, with no really sharp and divisive issues. In speeches that sometimes showed flashes of the fighting Pattullo of old, he defended the need for the vote in order to give his government the strength to deal with the federal government and to co-operate in winning the war. Before the campaign was over he had already scheduled a trip to Ottawa to discuss taxing arrangements. There were some issues he could not dwell upon. He was personally in favour of conscription and would have liked to have said so as a measure of his commitment to the war effort, but he was warned not to say anything that might embarrass the federal government on this delicate issue.[132] So he travelled the province, talking to British Columbians about roads and bridges, the possibility of annexing the Yukon, and of oil exploration in the north.

When the vote was counted it was evident that, although the government had not lost the election, it had not really won it either. The Liberals did have more seats than the other two parties. As usual they had failed to get a majority of the popular vote, but this time their credibility was further undermined by the fact that the CCF had polled more votes than the Liberals by a margin of slightly less than 2000. In Prince Rupert, where the Conservatives did not run a candidate, the CCF had been confident they would upset the premier and, in the event, they very nearly did. The outcome was in doubt until the final count when Pattullo was ahead of the CCF challenger, George Weaver, by just over one hundred votes. Province-wide, the Liberals had twenty-one seats, the CCF was second with fourteen, and the Conservatives had twelve. Tom Uphill, the perennial independent member from Fernie, made up the number to forty-eight. Significantly, Pattullo's party did not win a single seat in the Vancouver area with the exception of the re-election of Wells Gray in New Westminster. Two cabinet ministers, George Weir and Gordon Wismer, were defeated. In Victoria City, by contrast, John Hart won comfortably and brought two other Liberals in on his coat-tails.[133] The only part of the province from which Pattullo could draw any consolation was the north, which had remained solidly Liberal.

In the aftermath of the election, Pattullo's immediate reaction was that he would carry on with his minority government, at least until the legislature had met. As far as he was concerned, he had been re-elected with the largest number of seats and so he would continue as premier until he was defeated in the house. Constitutionally speaking he was correct, but politically the situation was not so clear. Nevertheless the premier went ahead with arrangements for his trip to Ottawa to discuss taxing arrangements with the federal government. Meanwhile, like a chorus in a Greek tragedy, the supporters of coalition began to recite their lines.

The clamour was instant. The *Vancouver Province* led the way the day after the election with an editorial calling for a coalition government and another item suggesting that John Hart was the likely leader.[134] Within a couple of days all the major newspapers in the province had joined the call and the Winnipeg *Free Press* and the *Globe and Mail* had also chimed in.[135] Pat Maitland immediately announced that he was in favour of the three-party coalition and Harold Winch equally quickly said that the CCF would not join such a union.[136] The veteran Victoria reporter Bruce Hutchison reduced the election to the single, simple issue of Pattullo's response to the Rowell-Sirois Commission. He then reasoned that, because the other two parties won more seats than the Liberals, most British Columbians opposed the way Pattullo dealt with the federal government.[137] The argument turned on the assumption that Conservatives and CCF voters had more in common than they had dividing them, which seemed an unlikely proposition. But it was a confused political situation. Pattullo responded to it all by saying that the call for a coalition, even before the returns were complete in some ridings, was only a 'rush act.'[138] The new legislature would meet in the first week of December, the earliest it was legally possible, and in the meantime he was off to Ottawa. Many felt that Pattullo did not have a mandate to represent the province in negotiations with the federal government and that he should sort out the political situation at home first. Observers also made much of the fact that Pattullo and Hart left for the east on separate trains.

Realizing he had a fight on his hands, Pattullo the public politician could still rise to the occasion. Torchy Anderson, a reporter who travelled with him to Ottawa, wrote that anyone who thought that Duff Pattullo was finished had better think again. He was sounding chipper and confident: a 'pretty frisky political corpse' in Anderson's opinion.[139] Duff himself said he had never been happier and he was now 'going to have more fun than a barrel of monkeys.'[140] In private the jolly front was difficult to maintain and Mackenzie King thought he was a very different person from the one he had been when he was securely in office. The prime minister saw Pattullo as 'chastened and subdued' though, as usual, King may have been seeing what he was looking for. The two conferred on the political situation in British Columbia and King agreed that Pattullo should resist all efforts to form a coalition, and certainly do nothing before the house met. Pattullo and Hart worked out a draft agreement on taxation with the Department of Finance and Duff returned to British Columbia on 8 November. Hart stayed in Ottawa to work on the fine print of the agreement and, he later revealed, he was urged by eastern financial interests to push for a 'stable,' which was to say coalition, government.[141]

Once again Pattullo had been absent from his province at a critical political moment and he now returned to face a delicate situation. If political survival were the objective, the coalescing of forces demanded some flexibility and willingness to negotiate and listen to others. But that was not Pattullo's way. Determination and single-mindedness had served him well in the past and he assumed they would again. There was absolutely no possibility he would even consider being part of a coalition, so to that extent the way before him was clear. He returned to the coast knowing that efforts were being made to form a union of Liberals and Conservatives under another leader. He still did not believe 'there could be sufficient deserters to carry out nefarious designs.' He realized his role at the Ottawa conference had hurt him politically but, if anything, he thought the opposition of the oil interests was more significant. He felt sure that at least 'one gentleman' from the business community 'would spend a large amount of money "to get even." '[142] Pat Maitland was also working on the idea of a coalition behind the scenes. He reiterated the idea of a three-party government in writing to Harold Winch and he was developing support for coalition in his own party. There is no direct evidence he had discussed the matter with prominent Liberals, though it is hard to imagine he had not.[143] While Pattullo knew his enemies were closing in on him, he still believed he could hold them off. This time his optimism was misplaced.

Matters came to a head on 14 November when Pattullo tried to form a new cabinet. The first move was made by George Pearson, who had leadership ambitions of his own. Pattullo had asked Pearson to relinquish his beloved labour portfolio and take the positions of provincial secretary and minister of education. William Asselstine would then become minister of labour. On the day the cabinet was to be sworn in, Pearson announced that this arrangement was unacceptable. He wrote to Pattullo that he thought steps should be taken to form a union government and released the letter to the press.[144] At the same time, Hart made public his support for a coalition with the Conservatives, though he did not submit his resignation immediately. At this stage Hart may have felt there was still some point to discussing the coalition idea with Pattullo. It was a very confusing day. In the midst of it all Norman Whittaker, who was to become attorney-general, was not informed of the swearing-in ceremony and arrived at Government House fifteen minutes late. The next day the two other Liberal members from Victoria declared themselves in favour of a coalition. Herbert Anscomb, a prominent Conservative who had fought with the Liberals for years over financial policy, now said he would be willing to serve as minister of finance under Hart.[145] Momentum was building.

The next development came a couple of days later. Hart continued to press for a coalition and so Pattullo asked for, and received, his resignation from the cabinet.[146] The same day William Asselstine, who had just been sworn in, now changed his mind and offered his resignation. Two days later Norman Whittaker resigned and he was followed by K.C. MacDonald. As the cabinet collapsed around him, Pattullo either looked for replacements or assumed the vacated positions himself. At one point he held three major portfolios in addition to the premiership. It was still his intention to 'go it alone': to hang on until the legislature met, which it was scheduled to do on 4 December. He argued that the people had not given him a mandate to form a coalition. He had been elected a Liberal and a Liberal he would remain.

Other Liberals had other views, however, and the political situation was fast moving beyond his grasp. The Vancouver gang were sharpening their knives. John W.deB. Farris had been contemplating the role that the lieutenant-governor might play in the situation and he told Ian Mackenzie that everything that Pattullo had recently done 'has been wrong and indicates a mentality not normal.' Pattullo's moods may have been, as the editor of the *Sun* observed, alternating between frivolity and anger, but there was no reason to think he had lost his grip on himself.[147] On the contrary, he had set a course based on his political principles and commitment to Liberalism, and now he was merely following it through to its conclusion. While such determination may have seem abnormal to those who thought it better to bend with the prevailing wind, for Duff Pattullo it was the only way to respond to the situation. He could not change at this late stage in his life. He reminded people that during all his years in the legislature he had been constantly under attack for one thing or another, whether it had been the Vancouver water supply or the Pattullo Bridge.[148] The current assault was not new, only more severe, and he would still rather fight than quit.

On 18 November Dr W.J. Knox, the president of the provincial Liberal party, announced there would be a party convention in Vancouver two days before the legislature was to open. The meeting, he said, was called to discuss the 'momentous events' of recent days and the differences of opinion between Liberal members of the legislature.[149] The real purpose of the meeting was to present a resolution in favour of a coalition government to the rank and file. Pattullo expected his opponents would be busy organizing and would gather together as many proxy votes as possible. He told Mackenzie King he did not have the time or the money to gather together any proxies, but he hoped he could persuade Liberals by the force of his argument. He knew that, at his age, his remaining term in office 'would be short at longest, but I am greatly concerned,' he wrote to the national leader, 'that the action of men who were in my cabinet and other prominent Liberals will result in splitting the Liberal Party in a way that will keep them out of office in this Province for a generation.' Looking back he remembered how in 1933 some of these same people – 'Hart, Pearson the Farrises and others' – had favoured a coalition while he had stood alone against the idea.[150]

When the convention opened in the Aztec ballroom of the Hotel Georgia on the morning of Tuesday, 2 December, Pattullo was greeted with cheers and resounding applause from the six or seven hundred delegates. It was a much more enthusiastic welcome than many expected him to receive. As he took his seat he said, surely a little tongue in cheek, 'I hope and expect that we are going to have a very interesting and enjoyable day.'[151] Immaculately dressed as always, the premier looked fit and ready for the fray as he sat through the opening speeches. Byron Johnson, who had been a Liberal member for Victoria until he was defeated in 1937, moved a resolution calling for the formation of a coalition government. For four hours, all through the afternoon, the arguments for and against were made. Pattullo listened to his former cabinet ministers speak in favour of a coalition and then he rose to address the convention himself. It was a feisty, fighting, Pattullo speech. He made it clear he did not intend to be subject to the ten-minute rule on speeches but, as leader of the party, would speak for as long as he wished. He lambasted the former ministers who had deserted him for their lack of courage. They should, he said, have stayed on and faced the house. But his biggest concern was the future of the Liberal party. He repeatedly warned that a coalition would be the ruin of the party in British Columbia: 'the great Liberal party would start downhill and it wouldn't come up for a generation.

Never again would it be a force in British Columbia.' He predicted that the more progressive elements in the Liberal party would move to the CCF. He spoke of his government's initiative to explore for oil in the Peace River country and how if there were Tories in the government that public project would be turned over to private enterprise. A coalition government, he said, would bring a definite move to the right. As he sat down he received another thunderous ovation from the assembled multitude.[152] This was the Duff Pattullo who had put the party back together in the early 1930s and led them through so many difficult years, the man they knew and respected even if they did not love him. He had made his case as forcefully as he could and now it was up to the rank and file. The delegates voted at five in the afternoon and the convention recessed while the ballots were counted.

When the convention reconvened to hear the results at 7:30 it was clear that many who had cheered Pattullo's speech did not share his views. The vote was 477 to 312 in favour of the coalition resolution. It was closer than many anticipated going into the convention, partly because there was still a lot of support for Pattullo outside the main centres. But there was no doubt that the leader had lost. Many Liberals were concerned about a minority government. They did not want the party to face an uncertain situation in the legislature and they were scared of another election right away. And, after he had been in power for so long, there were many who simply wanted to get rid of Pattullo.

The party had expressed itself and the leader's response was immediate. He listened stoically to the announcement of the vote that effectively ended his political career and a minute later he rose to speak. 'You have given your verdict, which I accept. But you must remember you are now no longer Liberals – you are coalitionists. I cannot allow my name to be submitted to the convention in any capacity whatsoever. I have so decided because I accept your verdict.' There was a moment of silence. Then Pattullo stepped down from the platform, and, waving his hand and saying, 'Good-bye, boys and girls,' he headed for the door. As he left that hall a woman said to him, 'It's a dirty trick,' while another delegate was heard to say, 'Thank God he's gone – he's a dictator.'[153]

Whatever people thought of Pattullo, they knew the party would not be the same without him as leader. One supporter later wrote to him that 'a pall seemed to settle over the meeting when you left and remained with the delegates during the balance of the evening.'[154] Once Pattullo had made his exit there was only one candidate for the leadership and John Hart was duly elected. The convention also passed a dozen uninspired policy resolutions. The following day Pattullo met with the caucus in Victoria. He released all the Liberal members, including the cabinet ministers, from any obligation to himself as premier. They were now free to carry out the wishes of the Liberal convention and form a coalition government.

It was appropriate that the last scenes of Pattullo's premiership should be played out in the Legislative Assembly that had been the centre of his life for twenty-five years. Two days after the Liberal convention, on 4 December 1941, the legislature opened for the first session of British Columbia's twentieth parliament. All eyes in the crowded gallery were on the premier. Pat Maitland tried to steal the show by barging in with what he knew to be a futile appeal for the three-party coalition. He did so, he claimed, not out of selfishness, but 'from a strong sense of duty.'[155] There was also an agenda of formalities to go through. But this was Pattullo's hour, as he took centre stage for his epilogue.

Pattullo spoke, observers said, like a benign and dignified father saying farewell to his children.[156] He greeted all the elected members and congratulated the leaders of the two opposition parties on their gains in the recent election. He commented on the increased number of women in the legislature and the importance of their contribution. He thanked the people of Prince Rupert for their constant support through his long political career. He then said he would relinquish the premiership the following week and would recommend to the lieutenant-governor that John Hart be called upon to form a new administration. He therefore moved an adjournment of the house until 8 January 1942. With that, he walked from the legislative chamber for the last time as premier.[157]

As the captain departed, the tumult and the shouting died and many British Columbians paused to reflect on what seemed like the end of an era. The moment was brief, for within days the province would be caught up in the maelstrom of a Pacific war. But Pattullo had been at the centre of British Columbia politics for so long that he had become an institution. He had come to prominence as a cabinet minister during the postwar reconstruction of the late 1910s and the economic uncertainties of the 1920s. As leader of the opposition he had revitalized the Liberal party and forged a strong alternative to the Conservative approach to the depression. Then he had led the province through the turbulent 1930s, asserting its rights through depression and war. He had become so closely identified with his province that he had become simply Duff Pattullo of British Columbia. Some, watching as Pattullo took his leave as premier, wondered what was the secret of his downfall, what was the weakness of judgement that undermined his leadership. For others the question had already been answered. Thomas King, one of the few cabinet ministers to remain loyal to the end, said of the premier after he left the Liberal convention: 'His strength is his only weakness.'[158]

CHAPTER 9

Looking Back

'So much there was that might have been'

After twenty-five years in the Legislative Assembly of British Columbia, Duff Pattullo was a private member for the first time. Though his premiership ended in a moment, the political instincts of a lifetime could not be immediately suppressed. They were as strong the day after he resigned as premier as they were the day before. He turned sixty-nine in January 1942, but he still had plenty of vigour and drive and, suddenly, all of that energy had nowhere to go. He had reached a stage in life when many would put the world of public affairs behind them and find fulfilment in the domestic and private sphere. While such a transition is never easy, for Pattullo it was particularly difficult. Until now politics had been his life. Having devoted himself to his public career rather than to nurturing personal relationships, he did not have those full and vital emotional resources to draw on. As they often are for men who have been active in public life, Pattullo's retirement years were more tense and trying than gentle and golden.

So he clung to politics. He could have resigned his seat and got out altogether, but he stayed on as the member for Prince Rupert. As well as simply needing something to do, he retained his seat for financial reasons. Although he was not poor, the endless political campaigns had been very expensive and he had always been generous with gifts. So he was not particularly wealthy either, and felt he still needed an income. Partly, though not entirely, for this reason he would have preferred a seat in the Canadian Senate to the back benches of the British Columbia legislature. He had already raised the possibility of some federal position with Mackenzie King when he was in Ottawa at the end of October 1941.[1] The day of his last appearance in the legislature as premier, Pattullo wrote King about a Senate appointment, just as his father had done twenty years before. While he did not want to see any other candidate disappointed, he told the prime minister he was 'not able to recall anyone whose record is quite as outstanding as my own.' King replied that he would discuss the matter with his colleagues, but he was clearly cool to the idea. He noted that, while he did not necessarily share the view, many still held Pattullo responsible for the failure of the dominion-provincial conference. He doubted that such an appointment would be possible.[2]

Duff first pressed and later pleaded on the matter. He replied to King that he did not think it was a healthy situation if any provincial politician who 'does not conform to the dictation of Ottawa authority' was to be denied consideration. He claimed that even 'the Sun newspaper stated that the people of the Province would unanimously approve of my being given preferment for my long and splendid service, though I must admit that the Sun is usually a liar. This may be the exception.' He also wrote to Ian Mackenzie to ask if he would push the issue. He was more blunt with Mackenzie, telling his former colleague that 'if any manipulating coalitionist is appointed, I surely will feel very hurt.' On a more personal note, he admitted to both men in Ottawa that he 'would like to end my days in quiet dignity and honour.'[3] But it was all to no avail and Pattullo was refused a seat in the Senate. King did not select anyone who had been at the forefront of the drive for a coalition government in British Columbia, but Pattullo took little comfort from the appointment of Gerry McGeer to fill the British Columbia vacancy in the upper house.

Pattullo stayed on in the provincial legislature. He took King's decision as final, believing if he were not appointed to the Senate early in 1942 he would be too old later. He also felt that at his time of life he could not launch into a new career, say in some area of business. Relegated to the back benches in the house, he no longer commanded centre stage. Yet when he took the floor he could still turn on crackling performances just as he had done in his prime. Now, however, he was fighting old battles and defending old issues. When he spoke other members stopped to listen, but they did not take much notice. He would be described as the 'Ripple Rock in the political narrows': a splendid anachronism, fixed and unrelenting as the tides moved and surged around him.[4]

British Columbia politics underwent a sea-change as Pattullo was ejected from the premiership. Once the old leader was gone, Hart and Maitland began to haggle in earnest over the details of the coalition. The two held discussions and exchanged letters over the weekend of 6 and 7 December 1941. Maitland raised a number of policy stipulations, but Hart argued that they were 'starting with a clear sheet.' He did not want to commit himself to anything specific, though he was sure there were 'no fundamental differences between us.' The Liberal leader did, however, find it necessary to lecture the inexperienced Maitland on the limitations of provincial jurisdiction when it came to mobilizing the war effort. The real issue between the two politicians was the number of positions that each party would have in the coalition cabinet. Maitland argued that the new government ought to be founded on the notion of equal responsibility and therefore there should be equal representation in cabinet. Hart, of course, was not going to give up a majority so easily and he maintained that portfolios should be allocated in proportion to the number of members each party had in the legislature.[5] The issue of balance in the coalition cabinet was somewhat diminished, however, by the Japanese attack on Pearl Harbor that same weekend. Amidst the ensuing panic on the west coast, Maitland quickly came to an agreement with Hart on the composition of the cabinet.

The new government was sworn in on 10 December. The Executive Council was made up of five Liberals and three Conservatives. While the formation of the coalition was accompanied by a great deal of rhetoric about the need for a government of unity to win the war, its real function was to keep the CCF out of power. At the same time, by conceding the role of official opposition, the coalition actually enhanced the position of the CCF. Duff Pattullo's reformist Liberal government had held the middle ground of British Columbia politics. Now the centre had fallen apart, and, as the coalition moved towards the right, the extremes that are often said to characterize west-coast politics became more and more apparent. The advent of the CCF in 1933 had created the possibility of polarization, but it took the decline of reform to bring it about. And, while the party labels would change, the Liberal-Conservative coalition of 1941 was only the first of many.

For his part, Duff Pattullo remained adamantly opposed to the coalition. He told King it was 'an Administration conceived in perfidy and, to mix metaphors, now purring in self-adulation.'[6] At a personal level, he felt some bitterness at being ousted as premier by his former colleagues. Perhaps because they had been so closely associated for so long, Duff seemed unable to forgive John Hart for his role in the events of late 1941. He would frequently refer to Hart as a double-crosser and this attitude was the one big exception to his general rule that politicians should not hold personal grudges. The day before the coalition was sworn in, Duff wrote to one J.R. Laurier in Montreal. The man was no relation to Sir Wilfrid but, as Pattullo noted, he bore a wonderful name. Duff recalled the 1917 Liberal convention in Winnipeg and the effort to depose the old leader. 'It was,' he said, 'a cruel action coming towards the end of a remarkable career.'[7] Clearly he was not only writing about the Liberal leader he had always most admired.

For Duff Pattullo this new world of British Columbia politics was not a very brave one. Soon after the session got underway early in the new year the government introduced a resolution that called on the house to approve the formation of the coalition at this time of national peril. On 19 January 1942, his sixty-ninth birthday, Pattullo rose to speak as the only member in the legislature opposing the motion. He sported the Liberal colours in the form of a red rose in his lapel and wondered aloud what the colour of the coalition might be.[8] Whatever its political stripe this union government was unnecessary and ill-advised, he asserted. Co-operation in the interests of the war effort could have been achieved through the house committees. This coalition was the product of fear. The Liberals and Conservatives were afraid that the ' "goblins would get them if they did not watch out," the particular goblin being the CCF.' And the CCF members, he claimed, were afraid their numbers would be diminished if another election were held. After the Liberal party had managed the political economy of the province for most of the last twenty-five years, and after he had had such a long career in that party, do you think, he asked the house, 'that I could lightly see the Liberal Party disappear.'[9] He strongly objected to being described as an independent in the legislature. As far as he was concerned, he was the only Liberal left.

He was deeply concerned that his party would be crushed in the new alignment of British Columbia politics. Later in the year he published a little political tract called 'Wither the Liberal Party' in a effort to warn others of the danger. He argued that it had been the purpose of the CCF to drive the Liberals and the Conservatives together. Toryism was dying so the CCF wanted to link the Liberal party to it, while, for their part, the Conservatives needed a new lease on life. The CCF hoped, according to Pattullo, that, with the formation of the coalition, more progressive Liberals would vote for them. Right now winning the war was important, but once the conflict was over there would be a need for major new social and economic policies to deal with the problems and opportunities of reconstruction. There would be a demand, he believed, for the reformist Liberalism that his party had represented. He predicted that, after the war, there would be a deadlock between extremes in British Columbia, along with continued pressure from the federal government for greater centralization. The Liberal party would have to combat that situation with all its strength if it were to remain a factor in provincial politics. He therefore advised all local workers to keep the Liberal organizations intact so that, at the proper time, the party could take effective action.[10] Unfortunately for the party, few heeded his call to arms. Some Liberals were bemused by the coalition. The Vancouver businessman, Victor Odlum, wrote to Maitland that 'it does seem strange ...

to see you and John Hart in a single bed with one thin sheet to cover you.' Other prominent party members, particularly those responsible for bringing about the marriage of convenience, were perfectly happy with the new arrangement. Wendell Farris thought the new government was doing just fine: 'at least,' he remarked, 'I hear little about them, which is always a good sign.'[11]

Pattullo, who still believed that elected representatives should make themselves heard, spent much of his time defending his record and reiterating old issues. In the same speech in which he attacked the coalition, he also touched on many of the points to which he would consistently return as a private member. He was still convinced that the virulent attacks on him at the end of his premiership were instigated by the financial interests behind the oil companies. Now that big business in British Columbia had achieved its long-standing goal of a coalition government, the regulations that Pattullo had passed to control the oil industry were revoked. He fought fiercely alongside the CCF when, later in the same session, the government passed an amendment to his Coal and Petroleum Act to allow private companies to drill for oil in the Peace River country.[12] He warned British Columbians that private exploitation would mean that the resource would be lost forever to the people and so the public should demand public ownership. His request later in the year for a referendum on the question of public involvement in oil exploration was politely but firmly rejected by Hart. His advocacy of government control of the petroleum industry was anathema to the Conservatives in the coalition and, over the next few years, the whole program was compromised away. It was clear evidence in Pattullo's mind that the coalition was not a new Liberalism but simply 'a patched-up Toryism.'[13]

He also constantly harped on the Rowell-Sirois Commission and its aftermath in a effort to rescue his reputation. While he had always been prepared to co-operate with Ottawa, he insisted he had to protect British Columbia's interests, particularly in the area of income tax. If he were wrong in the stand he took in Ottawa, he said, 'a remedy can still be applied. But let us suppose that I had agreed to surrender in perpetuity our right to impose income tax, do you think that situation could ever be remedied? Do you think Ottawa would ever restore our position? The question answers itself.' He had simply stood up against those eastern interests which, instead of co-operation, wanted to control the provinces.[14] He was particularly bitter towards the financial managers in Ottawa who had tried to perpetrate plan 1. He noted in a letter to King that Clifford Clark, the deputy minister of finance, had said that Pattullo had 'bust his programme.' He thought that Clark meant well enough, but even 'the self seeking financial interests have led themselves to believe that they are actuated and acting solely for the good of everybody concerned and that the poor boobs running political affairs are the real stumbling block to progress, to which deterrent, it seems, our so-called democratic system peculiarly lends itself.'[15]

He often harkened back to the political issues that had defined his career. He still believed there 'is an Empire in Northern British Columbia and Yukon' and he remained a strong advocate of the development of the north.[16] He defended his plan to annex the Yukon but was unimpressed with the construction of the Alaska Highway in 1942. The road that the federal government had rejected as a depression panacea was now built as a strategic route and, as Pattullo bitterly observed, put through in great haste and in the wrong place.[17] In the house he reminded members of other old battles he had fought and won, such as those over the Pattullo Bridge, the Capilano watershed, and the university endowment lands. Some issues he now pushed to greater lengths than when he had been in power. He introduced an amendment to the Libel and Slander Act that would oblige newspapers that printed criticism of an individual also to publish a rebuttal. Not surprisingly, this gambit produced cries that he was attempting to gag the press.[18] He followed the trend of his earlier labour policies to the conclusion that strikes were a form of civil war and then suggested that arbitration boards be the court of final appeal and that strikes be banned.[19]

But it was to the Rowell-Sirois Commission and British Columbia's right to a share of income tax that he constantly returned. In countless speeches and letters to editors he doggedly pursued the issue. His obsession arose partly from his wish to clarify the past and partly from his concern for the future, and it was fueled by the feeling he had little influence over either. He was still convinced he was absolutely right in the stand he took against the Rowell-Sirois recommendations. When the Vancouver *Province* continued to describe him as having been 'intransigent' in 1941 he retorted by saying the word was too mild.[20] The new taxing arrangement conceived by Ottawa when the conference collapsed was put in place early in 1942. The federal government now collected income tax and British Columbia received an amount equal to the tax levied in 1941. Pattullo was determined that the province should not completely surrender its right to income tax.

He remained convinced that, when the federal government faced the issue of postwar reconstruction, there would be a renewed drive towards centralization. He wrote and published two pamphlets, one in 1943 and another on the eve of a dominion-provincial conference in 1945, urging British Columbians to resist the demands of the centralizers. The province must insist, he argued after going over the history of the matter, that it continue to have a just share of income tax levied in British Columbia, even though the federal government was now the collection agent. Retention of its rights in the income-tax field was absolutely crucial to the welfare of the province. British Columbians, if not all Canadians, must resolve to live 'in divided unity as our natural conditions dictate, rather than set up a legalistic unity of disharmony and discord.' Duff Pattullo had certainly lost none of his joy for his adopted place or his enthusiasm for the periphery. 'I think of this great and glorious Province, anchored on the edge of the Pacific, as the western bulwark of Canada, vibrant with a self-reliant and energetic people.' But his exhilaration was tempered with a warning: 'If we hand over our money power exclusively to the jurisdiction of the federal authority we will place ourselves in the position of a poor relation.'[21]

The sad thing was that fewer and fewer people were taking notice. The first few times he spoke in the house after his resignation as premier, the members of the coalition were on edge as he began and felt relieved when he sat down. But he soon began to lose credibility. After a couple of years he seemed repetitive rather than merely retrospective. During the 1943 legislative session Pat Maitland noted that old Duff was up again for his 'annual "when I was" speech.' To his opponents he became an irritant rather than a threat, though Pattullo knew all along that, having 'succeeded in knocking the "Hon." off me, they would like nothing better than to kick me in the M.L.A.'[22]

The next provincial election was called for the fall of 1945. The long years of war and sacrifice were over and British Columbians were anticipating new and better times. There seemed little point in dwelling on the past. Yet Duff Pattullo still had things to prove. After considerable thought he decided to run again in Prince Rupert. He spent more than a month in the riding up to election day on 25 October. He ran as an independent Liberal and, though he was endorsed by the local executives of the two coalition parties, he knew he had a real fight on his hands. The two old parties had done little to boost the voters' list while the CCF, he claimed, had added some two thousand of their supporters. Moreover, a 'gentleman down south,' as he referred to Hart, had tried to prevent his nomination and, although the ploy had been unsuccessful, Liberal ranks in Prince Rupert were divided. Though he hoped the picture was 'perhaps not quite as bad as it sounds,' this time he was realistic rather than optimistic about his chances. He had apparently told at least one reporter over a year before that he thought his day was done, and, in the midst of the campaign in Prince Rupert, he wrote to Doris to warn the family that 'none of you must be disappointed at the result.'[23]

On election day his defeat was decisive. He had always argued that none of his string of election victories in the riding had been as easy as it looked from the outside. Now he was overwhelmed by the working-class vote that had always been a major factor in Prince Rupert. The CCF candidate, William Brett, had a plurality of more than 500 over Pattullo. Province-wide, the coalition had done well by winning thirty-seven of the forty-eight seats and the CCF had been reduced from sixteen to ten.[24] If anything, Pattullo was more concerned about the growing strength of the coalition and therefore the increased risk of the submergence of the Liberal party in the province. Once the election was over, he was philosophic about his own loss in Prince Rupert. The people of the area had chosen him as their representative seven times over a period of nearly thirty years. He had, he said, simply gone to the well once too often.

Now it was over. He was out of active politics for good. Tributes came in from friends and opponents alike. John Hart wrote a sanctimonious letter noting how their 'long association has made ties which are impossible to break.' Even CCF leader Harold Winch communicated his personal appreciation for the service Duff had given to the country for so many years 'and also for the unfailing courtesy you have extended to us at all times.'[25] Several years before, Bruce Hutchison had written what could be his political eulogy: 'he has been a great man in our public affairs in British Columbia, a bold and striking figure who will long be legendary here, a man who was often mistaken but never was afraid.'[26] Certainly everyone in Victoria, whether or not they liked him or agreed with him, knew that the legislature would be a very different place without Duff Pattullo. That particular, pungent flavour he had given to provincial politics was gone.

With the passing of the politician we are left with the man, and the last years of his life were not especially happy ones. He spent some time in the press gallery in Victoria writing newspaper articles. Many were published in the *Vancouver News Herald*, but they were usually pieces of self-justification.[27] Without meaningful work his world seemed empty, and his family provided little consolation. His marriage suffered from years of neglect and Lillian had her own cross to bear. By now she was nearly always doubled up with the pain of arthritis, there were times when she could neither stand nor sit in comfort, and she frequently had to crawl to get around the house. Duff sympathized to a degree, but sometimes felt she exaggerated her illness or at least could do more to help herself. He thought the two hundred cigarettes she smoked every week did not improve her health. He sometimes contemplated making a deal that he would give up drinking if she would stop smoking, but on second thought he remembered his wife was a determined woman and might take him up on the offer. When Lillian and her friends began to discuss aches and pains, to Duff it seemed the 'appropriate time to order the drinks.'[28] Some of his callousness towards Lillian's ailments arose from the frustration of having watched her suffer for years without being able to do anything to help. There were moments of affection between them. They celebrated their fiftieth wedding anniversary in 1949 and Duff commented to his sister that there 'must be something to my wife when she stood me for fifty years.' But such interludes were rare, and they spent more time arguing and fighting.[29]

All was not always well with the rest of the family either. Duff had a falling out with his daughter in the early 1950s. Doris had endured an increasingly unhappy marriage and contemplated separating from her husband, but her father shared the common view of the day that having made one's bed one should lie on it. It was, after all, what he had done. Doris felt badly because of her sense she had failed her parents.[30] There had been an even sharper break with his brother George a few years earlier. George had been an alcoholic for some time and his drinking was a response to a mental disorder. His condition grew worse and on a couple of occasions he nearly drank himself to death. In December 1946 Duff visited his brother in Florida and was shocked at the state he was in. Still believing 'we must all be our brother's keeper,' he advised George that, in his own best interests, he should get psychiatric help. George was enraged, and he cut off all contact with his brother. He wrote Duff a nasty, drunken note saying he did not want to see him ever again. In spite of his own success, George had always been jealous of Duff's achievements, though the bottom line of defence for George was that Duff had never made any money. Now all the animosity came out. Duff felt sorry for George, knowing that his brother could not help himself. 'No one,' wrote Duff of George, 'can be happy when they are ugly inside.'[31] A few years later George relented and the brothers wrote to each other again on occasion, but their close friendship was broken.

Duff did keep in touch by letter with his sisters in Ontario and he visited them whenever he could get back east. There was a special affection between him and his elder sister, Ethelwyn Ballantyne, or Wynnie as he called her. In contrast perhaps to the tempests of his own career, Duff thought his sister had 'sailed life's seas so beautifully.' On 14 September 1947 he wrote to her and recalled how, on that day fifty years ago, they had been together at Burnside. It had been his sister's wedding day.[32] Such memories were of times that seemed so long ago. In the immediate present Duff continued to get the most pleasure from his three granddaughters, Anne, Beth, and Clare. He always wrote and spoke of them with great fondness. For years he had been anxious to be alive when they grew up and now he wanted to survive until they had got to the top in their respective spheres. Never, he once reminded them as he had so often done himself, 'be satisfied with mere mediocrity.'[33]

For some people a circle of firm friends can provide the emotional support a family lacks. Like many political leaders, however, Pattullo ended up with numerous acquaintances and few really close friends. He kept up a considerable correspondence during retirement with people he knew through the mail. His letters are full of good-natured banter, but they do not bespeak of intimacy and confidence. Duff, it seems, revealed more of his inner self in the verse he wrote in his old age. One of these poems was simply called 'Alone':

Alone, far out
There is a light
Shines not for me
I am alone.

Alone, no trustful hand
No understanding mind
To feel the glow
I stand alone.[34]

In his loneliness, he looked back on his full and active life and reflected on how it might have been different. He tried to remain optimistic and look to the future. In a poem called 'Soliloquy' he wrote:

So much there was that might have been
And yet so much there was
I'll look ahead and not behind
The future yet unseen.[35]

And yet, as he noted in a letter written in June 1948, 'when one reaches three score ten and one half, retrospect and prospect do not seem so far apart.'[36] It was probably during this time that he wrote the series of autobiographical letters under the name of John Burnaby in which he describes his leaving Woodstock for New York: the time when his life seemed open and full of possibilities. It is perhaps significant that the 'fictional' Burnaby breaks off his engagement with 'Lilian' as he leaves in search of greater things.[37]

At times when his house seemed 'chuck full of hush' he recalled his Yukon days.[38] He still looked back on that exciting, formative period as the best time of his life. He sometimes heard from the voices of his past. He wrote to Billy Radford, his old business partner up north, to ask what had happened to the records from their Dawson office. He mentioned Martha Black, who they had both known in Dawson and who later became a federal member of parliament. She was living in Victoria and Duff had escorted her over to a sitting of the British Columbia legislature. Radford replied wondering how those like Duff and Martha Black, who had given much of their 'time talents and loyalty to party politics,' would frankly assess their lives. 'Can you (and me too) say we have fought the good fight, run the straight race or – after all – have we been on the wrong track all the time and our contribution to our times been secondary and meaningless?' Duff replied he would not have changed anything under the conditions as they appeared at the time. Political parties were merely a means to an end, and not an end in themselves. But it was also true he was 'too conscientious or something' to ever be quite satisfied. He was always aware that he might have achieved more. 'Nevertheless,' he concluded, 'there are some landmarks which the doublecrossers cannot expunge.'[39] He was particularly proud of the fact that he had stood firm in 1933 and, that time around at least, saved the

Liberal party from the clutches of a coalition. Though he always had to fight hard for every achievement, looking back on it all he still reckoned that, compared to the current crop of provincial politicians, 'I had more fun than they are now having.'[40]

Though he was out of politics, he continued to take an interest in what was going on. Occasionally he spoke out publicly, as in June 1949 when he addressed British Columbians on radio in support of the Liberals in the federal election. He spoke very highly of the new federal Liberal leader, Louis St Laurent, and he also spent a good deal of time expounding the old Pattullo verities. He could see no reason to change the name of the Liberal party as the Conservatives had done. 'The term Liberal is a beautiful word and all embracing.' Progressive Conservative seemed to him to be a contradiction in terms, 'unless they really mean that they become more conservative progressively.' He warned voters not to be taken in by such imprecise labels and, to make the point, he told the listeners a political parable. 'In the old days,' he began, 'there were Grits and Tories. The Grits were the reformers ...'[41]

Mostly he commented on political developments in private. Naturally enough, he often compared the present situation with his own experience. A number of people urged him to write his memoirs, but he felt that, while it would be an exciting book if he told his version of the truth in his own way, a lot of people would be hurt. So he resisted the notion and expressed his views more confidentially. By 1949 Pat Maitland had passed away and John Hart had resigned as premier to be replaced by Byron (Boss) Johnson. Duff ran into the premier one day and was prompted to write 'A Reflection':

> A few days ago I met a man in a place where all men meet sooner or later, a washroom. The man was Boss Johnson, our premier.
>
> I said 'Hello Boss, I'll bet that you are mighty glad that the work of the session is over.' Boss nodded and looked so rugged and fresh that I further observed, 'but you have no troubles, you are rolling in money to carry out your proposals. Now, during all my time, we were always short of money and had to fight every inch of the way in connection with everything we did.' The contrast seemed to strike the Premier.

He raised his eyebrows and replied 'that's so you did.' The Premier then rushed away to greet the Lieutenant Governor who was to give his consent to the bills which the legislature had passed and prorogue the legislature.

I sauntered out to my car with a reflection on the budget of 1916–7 which we inherited when we took office in 1916. Estimated receipts were less than six million dollars and estimated expenditures just over eleven millions.

With a further reflection of how little the public understands or is able to recall all that has transpired, I jumped into my car and reflected upon the new speed limit of fifty miles an hour.[42]

Pattullo took little consolation in watching many of his predictions about British Columbia politics come true. He always expected the coalition would crumble and he feared the Liberal party would go down with it. When Hart resigned as leader of the coalition in 1947, Duff thought he was getting out while the going was good. By 1949 he described provincial politics as a 'jumble,' with few people liking the coalition but many scared to death of the CCF. He was 'counting on getting some kick out of I told you so stuff, if that kind of stuff ever affords much of a kick.' Duff was saddened, but not surprised, when the 1952 and 1953 elections brought the Social Credit Party, under W.A.C. Bennett, to power. 'What a licking the Libs and Cons got. The coalition ended up as I expected it would.' After the confused 1952 election was over, he wrote bitterly to a relative in Ontario: 'We are balled up politically here. The clever boys made a fine hash of it.'[43]

Nor did he take much joy from those who wrote to him now, ten years after the fact, to say he had been right after all about the Rowell-Sirois report and the coalition. 'Mory' Moriarty, a veteran reporter who had known Pattullo since 1916, told him the political sagacity he had shown in 1941 was being recognized more and more by politicians today. 'Had the weak ones supported you then, the present-day schmozzle wouldn't exist.' The same reporter also seethed with anger when he thought of the barbs thrown at Pattullo over his efforts to find oil in the Peace River country. 'You had the right hunch, Chief, but the people were dumb.'[44] Even Bruce Hutchison, whose growing commitment to national affairs had led him to be very critical of Pattullo in 1941, now had second thoughts. He was wondering again, 'as I did so often wonder since reaching the age of discretion, whether I treated you justly as a public figure. I fear the answer to that question leaves a little scar on my conscience.'[45] But there was scant solace for an old politician in the knowledge that some thought he was right in retrospect.

The polarization that Pattullo had predicted twelve years earlier was now a fact of political life in British Columbia. As far as Pattullo was concerned, Social Credit was just another Tory party and the CCF was moving further to the left all the time. He had forecast in 1941 that the formation of the coalition would keep the Liberals out of office in British Columbia for a generation. Now it seemed he had been too optimistic. 'The results of the coalition will be with us not only ten years but in perpetuity.'[46] His beloved Liberal party to which he had given much of his life was only a minor factor in provincial politics and, with it, the middle-of-the-road reformism that Pattullo had represented also seemed lost. As the new politics in British Columbia were unfolding it occasionally crossed Duff's mind that he should be back in the game. 'If I were a reversal in figures in age,' he wrote in 1948 when he was seventy-five, 'I would give some of the boys a razzle dazzle for their money.'[47] Though they occurred to him more than once, such thoughts were only momentary.

Perhaps because, from Pattullo's point of view, there was little to write home about in British Columbia politics, he maintained an interest in wider affairs. In retirement he sometimes did what he had studiously avoided when he was in office and made personal comments about other leaders he had known. During the lengthy process leading up to Mackenzie King's resignation as prime minister on 15 November 1948, Pattullo expressed his ambivalence about his erstwhile antagonist. 'I have always had some reservations regarding Willie King,' he wrote. In contrast to the prime minister, Duff had 'never been able to communicate with Deadeye, a dog which we worshipped when we were youngsters.' On a more serious level, he would prefer to give King 'my power of attorney to deal with foreign policy than to any other leader in sight.' Yet, at the same time, he thought that, domestically, King had been lucky 'in never having had good leadership against him.' And, as a man, 'there is still something lacking. He is not a finished article.' If he had 'possessed the missing link' he might have gone down as Canada's greatest prime minister, but Pattullo believed he would be forgotten when the memory Macdonald and Laurier still shone.[48]

Duff also continued to be a keen observer of American politics. He was unimpressed with the Cold War hysterics in the United States during the early 1950s. His brother George wrote a number of books through the decade that bemoaned the passing of the true American spirit. George firmly believed that the United States was weakly abrogating its responsibilities in the face of international communism.[49] Duff, by contrast, thought the anti-communist crusade was just people crying, 'Whose afraid of the big bad wolf?' He did, however, take cold comfort from the extent to which it showed 'they have as many dunderheads over there as we have here.' He believed that the American president, Dwight Eisenhower, would have his work cut out for him and would need the good men he had around him. 'I think,' Duff added, 'he has some load to carry in Nixon.'[50]

As he grew older, Pattullo became acutely aware of the passage of time. He wrote to George just before Christmas 1951 that 'another year is about to cast itself from the chain of the ages and fall into the abyss of the past.' Or, as he remarked in another letter, 'time certainly fugits.' By the early 1950s, with the passing of friends and relatives, he was constantly writing letters of condolence. 'The old timers are fast passing and it looks as if I shall soon be the oldest man in the world.' He did not forget that passing time also brought renewal. He often wrote notes to newborn children to express his pleasure at their coming. 'I am surely delighted,' he wrote to one, 'to learn of your arrival to this wonderful world of adventure and interest.'[51] And yet it seemed he was losing more old friends than he was gaining new ones.

His own health was beginning to fail him by his late seventies.

Having been in robust physical condition throughout his life he did not take kindly to the effects of old age. He had to have a hernia operation in 1948. He had contracted the problem twenty-five years ago when, on a campaign tour, he had done a strong-arm act by lifting some hundred-pound smelter bars in Trail. It had not bothered him until now, but he decided it should be treated while he had the chance. By his own account he was pretty chipper through the process. The operation was done under local anaesthetic so he heard the whole performance. 'The two nurses who wheeled me out were very decidedly brunettes. I warned them that I was not a gentleman, because I did not prefer blondes. I saw a very striking blonde nurse afterwards and wondered if I should not have made some qualifications in my observations to the brunettes.'[52] In one of his boys-will-be-boys letters to George he observed that 'when the time comes when I can no longer admire a good looking woman I want to pass out.'[53] But such boyish joy in life became more difficult to sustain in the face of more serious maladies.

In early 1951, a few days after his seventy-eighth birthday, he reported that 'Mrs Lumbago intermittently tries to flirt with me' and her 'fellow Arthritis seems to be a confirmed molester.' He had occasionally suffered briefly from arthritic pain before. In the past, he had put his quick recovery down to the fact that he refused to stop drinking, but the remedy now seemed to be less effective. The failure of the medication was not, in itself, a problem. As far as Duff was concerned, no one had ever 'proven that mere long life is preferable to a measure of indulgence.' There were, however, times when he was in extreme pain. 'The Rheu gang are a tough bunch,' he concluded after a particularly severe bout. 'They don't kill you but keep you alive to torture you.'[54] In 1951 he had a attack that was so severe he was completely immobilized and had to be taken by ambulance to hospital where all he could do was lie and look up at a spot on the ceiling. He recovered and had a respite, but other attacks followed. Lillian was also chronically ill and in and out of hospital. Then in early 1955 Duff was carrying a bundle of magazines down the stairs, missed his footing, and fell.

That mishap put him in hospital for a week. He was not bouncing back as he used to do and began admitting to a lack of energy.

He turned eighty-three on 19 January 1956. There were the usual birthday interviews by reporters. He said once more he would 'like to be in the game again and give the boys some of the old razzle-dazzle.'[55] Yet he knew it would never be. The realization perhaps led him to the thought that his useful life was over. He had confided in George several years before that 'I should think that people who are helpless and can no longer be of assistance to others would want to pass out. I think that we should stick it out to the last drop of our usefulness, after that it is about time to pass on.'[56] There was a small family gathering for his birthday at Doris's place in the evening. As he left, standing by his car, he looked away into the distance and said quietly, as if to himself, that it was time for him to go.

Alone, so be that time
And tide ebb out
I cross the bar
I go alone.[57]

Duff Pattullo died after a short illness in St Joseph's Hospital in Victoria on the evening of Thursday, 29 March 1956. He was survived by Lillian, who lived on for several years, his daughter Doris, and his three grand-daughters and their families. His funeral, on Easter Monday, was at St Andrew's Presbyterian Church just a short distance from the British Columbia legislative buildings that for thirty years had been the centre of his life and work. The line of succession in British Columbia politics was highlighted as Premier W.A.C. Bennett, who had always rather admired Pattullo, cut short his vacation to be present. The assembled congregation of three or four hundred included family, friends, and political associates. They all joined in singing a hymn that did not so much mourn his death as celebrate his life. It was Duff Pattullo's favourite.

Dare to be a Daniel!
  Dare to stand alone!
Dare to have a purpose firm!
  Dare to make it known![58]

Duff Pattullo at about three years old

Duff Pattullo's father, George R. Pattullo

And mother, Mary Rounds Pattullo

The Pattullo family home, Burnside

Father and sons: George R. Pattullo with James and George Pattullo, probably taken about 1880

The wedding of Duff's eldest sister, Ethelwyn, to Adam Ballantyne in September 1897 was the last time that the Pattullo family was all together at Burnside.
Duff Pattullo is standing one row back between the bride and groom.

OPPOSITE

top Pattullo as a young man taken before he left Woodstock in 1897

bottom Duff Pattullo's uncle, Andrew Pattullo

The Walsh party leaving Vancouver for the Yukon on the *Quadra*, October 1897. Pattullo is standing third from the left along the rail.

Pattullo, second from left in back row, on the way to Dawson City with a group of government officials and their Indian packers

The Dawson City tennis club with Pattullo standing second from the right with his hand on the railing

The 1904 Yukon hockey team, with Pattullo third from the left in the back row

Duff, Doris, and Lillian, taken in Prince Rupert

Doris, sitting at the bottom of the balustrade,
was having a birthday party on the day this photo was taken
in front of her father's Prince Rupert office building.
The family lived on the second floor.

In this photo of the first Prince Rupert City Council, Pattullo is sitting next to the mayor, Alfred Stork, second and third from the left in the front row, and George Naden is on the left of the back row.

OPPOSITE

Pattullo brought the first motor car into Prince Rupert, but it was more a means of self-promotion than transportation.

Duff's brother, James B. Pattullo, in the uniform of the Seaforth Highlanders

Pattullo when he was minister of lands

The cartoonist Jack Boothe drew this caricature of Pattullo in 1931
when Duff was leader of the opposition
and many thought he was at his best in the house.

OPPOSITE

Pattullo speaking to the crowd at Brockton Point on the occasion of the City of Vancouver's Golden Jubilee in 1936

T.D. Pattullo, taken while he was premier

Pattullo was the first British Columbia premier to travel extensively by air.

Pattullo had this photograph of himself and Lillian waiting to greet the King and Queen on the steps of the legislature in 1939 made into a set of playing cards.

Prime Minister W.L. Mackenzie King giving his opening address to the dominion-provincial conference in the House of Commons, 14 January 1941. Pattullo is in the middle of the row of premiers facing the camera.

OPPOSITE

This Jack Boothe cartoon captures the largely mistaken view of the press at the time, and historians since, of Pattullo's role at the dominion-provincial conference on the Rowell-Sirois report.

The official photograph taken at the dominion-provincial conference in Ottawa, 14 January 1941.
Standing, left to right, W.J. Patterson (Saskatchewan), Pattullo, J. Bracken (Manitoba), T.A. Campbell (Prince Edward Island), W. Aberhart (Alberta), and seated, A.S. Macmillan (Nova Scotia), M.F. Hepburn (Ontario), W.L. Mackenzie King (prime minister), A. Godbout (Quebec), and J.B. McNair (New Brunswick)

An informal moment during a tense two days: Pattullo, King, and Godbout at the dominion-provincial conference on the Rowell-Sirois commission

'Looking Back' – a studio portrait taken after Pattullo retired from politics

Notes

Abbreviations

AO	Archives of Ontario
BCARS	British Columbia Archives and Records Service
GRPP	G.R. Pattullo Papers
NA	National Archives of Canada
PP	T.D. Pattullo Papers
TDP	T.D. Pattullo
UBCL	University of British Columbia Library
UTA	University of Toronto Archives
WLMK	William Lyon Mackenzie King
YGR	Yukon Government Records
YTA	Yukon Territorial Archives

Preface

1 Some of the exceptions are John Kendle, *John Bracken: A Political Biography* (Toronto: University of Toronto Press 1979); David Mitchell, *W.A.C. Bennett and the Rise of British Columbia* (Vancouver: Douglas & McIntyre 1983); Margaret Conrad, *George Nowlan: Maritime Conservative in National Politics* (Toronto: University of Toronto Press 1986); Norman Ward and David E. Smith, *Jimmy Gardner: Relentless Liberal* (Toronto: University of Toronto Press 1990). Interestingly, of these four, three had federal careers.

2 In his book *The Ottawa Men*, Granatstein twice refers to 'Premier Hart of British Columbia' in the 1930s. Hart later became premier, but from 1933 to 1941 he was Pattullo's minister of finance. Eastern historians, like Ottawa men at the time, would perhaps prefer it if Hart had been premier of British Columbia, but west-coast voters had other ideas. See J.L. Granatstein, *The Ottawa Men: The Civil Service Mandarins* (Toronto: Oxford University Press 1982), 56 and 57–8.

3 For these various comments see H. Blair Neatby, *William Lyon Mackenzie King: 1932–1939: The Prism of Unity* (Toronto: University of Toronto Press 1976), 48 and 117, and 'The Liberal Way: Fiscal and Monetary Policy in the 1930s,' in Michiel Horn, ed., *The Depression in Canada: Responses to Economic Crisis* (Toronto: Copp Clark Pitman 1988), 260.

4 Margaret A. Ormsby, 'Neglected Aspects of British Columbia's History,' *British Columbia Library Quarterly* 23 (April 1960): 10

5 Martin Robin, *The Rush for Spoils: The Company Province, 1871–1933* (Toronto: McClelland and Stewart 1972), and *Pillars of Profit: The Company Province, 1934–1972* (Toronto: McClelland and Stewart 1973)

6 Margaret Ormsby, 'T. Dufferin Pattullo and the Little New Deal,' *Canadian Historical Review* 43 (Dec. 1962): 277–97

7 Owram has pointed out that the Rowell-Sirois report began with an historical overview and that the historians who wrote it developed an interpretation that has 'assumed a central role in the historiography of English Canada.' See Doug Owram, *The Government Generation: Canadian Intellectuals and the State, 1900–1945* (Toronto: University of Toronto Press 1986), 245–7.

8 For a description of such individuals see A.O.J. Cockshut, *The Art of Autobiography in 19th and 20th Century England* (New Haven and London: Yale University Press 1984), 120. Conrad uses the same source to make the same point in her biography of another regional politician; see *Nolan*, xv–xvi.

9 Cf Bernard Malamud, *Dubin's Lives* (New York: Avon Books 1980), 20–1

Chapter 1: Woodstock

1 Upper Canada Land Petitions, P 12/123, vol. 4049, York 1820, National Archives of Canada (NA)

2 Census, Canada West, 1851, Township Caledon, County Peel, 111, NA

3 Abstract Index to Deeds, Blenheim Township, Oxford County, vol. A, 187, Archives of Ontario (AO)

4 Wadsworth, Unwin, and Brown, *Topographical and Historical Atlas of*

the County of Oxford, Ontario ... (Toronto: Walker and Miles 1876), 51

5 New Westminster *Mainland Guardian*, 11 Jan. 1879

6 *Woodstock Sentinel*, 3 Jan. 1873

7 Abstract Index of Deeds, Blenheim Township, Oxford County, vol. B, 237

8 Brian Dawe, *'Old Oxford Is Wide Awake!' Pioneer Settlers and Politicians in Oxford County, 1793–1853* (np: John Deyell Coy 1980), 3–10, 43–5

9 John Ireland, 'Andrew Drew and the Founding of Woodstock,' *Ontario History* 66 (Dec. 1968): 229–45

10 Dawe, *'Old Oxford,'* 47, 55, 75, 89–90

11 *Fisher & Taylor's Gazetteer and General Directory of the County of Oxford 1874–5* ... (Toronto: Fisher & Taylor [1874]), 94

12 *Daily Sentinel-Review*, 1 Oct. 1920

13 *Woodstock Sentinel*, 24 Jan. 1873

14 Ibid., 18 Oct. 1872

15 Assessment Roll, Woodstock, 1873, St Patrick's ward, 11, AO

16 Ibid., 1879 and 1880, St John's ward, 14, 13

17 T.D. Pattullo (TDP) to Wynnie, 8 Aug. 1953, Pattullo Papers, Add MSS 3 (PP), vol. 58, file 34, British Columbia Archives and Records Service (BCARS)

18 TDP to Wynnie, 14 Jan. 1949, PP, vol. 58, file 34

19 TDP to Margaret, 23 July 1951, Collison collection

20 M. Pattullo to her children, undated, Collison collection

21 TDP to Mrs A.W. Ballantyne, 8 April [1945], PP, vol. 22, file 1

22 TDP to Pearl, 14 Nov. 1950, Collison collection

23 TDP to Wynnie, 8 May 1948, Collison collection

24 *Oxford County Directory, 1881* ... ([Ingersoll]: Crotty & Dort 1881), 285

25 See Brian P.N. Beaven, 'Partisanship, Patronage and the Press in Ontario, 1880–1914: Myths and Realities,' *Canadian Historical Review* 64 (1983): 329; Andrew Pattullo to Clifford Sifton, 26 July 1897, Sifton Papers, MG 27 II, D 15, vol. 30, NA

26 *Daily Sentinel-Review*, 1 Oct. 1920

27 *Woodstock Sentinel*, 16 June 1871; and editorial, 30 Jan. 1874

28 Ibid., editorial, 15 Nov. 1872

29 TDP, radio speech, 13 June 1940, PP, vol. 65, file 5

30 Toronto *Globe*, 7 July 1876

31 See David Lee, 'The Dominion General Election of 1878 in Ontario,' *Ontario History* 51 (1959): 174–90.

32 TDP to Taschereau, 18 July 1952, PP, vol. 59, file 7; C.R.W. Biggar, *Sir*

Oliver Mowat Q.C., L.L.D., G.C.M.G., P.C.: A Biographical Sketch (Toronto: Warwick Bros. and Rutter 1905), vol. 2, 656. The year before this biography was published, Biggar wrote to George Pattullo asking for his critical judgment on it. Biggar to G.R. Pattullo, 17 March 1904, G.R. Pattullo Papers (GRPP), file 6, BCARS

33 The actual figures were $2880.12 for 1894, $2495.28 for 1895, and $2452.33 for 1896. See Ontario, Inspector of Registry Offices, Payments to Municipalities and Net Income of Registrars of Deeds for the Year 1896, 1895, 1894, *Annual Report of the Inspector of Registry Offices for the Year 1895* (Toronto: Warwick Brothers and Rutter 1896); Mowat to G.R. Pattullo, 13 May 1886, GRPP, file 6.

34 Christopher Armstrong, 'The Mowat Heritage in Federal-Provincial Relations,' in Donald Swainson, ed., *Oliver Mowat's Ontario: Papers Presented to the Oliver Mowat Colloquium Queen's University. November 25–26, 1970* (Toronto: Macmillan of Canada 1972), 93

35 Biggar, *Mowat*, vol. 1, 408–11

36 *Woodstock Sentinel*, editorial, 13 Sept. 1872; TDP to Pearl, 14 Sept. 1952, PP, vol. 59, file 7

37 G.R. Pattullo to Greenway, 14 Feb. 1888, Thomas Greenway Papers, MG 13E, item 1432, Provincial Archives of Manitoba

38 H.V. Nelles, *The Politics of Development: Forests, Mines & Hydro-Electric Power in Ontario, 1849–1941* (Toronto: Macmillan of Canada 1974), 27, 102–3

39 For a general summary of Mowat's policies see A. Margaret Evans, 'The Mowat Era, 1872–1896: Stability and Progress,' in Edith G. Firth, ed., *Profiles of a Province: Studies in the History of Ontario* (Toronto: Ontario Historical Society 1967), 97–106, and 'Oliver Mowat: Nineteenth Century Liberal,' in Swainson, ed., *Mowat's Ontario*, 34–51.

40 Armstrong, in Swainson, ed., *Mowat's Ontario*, 118

41 *Toronto Daily Star*, 30 Dec. 1903

42 Margaret Prang, *N.W. Rowell: Ontario Nationalist* (Toronto and Buffalo: University of Toronto Press 1975), 102

43 Memorandum by G.R. Pattullo, March 1886, Niagara Falls Park Papers, MU 2194, AO. For a discussion of these developments see Gerald Killan, 'Mowat and a Park Policy for Niagara Falls 1873–1887,' *Ontario History* 70 (1978): 115–35.

44 Minutes County of Oxford Historical Society, 15 and 27 Jan. 1897, Oxford Museum, Woodstock

45 For this point and much of the information in this paragraph see Gerald

Killan, *Preserving Ontario's Heritage: A History of the Ontario Historical Society* (Ottawa: Love Printing 1976), 61, 49–136.

46 Memorandum by G.R. Pattullo, 12 May 1905, quoted in ibid., 129

47 Pattullo to Coyne, 3 Sept. 1918, James Henry Coyne Papers, University of Western Ontario Library

48 George R. Pattullo, 'Leaves from an Unpublished Volume (The President's Address, June 16th, 1919),' Ontario Historical Society, *Papers and Records* 17 (1919): 5–10

49 *Daily Sentinel-Review*, 1 Oct. 1920

50 TDP to Sir Henry Thornton, 29 Dec. 1931, PP, vol. 31, file 25

51 G.R. Pattullo to TDP, 15 April 1886, Collison collection

52 TDP to Mr Wright, 3 May 1952, PP, vol. 59, file 8

53 Art Williams, *Bits & Pieces: A Montage of Woodstock, Ontario in Text and Pictures* (Woodstock: Art Williams and Edward Baker 1967), 17–18; *Directory of the Town of Woodstock Containing Alphabetical List of Names with Occupations, Places of Business and Residence* (Woodstock: Pattullo and Co 1888), 23

54 G.R. Pattullo to TDP, 15 April 1886, Collison collection

55 Lester Parmenter to TDP, 4 Nov. 1933, PP, vol. 52, file 16

56 TDP, press statement, 27 Dec. 1930, PP, vol. 39, file 6

57 Letter of I.M. Leven, principal, the collegiate institute, Woodstock, 8 Jan. 1902, PP, vol. 1, file 14

58 TDP, undated newspaper article, PP, vol. 60, file 17

59 TDP to Mr Ball, 30 Dec. 1952, PP, vol. 59, file 8

60 TDP to Wynnie, 28 March 1948, Collison collection; TDP to G.R. Pattullo, undated [1894], GRPP, file 1

61 TDP to G.R. Pattullo, undated [1896], GRPP, file 1

62 Ibid.

63 John Burnaby to Sibil, 15 May 1892, and John Burnaby to Lilian, 18 June 1892, PP, vol. 1, file 1

64 John Burnaby to Sibil, 7 July 22 Aug. and 15 Sept. 1892, PP, vol. 1, file 1

65 Ibid.

66 John Burnaby to Sibil, 26 Sept. 1892, PP, vol. 1, file 1

67 Ibid., Oct. 1892, PP, vol. 1, file 1

68 Ibid., 10 Dec. 1892, PP, vol. 1, file 1

69 Ibid., 30 Oct. 1892, PP, vol. 1, file 1

70 TDP to 'L.G.,' 17 Sept. 1950, PP, vol. 59, file 2

71 Assistant secretary, Department of the Interior, to TDP, 16 Sept. 1897, GRPP, file 1

72 *Daily Sentinel-Review*, 15 Sept. 1897

Chapter 2: Dawson City, Yukon

1 Robert Service, 'The Men That Don't Fit In,' *The Best of Robert Service* (Toronto: McGraw-Hill Ryerson 1953), 23
2 *The Woodstock Sentinel*, 9 Feb.–29 March 1872; New Westminster *Mainland Guardian*, 11 Jan. 1879
3 TDP to G.R. Pattullo, May 1898, GRPP, file 2, BCARS
4 TDP to G.R. Pattullo, undated, PP, vol. 1, file 8, BCARS
5 TDP to G.R. Pattullo, 27 Sept. 1897, GRPP, file 1
6 TDP in *Weekly Sentinel-Review*, 22 Oct. 1897
7 Ibid.
8 TDP to G.R. Pattullo, 27 Sept. 1897, GRPP, file 1
9 TDP in *Weekly Sentinel-Review*, 22 Oct. 1897
10 TDP, undated notes on the Yukon, PP, vol. 60, file 1; TDP to G.R. Pattullo, 5 Oct. 1897, GRPP, file 1
11 TDP in *Weekly Sentinel-Review*, 5 Nov. 1897
12 TDP, undated notes on the Yukon, PP, vol. 60, file 1
13 TDP in *Weekly Sentinel-Review*, 5 Nov. 1897
14 Ibid. The woman's name was actually spelt Scovel.
15 See Pierre Berton, *Klondike: The Last Great Gold Rush, 1896–1899* (Toronto: McClelland and Stewart 1974), 143.
16 TDP in *Weekly Sentinel-Review*, 5 Nov. 1897
17 Ibid.; TDP to G.R. Pattullo, 5 Oct. 1897, GRPP, file 1
18 TDP to G.R. Pattullo, 5 Nov. 1897, GRPP, file 1
19 TDP to G.R. Pattullo, 9 Oct. 1897, GRPP, file 1
20 Ibid.
21 Ibid.
22 Ibid.
23 TDP to G.R. Pattullo, 31 Oct. 1897, GRPP, file 1
24 TDP to the editor of *Mayfair*. (Montreal), 16 April 1951, Collison collection
25 TDP to G.R. Pattullo, 18 Nov. 1897, GRPP, file 1, published in *Weekly Sentinel-Review*, 22 March 1898
26 TDP to G.R. Pattullo, 28 Nov. 1897, GRPP, file 1
27 TDP to G.R. Pattullo, 5 Dec. 1897, GRPP, file 2
28 TDP to G.R. Pattullo, 20 March 1898, GRPP, file 1
29 TDP in *Weekly Sentinel-Review*, 29 March and 3 May 1898
30 Ibid., 3 May 1898

31 TDP to G.R. Pattullo, 17 Feb. 1898, GRPP, file 2
32 Ibid.
33 TDP to G.R. Pattullo, 18 April 1898, GRPP, file 2
34 Letter of TDP, May 1898, PP, vol. 1, file 7
35 Ibid.
36 Ibid.
37 TDP to Mr Peterson, 26 Aug. 1948, Collison collection
38 TDP in *Weekly Sentinel-Review*, 26 July 1898
39 Ibid.
40 Ibid.
41 Morris Zaslow, *The Opening of the Canadian North, 1870–1914* (Toronto and Montreal: McClelland and Stewart 1971), 109
42 Walsh to Sifton, 14 June 1898, Sifton Papers, vol. 295, NA
43 David R. Morrison, *The Politics of the Yukon Territory, 1898–1909* (Toronto: University of Toronto Press 1968), 14
44 William Rodney, *Joe Boyle: King of the Klondike* (Toronto:McGraw-Hill Ryerson 1974), 31–40
45 *Daily Sentinel-Review*, 6 Sept. 1898
46 Berton, *Klondike*, 295
47 TDP to Tom, 3 Oct. 1948, Collison collection
48 Barristers and Solicitors Roll 1898–1950, Yukon Government Records (YGR), series 8, vol. 39, Yukon Territorial Archives, Whitehorse (YTA)
49 TDP to Mrs Fordham Johnson, 19 March 1952, PP, vol. 59, file 6
50 Tappan Adney, *The Klondike Stampede* (New York and London: Harper & Brothers 1900), 437–8
51 TDP to Sifton, 18 Nov. 1898, Sifton Papers, vol. 50
52 G.R. Pattullo to Sifton, 13 Sept. 1898, ibid.; *Weekly Sentinel-Review*, 18 Nov. 1898
53 Ogilvie to Sifton, 12 Nov. 1898, Sifton Papers, vol. 295
54 Ogilvie to Sifton, 4 Feb. 1899, ibid.; and D.J. Hall, *Clifford Sifton*, vol. 2: *A Lonely Eminence, 1901–1929* (Vancouver: University of British Columbia Press 1985), 3
55 Sifton to Ogilvie, 15 Feb. and 24 March 1899, Sifton Papers, vols. 230 and 231
56 TDP to Senkler, 21 April and 1 May 1899, YGR, series 1, vol. 9
57 TDP to Sifton, 13 Sept. 1899, Sifton Papers, vol. 69
58 TDP to Sifton, 23 May 1899, ibid.
59 TDP to Sifton, 13 Sept. 1899, ibid.
60 Ibid.
61 Ibid.

62 Sifton to G.R. Pattullo, 4 July 1899, ibid., vol. 233
63 *Klondike Nugget*, 16 Aug. 1899; Report of Ogilvie, 20 Sept. 1899, Canada, *Sessional Papers*, 8th Parl., 5th sess., 1900, no. 33u, 9
64 J.B. Pattullo to G.R. Pattullo, 25 June 1899, GRPP, file 7
65 Ogilvie to Sifton, 13 Feb. 1899, Sifton Papers, vol. 295
66 TDP to Sifton, 23 May 1899, ibid., vol. 69
67 Ibid.
68 G.R. Pattullo to Sifton, 3 July 1899, ibid.
69 Sifton to TDP, 2 Oct. 1899, ibid., vol. 234
70 Ogilvie to Sifton, 3 June 1899, ibid., vol. 295
71 Certificate no. 3190, 12 April 1898, Index of Free Miners' Certificates, YTA
72 TDP to G.R. Pattullo, 11 Feb. 1901, GRPP, file 2
73 *Klondike Nugget*, 6 Dec. 1899
74 J.B. Pattullo to G.R. Pattullo, 12 Feb. 1900, GRPP, file 7
75 [Martha L. Black], *My Seventy Years* ... (London: Thomas Nelson and Sons 1938), 175
76 TDP to Sifton, 9 Nov. 1899, Sifton Papers, vol. 69; J.B. Pattullo to G.R. Pattullo, 12 Feb.1900, and TDP to G.R. Pattullo, 11 Feb. 1901, GRPP, files 7 and 2
77 Ogilvie to TDP, 6 Dec. 1899, YGR, series 1, vol. 77
78 TDP to Sifton, 3 Oct. 1900, Sifton Papers, vol. 87
79 TDP to Sifton, 3 Oct. 1900, and Sifton to TDP, 19 Dec. 1900, ibid.
80 *Daily Klondike Nugget*, 19 Nov. 1900; *Daily Sentinel-Review*, 14 July 1900
81 *Daily Klondike Nugget*, 12, 14 April, 10, 25 May 1900, and 3 Oct. 1901
82 *Dawson Daily News*, 9 March 1902; *Semi-Weekly Nugget*, 30 Nov. 1901
83 *Daily Klondike Nugget*, 15 Nov. 1901
84 For the details on the administration building see Margaret E. Archibald, 'A Structural History of the Administration Building, Dawson, Yukon Territory,' Department of Indian and Northern Affairs, National Historic Parks and Sites Branch, Manuscript Report Number 217, 1977, 42–5, 137.
85 Dawson City, Directory of Existing Structures, catalog no. 5-10-4, Parks Canada Archives, Dawson City
86 TDP to Senkler, 1 May 1899, YGR, series 1, vol. 9
87 Lewis Green, *The Gold Hustlers* (Anchorage: Alaska Northwest Publishing Company 1977), 33
88 TDP to J.H. Ross, 14 Feb. 1902, Sifton Papers, vol. 130
89 Ibid.; *Daily Klondike Nugget*, 18 Feb. 1902; see also TDP to J.H. Ross, 8 Jan. 1902, PP, vol. 1, file 13.

90 J.B. Pattullo to Wynnie, 13 Aug. 1920, GRPP, file 7
91 *Daily Klondike Nugget*, 23, 27 Jan. 1902; TDP to G.R. Pattullo, 2 Feb. 1901, GRPP, file 2; Sifton to G.R. Pattullo, 9 Oct. 1901, and Sifton to A. Pattullo, 21 Nov. 1901, Sifton Papers, vol. 245
92 Smart to Sifton, 15 Sept. 1902, Sifton Papers, vol. 133; Hall, *Sifton*, vol. 2, 3–4; Morrison, *Politics*, 48
93 Senkler to Smart, 8 Sept. 1902, Smart to Acting Commissioner Z.T. Wood, 27 Oct. 1902, and TDP to Sifton, 1 Nov. 1902, Sifton Papers, vol. 130
94 Certificate signed by C.D. Macaulay, 6 Oct. 1902, PP, vol. 1, file 14
95 Letter of TDP, May 1898, PP, vol. 1, file 7
96 *Daily Klondike Nugget*, 15 and 3 Nov. 1902
97 TDP to G.R. Pattullo, 18 Dec. 1902, GRPP, file 3
98 Sifton to A. Pattullo, 17 Dec. 1902, Sifton Papers, vol. 249
99 A. Pattullo to Sifton, 13 Feb. 1903, and Sifton to Rothwell, 7 March 1903, ibid., vols. 249 and 251
100 TDP to G.R. Pattullo, 28 March 1903, GRPP, file 2
101 Index of partnerships, YGR, series 8, vol. 36
102 Margaret Archibald, 'A Substantial Expression of Confidence: The Structure and Use of the Northern Commercial Company Store in Dawson, Y.T., 1897–1951,' unpublished manuscript, Parks Canada, 1980, 1–10
103 Zaslow, *Opening*, 145
104 J.B. Pattullo to G.R. Pattullo, 10 Nov. 1904, GRPP, file 7
105 TDP to G.R. Pattullo, 11 Feb. 1901, GRPP, file 2
106 J.P. Smith to TDP, 30 May 1951, and TDP to J.P. Smith, 17 July 1951, Collison collection
107 *Semi-Weekly Klondike Nugget*, 9 May 1901
108 *Daily Klondike Nugget*, 7 June 1901
109 *Dawson Daily News*, 17 Jan. 1905
110 *Daily Klondike Nugget*, 25 March 1903
111 Ibid., 17 Dec. 1902
112 Ibid., 5 Feb. 1903; *Yukon Sun*, 10 Dec. 1903
113 *Yukon Sun*, 31 Dec. 1903, 10 Jan. 1904; see also Hal Guest, 'The Political Apprenticeship of Thomas Dufferin Pattullo,' *BC Studies* 58 (summer 1983): 59, which deals with this period of Pattullo's career but is factually unreliable.
114 Guest, 'Political Apprenticeship,' 60
115 Congdon to W.S. Fielding, 21 Sept. 1904, W.S. Fielding Papers, MG 2, vol. 509, folder 29; Public Archives of Nova Scotia; Congdon to Smart, 2 June 1904, Sifton Papers, vol. 156

116 TDP to Sifton, 29 March 1904, Sifton Papers, vol. 169
117 Congdon to Fielding, 21 Sept. 1904, W.S. Fielding Papers, vol. 509, folder 29: TDP to Sifton, 12 May 1904, Sifton Papers, vol. 169
118 Cf Guest, 'Political Apprenticeship,' 58
119 TDP to Sifton, 29 March 1904, Sifton Papers, vol. 169
120 Guest, 'Political Apprenticeship,' 60 and 62
121 Resolution of the Yukon Liberal Association, 8 April 1904, Sifton Papers, vol. 169; Morrison, *Politics*, 59–60
122 TDP to Laurier, 1 June 1904, PP, vol. 2, file 2; J.C. Noel to Laurier, 9 April 1904, Sir Wilfrid Laurier Papers, MG 26 G, vol. 312, NA
123 Morrison, *Politics*, 60
124 TDP to Sifton, 10 July 1904, Sifton Papers, vol. 169; Laurier to TDP, 25 July 1904, PP, vol. 2, file 2
125 TDP to Sifton, 12 May and 3 July 1904, Sifton Papers, vol. 169
126 *Dawson Daily News*, 10 Sept. 1904
127 For an account of these events see Guest, 'Political Apprenticeship,' 64–5.
128 TDP to Sifton, 29 March 1904, Sifton Papers, vol. 169
129 J.B. Pattullo to G.R. Pattullo, 10 Nov. 1904, GRPP, file 7
130 TDP to Laurier, 8 June 1904, PP, vol. 2, file 2
131 TDP to Sifton, 21 Dec. 1904, Sifton Papers, vol. 169; Morrison, *Politics*, 67
132 TDP to Sifton, 9 July 1904, Sifton Papers, vol. 169
133 TDP to Sifton, 21 Dec. and 29 March 1904, ibid.
134 Morrison, *Politics*, 80
135 Laurier to TDP, 15 Feb. 1906, PP, vol. 2, file 9
136 T.A. Rickard, *Through the Yukon and Alaska* (San Francisco: Mining and Scientific Press 1909), 183–7
137 Robert Service, 'The Spell of the Yukon,' *Best of Robert Service*, 1
138 TDP, 'Over the Chilkoot,' PP, vol. 60, file 1
139 TDP, speech, 24 Nov. 1937, PP, vol. 55, file 22
140 TDP to Mary Lee Davis, 5 Jan. 1938, PP, vol. 32, file 3; Mary Lee Davis, *Sourdough Gold: The Log of a Yukon Adventure* (Boston: W.A. Wilde Company 1933); Davis to TDP, 15 Jan. 1938, PP, vol. 32, file 3
141 TDP to G.R. Pattullo, 5 Dec. 1897, GRPP, file 2; *Weekly Sentinel-Review*, 29 March 1898; Davis, *Sourdough Gold*, 61, 197, and 342
142 TDP to Mrs Fordham Johnson, 19 March 1952, PP, vol. 59, file 6
143 With apologies to Leonard Cohen, 'The Stranger Song,' Project Seven Music, 1966

Chapter 3: Prince Rupert

1 TDP to Laurier, 18 Sept. 1908, Laurier Papers, vol. 534, NA

2 Memorandum of Association of the Prince Rupert Construction Company, 26 Oct. 1908, PP, vol. 2, file 14, BCARS
3 J.B. Pattullo to TDP, 10 Oct. 1908, PP, vol. 2, file 14
4 For a more detailed look at George Pattullo's career during this period see Robin Fisher, 'Duff and George Go West: A Tale of Two Frontiers,' *Canadian Historical Review* 68 (Dec. 1987): 507–15.
5 TDP to Radford, 8 Feb. 1909, PP, vol. 2, file 14
6 J.B. Pattullo to TDP, 10 Oct. 1908, ibid.
7 TDP to Wynnie, 4 March 1951, PP, vol. 59, file 5
8 TDP to Radford, 2 Nov. 1908 and 8 Feb. 1909, PP, vol. 2, file 14
9 TDP to Radford, 19 Feb. 1909, ibid.
10 TDP to general manager, Grand Trunk Pacific Railway, and TDP to W.H. Biggar, 8 Feb. 1909, PP, vol. 3, file 2; E.J. Chamberlain, vice-president and general manager, Grand Trunk Pacific Railway, to D'Arcy Tate, assistant solicitor, 16 Feb. 1909, and Tate to Chamberlain, 19 March 1909, Canadian National Railway Papers, RG 30, vol. 3271, file A474, NA
11 Victoria *Times*, 3 Dec. 1949; TDP to Radford, 28 April 1909, PP, vol. 3, file 7; TDP to Mr Kelly, 12 April 1952, PP, vol. 59, file 6
12 TDP to Radford, 16 Feb. 1909, PP, vol. 3, file 7, and 19 Feb. 1909, PP, vol. 2, file 14; Radford to TDP, 29 May 1909, PP, vol. 3, file 7
13 J.B. Pattullo to TDP, 6 April 1909, TDP to J.B. Pattullo, 26 March 1909, and TDP to Radford, 28 April 1909, PP, vol. 3, file 6; TDP to Radford, 20 March 1909, PP, vol. 2, file 14
14 F.W. Morse to D'Arcy Tate, 19 Feb. 1909, Grand Trunk Pacific Legal Files, Canadian National Railway Papers, vol. 3265
15 Minutes of Directors' Meeting, Grand Trunk Pacific Development Company, 26 March and 14 May 1909, Canadian National Railway Papers, vol. 1073
16 TDP to Horne, 15 Sept. 1909, PP, vol. 3, file 17
17 TDP to J.B. Pattullo, 21 June 1909, PP, vol. 3, file 6
18 A.W. Ballantyne to TDP, 13 Sept. 1909, PP, vol. 3, file 1; TDP to Stauf, 23 June 1909, PP, vol. 3, file 10
19 TDP to J.B. Pattullo, 21 June and 6 Nov. 1909, PP, vol. 3, file 6
20 *The Empire*, 12 June 1909
21 TDP to Horne, 15 Sept. 1909, PP, vol. 3, file 17; TDP to J.B. Pattullo, 14 Sept. 1909, PP, vol. 3, file 6
22 TDP to Horne, 15 Sept. 1909, PP, vol. 3, file 17
23 TDP to Radford, 28 April 1909, PP, vol. 3, file 7
24 TDP to J.B. Pattullo, 21 June 1909, PP, vol. 3, file 6
25 *The Empire*, 12 June 1909
26 TDP to J.B. Pattullo, 14 Sept. 1909, PP, vol. 3, file 6

27 TDP to J.B. Pattullo, 10 June 1910, PP, vol. 4, file 4

28 TDP to Radford, 18 Sept. 1910, PP, vol. 4, file 5; and 3 Jan. 1911, PP, vol. 5, file 4

29 Radford to TDP, 1 Feb. 1911 and 12 March 1910, PP, vol. 5, file 4, and vol. 4, file 5

30 Minutes of Directors' Meeting, Grand Trunk Pacific Development Company, 26 May 1909, Canadian National Railway Papers, vol. 1073

31 G.S. Turner to TDP, 24 March 1910, PP, vol. 4, file 24

32 TDP to J.B. Pattullo, 18 June 1910, PP, vol. 4, file 4; TDP to Radford, 30 June 1910, PP, vol. 4, file 5

33 The actual figures were 3030 males and 1154 females; Canada, *Fifth Census of Canada 1911* (Ottawa: King's Printer 1912), vol. 1, 38.

34 *Daily News*, 20 Nov. 1911

35 *Prince Rupert Optimist*, 13, 20, and 22 Aug. 1910

36 For a discussion of McBride's attitude to railway companies see Patricia E. Roy, 'Progress, Prosperity and Politics: The Railway Policies of Richard McBride,' *BC Studies* 47 (autumn 1980): 3–28.

37 McBride to Tate, 14 June 1909, Grand Trunk Pacific Legal Files, Canadian National Railway Papers, vol. 3285

38 TDP et al. to McBride with enclosure to the attorney-general, 2 March 1910, British Columbia, Premier, Papers, GR 441, vol. 38, file 3, BCARS

39 'An Act to Incorporate the City of Prince Rupert,' British Columbia, *Statutes of the Province of British Columbia* (Victoria: R. Wolfenden 1910), 10 Ed. 7, c.41

40 J.B. Pattullo to TDP, 26 April and 1 June 1910, PP, vol. 4, file 4

41 Patricia E. Roy, *A White Man's Province: British Columbia Politicians and Chinese and Japanese Immigrants, 1858–1914* (Vancouver: University of British Columbia Press 1989), 256

42 J.B. Pattullo to TDP, 1 June 1910, PP, vol. 4, file 4; *Prince Rupert Optimist*, 21 May 1910

43 TDP to J.B. Pattullo, 18 June 1910, PP, vol. 4, file 4

44 *Prince Rupert Optimist*, 13 July 1910

45 D'Arcy Tate to McBride, 12 May 1910, British Columbia, Premier, Papers, vol. 39, file 1

46 Tate to McBride, 1 Aug. 1910, ibid.

47 *Prince Rupert Optimist*, 4 Nov. 1910

48 Prince Rupert Council Minutes, 29 Sept. 1910, Minutes of the Council Meeting of the Corporation of Prince Rupert, BC (hereafter Minutes), vol. 2, 82, Prince Rupert City Hall

49 *Prince Rupert Optimist*, 8 Oct. 1910

50 Ibid., 30 Sept. 1910; Prince Rupert Council Minutes, 6 and 10 Oct. 1910; Minutes, vol. 2, 92, 95–6

51 *Prince Rupert Optimist*, 6 Sept., 7 Oct., and 4 and 5 Nov. 1910

52 Ibid., 7 Oct. 1910

53 Ibid., 23 Nov. and 16 Dec. 1910. A similar agreement was ratified by the Prince Rupert Council and the Grand Trunk Pacific the following year; see Minutes of Meeting of Directors of the Grand Trunk Pacific Development Company, 8 Aug. 1911, Canadian National Railway Papers, vol. 1073.

54 See Christopher Armstrong and H.V. Nelles, *Monopoly's Moment: The Organization and Regulation of Canadian Utilities, 1830–1930* (Toronto: University of Toronto Press 1986), 141–86.

55 Prince Rupert Council Minutes, 16 Aug. 1910, Minutes, vol. 2, 7; Pattullo to editor *Daily News* [4 Dec. 1948?], PP, vol. 58, file 29

56 M.M. Stephens to W. Manson, 15 Jan. 1910, British Columbia, Premier's Papers, vol. 38, file 3

57 *Prince Rupert Optimist*, 8 Aug. 1910; 'A By-Law to Regulate the Measuring and Weighing of Fuel, and to Prevent the Adulteration of Food Stuffs,' By-Law no. 17, 13 Aug. 1910, Prince Rupert By-Laws, Prince Rupert City Hall

58 *Prince Rupert Optimist*, 11 May 1910; undated newspaper article, PP, vol. 60, file 17; TDP to John, 26 Feb. 1948, Collison collection

59 *Prince Rupert Optimist*, 27 and 29 July 1910

60 Ibid., 29 Dec. 1910

61 TDP to Radford, 4 Feb. 1911, PP, vol. 5, file 4

62 *Prince Rupert Optimist*, 8 Dec. 1910

63 Ibid., 7 May 1910; TDP to Radford, 4 Feb. 1911, PP, vol. 5, file 4

64 *Prince Rupert Optimist*, 13 March 1911

65 TDP to Radford, 11 March 1911, PP, vol. 5, file 4

66 Prince Rupert City Council Minutes, 13 March 1911, Minutes, vol. 2, 266; *Prince Rupert Optimist*, 14 March 1911

67 TDP to Radford, 4 Feb. 1911, PP, vol. 5, file 4

68 *Prince Rupert Optimist*, 3 April 1911; TDP to Radford, 11 March 1911, PP, vol. 5, file 4

69 TDP to Radford, 8 April 1911, PP, vol. 5, file 4

70 TDP to Radford, 8 May 1911, ibid.

71 R.V. Winch to TDP, 26 June 1912, PP, vol. 6, file 4; TDP to Winch, 30 June 1912, PP, vol. 6, file 3

72 TDP to Radford, 4 June 1911, PP, vol. 5, file 4

73 TDP to Radford, 5 Oct. 1912, PP, vol. 6, file 3

74 *Daily News*, 30 Nov. 1912
75 Ibid., 17 Jan. 1913
76 Ibid., 21 Jan. 1913
77 Ibid., 7 Feb. 1913
78 Ibid., 27 Feb. 1913
79 TDP to Chamberlain, 19 and 23 April 1913, PP, vol. 7, file 5
80 Prince Rupert Council Minutes, 7 May 1913, Minutes, vol. 3, 362–3
81 *Canadian Annual Review of Public Affairs, 1913* (Toronto: Annual Review Publishing Company 1914), 34–5
82 *Evening Empire*, 4 June, 31 May, and 18 July 1913
83 Ibid., 2 June 1913
84 TDP to Radford, 30 Nov. 1913, PP, vol. 2, file 14
85 The assessment rolls for 1914 were reprinted in the *Evening Empire*, 4 May to 10 June 1914.
86 Minutes of Directors' Meeting, Grand Trunk Pacific Development Company, 12 Oct. 1915, Canadian National Railway Papers, vol. 1074
87 Radford to TDP, 17 Sept. 1913, PP, vol. 2, file 14
88 TDP to Radford, 5 Oct. 1913, ibid.
89 TDP to Stauf, 3 Feb. 1914, PP, vol. 8, file 6; TDP to J.B. Pattullo, 20 Oct. 1914, and TDP to J.B. Pattullo, 8 July 1914, PP, vol. 8, file 3
90 TDP to J.B. Pattullo, 28 Nov. 1909, PP, vol. 3, file 6
91 *Daily News*, 22 Jan., 20 Feb., and 4 April 1914
92 Ibid., 8 Sept. 1914; TDP to J.B. Pattullo, 24 Feb. 1915, PP, vol. 8, file 20
93 TDP to J.B. Pattullo, 24 Feb. 1915, PP, vol. 8, file 20
94 J.B. Pattullo to TDP, 21 Feb. 1915, PP, vol. 8, file 20
95 TDP to J.B. Pattullo, 24 Feb. 1915, ibid.
96 Ibid.
97 *Daily News*, 12 March 1915
98 TDP to J.B. Pattullo, 24 Feb. 1915, PP, vol. 8, file 20
99 *Daily News*, 6 April 1915
100 TDP to Brewster, 20 April 1915, PP, vol. 8, file 18
101 J.B. Pattullo to TDP, 30 April 1915, PP, vol. 8, file 20
102 TDP to Horne, 3 June and 16 July 1915, PP, vol. 8, files 19 and 2.
103 Radford to TDP, 24 June 1915, PP, vol. 8, file 21
104 TDP to Radford, 7 July 1915, ibid.
105 TDP to Horne, 22 April 1915, ibid.
106 TDP to Gordon Joliffe, 20 June 1950, PP, vol. 59, file 1
107 TDP to Brewster, 8 Oct. 1915, PP, vol. 8, file 20
108 *Daily Sentinel-Review*, 9 March 1916
109 TDP to Horne, 20 Oct. 1915, PP, vol. 8, file 19
110 TDP to J.B. Pattullo, 15 Jan. 1916, PP, vol. 9, file 5

111 TDP to J.B. Pattullo, 10 March 1916, and J.B. Pattullo to TDP, 4 April 1916, ibid.
112 TDP to J.B. Pattullo, 16 March 1916, ibid.
113 Ibid.
114 *Daily News*, 16 June 1916
115 Ibid., 15 July 1916
116 Ibid., 26 Aug. 1916
117 Ibid., 21 Aug. 1916
118 Ibid., 28 Aug. 1916
119 Ibid., 25 Aug. 1916
120 Ibid., 14 Sept. 1916
121 Ibid., 15 Sept. 1916; *Electoral History of British Columbia* (Victoria: Elections British Columbia 1988), 126
122 *Electoral History of British Columbia*, 123
123 *Daily News*, 23 Sept. 1916
124 Unsigned letter to Brewster, 6 Oct. 1916, PP, vol. 8, file 18
125 *Daily News*, 18 Sept. 1916, quoting the Vancouver *Province*
126 TDP income tax return 1918, PP, vol. 10, file 21; J.B. Pattullo to TDP, 4 April 1916, PP, vol. 9, file 5
127 TDP to Brewster, 15 Nov. 1916, PP, vol. 9, file 1
128 McCaffery to TDP, 10 Oct. 1916, PP, vol. 4, file 6
129 *Electoral History of British Columbia*, 7
130 *Daily News*, 29 Dec. 1916
131 TDP to J.B. Pattullo, 10 March 1916, PP, vol. 9, file 4

Chapter 4: Minister of Lands

1 Interview with Doris Collison, 6 Jan. 1980
2 G.R. Pattullo to William Lyon Mackenzie King (WLMK), 20 Sept. 1919, King Papers, MG 26, J 1, NA
3 'Estimate of Revenue and Receipts of the Province of British Columbia for the Fiscal Year Ending 31st March 1918,' British Columbia, *Sessional Papers*, 14th Parl., 1st Sess., 1917, E10; TDP bank books, PP, vol. 10, file 5, BCARS
4 Interview with Ethelwyn Zimmerman and Tom Lownsbrough, 23 Nov. 1980
5 Russell R. Walker, *Politicians of a Pioneering Province* (Vancouver: Mitchell Press 1969), 48–50
6 Patricia E. Roy, 'John Hart,' in *The Canadian Encyclopedia* (Edmonton: Hurtig Publishers 1985), vol. 2:796
7 *Canadian Annual Review, 1917*, 830–1

8 *Daily Province*, 20 March 1917, 4

9 *Synopsis of Legislation Enacted by the Legislature of British Columbia: The Sessions of 1917, 1918 and 1919*, PP, vol. 10, file 11

10 See, for example, TDP, speech, 3 May 1929, PP, vol. 12, file 8.

11 TDP, undated speech to the Vancouver Real Estate Exchange, PP, vol. 12, file 8

12 *Victoria Daily Times*, 25 June 1918

13 Interview with J.W. deB. Farris, 15 Sept. 1958, quoted in John Neil Sutherland, 'T.D. Pattullo as a Party Leader,' (MA thesis, University of British Columbia, 1960), 6; Royal L. Maitland, 'House Log,' 31 Jan. 1929, Maitland Family Papers, box 8, file 1, Add. Ms 781, BCARS

14 Article by Torchy Anderson, *Vancouver Daily Province*, 16 Sept. 1941

15 TDP, speech to Canadian Club, 12 Jan. 1924, PP, vol. 12, file 10; *Victoria Daily Times*, 24 June 1922

16 See, for example, *Victoria Daily Times*, 22 Feb. 1922 and 23 Nov. 1927.

17 *Daily News*, 6 Jan. 1917; J.W. Jones, undated speech, J.W. Jones Papers, Add. Ms 23, vol. 6, file 1, BCARS

18 This point, along with a summary of his department's work, is in TDP to Oliver, 2 March 1921, British Columbia, Premier Papers, GR 441, vol. 345, file 6, BCARS

19 'An Act to Provide for the Proportionate Allotment of Lands Held from the Crown under Agreements to Purchase,' British Columbia, *Statutes* 1918, 8 Geo. 5, c. 69; *Synopsis of Legislation*, PP, vol. 10, file 11

20 TDP, speech during debate on 1923 throne speech, PP, vol. 12, file 10

21 I have argued this case in more detail in Fisher, 'Duff and George Go West,' 501–28.

22 TDP, speech to Building and Construction Industries Exchange, Vancouver, undated (1926–8), PP, vol. 23, file 14; TDP speech, undated (1920), PP, vol. 12, file 10

23 Pattullo to minister of agriculture, 13 Dec. 1916, British Columbia, Premier, Papers, vol. 336, file 8

24 'An Act to Promote Increased Agricultural Production,' British Columbia, *Statutes* 1917, 7 and 8 Geo. 5, c. 34

25 TDP to Barrow, 18 Aug. 1917, British Columbia, Premier, Papers, vol. 190, file 1126

26 TDP to Brewster, 14 Nov. 1917, British Columbia, Premier, Papers, vol. 335, file 6

27 TDP to Maxwell Smith, 19 Feb. 1918, British Columbia, Land Settlement Board, Papers, GR 929, vol. 12 file 11, BCARS

28 TDP to Oliver, 26 Sept. 1918, British Columbia, Premier, Papers, vol. 339, file 8
29 TDP, speech on natural resources conservation and immigration, undated [1926], PP, vol. 12, file 8
30 TDP to Arthur Meighen, 6 Oct. 1921, British Columbia, Premier, Papers, vol. 345, file 6
31 *Daily Colonist*, 2 Nov. 1921; TDP, speech on natural resources conservation and immigration, undated [1926], PP, vol. 12, file 8; on eugenics and immigration more generally see Angus McLaren, *Our Own Master Race: Eugenics in Canada, 1885–1945* (Toronto: McClelland and Stewart 1990), 46–67.
32 *Victoria Daily Times*, 2 Oct. 1917
33 'An Act to provide for the Settlement of Differences between the Governments of the Dominion and the Province respecting Indian Lands and Indian Affairs in the Province of British Columbia,' British Columbia, *Statutes* 1919, 9 Geo. 5, c. 32; Paul Tennent, *Aboriginal Peoples and Politics: The Indian Land Question in British Columbia, 1849–1889* (Vancouver: University of British Columbia Press, 1900), 98–9
34 TDP to Meighen and TDP to Borden, 26 Nov. 1919, British Columbia, Premier, Papers, vol. 341, file 8
35 Paul Koroscil, 'Soldiers, Settlement and Development in British Columbia, 1915–1930,' *BC Studies* 54 (summer 1982): 68–9
36 Koroscil focuses almost entirely on Oliver's contribution to and responsibility for the scheme. Ibid., 86–7
37 TDP to Jack Strickland, Vancouver *Province*, 3 Jan. 1945, PP, vol. 65, file 12
38 Most of the points made in this paragraph are based on David R.B. Dendy, 'One Huge Orchard: Okanagan Land and Development Companies Before the Great War' (BA essay, University of Victoria, 1976), particularly 63–4.
39 T.W. Stirling, president Kelowna Land and Orchard Company, to TDP, 6 June 1919, and TDP to W.M. Maclachlan, manager Central Okanagan Lands Ltd, 24 July 1919, PP, vol. 11, file 5
40 TDP to Oliver, 25 May 1920, PP, vol. 343, file 3
41 J.D. Mclean to Oliver, 28 July 1920, PP, vol. 12, file 12
42 TDP to Oliver, 2 June 1923, British Columbia, Premier, Papers, vol. 349, file 3
43 Oliver to TDP, 8 Sept. 1923, ibid.
44 On Wallachin see Nelson Riis, 'The Wallcahin Myth: A Study of Settlement Abandonment,' *BC Studies* 17 (spring 1973): 3–25.

45 TDP to Oliver, 14 Sept. 1923, British Columbia, Premier, Papers, vol. 349, file 3

46 Stephen Gray, 'Forest Policy and Administration in British Columbia, 1912–1928' (MA thesis, Simon Fraser University, 1982), 7. Gray here cites H.V. Nelles, *The Politics of Development: Mines & Hydro-Electric Power in Ontario, 1849–1941* (Toronto: Macmillan of Canada 1974), 428.

47 For an account of these developments see R. Peter Gillis and Thomas R. Roach, *Lost Initiatives: Canada's Forest Industries, Forest Policy and Forest Conservation* (New York: Greenwood Press 1986), 140–52; and Robert Howard Marris, 'Pretty Sleek and Fat: The Genesis of Forest Policy in British Columbia, 1903–1914' (MA thesis, University of British Columbia, 1979), 76–99.

48 *Daily Colonist*, 11 April 1918

49 *Vancouver Sun*, 7 March 1918; TDP, press statement, undated [Jan. 1918?], PP, vol. 60, file 1

50 Gillis and Roach, *Lost Initiatives*, 152–3

51 Oliver to TDP, 16 June 1921, British Columbia, Premier, Papers, vol. 345, file 6

52 TDP to Oliver, 20 Nov. 1922, and Oliver to TDP, 21 Nov. 1922, British Columbia, Premier, Papers, vol. 345, file 6; T.D. Pattullo, 'Reafforestation in Relation to the Lumber Industry,' *British Columbia Lumberman*, 9 (Feb. 1925): 42

53 John Herd Thompson with Allen Seager, *Canada 1922–1939: Decades of Discord* (Toronto: McClelland Stewart 1985), 77–8

54 Fraser River Syndicate to TDP, 16 Dec. 1920, and E.J. Palmer (Canada Cement Company) to TDP, 15 Feb. 1921, PP, vol. 12, file 2; TDP to F.P. Jones, 21 Nov. 1921, PP, vol. 12, file 2

55 P.Z. Caverhill to TDP, 17 Oct. 1921, and Naden to TDP, undated memo, PP, vol. 12, file 2

56 These concessions are outlined in Caverhill to TDP, 8 Dec. 1921, PP, vol. 12, file 2

57 Angus Mclean to TDP, 29 June 1922, PP, vol. 12, file 2

58 *Vancouver Sun*, 26 Nov. 1926

59 'Forest Act Amendment Act, 1921,' British Columbia, *Statutes* 1921, 11 Geo. 5, c. 28

60 TDP to Jones, 8 April 1927, and Jones to TDP, 25 March 1927, PP, vol. 12, file 2

61 Gray, 'Forest Policy,' 174; 'Appendix to Forest Branch Annual Report 1940, Consolidated Statistical Tables 1912–1940,' British Columbia, *Sessional Papers*, 20th Parl., 1st Sess., 1942, F60, table 2

62 'Appendix to Forest Branch Annual Report 1940'; Gray, 'Forest Policy,' 11
63 'Timber Royalty Act,' British Columbia, *Statutes* 1914, 4 Geo. 5, c. 76
64 Gray, 'Forest Policy,' 29
65 TDP to Executive Council, 30 Nov. 1923, PP, vol. 16, file 6; TDP, address on timber royalties, undated [1925], PP, vol. 23, file 1a
66 William McNeill, report of royalty committee to Timber Industries Council, 9 March 1923, British Columbia, Council of Forest Industries, Papers, vol. 44, file 5, UBCL; Gray, 'Forest Policy,' 34; Minutes of meeting of Timber Industries Council royalty committee and Department of Lands, 12 April 1923, vol. 38, file 6, ibid.
67 These points are made by Gray, 'Forest Policy,' 34–5.
68 TDP to president and members of the Executive Council, 30 Nov. 1923, British Columbia, Premier, Papers, vol. 349, file 3
69 McNeill to TDP, 24 Oct. 1924, PP, vol. 16, file 6
70 'Forest Act Amendment Act,' British Columbia, *Statutes* 1924, 15 Geo. 5, c. 20
71 TDP, speech on timber royalties, undated [1925], PP, vol. 23, file 1a
72 McRae, open letter to Oliver, *Daily Colonist*, 7 Dec. 1924
73 *Vancouver Sun*, 9 Dec. 1924
74 TDP, speech on timber royalties, undated [1925], PP, vol. 23, file 1a
75 Ibid.
76 *Victoria Daily Times*, 14 Dec. 1922
77 Ibid.
78 *Daily Colonist*, 2 June 1926; *Vancouver Daily Province*, 2 June 1926; 3 June 1926
79 *Victoria Daily Times*, 2 June 1926
80 *Vancouver Daily Province*, 31 May 1926; *Victoria Daily Times*, 2 June 1926
81 *Victoria Daily Times*, 29 July 1926; *Vancouver Daily Province*, 30 July, 4 Aug. 1926
82 TDP, speech, undated [1926?], PP, vol. 12, file 8
83 Ibid., [1927–8]

Chapter 5: Party Spokesman

1 R.G. Large, *Prince Rupert: A Gateway to Alaska* (Vancouver: Mitchell Press 1960), 56–9; *Daily Colonist*, 2 April 1921, 9, and 31 July 1923
2 *Electoral History of British Columbia*, 143
3 Cost of general elections as shown by districts – Dec. 1920, PP, vol. 12, file 6

4 Perry to Oliver, 10 Nov. 1921, PP, vol. 13, file 18. The Fort George riding centred on Prince George.

5 Oliver to TDP, 30 Dec. 1921, PP, vol. 13, file 18; Perry to TDP, 6 Jan. 1922, and TDP to Perry, 12 Jan. 1922, PP, vol. 14, file 2

6 Ian Parker, 'The Provincial Party,' *BC Studies* 8 (winter 1970–1): 17–28; and Margaret A. Ormsby, 'The United Farmers of British Columbia: An Abortive Third-Party Movement,' *British Columbia Historical Quarterly* 17 (1953): 53–73

7 Joseph Oliver to Oliver, 13 Dec. 1923, PP, vol. 17, file 16

8 Oliver to K. Campbell, member for Nelson, 12 Feb. 1924, PP, vol. 18, file 19

9 TDP, speech, undated [1917], PP, vol. 12, file 10

10 TDP, speech to B.C. Products Bureau of the Vancouver Board of Trade, 21 Oct. 1927, PP, vol. 23, file 14

11 Memo from the Office of the District Forester, Prince Rupert, 5 Feb. 1924, PP, vol. 18, file 7

12 TDP, speech to the Gyros, Prince Rupert, Nov. 1926, PP, vol. 12, file 10

13 The quotations in this paragraph are from TDP, speech during the dominion election campaign, 14 Sept. 1926, PP, vol. 23, file 14; TDP, speech in Prince Rupert, 3 May 1929, and speech to Vancouver Liberal Association, 21 Nov. 1929, PP, vol. 12, file 8.

14 TDP, speech, undated [1920?], PP, vol. 12, file 10

15 TDP, speech to B.C. Products Bureau of Vancouver Board of Trade, 21 Oct. 1927, PP, vol. 23, file 14

16 *Searchlight*, no. 6; *Vancouver Sun*, 16 Nov. 1923; *Daily Colonist*, 16 Nov. 1923

17 Oliver to ministers, 27 Feb. 1924, PP, vol. 17, file 12; Manson to Oliver, 2 April 1924, PP, vol. 18, file 19

18 Oliver to TDP, 9 April 1924, PP, vol. 18, file 19

19 J.H. King to TDP, 4 June 1824, and TDP to Oliver, 5 June 1924, PP, vol. 18, file 5

20 TDP to Oliver, 17 June 1924, PP, vol. 18, file 20

21 *Electoral History of British Columbia*, 149–55

22 Margaret to TDP, and Pearl to TDP, 21 June 1924, PP, vol. 18, file 3

23 E.C. Henniger to Oliver, 30 June 1924, PP, vol. 18, file 18

24 Oliver to WLMK, 26 June, 21 and 23 July 1924, King Papers, MG 26, J 1, vol. 106, NA

25 Oliver to Odium, 19 Nov. 1926, Victor Odium Papers, MG 30, E 300, vol. 9, NA; James Morton, *Honest John Oliver: The Life Story of the Honourable John Oliver Premier of British Columbia 1918–1927* (London: J.M. Dent and Sons 1933), 157

26 TDP, speech in the legislature, undated [1923], PP, vol. 12, file 10

27 Unsigned [A.M. Manson] to Oliver, 21 July 1924, PP, vol. 18, file 20
28 *Daily Colonist*, 22 Nov. 1924
29 Ibid., 5 Dec. 1925
30 TDP to Louis St Laurent, 23 Jan. 1948, St Laurent Papers, MG 26L, vol. 163, file 220–5, NA. I am grateful to Robert Bothwell for drawing my attention to this letter. For an account of the Winnipeg convention see John English, *The Decline of Politics: The Conservatives and the Party System 1901–20* (Toronto and Buffalo: University of Toronto Press 1977), 141–4; Hall, *Sifton*, vol. 2, 283–6.
31 TDP to WLMK, 6 and 7 Dec. 1921, King, Papers, MG 26, J 1, vol. 65
32 G.R. Pattullo to WLMK, 8 and 13 Dec. 1921, ibid.
33 WLMK to G.R. Pattullo, 11 Oct. 1919, GRPP, file 6, BCARS
34 WLMK, diary, 1 and 2 Oct. 1920, King Papers, MG 26, J 13
35 WLMK to TDP, 15 Sept. 1921, PP, vol. 13, file 18
36 TDP to King, 6 and 7 Dec. 1921, King Papers, MG 26, J 1, vol. 65; Thompson with Seager, *Canada 1922–1939*, table 1a, 333
37 J.G. Turgeon to J.H. King, 8 May 1924, King Papers, MG 26, J 1, vol. 110
38 Turgeon to WLMK, 4 March 1922, and 13 May 1925, King Papers, MG 26, J1, vols. 82 and 126
39 TDP, speech, 1925, PP, vol. 21, file 3. For an uncritical account of McGeer see David Ricardo Williams, *Mayor Gerry: The Remarkable Gerald Gratton McGeer* (Vancouver: Douglas & McIntyre 1986).
40 Thompson with Seager, *Canada 1922–1939*, table 1b, 334
41 WLMK to W.A. MacDonald, 11 Nov. 1925, King Papers, MG 26, J 1, vol. 135
42 TDP, speech, 14 Sept. 1926, PP, vol. 23, file 14
43 Thompson with Seager, *Canada 1922–1939*, table 1c, 335
44 W.A. MacDonald (secretary, Young Liberal party) to Oliver, 11 Oct. 1924, PP, vol. 18, file 21, BCARS; MacDonald to WLMK, 5 Nov. 1925, King Papers, MG 26, J 1, vol. 118
45 *Vancouver Sun*, 7 Aug. 1924
46 Ibid., 19 Sept. 1924
47 'An Act to Incorporate the Greater Vancouver Water District,' British Columbia, *Statutes*, 1924, 5 Geo. 5, c. 22; TDP to Oliver, 28 July 1925, Premier, Papers, GR 441, vol. 352, file 17, BCARS; TDP, undated newspaper article, PP, vol. 60, file 17
48 TDP, speech in house, 1925, PP, vol. 20, file 6
49 For example, Charles Woodward to Oliver, 11 July 1925, PP, vol. 21, file 10
50 *Daily Colonist*, 18 Nov. 1925; marginal note on E.A. Cleveland to TDP, 16 Feb. 1926, PP, vol. 22, file 4; *Vancouver Sun*, 27 May 1927
51 *Vancouver Daily Province*, 8 June 1926

52 Ibid., 23 Aug. 1926
53 Ibid., 23 Feb. 1927
54 Woodward to Oliver, 14 May 1927, and Woodward to MacLean, 11 July and 4 Aug. 1927, PP, vol. 24, files 20 and 17; *Vancouver Daily Province*, 10 Feb. 1927
55 Ibid., 12 Dec. 1924
56 *Daily Colonist*, 13 July 1925; Pattullo to Oliver, 7 Feb. 1925, British Columbia, Premier, Papers, GR 441, vol. 250, file 110; *Vancouver Sun*, 9 Feb. 1925
57 *Vancouver Daily Province*, 29 March 1928
58 Notes on meeting of Liberals, 5 Oct. 1926, PP, vol. 22, file 13; *Daily Colonist*, 1 Dec. 1926
59 'An Act to provide for Old Age Pensions,' British Columbia, *Statutes*, 1927, 17 Geo. 5, c. 50
60 'An Act Respecting the Marketing of Fruit and Other Produce,' British Columbia, *Statutes*, 1927, 17 Geo. 5, c. 54; Martin Robin, *The Rush for Spoils: The Company Province, 1971–1933* (Toronto: McClelland and Stewart 1972), 224
61 *Vancouver Daily Province*, 4 Feb. 1927
62 Ibid., 10 Feb. 1927
63 *Daily Colonist*, 2 Feb. 1927; *Vancouver Daily Province*, 15 Nov. 1933
64 Danvers Osborn to MacLean, 21 Jan. 1928, PP, vol. 28, file 2
65 *Daily Colonist*, editorial, 1 Dec. 1926
66 TDP to Oliver, 14 June 1927, PP, vol. 75, file 18
67 TDP to Robert Oliver, 21 June 1927, PP, vol. 75, file 18
68 TDP to Oliver, 29 July 1927, PP, vol. 75, file 18
69 Danvers Osborn to MacLean, 21 Jan. 1928, PP, vol. 28, file 2
70 *Vancouver Daily Province*, 3 Feb. 1928; *Victoria Daily Times*, 3 Feb. 1928
71 W.F. Hanbury to MacLean (telegram), 22 June 1928, J.D. MacLean Papers, Add. Ms 139, file 3, BCARS
72 MacLean to WLMK, 17 April 1928, King Papers, MG 26, J 1, vol. 154; TDP to MacLean, 7 May 1928, PP, vol. 28, file 7
73 [British Columbia Liberal Association], *What Liberalism Has Done for the Masses: A Synopsis of Labour and Social Legislation Enacted in British Columbia Since 1916* [Vancouver: British Columbia Liberal Association 1928]
74 TDP, speech, 1928, PP, vol. 27, file 3
75 MacLean to Woodward, 16 May 1928, MacLean Papers, Add. Ms 139, file 3

76 *Vancouver Daily Province*, 10 Nov. 1927
77 Robin, *Rush for Spoils*, 229–30
78 MacLean to Liberal candidates, 20 June 1928, PP, vol. 29, file 11; TDP, speech, 1928, PP, vol. 27, file 3
79 Ibid.
80 MacLean to all candidates, 16 July 1928, MacLean Papers, Add. MS 139, file 2
81 McGeer to WLMK, 27 Sept. 1927, King Papers, MG 26, J 1, vol. 145
82 TDP to MacLean, 16 July 1928, MacLean Papers, Add. MS 139, file 2
83 J.H. King to WLMK, 13 July 1928, King Papers, MG 26, J 1, vol. 153
84 W.F. Hanbury to WLMK, 19 May 1928, MacLean Papers, Add. MS 139, file 3
85 *Electoral History of British Columbia*, 163
86 *Victoria Daily Times*, 20 July 1928
87 Robin, *Rush for Spoils*, 230; *Electoral History of British Columbia*, 149 and 159
88 MacLean to WLMK, 26 July 1928, King Papers, MG 26, J 1, vol. 154

Chapter 6: Leader of the Opposition

1 For figures on forestry production see Consolidated Statistical Tables 1912–1940, Appendix to Forest Branch Annual Report 1940, British Columbia, *Sessional Papers*, 20th Parl., 1st Sess., 1942, F60, table 2; and for overall production, Economic Council of British Columbia, *Statistics of Industry in British Columbia* (Victoria: Economic Council of British Columbia 1935), unpaginated [7].
2 MacLean to WLMK, 26 July 1928, King Papers, MG 26, J 1, vol. 154, NA
3 S.L. Howe to TDP, 18 and 28 Dec., and TDP to Howe, 20 Dec. 1928, PP, vol. 26, files 7 and 8; *Victoria Daily Times*, 2 Jan. 1929
4 See, for example, J.J. Gillis to TDP, 1 Jan. 1929, PP, vol. 26, file 22
5 TDP to M.E. Smith, 13 Dec. 1928, PP, vol. 26, file 22
6 *Daily Victoria Times*, 22 Jan. 1929
7 TDP to Mrs J.W. deB. Farris, 4 June 1930, PP, vol. 30, file 38
8 TDP, speech, 15 Nov. 1929, PP, vol. 12, file 8
9 *Vancouver Sun*, 16 Dec. 1929; J.J. Gillis to TDP, 20 Dec. 1929, PP, vol. 32, file 2, Woodward to WLMK, 2 Jan. 1930, King Papers, MG 26, J 1, vol. 223
10 See, for example, TDP to W. Turnbull, 10 June 1930, PP, vol. 37, file 20.
11 Patmore to WLMK, 16 May 1930, King Papers, MG 26, J 1, vol. 179
12 WLMK to TDP, 4 June 1930, ibid.

13 WLMK, diary, 2 June and 4 July 1930, King, Papers, MG 26, J 13

14 See, for example, F. Frisby (secretary South Slocan and District Liberal Association) to TDP, 4 April 1929, PP, vol. 34, file 14.

15 Thompson and Seager, *Canada 1922–1939*, 335–6

16 The estimated values were $378,213,668 for 1929 and $179,771,012 for 1932. See Economic Council of British Columbia, *Statistics of Industry in British Columbia*, unpaginated.

17 Here the estimated values were $93,301,000 in 1929 and 39,155,000 in 1932. 'Consolidated Statistical Tables,' British Columbia, *Sessional Papers*, 20th Parl., 1st Sess., 1941–42, F60, table 2.

18 Canada, Dominion Bureau of Statistics, *Seventh Census of Canada, 1931* (Ottawa: King's Printer 1934), vol. VI, 3

19 Tolmie to Colonel Andrew Thompson, 29 Dec. 1931, S.F. Tolmie, Papers, vol. 4, file 10, University of British Columbia Library (UBCL)

20 See Bettina Bradbury, 'The Road to Receivership: Unemployment Relief in Burnaby, North Vancouver City and District and West Vancouver, 1929–1933' (MA thesis, Simon Fraser University, 1975); E.F. Jones, Prince Rupert city clerk, to TDP, 16 March 1932, PP, vol. 31, file 15; Large, *Prince Rupert*, 62–3.

21 This point is made by H. Blair Neatby, *The Politics of Chaos: Canada in the Thirties* (Toronto: Copp Clark Pitman 1986), 49.

22 *Vancouver Daily Province*, 14 Dec. 1929

23 TDP to Mary Lownsborough, 10 Jan. 1933, PP, vol. 45, file 14

24 Agreement to purchase 951 Beach Drive, N.W. Whittaker (soliciter) to TDP, 24 Nov. 1932, and TDP to N.W. Whittaker, 6 May 1933, PP, vol. 49, file 2.

25 TDP to Margaret Morgan, 18 Feb. 1933, PP, vol. 51, file 12

26 Bruce Hutchison in the *Vancouver Daily Province*, 2 Oct. 1932

27 TDP to Mary Short, 22 Dec. 1931, PP, vol. 41, file 30

28 Wynnie (Ethelwyn Ballantyne) to TDP, 28 July 1932, PP, vol. 45, file 4

29 TDP to J.R. Short, 17 Dec. 1932, PP, vol. 41, file 30

30 TDP to Neil Pattullo, 28 July 1930, PP, vol. 37, file 4

31 *Victoria Daily Times*, 29 Feb. 1928

32 *Vancouver Daily Province*, 15 Nov. 1933

33 *Vancouver Sun*, 4 April 1929

34 Ibid., 27 March 1929; TDP to C.Y. Peck (Conservative member for The Islands), 5 June 1930, PP, vol. 41, file 16; *Vancouver Daily Province*, 3 Nov. 1933

35 W. Turnbull to TDP, 11 July 1930, PP, vol. 37, file 20

36 *Vancouver Sun*, 2 March 1964; *Vancouver Daily Province*, 3 March 1964

37 Pattullo calculated that it cost $1000 a month to run the headquarters. TDP to Manson, 18 April 1932, PP, vol. 46, file 17
38 For the details of the Liberal party structure I have relied heavily on Sutherland, 'Pattullo,' 17–25 and 142.
39 TDP to J.F. Guimont (Nelson), 17 Nov. 1931, PP, vol. 35, file 1
40 See, for example, Dugald Donaghy to WLMK, 31 Jan. 1929, King Papers, MG 26, J 1, vol. 161.
41 TDP to George Pattullo, 9 March 1931, George Pattullo to TDP, 18 March 1931, and TDP to George Pattullo, 24 March 1931, PP, vol. 41, file 19
42 TDP to Wynnie (Ethelwyn Ballantyne), 21 Jan. 1952, Collison collection
43 TDP to Moodie, 19 Nov. 1931, PP, vol. 41, file 3
44 TDP to Manson, 7 May 1931, PP, vol. 41, file 2
45 TDP to Manson, 10 May 1932, PP, vol. 46, file 17
46 Moodie, 'Memorandum on Organization Essential to Party Success,' 24 Sept. 1930, PP, vol. 36, file 42
47 TDP to J.J. Gillis, member for Yale (and all other Liberal MLAS), 25 June 1929, PP, vol. 30, file 18
48 TDP to Patmore, 8 April and 11 May 1931, PP, vol. 41, file 22
49 Senator Hewitt Bostock to WLMK, 21 Jan. 1929, King Papers, MG 26, J 1, vol. 191
50 For a detailed description of this process see Moodie to H.F. Glassey, secretary, Prince Rupert Liberal Association, 15 Dec. 1930, PP, vol. 35, file 7; and TDP to L.L. Adams, president, Lillooet Liberal Association (and all other ridings), 26 Jan. 1931, PP, vol. 34, file 1.
51 TDP to Adams (and all other ridings), 7 Feb. 1931, PP, vol. 34, file 1
52 TDP to Fred W. Stirling, 8 April 1931, PP, vol. 41, file 28; *Vancouver Daily Province*, 22 May 1932; TDP to Adams (and all other ridings), 13 May 1932, PP, vol. 34, file 1
53 TDP to J.H. King, 21 Sept. 1929, PP, vol. 30, file 25; TDP to M.P. McCaffery, 31 Oct. 1931, PP, vol. 41, file 6
54 *Vancouver Sun*, 2 Nov. 1931
55 TDP to Turnbull, 1 June 1932, PP, vol. 47, file 20; *Vancouver Sun*, 17 May 1932
56 TDP to Harry H. Carlin, 29 Aug. 1931, PP, vol. 34, file 19; press release, 1 Sept. 1931, PP, vol. 44, file 1
57 TDP to L.A. Hanna (MLA for Alberni), 20 June 1931, PP, vol. 40, file 25
58 TDP to Gillis, 17 Dec. 1932, PP, vol. 45, file 22
59 TDP, press statements, 16 June 1930 and 18 Nov. 1938, PP, vol. 39, file 6, and vol. 44, file 1
60 Norman Senior to TDP, 5 Nov. 1930, and TDP to Senior, 6 Nov. 1930, PP,

vol. 37, file 15; TDP to Senior, 27 April and 28 June 1933, PP, vol. 52, file 3; TDP to Cromie, 10 Jan. 1933, PP, vol. 50, file 12

61 TDP, radio address, 6 April 1931, PP, vol. 65, file 1a; *Victoria Daily Times*, 7 April 1931

62 *Vancouver Daily Province*, 3 May 1931; TDP to William Turnbull, 22 April 1931, PP, vol. 42, file 3

63 TDP to H.C. Wrinch (MLA for Skeena), 6 Nov. 1930, PP, vol. 37, file 26

64 Tolmie to B.W. Howard, 9 Nov. 1931, Tolmie Papers, vol. 2, file 17

65 Moodie to TDP, 17 Nov. 1931, PP, vol. 41, file 3

66 TDP to Thomas King, and TDP to WLMK, 21 Dec. 1931, PP, vol. 40, file 31

67 Tolmie to B.W. Howard, 23 Dec. 1931, Tolmie Papers, vol. 2, file 17

68 TDP to Thomas King, 15 July 1932, PP, vol. 46, file 8

69 TDP to H.G. Perry, 13 Sept. 1932, PP, vol. 47, file 9; and W.O. Fulton (Prince Rupert) to TDP, PP, vol. 45, file 20a

70 Manson to TDP, 8 Oct. 1932, PP, vol. 46, file 17

71 TDP to J.F. Hutchcroft, 6 Oct. 1932, PP, vol. 46, file 1

72 *Vancouver Sun*, 3 Oct. 1932

73 Ibid.

74 WLKM, diary, 4 Oct. 1932, King Papers, MG 26, J 13

75 *Vancouver Sun*, editorial, 3 Oct. 1932; King, diary, 3 March 1933, King Papers, MG 26, J 13

76 TDP to Gillis, 29 Nov. 1932, PP, vol. 45, file 22; WLMK to McGeer, 9 Dec. 1930, King Papers, MG 26, J 1, vol. 177

77 TDP to Brenton Brown, 2 April 1932, PP, vol. 45, file 8

78 Cf Margaret A. Ormsby, 'T. Dufferin Pattullo and the Little New Deal,' *Canadian Historical Review* 43 (Dec. 1962): 278; and Martin Robin, *Pillars of Profit: The Company Province, 1934–1972* (Toronto: McClelland and Stewart 1973), 9.

79 Ormsby, 'Pattullo and the Little New Deal,' 286; Williams, *Mayor Gerry*, 124–5

80 TDP to McGeer, 21 Jan. 1933, PP, vol. 51, file 16; Keynes to McGeer, 25 Nov. 1931, King Papers, MG 26, J 1, vol. 192; for McGeer's ideas see G.G. McGeer, *The Conquest of Poverty or Money: Humanity and Christianity* (Gardenville, Quebec: Garden City Press 1935); TDP to McGeer, 28 Nov. 1932, and McGeer to TDP, 30 Nov. 1932, PP, vol. 46, file 23; Williams, *Mayor Gerry*, 125; interview with Bruce Hutchison, 28 July 1982

81 TDP, address at University of British Columbia, 9 May 1935, PP, vol. 65, file 1a

82 TDP, radio address, 20 April 1931, PP, vol. 44, file 12; TDP to J.A. Campbell, 21 Feb. 1933, PP, vol. 50, file 9

83 TDP to C.W. Craig, 2 March 1933, PP, vol. 50, file 5; TDP address on social

legislation, 21 April 1931, PP, vol. 44, file 12; TDP radio address, 30 June 1932, PP, vol. 49, file 15

84 TDP to Mabel Cook, 7 June 1933, PP, vol. 50, file 8; TDP to Cromie, 10 June 1932, PP, vol. 45, file 14

85 TDP to the editor of the *Financial Post*, 30 Jan. 1936, PP, vol. 64, file 5; TDP to Cromie, 2 June 1932, PP, vol. 49, file 8; TDP to Cromie, 10 June 1932, PP, vol. 45, file 14

86 See Doug Owram, 'Economic Thought in the 1930s: The Prelude to Keynesianism,' *Canadian Historical Review* 65 (Sept. 1985): 364.

87 TDP to McGeer, 28 Nov. 1932, PP, vol. 46, file 23

88 Resolutions Passed by the Convention of the British Columbia Liberal Association held in Vancouver, 3 and 4 October 1932, PP, vol. 62, file 15

89 TDP to Hutchison, 20 Feb. 1933, PP, vol. 50, file 20

90 Turnbull to TDP, 24 March and 9 April 1931, PP, vol. 42, file 3

91 Bruce Hutchison in *Victoria Daily Times*, 25 Jan. 1929

92 R.L. Maitland, 'House log,' 24 Jan. 1929, Maitland Family Papers, Add. Ms 781, vol. 8, file 1, BCARS; *Victoria Daily Times*, 25 Jan. 1929

93 TDP, reply to budget speech, 17 March 1932, PP, vol. 49, file 16; *Vancouver Sun*, 1 Feb. 1962; TDP, reply to budget speech, 23 Feb. 1929, PP, vol. 33, file 13; *Victoria Daily Times*, 31 Jan. 1930

94 *Victoria Daily Times*, 31 Jan. 1930; Maitland, 'House log,' 6 March 1930, vol. 8 file 2

95 *Vancouver Sun*, 26 Feb. 1929

96 *Vancouver Daily Province*, 7 March 1929

97 *Vancouver Sun*, 23 Feb. 1929

98 See, for example, Tolmie to John J. Banfield, 11 June 1931, Tolmie Papers, vol. 5, file 13

99 TDP to Watt, 11 June 1929, PP, vol. 32, file 1

100 TDP to E.C. Stevens (Skidegate), 1 Feb. 1929, PP, vol. 31, file 23; TDP to Watt, 8 and 14 Feb. 1930, PP, vol. 38, file 1; Maitland, 'House log,' 7 Feb. 1930, vol. 8, file 2

101 TDP to E.G. Lucas, 20 March 1931, PP, vol. 40, file 10

102 TDP, speech during budget debate, 6 March 1930, PP, vol. 39, file 12

103 Maitland, 'House log,' 24 March 1930, vol. 8, file 2

104 Jones to Tolmie, 10 Dec. 1930, Tolmie Papers, vol. 7, file 3

105 Maitland, 'House log,' 5 March 1931, vol. 8, file 3

106 TDP to Turnbull, 22 April 1931, PP, vol. 42, file 3; *Vancouver Sun*, 24 March 1931; *Vancouver Daily Province*, 7 March 1931

107 Tolmie to MacMillan, 15 April 1932, PP, vol. 47, file 19

108 [British Columbia], *Report of the Committee Appointed by the Govern-*

ment to Investigate the Finances of British Columbia (Victoria: King's Printer 1932), 1–55. For summaries of the Kidd Commission's recommendations see Robert Edmund Groves, 'Business Government: Party Politics and the British Columbia Business Community, 1928–1933' (MA thesis, University of British Columbia, 1976), 143–6; and Robin, *The Rush for Spoils*, 239–43.

109 Cf Robin, *The Rush for Spoils*, 214–42.

110 TDP to MacMillan, 9 July 1932, and MacMillan to TDP, 13 July 1932, PP, vol. 46, file 20; Tolmie to TDP, 30 Aug. 1932, PP, vol. 47, file 19

111 TDP to Kate, 15 Sept. 1932, PP, vol. 45, file 19

112 H.F. Angus, 'The Kidd Report in British Columbia,' *Canadian Forum* 13 (Nov. 1932): 47

113 *British Columbia Financial Times*, 17 Sept. 1932

114 TDP, press statement, 16 June 1932, PP, vol. 49, file 8

115 Minutes of a meeting of the Rotary Club of Prince Rupert, 7 April 1932, PP, vol. 48, file 17; Tolmie to R.B. Bennett, 19 Sept. 1932, Tolmie Papers, vol. 5, file 7

116 *Vancouver Province*, 11 June 1932

117 Tolmie to Byron W. Howard, 30 Sept. 1932, Tolmie Papers, vol. 2, file 18

118 Walter Scott, 'The Lady of the Lake,' canto 5, stanza 10

119 TDP to H.F. Pullen, editor of the Prince Rupert *Daily News*, 2 Aug. 1932, PP, vol. 47, file 12

120 TDP, speech to Laurier Club of Vancouver, 29 April 1932, PP, vol. 49, file 15

121 TDP to W.H. Malkin, 21 Sept. 1932, PP, vol. 46, file 15; see also TDP to Turnbull, 31 March 1933, PP, vol. 52, file 7; and TDP to R.R. Burns, 12 July 1932, PP, vol. 35, file 10.

122 TDP to J. Boyd McBride, secretary, Provincial Liberal Association of Alberta, 19 May 1932, PP, vol. 46, file 21; TDP to Pullen, 2 Aug. 1932, PP, vol. 47, file 12

123 TDP to Tolmie, 13 Sept. 1932, PP, vol. 47, file 19

124 TDP to Tolmie, 28 March 1933, and Tolmie to TDP, 27 March 1933, PP, vol. 52, file 6; TDP, press statement, 15 Sept. 1932, PP, vol. 49, file 8

125 TDP, radio address, 30 June 1932, PP, vol. 49, file 15; TDP to presidents of Liberal associations, 11 July 1932, PP, vol. 48, file 10

126 Pullen to TDP, 4 June and 30 July 1932, and Patmore to TDP, 26 July 1932, PP, vol. 47, files 12 and 7; TDP to WLMK, 22 Nov. 1941, PP, vol. 58, file 2

127 *Vancouver Daily Province*, 19 Jan. 1933

128 Bruce Hutchison, *Vancouver Daily Province*, 22 Jan. 1933
129 TDP to Margaret Morgan, 12 Jan. 1933, PP, vol. 51, file 12; TDP, press statement, 13 Jan. 1933, PP, vol. 53, file 16
130 Senior to TDP, 18 Jan. 1933, PP, vol. 52, file 3
131 Maitland, 'House log,' 28 Feb. 1933, vol. 8, file 5
132 TDP, reply to budget speech, 16 March 1933, and reply to throne speech, 27 Feb. 1933, PP, vol. 53, file 22; TDP to Perry, 24 Feb. 1933, PP, vol. 51, file 29
133 Bennett to Tolmie, 9 March 1933, R.B. Bennett Papers, MG 26K, vol. 569, NA
134 TDP, reply to budget speech, 16 March 1933, PP, vol. 53, file 22
135 Ibid.
136 TDP to J.F. Huchcroft, 1 April 1933, PP, vol. 50, file 20; *Vancouver Daily Province*, 1 April 1933
137 Maitland, 'House log,' 6 and 7 April 1933, vol. 8, file 5
138 TDP, press statements, 5 July and 2 Aug. 1933, PP, vol. 53, file 16; *Vancouver Daily Province*, 7 July 1933
139 See, for example, Ian D. Parker, 'Simon Fraser Tolmie: The Last Conservative Premier of British Columbia,' *BC Studies* 11 (fall 1971): 35.
140 TDP, press statement, 11 Aug. 1933, PP, vol. 53, file 16; *Vancouver Sun*, 11 Aug. 1933
141 TDP to Mary Ellen Smith, 31 March 1933, PP, vol. 52, file 4
142 McGeer to Pattullo, 18 Aug. 1933, PP, vol. 51, file 16
143 See, for example, A.E. Munn (member of parliament) to TDP, 7 April 1933, and TDP to Munn, 13 April 1933, PP, vol. 51, file 13.
144 TDP to C. Ewart, 2 May 1933, PP, vol. 34, file 19
145 For an account of these developments see Walter D. Young, 'Ideology, Personality and the Origin of the CCF in British Columbia,' *BC Studies* 32 (winter 1976–7): 139–52; and on the last point Dorothy G. Steeves, *The Compassionate Rebel: Ernest Winch and the Growth of Socialism in Western Canada* (Vancouver: J.J. Douglas 1977), 89.
146 Tolmie to W. Graham Gillam, 4 Oct. 1933, Tolmie Papers, vol. 2, file 2; Jones to Colonel A.M. Brown, 7 Nov. 1933, J.W. Jones Papers, Add. Ms 23, vol. 2, file 4, BCARS
147 H.R. MacMillan to TDP, 23 May 1933, TDP to MacMillan, 25 May 1933, PP, vol. 51, file 14
148 P.C. Sanford (secretary, South Main Liberal Association) to TDP, 21 March 1933, PP, vol. 35, file 9; Pullen to TDP, 4 June 1932, PP, vol. 47, file 12; T.R. Tomlinson, 6 April 1933, PP, vol. 52, file 5; Manson to TDP, 1 Sept. 1933, PP, vol. 35, file 6

149 TDP to Cromie, 28 Aug. 1933, PP, vol. 50, file 12

150 P.W. Luce in *Saturday Night*, 21 Oct. 1933; there were, in all, 209 candidates. See *Electoral History of British Columbia*, 173–80.

151 WLMK to T.A. Crerar, 12 June 1933, T.A. Crerar Papers, vol. 119, Queen's University Archives; *Victoria Daily Times*, 26 Aug. 1933

152 TDP to J.J. Gillis, 14 Aug. 1933, PP, vol. 50, file 18

153 Tolmie to B.W. Howard, 5 Oct. 1933, Tolmie Papers, vol. 2, file 18; Margaret A. Ormsby, *British Columbia: A History* (Toronto: Macmillan 1958), 453, citing *Vancouver Sun*, 21 Oct. 1933

154 TDP to Pullen, 25 May 1933, PP, vol. 51, file 31

155 TDP to D. McPherson, 1 Sept. 1933, PP, vol. 34, file 21

156 *Vancouver Daily Province*, 22 July 1933

157 *Vancouver Sun*, 20 Sept. 1933

158 Ibid., 27 Sept. 1933; 'A Brief Synopsis of Liberal Policy,' Aug. 1933, PP, vol. 53, file 12; *Vancouver Daily Province*, 23 Oct. 1933

159 *Vancouver Daily Province*, 12 Oct. 1933

160 George to TDP, 18 Sept. 1933, PP, vol. 51, file 27

161 *Electoral History of British Columbia*, 173–80

162 Turgeon to WLMK, 13 Nov. 1933, and McGeer to WLMK, 1 Nov. 1933, King Papers, MG 26, J 1, vols. 198 and 197

163 See, for example, Jones to H.H. Stevens, 7 Nov. 1933, Jones, Papers, Add. Ms 23, vol. 2, file 4

164 *Vancouver Daily Province*, 6 Nov. 1933

165 Maitland to TDP, 4 Nov. 1933, PP, vol. 51, file 8

166 *Vancouver Daily Province*, 3 Nov. 1933

167 *Daily Sentinel-Review*, 3 Nov. 1933

168 George Pattullo to TDP, 3 Nov. 1933, PP, vol. 52, file 16

169 George Pattullo to Wynnie Ballantyne, undated [Nov. 1933], Collison collection

170 McGeer to TDP, 3 Nov. 1933, PP, vol. 51, file 16

171 WLMK to TDP, 4 Nov. 1933, PP, vol. 75, file 1; WLMK to T. Reid, 17 Nov. 1933, quoted in H. Blair Neatby, *William Lyon Mackenzie King, 1932–1939: The Prism of Unity* (Toronto: University of Toronto Press 1976), 49

172 B.R. Dusenbury (president, Vancouver Yukoners' Association) to TDP, 3 Nov. 1933, PP, vol. 52, file 11

Chapter 7: Politics of Reform

1 *Vancouver Sun*, 15 Nov. 1933

2 Ibid., 3 Nov. 1933; *Vancouver Daily Province*, 3 Nov. 1933

3 Economic Council of British Columbia, *Statistics of Industry in British Columbia*, unpaginated [7]

4 The actual figure was 47 per cent. See Royal Commission on Dominion-Provincial Relations, *Report of the Royal Commission on Dominion Provincial Relations*, Book I: *Canada: 1867–1939* [Ottawa: King's Printer 1940], 150.

5 Canada, Dominion Bureau of Statistics, *Seventh Census ... 1931*, vol. VI, 3. The national figure had increased since 1931 and there is no reason to think that British Columbia did not reflect the trend. See James Struthers, *No Fault of Their Own: Unemployment and the Canadian Welfare State, 1914–1941* (Toronto: University of Toronto Press 1983), 215.

6 Ormsby, *British Columbia: A History*, 457

7 For Vancouver figures on these points see John Douglas Belshaw, 'The Administration of Relief to the Unemployed in Vancouver during the Great Depression,' (MA thesis, Simon Fraser University, 1982), 81–2, 98 and 121.

8 Robert Bothwell, John English, and Ian Drummond, *Canada, 1900–1945* (Toronto: University of Toronto Press 1987), 258

9 TDP, speech, 6 June 1934, PP, vol. 65, file 19; TDP to WLMK, 9 Aug. 1934, PP, vol. 69, file 12

10 TDP, press statement, 2 March 1933, PP, vol. 53, file 16

11 Peebles to TDP, 27 Dec. 1950, PP, vol. 59, file 2

12 *Victoria Daily Times*, 19 Jan. 1934

13 TDP to T.C. Morgan, 28 Sept. 1934, PP, vol. 32, file 3

14 *Victoria Daily Times*, 19 Jan. 1934

15 TDP, congregation address at University of British Columbia, 9 May 1935, and radio speech, 20 Sept. 1935, PP, vol. 65, file 1b

16 Bruce Hutchison, in *Vancouver Daily Province*, 2 Dec. 1933

17 TDP to WLMK, 17 Nov. 1933, PP, vol. 75, file 1

18 The phrase is used by Ormsby, 'T. Dufferin Pattullo and the Little New Deal,' 277–97.

19 TDP to George Pattullo, 14 Aug. 1936, Collison collection

20 TDP to WLMK, 29 Nov. 1933, PP, vol. 75, file 1

21 McGeer to WLMK, 1 and 14 Nov. 1933, King Papers, MG 26, J 1, vol. 197, NA

22 *Vancouver Sun*, 27 Nov. 1933

23 TDP to WLMK, 29 Nov. 1933, PP, vol. 75, file 1

24 See, for example, *Vancouver Sun*, 16 Nov. 1933; TDP, memo to deputy provincial secretary, 14 Nov. 1933, PP, vol. 67, file 7.

25 Hart to Edgar N. Rhodes, federal minister of finance, 26 Feb. 1934, PP, vol. 69, file 11; *Canadian Annual Review 1934*, 336
26 TDP to Logan and Logan to TDP, 28 Nov. 1933, PP, vol. 74, file 3; and Logan to Bennett, 25 Nov. 1933, Bennett Papers, MG 26K, vol. 570, NA
27 TDP to George Pattullo, 19 Oct. 1932, PP, vol. 47, file 6
28 Billy McJames (of the *Edmonton Bulletin*) to TDP, 14 Oct. 1933, Collison collection
29 TDP to Bennett, 12 Dec. 1933, PP, vol. 74, file 3
30 TDP to Logan, 1 Dec. 1933, PP, vol. 74, file 3
31 WLMK to TDP, 4 Nov. 1933, PP, vol. 75, file 1
32 Thomas White to TDP, 13 Dec. 1933, PP, vol. 74, file 13
33 TDP to Bennett, 18 Dec. 1933, PP, vol. 69, file 10
34 TDP to Logan, 1 Dec. 1933, PP, vol. 74, file 3
35 For a brief history of British Columbia's claims see R.M. Burns, 'British Columbia and the Canadian Confederation,' in Patricia E. Roy, ed., *A History of British Columbia: Selected Readings* (Toronto: Copp Clark Pitman 1989), 159–61.
36 TDP to Bennett, 18 Dec. 1933, PP, vol. 69, file 10; *Vancouver Sun*, 2 Dec. 1933, 12
37 Minutes of meeting of four western premiers, 4 Dec. 1933, PP, vol. 53, file 4; Resolutions Passed at Inter-Provincial Conference Held in Victoria ... 4 December 1934, John Bracken, Premier's Office Papers, MG 13, I 2, vol. 67, file 199, Provincial Archives of Manitoba
38 TDP, speech to the Empire Club of Toronto, July 1934, PP, vol. 65, file 1a
39 TDP, press interview, Jan. 1932, PP, vol. 64, file 1
40 [British Columbia], *British Columbia's Claim for Readjustment of Terms of Union*, 1–30; see also H. Alan Maclean (lawyer who prepared the brief) to TDP, 27 Dec. 1933, PP, vol. 63, file 3.
41 TDP, speech, 18 Aug. 1936, PP, vol. 55, file 10
42 *Victoria Daily Times*, 26 Jan. 1934; *Vancouver Province*, 29 Jan. 1934
43 TDP, press interview, Jan. 1934, PP, vol. 64, file 1; TDP, speech, 6 June 1934, PP, vol. 65, file 19
44 TDP to Bennett, 7 Feb. 1934, and Bennett to TDP, 26 Feb. 1934, PP, vol. 69, file 11; for a general account of this conference see Thompson with Seager, *Canada 1922–1939*, 254; Struthers, *No Fault of Their Own*, 109–11; and *Canadian Annual Review*, *1934*, 34–35.
45 *Vancouver Sun*, 6 Feb. 1934
46 *Vancouver Province*, 21 Feb. 1934
47 Ibid., 15 March 1934

48 For a summary of this legislation see Robin, *Pillars of Profit*, 13–14, which is largely based on *Canadian Annual Review, 1934*, 334–9.

49 'An Act to amend and consolidate the "Male Minimum Wage Act,"' 'An Act to amend and consolidate the Act respecting a Minimum Wage for Women,' and 'An Act to amend and consolidate the "Hours of Work Act, 1923,"' British Columbia *Statutes* 1934, 24 Geo. 5, c. 47, 48, and 30

50 'An Act to provide for the Marketing of Natural Products,' British Columbia, *Statutes*, 1934, 24 Geo. 5, c. 38

51 'An Act to provide for the Investigation of Matters of Economic Importance, and for the Creation of an Economic Council,' British Columbia, *Statutes*, 1934, 24 Geo. 5, c. 19

52 'An Act to amend the "Public Schools Act,"' British Columbia, *Statutes*, 1934, 24 Geo. 5, c. 58

53 'An Act to give Further Power to Courts with respect to Recovery of Money secured by Mortgage and Similar Matters,' British Columbia, *Statutes*, 1934, 24 Geo. 5, c. 49

54 'An Act to establish a Department of Municipal Affairs,' British Columbia, *Statutes*, 1934, 24 Geo. 5, c. 52

55 The estimates for 1934–5 provided for expenditure of $21,609,637 and revenue of $19,492,791, British Columbia, *Sessional Papers*, 18th Parl., 1st Sess., 1934, v4 and v8

56 Bennett to TDP, 25 March 1934, and TDP to Bennett, 26 March 1934, PP, vol. 69, file 11; TDP, press statement, 27 March 1934, PP, vol. 64, file 1

57 'An Act to provide for the Exercise by the Lieutenant-Governor in Council of certain Powers during the Interim between the Sessions of the Legislature,' British Columbia, *Statutes*, 1934, 24 Geo. 5, c. 60

58 See, for example, G. Sivertz in *Vancouver News Herald*, 17 March 1934

59 Pooley to Jones, 19 March 1934, Jones Papers, Add. Ms 23, vol. 2, file 3, BCARS

60 *Vancouver Province*, 21 March 1934; *Daily Colonist*, 20 March 1934

61 *Victoria Times*, 21 March 1934; *Vancouver Sun*, 21 March 1934

62 *Victoria Daily Times*, 21 March 1934

63 See, for example, *Daily Colonist*, 27 March 1934

64 Bennett to TDP, 24 March 1934, PP, vol. 69, file 11; Bennett to H.H. Stevens, 4 April 1934, Bennett Papers, MG 26K, vol. 570, NA

65 WLMK, diary, 26 March 1934, King Papers, MG 26, J 13

66 See, for example, Victor Odlum to TDP, 19 March 1934, Odlum Papers, MG 30, E 300, vol. 10, NA; Professor Henry Angus quoted in *Vancouver News-Herald*, 19 March 1934.

67 TDP to Mackenzie, 21 March 1934, PP, vol. 63, file 2
68 TDP to the earl of Bessborough, 7 April 1934, PP, vol. 69, file 3
69 *Vancouver Province*, 21 March 1934
70 *Vancouver Sun*, 14 July 1934
71 Bennett to TDP, and TDP to Bennett, 24 March 1934, PP, vol. 69, file 11
72 Edgar Rhodes (minister of finance) to Bennett, 12 Dec. 1933, Bennett Papers, MG 26K, vol. 570
73 Logan to Bennett, 4 April 1934, Bennett Papers, MG 26K, vol. 570; Hart to Rhodes, 26 Feb. 1934, PP, vol. 69, file 11
74 *Victoria Daily Times*, 23 April 1934
75 See WLMK, diary, 26 April 1934, King Papers, MG 26, J 13.
76 *Vancouver Sun*, 28 April 1934
77 *Vancouver Province*, 3 May 1934; TDP to Bennett, 3 May 1934, and Perley to TDP, 4 May 1934, PP, vol. 60, file 11
78 Bennett to TDP, 3 May 1934, PP, vol. 69, file 11
79 TDP to Perley, 7 May 1934, ibid.
80 TDP to Wynnie Ballantyne, 16 Nov. 1952, PP, vol. 59, file 8
81 TDP to WLMK, 9 Aug. 1934, PP, vol. 69, file 12
82 WLMK, diary, 20 Jan. 1934, King Papers, MG 26, J 13
83 Ibid., 25 April and 1 Aug. 1934
84 TDP to Perley, 7 May 1934, PP, vol. 69, file 11
85 Rhodes to Hart, 11 June 1934, TDP to Bennett, 11 July 1834, PP, vol. 69, file 12
86 TDP to Bennett, 6 July 1934, PP, vol. 69, file 12; Bennett to TDP, 6 July 1934, PP, vol. 69, file 12
87 *Vancouver Sun*, 4 May 1934; TDP to Perley, 7 May 1934, PP, vol. 69, file 11
88 See, for example, *Victoria Times*, 3, 4, 5 May 1934; Norman Senior in *Vancouver Sun*, 4 May 1934; *Vancouver Sun*, 14 May 1934.
89 Bruce Hutchison to Roy Brown, editor of the *Vancouver Province*, undated [April 1934], Bruce Hutchison Papers, University of Calgary Library
90 Ibid.
91 TDP, press statement, 6 April 1934, PP, vol. 64, file 1
92 For an account of Canadian developments see Doug Owram, *The Government Generation: Canadian Intellectuals and the State 1900–1945* (Toronto: University of Toronto Press 1986).
93 On Carrothers's career see the *Daily Colonist*, 30 Aug. 1931.
94 British Columbia, Coal and Petroleum Products Commission, *Report of the Commissioner the Honourable Mr. Justice M.A. Macdonald Relat-*

ing to the Petroleum Industry, volume 1 (Victoria: Charles F. Banfield 1937), v. For more detail on the background and work of this commission see Robin Fisher, 'Regulating Fuels in the Depression: The Coal and Petroleum Control Board of British Columbia,' *BC Studies* 66 (summer 1985): 3–27.

95 The attempt to introduce health insurance is one of the few aspects of the Pattullo program that has been well written up, though the focus of most of this work is either on the doctors who opposed the scheme or the experts who formulated it rather than on Pattullo's role. See C. David Naylor, *Private Practice, Public Payment: Canadian Medicine and the Politics of Health Insurance 1911–1966* (Kingston and Montreal: McGill-Queen's University Press 1986); Margaret W. Andrews, 'The Course of Medical Opinion on State Health Insurance in British Columbia, 1919–1939,' *Histoire sociale / Social History* 16 (May 1983): 129–41; and Allan Irving, 'The Doctors Versus the Expert: Harry Morris Cassidy and the British Columbia Health Insurance Dispute of the 1930s,' *BC Studies* 78 (summer 1988): 53–79.

96 In Vancouver the incomes of general practitioners had dropped from an average of $3742 in 1929 to $2361 in 1933 (see Irving, 'Doctors,' 65). That decline of 37 per cent was lower than the provincial average of 47 per cent (see above, note 4). Doctors in rural areas may well have been hit harder and received more payments in kind than big city doctors.

97 C. David Naylor, 'Canada's First Doctors' Strike: Medical Relief in Winnipeg, 1933–34,' *Canadian Historical Review* 67 (June 1986): 151–80, and *Private Practice*, 62.

98 Andrews, 'Medical Opinion,' 136

99 Weir, speech, 9 Oct. 1934, British Columbia, Premiers' Papers, GR 1222, vol. 5, file 1, BCARS

100 Weir to Barrow (and all Liberal members), 29 Sept. 1934, ibid., file 8

101 Weir to TDP, 24 Sept. 1934, ibid., file 1. Andrews, 'Medical Opinion,' 131–8, has shown that British Columbia doctors were in favour of health insurance, if it were in their interests, by the mid-1920s.

102 Struthers, *No Fault of Their Own*, 64. On Cassidy see also Irving, 'Doctors,' 54–7, and Naylor, *Private Practice*, 62.

103 Cassidy to Professor J.F. Parkinson, Harvard University, 21 Nov. 1934, Harry M. Cassidy Papers, Acc. no. B72-0022, vol. 16, file 1, University of Toronto Archives (UTA)

104 Weir to Pattullo, 22 Nov. 1934, PP, vol. 67, file 6

105 TDP to Weir, 5 Jan. 1935, British Columbia, Premiers' Papers, GR 1222, vol. 14, file 2. There is some difference of opinion among historians

about Bennett's sincerity when he gave the 'New Deal' talks. For a summary of reaction to the broadcasts see Thompson with Seager, *Canada 1922–1939*, 261–5.

106 For a description of this draft bill see Irving, 'Doctors,' 63–6.

107 Naylor, *Private Practice*, 72; Irving, 'Doctors,' 60

108 TDP to Weir, 2 Jan. 1936, British Columbia, Premiers' Papers, GR 1222, vol. 13, file 11

109 Cassidy to Peebles, 30 May 1935, Cassidy Papers, Acc. no. B72-0022, vol. 17, file 2

110 'An Act to Provide for the Establishment of a Provincial System of Health Insurance,' British Columbia, *Statutes*, 1936, 1 Ed. 8, c. 23; for the vote see British Columbia, *Journals of the Legislative Assembly of the Province of British Columbia ... Session 1936* (Victoria: Charles F. Banfield 1935), 136; and for a description of the final legislation see Irving, 'Doctors,' 72–3; and Naylor, *Private Practice*, 75–9.

111 On the particular projects see Mackenzie to TDP, 21 March 1934, PP, vol. 63, file 2.

112 TDP, press statement, 8 Dec. 1933, PP, vol. 64, file 1; *Vancouver Sun*, 8 Dec. 1933

113 TDP, press statement, 10 Sept. 1934, PP, vol. 64, file 1; *Victoria Times*, 10 Sept. 1934

114 *Vancouver Sun*, 22 March 1935

115 J.A.L. Waddell to Bennett, 18 Dec. 1934, and H.A. Stewart (minister of public works) to Bennett, 28 Dec. 1934, Bennett Papers, MG 26K, vol. 575

116 Strachan to TDP, 15 Sept. 1934, and Strachan to TDP, 18 Sept. 1934, PP, vol. 70, file 10

117 *Vancouver Sun*, 14 March 1935; *Vancouver Daily Province*, 19 and 20 March 1935

118 'An Act to provide for the Construction of a Bridge across the Fraser River at New Westminster,' British Columbia, *Statutes*, 1935, 25 Geo. 5, c. 26; for the vote see British Columbia, *Journals of the Legislative Assembly ... Session 1935*, 104–5.

119 *Victoria Daily Times*, 11 and 18 June 1935

120 TDP, radio speech, 29 March 1935, PP, vol. 65, file 1b; *Victoria Daily Times*, 9 July 1935

121 TDP to Stewart, 16 and 23 July 1935, PP, vol. 70, file 7; TDP, press statement, 29 July 1935, PP, vol. 64, file 1; *Victoria Daily Times*, 29 July 1935

122 TDP, press statement, 23 Aug. 1934, PP, vol. 64, file 1

123 Bennett to TDP, 31 Aug. 1934, and TDP to Bennett, 25 Sept. 1934, British Columbia, Premiers' Papers, GR 1222, vol. 124, file 3

124 Bennett to TDP, 5 Feb. 1935, and TDP to Bennett, 11 Feb. 1935, PP, vol. 69, file 15

125 TDP to McGeer, 12 Jan. 1935, and TDP to C. Jones (Vancouver city clerk), 14 Jan. 1935, British Columbia, Premiers' Papers, GR 1222, vol. 12, file 6; Williams, *Mayor Gerry*, 173–6; McGeer to Hart, 16 Jan. 1935, British Columbia, Premiers' Papers, GR 1222, vol. 12, file 6; TDP to Bennett, 4 March 1935, and TDP to Rhodes, 6 March 1935, PP, vol. 69, file 15

126 TDP to Bennett, 17 and 24 Dec. 1934, PP, vol. 69, file 13; Bennett to TDP, 3 March and 28 Dec. 1934, PP, vol. 69, files 11 and 13

127 TDP to Perley, 27 March 1935, PP, vol. 74, file 5

128 For an account of the strike and the trek see Thompson with Seager, *Canada 1922–1939*, 269–72.

129 Cromie to TDP, 23 Feb. 1935, PP, vol. 62, file 3a; also Nickerson to TDP, 20 May 1935, PP, vol. 63, file 7

130 Hutchison in the *Vancouver Daily Province*, 11 May 1935

131 TDP to Cromie, 25 Feb. 1935, PP, vol. 62, file 3a; TDP to Nickerson, 27 May 1935, PP, vol. 63, file 7

132 TDP to WLMK, 1 Sept. 1934, and WLMK to TDP, 8 Sept. 1934, PP, vol. 75, file 2

133 For the election results see Thompson with Seager, *Canada 1922–1939*, table 1e, 337.

134 TDP to WLMK, 19 Oct. 1935, PP, vol. 69, file 15

135 Cromie to TDP, 23 Feb. 1935, PP, vol. 62, file 3a

136 WLMK, diary, 27 Sept. 1935, King Papers, MG 26, J 13

137 *Victoria Daily Times*, 29 Nov. 1935

138 WLMK, diary, 12 Dec. 1935, King Papers, MG 26, J 13

139 *Vancouver Province*, 11 and 14 Dec. 1935

140 WLMK, diary, 13 Dec. 1935, King Papers, MG 26, J 13

141 Ibid., 25 and 28 March 1936; *Victoria Daily Times*, 23 April 1936

142 TDP to WLMK, 14 March 1936, PP, vol. 68, file 5; WLMK, diary, 7 April 1936, King Papers, MG 26, J 13

143 TDP to WLMK, 14 Feb. 1936, PP, vol. 69, file 17

144 WLMK, diary, 26 Feb. 1937, King Papers, MG 26, J 13

145 TDP to WLMK, 8 April 1936, PP, vol. 68, file 5

146 See, for example, WLMK, diary, 7 April 1936 and 26 Feb. 1937, King Papers, MG 26, J 13

147 Ibid., 11 May 1930, 17 Oct. 1935, 25 April 1934

148 TDP to H.G. [Perry?], 23 Oct. 1948, Collison collection

149 Neatby, *William Lyon Mackenzie King*, 157

150 Dunning to Hart, 16 Oct. 1936, PP, vol. 68, file 6

151 See, for example, *Victoria Daily Times*, 15 Feb. 1935.

152 *Vancouver Sun*, 30 March 1935; *Vancouver Daily Province*, 30 March 1935
153 TDP to George Pattullo, 17 May 1936, PP, vol. 55, file 12
154 George Pattullo to TDP, 3 Aug. 1936, PP, vol. 55, file 12; and 4 Aug. 1936, Collison collection
155 George Pattullo, 'Our Sentimentalists,' *Saturday Evening Post* 209 (28 Oct. 1936): 69, and *All Our Yesterdays* (San Antonio: Naylor Company 1948), 262 and 273
156 Fisher, 'Duff and George Go West,' 521–5
157 George Pattullo to TDP, 18 Nov. 1933, PP, vol. 52, file 16
158 *Vancouver Daily Province*, 7 March 1936
159 TDP to WLMK, 19 Oct. 1935, PP, vol. 69, file 15
160 *Vancouver Daily Province*, 30 May 1936
161 *Electoral History of British Columbia*, 182
162 Ibid., 27 June 1936
163 Young, 'Ideology, Personality and the Origin of the CCF,' 157–62
164 *Electoral History of British Columbia*, 182
165 *Victoria Daily Times*, 6 Nov. 1936
166 *Monetary Times*, 14 Nov. 1936; *Maclean's Magazine*, 15 Feb. 1937
167 TDP, press statement, 6 March 1937, PP, vol. 64, file 1
168 TDP to George, 14 Aug. 1936, Collison collection
169 F.J. Scully to TDP, 11 Dec. 1936, PP, vol. 76, file 9
170 TDP, press statement, 19 Jan. 1937, PP, vol. 32, file 3
171 The only provincial premier to survive through the decade was John Bracken of Manitoba who was re-elected in 1932 and 1936. He began as the leader of the United Farmers of Manitoba, formed a Liberal-Progressive coalition just before a provincial election in 1932, and after the 1936 election needed the support of Social Credit members to stay in power. See Kendle, *Bracken*, 125–6 and 145.
172 Cassidy to D.M. Keezer, president of Reed College, Portland, 4 Feb. 1936, and Cassidy to Professor King Gordon, 4 May 1936, Cassidy Papers, Acc. no. B72-0022, vol. 17, file 2
173 Weir to TDP, 6 Feb. 1937, PP, vol. 67, file 8
174 TDP to Hart, 10 Feb. 1937, Hart to TDP, 11 Feb. 1937, Weir to TDP, 15 Feb. 1937, Peebles to Gray (acting premier), 19 Feb. 1937, PP, vol. 67, file 8; TDP, press statement, 19 Feb. 1937, PP, vol. 64, file 1; *Victoria Daily Times*, 19 Feb. 1937; *Vancouver Daily Province*, 19 Feb. 1937
175 Cassidy to Gilbert Jackson (Bank of England), 21 April 1937, Cassidy Papers, Acc. no. B72-0022, vol. 17, file 3
176 TDP to WLMK, 5 Feb. 1936, PP, vol. 76, file 17; T.A. Crerar (minister of

the interior) to TDP, 5 March 1937, and TDP to Crerar, 8 March 1937, PP, vol. 76, file 17

177 See Crerar to WLMK, 27 Aug. 1937, King Papers, MG 26, J 1, vol. 233; and for a discussion of the separate schools issue in particular, Richard Stuart, 'Duff Pattullo and the Yukon Schools Question of 1937,' *Canadian Historical Review* 64 (March 1983): 25–44.

178 TDP, radio address, 25 May 1937, PP, vol. 65, file 3

179 *Victoria Daily Times*, 28 May 1937

180 *Vancouver Sun*, 21 May 1937

181 TDP, press statement, 29 May 1937, PP, vol. 64, file 1

182 *Prince Rupert Daily News*, 26 June 1937

183 *The Electoral History of British Columbia*, 183–9

184 *Maclean's Magazine*, 15 Feb. 1937; Robin, *Pillars of Profit*, 29–36

Chapter 8: Decline of Reform

1 *Vancouver Sun*, 24 March 1939

2 *Globe and Mail*, 3 June 1937

3 WLMK, diary, 10 Feb. 1937, King Papers, MG 26, J 13, NA

4 *Vancouver Sun*, 22 Oct. 1937; *Vancouver Daily Province*, 23 Jan. 1937

5 Maitland, 'House log,' 24 Nov. 1937, Maitland Family Papers, Add. Ms 781, vol. 8, file 6, BCARS

6 See Bruce Hutchison in *Victoria Daily Times*, 10 Nov. 1939, and *Vancouver Daily Province*, 23 Jan. 1937.

7 *Victoria Daily Times*, 5 Sept. 1936

8 TDP, convocation address at University of British Columbia, 27 Oct. 1937, PP, vol. 84

9 Pattullo Bridge Opening, New Westminster, 15 Nov. 1937, Acc. No. 3713:1, Aural History Division, BCARS; *Vancouver Sun*, 16 Nov. 1937

10 WLMK, diary, 4, 14, and 29 Nov. 1937, King Papers, MG 26, J 13

11 TDP, press statement, 17 Aug. 1937, PP, vol. 64, file 1

12 On New Deal spending in the American west see Richard Lowitt, *The New Deal and the West* (Bloomington: Indiana University Press 1984), passim; and Leonard J. Arrington, 'The Sagebrush Ressurection: New Deal Expenditures in the Western States, 1933–1939,' *Pacific Historical Review* 52 (Feb. 1983): 1–16. The phrase is Lowitt's (xvi).

13 Toast list for Pattullo's birthday dinner, 19 Jan. 1938, PP, vol. 61, file 6; *Vancouver Daily Province*, 20 and 21 Jan. 1938; *Vancouver News-Herald*, 20 Jan. 1938

14 *Victoria Daily Times*, 19 Jan. 1938

15 Ibid.
16 Ibid., 27 Aug. 1938; *Vancouver Daily Province*, 16, 26, and 27 Aug. 1938
17 Maitland, 'House log,' 30 Nov. 1937
18 Ibid., 9 Dec. and 29 Oct. 1937
19 TDP to Maitland, 29 July 1939, and Maitland to TDP, 31 July 1939, PP, vol. 63, file 4a
20 Maitland, 'House log,' 9 Dec. 1937
21 Interview with Harold Winch, 1 March 1973, interview no. 146, 27, BCARS; and interview with Harold Winch by author, 27 Sept. 1984
22 *Vancouver Sun*, 16 Nov. 1937
23 See, for example, TDP to Perley, 27 April 1935, PP, vol. 69, file 15.
24 Neatby, *William Lyon Mackenzie King*, 249–58 and 264–5; *Victoria Daily Times*, 4 June 1938; TDP, press statement, 15 June 1938, PP, vol. 64, file 2
25 Proceedings at conference between the Honourable T.D. Pattullo, premier of British Columbia, and a delegation from the single unemployed, 20 June 1938, PP, vol. 73, file 5; TDP to WLMK, 6 July 1938, PP, vol. 75, file 6
26 TDP to WLMK, 25 June 1938, PP, vol. 70, file 2
27 TDP to WLMK, 23 June 1938, PP, vol. 75, file 6; TDP, press statements, 15 June and 27 July 1938, PP, vol. 64, file 2
28 Proceedings at conference between the Honourable T.D. Pattullo, premier of British Columbia, and a delegation from various churches in the City of Vancouver, 20 June 1938, and Proceedings at conference between the Honourable T.D. Pattullo, premier of British Columbia, and a delegation from the Canadian Commonwealth Federation, 20 June 1938, PP, vol. 73, file 5; TDP, radio address, 25 July 1938, PP, vol. 65, file 4
29 Maitland, 'House log,' 10 Nov. 1937
30 *Victoria Daily Times*, 10 Nov. 1937; Hart to TDP, 1 Nov. 1938, British Columbia, Premiers' Papers, GR 1222, vol. 17, file 8, BCARS; *Victoria Daily Times*, 9 Nov. 1939; *Vancouver Sun*, 1 April 1939
31 *Electoral History of British Columbia*, 420–1. The calculation of the actual percentage of 58.78 excludes the rejected votes from the total cast.
32 Cassidy to Harold Innis, 13 April 1937, Cassidy Papers, Acc. no. B72-0022, vol. 17, file 3, UTA; Harry M. Cassidy, *Social Security & Reconstruction in Canada* (Toronto: Ryerson 1943), 23
33 Weir to TDP, 12 July 1939, PP, vol. 67, file 6
34 TDP to Weir, 13 July 1939, ibid.

35 'An Act to amend the "Workman's Compensation Act," ' British Columbia, *Statutes*, 1938, 2 Geo. 6, c. 67
36 'An Act to provide for the Regulation of Public Utilities,' and 'An Act Respecting Credit Unions,' British Columbia, *Statutes*, 1938, 2 Geo. 6, c. 47 and c. 12
37 'An Act respecting the Right of Employees to organize and providing for Conciliation and Arbitration of Industrial Disputes,' British Columbia, *Statutes*, 1937, 1 Geo. 6, c. 31; 'An Act to amend the "Industrial Conciliation and Arbitration Act," ' British Columbia, *Statutes*, 1938, 2 Geo. 6, c. 23; *Vancouver Sun*, 9 Dec. 1939; and Steeves, *Compassionate Rebel*, 119–20
38 TDP, press statement, 18 Oct. 1939, PP, vol. 64, file 2
39 British Columbia, Coal and Petroleum Products Commission, *Report of the Commissioner the Honourable Mr. Justice M.A. Macdonald Relating to the Coal Industry*, vol. II (Victoria: Charles F. Banfield 1937), passim, and for a summary of the findings, xi–xviii
40 Ibid., vol. I, 255. For a more detailed summary of these findings see Fisher, 'Regulating Fuels,' 11–16.
41 Macdonald to TDP, 3 Jan. 1936, PP, vol. 66, file 18
42 'An Act to provide for the Regulation and Control within the Province of the Coal and Petroleum Industries,' British Columbia, *Statutes*, 1937, 1 Geo. 6, c. 8
43 TDP, radio address, 15 May 1940, PP, vol. 64, file 2; TDP, press statement, 1 May 1940, PP, vol. 62, file 2
44 TDP to S.G. Blaylock (president Consolidated Mining and Smelting), 14 May 1940, British Columbia, Premiers' Papers, GR 1222, vol. 151, file 9
45 'An Act to amend the "Coal and Petroleum Products Control Act," ' and 'An Act to confer upon the Lieutenant-Governor-in-Council certain Authority in Relation to the Petroleum Industry in British Columbia,' British Columbia, *Statutes*, 1940, 4 Geo. 6, c. 1 and c. 3
46 TDP to J.L. Ralston (minister of finance), 1 May 1940, PP, vol. 72, file 5; TDP, radio address, 15 May 1940, PP, vol. 65, file 5
47 TDP to Crerar, 6 Oct. 1937, and Crerar to TDP, 8 Oct. 1937, PP, vol. 76, file 17
48 TDP to WLMK, 4 March 1937, King Papers, MG 26, J 1, vol. 239
49 TDP, press statement, 6 Sept. 1929, PP, vol. 33, file 9
50 WLMK, diary, 18 Oct. 1937, King Papers, MG 26, J 13
51 TDP to WLMK, 23 April 1938, PP, vol. 72, file 1
52 TDP to WLMK, 6 June 1938, and WLMK to TDP, 27 June 1938, PP, vol. 72, file 1; WLMK, diary, 3 May 1938, King Papers, MG 26, J 13

53 Interdepartmental Committee, Report to Council on the Proposal to Construct a Highway through British Columbia and the Yukon Territory to Alaska, nd (Aug. 1938), PP, vol. 72, file 1

54 TDP to WLMK, 6 July 1938, PP, vol. 75, file 6

55 For a more detailed account of Pattullo's efforts to build a highway to Alaska see Robin Fisher, 'T.D. Pattullo and the British Columbia to Alaska Highway,' in Kenneth Coates, *The Alaska Highway: Papers of the 40th Anniversary Symposium* (Vancouver: University of British Columbia Press 1985), 9–24.

56 TDP to WLMK, 17 Dec. 1937 and 28 Jan. 1939, PP, vol. 75, file 5, and vol. 72, file 1

57 TDP, press statement, 19 Sept. 1938, PP, vol. 64, file 2; Hepburn to TDP, 27 July 1937, and TDP to Hepburn, 9 Aug. 1937, PP, vol. 73, file 2

58 WLMK, diary, 6 Oct. 1937, King Papers, MG 26, J 13

59 Ibid., 16 Aug. 1937; Neatby, *William Lyon Macenzie King*, 246; Bothwell, Drummond, and English, *Canada 1900–1945*, 274; Granatstein, *Canada's War*, 170

60 TDP to WLMK, 17 Dec. 1937, 28 Jan. 1939, PP, vol. 75, file 5, and vol. 72, file 1

61 For an analysis of these men and their ideas see Owram, *The Government Generation*, 237–42; J.L. Granatstein, *The Ottawa Men: The Civil Service Mandarins 1935–1957* (Toronto: Oxford University Press 1982), 273–4; and David Warren Fransen, ' "Unscrewing the Unscrutable": The Rowell-Sirois Commission, the Ottawa Bureaucracy and Public Finance Reform 1935–1941,' (PHD thesis, University of Toronto, 1984), 41ff.

62 TDP to P. McD. Kerr, 11 June 1932, PP, vol. 46, file 5

63 TDP to WLMK, 10 Aug. 1937, PP, vol. 74, file 13; J.W.deB. Farris to Hart, 8 Sept. 1937, J.W. deB. Farris Papers, vol. 9, file 10, UBCL

64 S.E. Low (provincial treasurer of Alberta) to TDP, 20 May 1937, and TDP to Low, 25 May 1937, British Columbia, Premiers' Papers, GR 1222, vol. 138, file 6

65 British Columbia, *British Columbia in the Canadian Confederation: A Submission to the Royal Commission on Dominion-Provincial Relations by the Government of the Province of British Columbia* (Victoria: Charles F. Banfield 1938), iii and 351–4

66 He and the government finally agreed on $28,000 plus $1760.50 in disbursements; see Farris and Co to Gordon Wismer (attorney-general), 13 March and 17 May 1939, J.W. deB. Farris Papers, vol. 19, file 4, UBCL; TDP to Wismer, 19 May 1939, PP, vol. 68, file 8. For a disapproving account of Farris's performance see Fransen, ' "Unscrewing the Unscrutable," ' 179–92.

67 The phrase is Rowell's; see Rowell to Nell (Rowell), 22 March 1938, Newton Wesley Rowell Papers, MG 27 II, D 13, vol. 89, NA
68 Farris said that though he was a member of the Board of Trade he had never heard of the brief before it was presented. *Vancouver Sun*, 26 March 1938
69 Associated Boards of Trade of British Columbia, Submission to the Royal Commission on Dominion-Provincial Relations, no. 188; *Vancouver Daily Province*, 22 March 1938
70 Rowell to TDP, 28 March 1938, British Columbia, Premiers' Papers, GR 1222, vol. 95, file 2
71 TDP to editor of *Vancouver Province*, 20 Feb. 1939, PP, vol. 65, file 12
72 See Brian J. Young, 'C. George McCullagh and the Leadership League,' *Canadian Historical Review* 47 (Sept. 1966): 201–26; TDP, press statement, 1 Feb. 1939, PP, vol. 64, file 2.
73 *Victoria Daily Times*, 15 Feb. 1939. The wording in the *Times* is slightly different from the original, but the meaning is not. See *Globe and Mail*, 15 Feb. 1939.
74 *Vancouver Daily Province*, 17 Feb. 1939; Bruce Hutchison in *Victoria Daily Times*, 15 Feb. 1939
75 WLMK, diary, 29 and 30 May 1939, King Papers, MG 26, J 13; WLMK to TDP, 21 May 1939, and TDP to WLMK, 8 June 1939, PP, vol. 75, file 7; *Victoria Daily Times*, 8 Aug. 1939
76 TDP to George, 3 Oct. 1939, and George to TDP, 9 Oct. 1939, PP, vol. 57, file 7
77 *Victoria Daily Times*, 4 March 1940
78 See Owram, *The Government Generation*, 240–3; and Fransen, ' "Unscrewing the Unscrutable," ' 316ff and 460–1.
79 Mackenzie to TDP, 11 May 1940, PP, vol. 75, file 16
80 For summaries of plan I see *Report of the Royal Commission on Dominion-Provincial Relations*, Book II: *Recommendations*, 86; and J.L. Granatstein, *Canada's War: The Politics of the Mackenzie King Government, 1939–1945* (Toronto: Oxford University Press 1975), 161–2.
81 TDP to WLMK, 31 Oct. 1940, PP, vol. 70, file 4
82 WLMK to TDP, 2 Nov. 1940, PP, vol. 57, file 20
83 TDP, statement in the legislature, 7 Nov. 1940, PP, vol. 57, file 20
84 TDP, speech in the legislature, 14 Nov. 1940, PP, vol. 65, file 1a; *Victoria Daily Times*, 15 Nov. 1940
85 WLMK to TDP, 2 Nov. 1940, PP, vol. 70, file 4; TDP to WLMK, 5 Dec. 1940, PP, vol. 73, file 2
86 TDP to Hepburn, 8 Nov. and 10 Dec. 1940, and Hepburn to TDP, 5 Dec. 1940, PP, vol. 73, file 2; TDP to WLMK, 22 Dec. 1941, PP, vol. 58, file 2
87 WLMK to TDP, 28 Dec. 1940, PP, vol. 57, file 20

88 Carrothers to TDP, 16 Dec. 1940, British Columbia, Premiers' Papers, GR 1222, vol. 95, file 2

89 *Dominion-Provincial Conference Tuesday, January 14 1941 and Wednesday, January 15 1941* (Ottawa: King's Printer 1941), 1–10

90 Ibid., 38–41

91 Ibid., 74–5

92 Ibid., 81

93 WLMK, diary, 15 Jan. 1941, King Papers, MG 26, J 13

94 Ibid.

95 TDP to WLMK, 26 Jan. 1941, and WLMK to TDP, 28 Jan. 1941, PP, vol. 70, file 5

96 *Vancouver Daily Province*, 15 Jan. 1941

97 *Vancouver Sun*, 15 Jan. 1941; *Victoria Daily Times*, 15 Jan. 1941

98 B.A. McKelvie in the *Vancouver Daily Province*, 16 Jan. 1941, 16; also the editorial, 4

99 The most blatant example of this illogic is in Fransen, ' "Unscrewing the Unscrutable," ' 409–63, but see also, for example, Granatstein, *Canada's War*, 167–72; Christopher Armstrong, 'Ceremonial Politics: Federal-Provincial Meetings before the Second World War,' in R. Kenneth Carty and W. Peter Ward, eds., *National Politics and Community in Canada* (Vancouver: University of British Columbia Press 1986), 137–9.

100 Fransen, ' "Unscrewing the Unscrutable," ' 440–1; Armstrong, 'Ceremonial Politics,' 139; Granatstein, *Canada's War*, 170. For some it would seem that this is such a neat comment that it does not really matter who made it. As Fransen notes, Granatstein incorrectly attributes the phrase to federal cabinet minister T.A. Crerar.

101 Armstrong, for example, asserts that 'Hepburn had rallied T.D. Pattullo of British Columbia and William Aberhart of Alberta to oppose the changes.' He provides no evidence for this claim. See Armstrong, 'Ceremonial Politics,' 138. Donald Blake has Pattullo 'conspiring with William Aberhart and Mitchell Hepburn to wreck the dominion-provincial conference.' Donald Blake, 'Managing the Periphery: British Columbia and the National Political Community,' in Carty and Ward, eds., *National Politics*, 172

102 The mixed metaphor is to be found in Kendle, *Bracken*, 178.

103 *Victoria Daily Times*, 24 Jan. 1941; *Vancouver Sun*, 30 Jan. 1941

104 *Vancouver Daily Province*, 21 Jan. 1941; Turgeon to Mackenzie, 22 Jan. 1941, Ian Mackenzie Papers, MG 27 III, B 5, vol. 19, NA

105 Byron Johnson to Mackenzie, 17 Jan. 1941, Mackenzie Papers, MG 27 III, B 5, vol. 19

106 Pullen to TDP, 17 Jan. 1941, PP, vol. 64, file 6
107 WLMK, diary, 15 Jan. 1941, King Papers, MG 26, J 13
108 *Victoria Daily Times*, 3 Jan. 1941; Hart to TDP, 29 Jan. 1941, PP, vol. 68, file 8; *Victoria Daily Times*, 27 Jan. 1941
109 TDP, press statement, 31 Jan. 1941, PP, vol. 76, file 11
110 TDP, speech, 19 Feb. 1941, PP, vol. 65, file 6
111 TDP to W.J. Knox (president of British Columbia Liberal Association), 5 Feb. 1941, PP, vol. 63, file 1
112 See George Kidd et al., circular letter, 24 Feb. 1941, George Martin to Mackenzie, 28 Feb. 1941, and Mackenzie to Martin, 4 March 1941, Mackenzie Papers, MG 27 III, B 5, vol. 19.
113 Maitland, speech, 16 May 1940, Maitland Papers, Add. Mss 11, vol. 1, file 8, BCARS
114 *Vancouver Sun*, 10 May 1940
115 TDP to WLMK, 22 Dec. 1941, PP, vol. 58, file 2
116 TDP to Knox, 5 Feb. 1941, PP, vol. 63, file 1
117 Winnipeg *Free Press*, 12 Feb. 1941, PP, vol. 63, file 1
118 TDP to W. Farris, 7 April 1941, and Farris to TDP, 9 April 1941, W.B. Farris Papers, vol. 3, file 6, and vol. 6, file 8
119 TDP to George Pattullo, 5 Feb. 1941, PP, vol. 58, file 3
120 TDP to WLMK, 24 Feb. 1941, PP, vol. 68, file 4
121 *Vancouver Daily Province*, 19 and 20 March 1941; *Vancouver Sun*, 19 March 1941; *Victoria Daily Times*, 20 March 1941
122 Granatstein, *Canada's War*, 172–4; TDP, press statement, 29 April 1941, PP, vol. 64, file 3
123 TDP, press statement, 10 May 1941, PP, vol. 64, file 3; WLMK to TDP, 14 May 1941, PP, vol. 70, file 5; WLMK, diary, 1 July 1941, King, Papers, MG 26, J 13
124 *Victoria Daily Times*, 18 June 1941
125 TDP, press release, 22 July 1941, PP, vol. 62, file 8
126 *Vancouver Daily Province*, 22 July 1941; TDP, press release, 22 July 1941, PP, vol. 62, file 8
127 *Vancouver Daily Province*, 17 Feb. 1941; TDP, radio address, 13 March 1941, PP, vol. 65, file 6
128 TDP to J.L. Ralston, 22 July 1941, and Ralston to TDP, 28 July 1941, PP, vol. 62, file 9
129 T.W. Brown (Prince Rupert) to TDP, 28 Aug. 1941, PP, vol. 63, file 12
130 TDP to Charles Reid (Liberal organizer), 13 Aug. 1941, and TDP to James Mowat (and all Liberal candidates), 29 Sept. 1941, PP, vol. 63, file 1, and vol. 62, file 5
131 TDP to Edith B. Seager, 29 Oct. 1938, British Columbia, Premiers' Papers, GR 1222, vol. 140, file 7

132 Ernest Lapointe (federal minister of justice and attorney-general) to TDP, 8 Aug. 1941, PP, vol. 69, file 5
133 *Electoral History of British Columbia*, 193–9
134 *Vancouver Daily Province*, 22 Oct. 1941
135 *Winnipeg Free Press*, 23 Oct. 1941; *Globe and Mail*, 23 Oct. 1941
136 Maitland to TDP, 23 Oct. 1941, PP, vol. 62, file 16; *Victoria Daily Times*, 23 Oct. 1941
137 *Vancouver Sun*, 24 Oct. 1941
138 TDP, press statement, 24 Oct. 1941, PP, vol. 62, file 16
139 *Vancouver Daily Province*, 28 Oct. 1941
140 *Vancouver Sun*, 27 Oct. 1941
141 WLMK, diary, 31 Oct. 1941, King Papers, MG 26, J 13; *Vancouver Daily Province*, 3 Dec. 1941
142 Ibid., and TDP to WLMK, 3 Nov. 1941, PP, vol. 58, file 2
143 Maitland to Winch, 7 Nov. 1941, Maitland Papers, Add. Mss 11, vol. 3; Maitland to Howard Green, 13 Nov. 1941, Maitland Family Papers, Add. Ms 781, vol. 4, file 3
144 Pearson to TDP and TDP to Pearson, 14 Nov. 1941, PP, vol. 66, file 15; *Vancouver Daily Province*, 14 Nov. 1941
145 *Victoria Daily Times*, 14 and 15 Nov. 1941
146 Hart to TDP, 17 Nov. 1941, PP, vol. 66, file 8; *Victoria Daily Times*, 17 Nov. 1941
147 J.W. deB. Farris to Mackenzie, 17 Nov. 1941, Mackenzie Papers, MG 27 III, B 5, vol. 35, file B-70A; *Vancouver Sun*, 17 Nov. 1941
148 TDP, press statement, 20 Nov. 1941, PP, vol. 64, file 3
149 *Vancouver Daily Province*, 18 Nov. 1941
150 TDP to WLMK, 23 Oct. 1941, PP, vol. 58, file 2
151 *Victoria Daily Times*, 2 Dec. 1941
152 Ibid., 3 Dec. 1941
153 Ibid.; *Vancouver Daily Province*, 3 Dec. 1941
154 N. Fitzgerald to TDP, 8 Dec. 1941, PP, vol. 63, file 14
155 Maitland, 'House log,' 4 Dec. 1941, Maitland Family, Papers, Add. Ms 781, vol. 8, file 10
156 Hutchison in *Vancouver Sun*, 5 Dec. 1941
157 Ibid.; TDP, press statement, 4 Dec. 1941, PP, vol. 64, file 3; British Columbia, *Journals ... Session 1941–42*, 6
158 *Victoria Daily Times*, 3 Dec. 1941

Chapter 9: Looking Back

1 WLMK, diary, 31 Oct. 1941, King Papers, MG 26, J 13, NA

2 TDP to WLMK, 4 Dec. 1941, WLMK to TDP, 13 Dec. 1941, PP, vol. 58, file 2

3 TDP to WLMK, 22 Dec. 1941, PP, vol. 58, file 2; TDP to Mackenzie, 19 Jan. 1942, and TDP to WLMK, 19 Jan. 1942, PP, vol. 58, file 11

4 *Vancouver Daily Province*, 19 Feb. 1953

5 Hart to Maitland, 4 Dec. 1941, Maitland to Hart, 6 Dec. 1941, and Hart to Maitland, 7 Dec. 1941, Maitland Family Papers, vol. 2, file 9, and vol. 4, file 2, Add. Ms 781, BCARS. For an account of the formation of the coalition written largely from Maitland's point of view see John Gordon Terpenning, 'Maitland and the British Columbia Conservative Party: The Struggle for Political Identity and Survival,' (MA thesis, University of Victoria, 1988), 157–73.

6 TDP to WLMK, 30 Oct. 1942, PP, vol. 58, file 14

7 TDP to J.R. Laurier, 9 Dec. 1941, PP, vol. 63, file 14

8 *Victoria Daily Times*, 20 Jan. 1942

9 TDP, speech in the house, 19 Jan. 1942, PP, vol. 58, file 12

10 T.D. Pattullo, *Wither the Liberal Party* [Victoria: np 1942], 1–7; also TDP to Liberal associations of British Columbia, 9 Sept. 1943, PP, vol. 58, file 17

11 Odlum to Maitland, 24 July 1942, W. Farris to Odlum, 24 July 1942, Odlum Papers, vols. 8 and 4, MG 30, E 300, NA

12 TDP, speech in the house, 19 Jan. 1942, PP, vol. 58, file 12; *Victoria Daily Times*, 12 Feb. 1942

13 TDP, letter to editor, *Victoria Daily Colonist*, 6 March 1942; Hart to TDP, 25 April 1942, PP, vol. 58, file 10; TDP to editor of the *Sun*, 4 Aug. 1942, PP, vol. 64, file 5

14 TDP, speech in house, 19 Jan. 1942, PP, vol. 58, file 12

15 TDP to WLMK, 22 Dec. 1941, PP, vol. 58, file 2

16 TDP to H.G. Perry, 3 March 1942, PP, vol. 58, file 15

17 TDP to J.L. Ralston (minister of defence), 23 Nov. 1943, PP, vol. 73, file 9. Pattullo had favoured the more westerly Rocky Mountain Trench route north from Prince George.

18 *Victoria Daily Times*, 18 Feb. 1944; *Vancouver Daily Province*, 6 March 1944

19 T.D. Pattullo, *Let Us Reason Together: The Labour Problem* [Victoria: np 1946]; and T.D. Pattullo, *The Strike Situation* [Victoria: np 1946]

20 *Vancouver Daily Province*, 18 Jan. 1945

21 T.D. Pattullo, *Provincial Income Tax* (Victoria: np 1943), 8; and T.D. Pattullo, *Dominion-Provincial Conference* (Victoria: np 1945), 8

22 Maitland, 'House log,' 2 March 1943, Maitland Family Papers, Add. Ms 781, vol. 8, file 11, BCARS; TDP, speech in house, 19 Jan. 1942, PP, vol. 58, file 12

23 TDP to Doris, 28 Sept. 1945, Collison collection; James Dyer in the *Vancouver Sun*, 26 Oct. 1926
24 *Electoral History of British Columbia*, 203–9
25 Hart to TDP, 5 Nov. 1945, and Winch to TDP, 29 Oct. 1945, PP, vol. 58, file 21
26 Hutchison in the *Victoria Daily Times*, 10 Nov. 1939
27 See, for example, *Vancouver News Herald*, 25 Feb., 4 and 9 March, 10, 18, and 29 April 1946
28 TDP to Clara Laidlaw, 8 Jan. 1953, PP, vol. 59, file 9; TDP to David, 28 Feb. 1952, PP, vol. 59, file 6
29 TDP to Wynnie Ballantyne, 28 Nov. 1949, Collison collection; interview with Ethelwyn and Adam Zimmerman, 26 Nov. 1983
30 Doris to Daddy, 4 Feb. 1953, Collison collection
31 TDP to Kate Foster, 14 Jan. 1949, TDP to George Pattullo, 17 Dec. 1946, George Pattullo to TDP, Dec. 1946, and TDP to Wynnie, 22 Nov. 1951, Collison collection
32 TDP to Wynnie, 18 Oct. and 14 Sept. 1947, Collison collection
33 TDP to his granddaughters, 8 Jan. 1948, PP, vol. 58, file 34
34 'Alone' by TDP, Collison collection
35 'Soliloquy' by TDP, ibid.
36 TDP to Cora, 7 June 1948, ibid.
37 John Burnaby to Lilian, 12 June 1892, PP, vol. 1, file 1
38 TDP to Pearl Bowie, 6 May 1951, Collison collection
39 Radford to TDP, 19 April 1949, and TDP to Radford, 15 and 21 April 1949, PP, vol. 58, file 35
40 TDP to Margaret, 26 Jan. 1951, Collison collection
41 TDP, radio speech, 27 June 1949, ibid.
42 TDP, 'A Reflection,' 25 March 1949, PP, vol. 58, file 34
43 TDP to Pearl Bowie, 18 Nov. 1947, Collison collection; TDP to Kate Foster, 20 Jan. 1949, PP, vol. 58, file 34; TDP to George Pattullo, 21 March 1948, Collison collection; TDP to Mrs Hanson, 18 July 1952, PP, vol. 59, file 7; TDP to Ethelwyn Zimmerman, 10 Oct. 1952, PP, vol. 59, file 8
44 C. 'Mory' Moriarty to TDP, 9 May 1950 and 21 Nov. 1952, PP, vol. 59, files 1 and 8; see also M.E. Nichols to TDP, 21 Feb. 1949, PP, vol. 58, file 34
45 Hutchison to TDP, 21 May 1951, Collison collection
46 TDP to WLMK, 22 Nov. 1941, PP, vol. 58, file 2; TDP to Nonie and Lynette, 30 July 1952, PP, vol. 59, file 7
47 TDP to Mary Lownsbrough, 23 March 1948, Collison collection
48 TDP to Ethelwyn and Hartley Zimmerman, 10 Jan. 1952, TDP to Pearl Bowie, 30 Nov. 1947, TDP to Wynnie Ballantyne, 18 April 1948, Collison collection; and TDP to Eric Hamber, 11 Oct. 1950, PP, vol. 59, file 2

49 George Pattullo, *Era of Infamy* (San Antonio: Naylor Company 1952); George Pattullo, *Morning After Commeth* (San Antonio: Naylor Company 1954); George Pattullo, *Giant Afraid* (San Antonio: Naylor Company 1957)

50 TDP to Kate Foster, 14 March 1953, and TDP to Mary Lownsbrough, 14 Feb. 1953, PP, vol. 59, file 9

51 TDP to George Pattullo, 17 Dec. 1951, Collison collection; TDP to Wendle Farris, 2 Nov. 1952, PP, vol. 59, file 8; TDP to H.S. Tobin, 28 June 1950, PP, vol. 59, file 1; TDP to 'my dear young friend,' 4 Sept. 1949, Collison collection

52 TDP to Kate Foster, 12 Dec. 1948, PP, vol. 58, file 29

53 TDP to George Pattullo, 3 Feb. 1949, Collison collection

54 TDP to Pearl Bowie, 22 Jan. 1951, Collison collection; TDP to Pearl Bowie, 8 Aug. 1950, PP, vol. 59, file 2; TDP to Wynnie Ballantyne, 14 Jan. 1949, PP, vol. 58, file 34; TDP to Wynnie Ballantyne, 19 Jan. 1954, Collison collection

55 *Victoria Daily Times*, 19 Jan. 1956

56 TDP to George Pattullo, 26 June 1948, Collison collection

57 TDP, 'Alone'

58 *he Hymn Book* (New York: Presbyterian Church 1955), hymn 773

Illustration Credits

Mrs D. Collison: Pattullo at about three years old; as a young man before he left Woodstock; on the way to Dawson City; with Doris and Lillian; Doris's birthday party; the first Prince Rupert City Council; Pattullo as Minister of Lands; as Premier

Mrs E. Zimmerman: George R. Pattullo; Mary Rounds Pattullo; Burnside; the wedding of Duff's sister Ethelwyn; James B. Pattullo

Woodstock Museum: Father and sons; Andrew Pattullo

British Columbia Archives and Records Service: Walsh Party leaving Vancouver for the Yukon (HP2006); Dawson City tennis club (67211); the first motor car in Prince Rupert (1076); the first British Columbia premier to travel by air (42903)

Yukon Archives: the 1904 Yukon hockey team (3988)

Vancouver City Archives: caricature of Pattullo in 1931; Pattullo speaking to the crowd at Brockton Point 1936; Jack Boothe cartoon

Mrs B. Pattullo: playing cards; 'Looking Back'

National Archives of Canada: Mackenzie King giving his opening address 1941 (C26112); official photograph of the dominion-provincial conference 1941 (C7491); Pattullo, King, and Godbout (C62102)

A Note on Sources

As the notes indicate, the primary source of this biography has been the T.D. Pattullo Papers in the British Columbia Archives and Records Service in Victoria. The collection is an extensive one, comprising almost eighty boxes, and it includes correspondence, speeches, press releases, and newspaper clippings. Yet it is largely the record of Pattullo's public life. There are some private papers, but there is also evidence that personal letters were removed by a secretary when Pattullo left office. Fortunately the deficiency was partly made up by a smaller collection of personal letters that Duff Pattullo's daughter, Doris Collison, gave me as I started on this project. Historical research is not always a dignified process, and I had to get down on my hands and knees on her living-room floor to rescue some of these Pattullo letters from a waste-paper basket. Doris Collison had gone through them just prior to my first visit and discarded those that, to her, simply appeared to be uninteresting. She had no desire to protect her father in any way and was always extremely generous and open with information. This small collection of family letters, mostly written after Pattullo was premier, provided insights into the private man that the official Pattullo papers did not. I have designated these papers the Collison collection and they are now being placed in the British Columbia Archives and Records Service.

Other collections of papers that were essential to an understanding of Pattullo's life were found in the following archives:

Archives of Ontario

Abstract Index to Deeds
Baptismal Records, Knox Presbyterian Church, Woodstock
Niagara Falls Park
Mitchell Hepburn

British Columbia Archives and Records Service

British Columbia, Attorney-General
British Columbia, Coal and Petroleum Board
British Columbia, Commission on Coal and Petroleum Products
British Columbia, Land Settlement Board
British Columbia, Premiers' Papers
A.F. Buckham
J.W. Jones
Gerald McGeer
J.D. MacLean
Maitland Family
Royal L. Maitland
George R. Pattullo

National Archives of Canada

R.B. Bennett
Canada, Royal Commission on Dominion-Provincial Relations, 1937–9
Canadian National Railways
W.L.M. King
Wilfrid Laurier
Ian Mackenzie
National Health and Welfare
Victor W. Odlum
Newton W. Rowell
Louis St Laurent
Clifford Sifton
Upper Canada Land Petitions

Prince Rupert City Hall

Minutes of Council Meetings

Prince Rupert Public Library

Prince Rupert Board of Trade, Minutes

Provincial Archives of Manitoba

John Bracken
Thomas Greenway
W.L. Walsh

Public Archives of Nova Scotia

W.S. Fielding

Queen's University Archives

T.A. Crerar
Charles A. Dunning

Toronto Public Library

Pattullo family

University of British Columbia Library (Special Collections)

British Columbia Council of Forest Industries
Gerald McGeer
J.W.deB. Farris
W.B. Farris
Simon Fraser Tolmie

University of Calgary Library

Bruce Hutchison

University of Toronto Archives

Harry M. Cassidy

University of Victoria Library

Byron Johnson

University of Western Ontario Library

Ethel Canfield
James H. Coyne

Woodstock Museum

County of Oxford Historical Society, Minutes

Yukon Territorial Archives

Dawson Mining Record Books
Yukon Government Records

The documentary sources were supplemented with interviews, though it quickly became clear how few of Pattullo's contemporaries were still alive. There were already some interviews in the Sound and Moving Image Division of the British Columbia Archives and Records Service, and those with Doris Collison, Percy Richards, Dorothy Steeves, and Harold Winch were useful. I conducted my own interviews with Doris Collison on several occasions, and also with E.F. Stewart, Norman Whittaker, Harold Winch, Tom Lownsbrough, Beth Pattullo, and Ethelwyn and Adam Zimmerman. Three recordings of Pattullo speeches survive: a radio address from 17 June 1935 and another made at the opening of the Pattullo Bridge on 15 November 1937 are in the British Columbia Archives and Records Service, and one given in Montreal on 13 June 1940 is in the CBC Archives in Toronto.

The other sources used for this study – newspapers, secondary literature, and so on – are detailed in the notes.

Index